Saṅkalpasūryodaya

— A Literary Analysis

Saṅkalpasūryodaya

— A Literary Analysis

R. Laxmi

SHARADA

Sharada Publishing House
DELHI
2008

First Published 2008

ISBN: 978-81-88934-48-5

Published by:
Anjana Bansal
SHARADA PUBLISHING HOUSE
111, Vidya Vihar Apartment
Sector-9, Rohini, Delhi-110 085 (INDIA)
Ph.: +91-11-3292 1560, 2755 2102
E-mail: bansal_sph@rediffmail.com

Printed at:
Salasar Imaging System
Delhi

Śrī Vedānta Deśika

Foreword

Writing a piece of introduction to a learned work by a studious researcher under a competent guide, and on which judgment is already passed and a doctorate issued by an established, well known, University, is a highly embarassing task, as it further involves attempting a further estimate by a total outsider, if not an intruder !

Fortunately there is yet another angle of looking at it! It is no longer a work meant for examination by a panel of judges ! It is a piece of learning before a world, learned— may be in other fields — but not so well informed in the present chosen field of research (by the author), who is entitled to a good listening ! The pleasant duty of the introducer is to act as a good link between the author and the wider world of scholarship. If the task still involves an estimate of the present work, it is no longer for the purpose of 'examination', but the post-examination duty of critical admiration. There can be no possible objection to or inhibition for this, one hopes. It is to fulfil this task, that I am attempting these few words.

It is not easy to attempt a work on an outstanding Ācārya like Vedānta Deśika, who is unique as a combination of several fields of learning, several talents and gifts of arts — like the traditional *Śāstras,* Vedānta, Grammar, Mīmāṁsā, Poetry, Drama, the art of debate and disputation,

Āgama, Tamil lore, Prākṛt as well as Sanskrit, semantics, etymology, astrology and whatever else there is to learn and master over.

Here is a play representing man's victory of war over himself, of vanquishing forces of lust, ignorance, egoism, and selfishness, thanks to the Grace of God, rising like the rays of the morning Sun, to dispel the darkness of the just finished night, leading him to final emancipation from all cycles of sorrow once and for all. The language is that of allegory, the characters all symbolic, and the 'action' significant of Vedāntic meanings and overtones at every step of progress. It is not easy to write such a play, in the first instance, and it is much less easy to put it to dramatic aplause unless its spectators are learned, equally, about its philosophical content and its literary mode of representation, on the stage. For, the play is meant more for mental performance than for physical representation, as the story itself is not about any actual historical king or queen, trying to assert themselves unto their emerging freedom from a real seige which is over as a historical fact ! It is a story, –if it can be ever called one !– unfinished in its larger generalities, though getting finished in individual particularities, in the cases of the devout, faithful and wise *prapannas*, seeking refuge in the Lord's saving Grace. The Sun does not rise all over the world at once, in one moment of total illumination, does he? So that, darkness *does* persist over some part of the world or the other, while the Sun is continually rising over the globe, in the tireless effort of dispelling all darkness, one Day ! That is one aspect of the pregnant meanings of the title of the play. The urge of the *Bhagavan* to save all sinners and sufferers is there as a 'given', a *Siddha upāya*, to use a technical Vedāntic term; but the effort, however meagre in measure, to deserve this deliverance from darkness or sorrow, is wanting, even in a token-form, as *Sādhya upāya*, as a means to that Destiny. The poet uses two analogies to suggest this :

1. that of the rays of the Sun ready to dispel darkness, and

2. that of Lord Rāma ready to save Sītā, in the Holy Epic.

Both have been pressed into service in the present play, with great force and beauty.

[1] The first is an eye-catcher, even in the title of the play, apart from amplifications through dialogues, characters and situations within the text itself. What are its implifications in terms of the central theme of the play ?

There was an earlier play by the title *Prabodha Candrodaya* by one Krishna Miśra, with an Absolutistic Monistic theme, to which the present play by Deśika is said to be a reply. This matter is referred to in the present work also. This other play, naturally views that human bondage to nescience is due to the non-realisation of the Absolute identity between the Individual Self and the Universal Self, as in reality there is only one such Self, with no second to it. Bondage is due to ignorance, and liberation is through such knowledge, and so the title symbolically suggests that "the rise of moonlight of this knowledge of non-duality" — [*prabodha* = knowledge, *candrodaya* = moonrise] is instrumental for liberation. Given this philosophy, there is nothing wrong with such dramatic representation.

But is this philosophy correct ? How to counter a philosophical thesis couched in dramatic languag ? Śrī Vedānta Deśika addresses both these tasks in the course of the present play without violating the grammar of aesthetics or Arts. Direct criticism of Monism can be seen in his numerous metrical works like *Tattvamuktākalāpa, Adhikaraṇa*

Sārāvaḷī, and in prose treatises like *Tattvaṭīkā, Nyāyasiddhāñjana, Tatparya-Candrikā, Śata Dūṣaṇī, Sarvārthasiddhi* and others. That is freedom as per the science of disputations. But even in the praise poems of the Lord like *Nyāsa Tilakam, Nyāsa Viṁśati, Varadarāja Pañcāśata, Dayā Śatakam* etc. (the several *stotras,* so to call them) the Ācārya establishes the alternative tenets of Organic Monism by criticising Absolutistic Monism without violating the limits of poetry. His *Yatirāja Saptati*, a hymn in seventy verses, in praise of *Rāmānuja* is especially replete with philosophical ideas, as the context is to praise the Ācārya for his great services in the realm of Vedantic thought. All this may be easy in a way, as there are conventions behind such attempts. But in drama it is not easy, as the poet cannot directly talk, freely ! He must always speak through characters, and create contexts for such occasion. So Deśika has improvised on the theme, parallelly to that of *Prabodha Candrodaya*, by substituting an alternate set of characters, situations, dialogues, and their imports. That is the work that expects commendation and amplification here.

It does not mean that the present play is derivative in status. If it is so, it is only inversely, and incidentally. For you can read this play independently as an embodiment of a totally different view of the philosophical world, and any presuppositions of a *prima facie* view can be had, within the play itself. You read that other play, if you do, for your additional pleasure of realising the larger textual contrast; but if you do not, there is no harm, you do not suffer from any handicap !

Let us for a moment meditate on the significance of the Title itself; and make, these observations in response; in contrasts :

(1) True and complete clearance of darkness can

happen only through Sunlight and not Moonlight, which however, is only the next best alternative.

(2) But even moonlight is not efficient without the Sun and his light, as the moon is only a reflector, and not self-luminous like the Sun, and so Sunlight is the better, more lasting and more efficacious apart for dispelling darkness.

(3) Self-efforts, mere 'Self-realisation', however important as a step in the final act of liberation, are not self-sufficient. What is required is a higher elevating Agency, waiting to save all that can be saved. The self must realise not only its true ideal nature, but must actually be restored to its true status.

(4) The act of liberation involves not merely knowledge, but a whole process of transformation, sublimation, in body, mind and deed, which is more than any individual can undertake for himself in full. The individual must cooperate, no doubt, by self-purification, a readiness to be saved, an abject state of helplessness in the absence of Divine Intervention, and a threefold application, in body, mind and deed, for such Saving Grace to Descend on him.

(5) But the Saving Agency can be none other than God, ever ready to save the sufferer, expecting at least a token act of self-surrender, as without it, saving all indiscriminately would amount to partiality and un kindliness.

(6) Why does the All-merciful require such tokens from the hapless, from those condemned to cycles of sorrow ? Is He not All-knowing, All-powerful to overcome all impediments in so saving the world of lives ? True, but bondage is self-inflicted and God is only a sanctioning authority for those who so desire bondage ! God does not

like it, but cannot help it, as life consists in freedom, which means freedom for wrong choices also by the individual !! Any salvation, must, therefore involve this mischievous freedom that now requires to be surrendered, and not independently of it, or compulsorily. That is the meaning of *Prapatti*. God is willing to save, as a *siddhopāya*. Man must also will to be saved, and *prapatti* or *bhakti* are tokens as *sādhyopāya*. When the two coincide, there arises the *urge* for God to act, to liberate the sinner, and the rise of this *urge* is *Saṅkalpasūryodaya*.

[2] See the import of the second analogy also, reinforcing the same idea. The Holy Epic is pregnant with the very allegorical overtones : Sītā devī represents man both in bondage and liberation, later on. But how ?

She is enamoured after the elusive beauties of a bewitching and unnatural deer — *Mārīca*. Likewise the self is allured by the false attractions of joy of *Saṁsāra* which is *marīcika*, even for namesake ! She forgets the Divine Beauties of her Lord for a moment and is ensured by this false appearance. It is her own choice — that she wants it to be caught. She banishes Lord Rāma, in her own express orders. When the self banishes God form its sight, Nescience or *Avidyā* appears before it rearing all its ten big heads, like *Rāvaṇa*. Literally, *Rāvaṇa* means an agency that makes us cry for impossibilities, for unrealities and discomforts in the final counting – *Ravayati, asatpralapān Kārayati* – as the commentator Govinda Raja explains. This is the aspect of the self's bondage symbolised in the episode of the kidnapping of *Sītā* by *Rāvaṇa*.

See where *Sītā* is imprisoned; it is an island; our body, symbolically, floating in the sea of all-enveloping sorrow and transmigration. Further, it is a 'pleasure grove', –*Aśoka vana*– where *Sītā* suffers maximum sorrow ! See the significance :

the *hṛdaya*, the seat of the self is not meant as a place of punishment, but in fact it turns out to be a virtual prison ! That is the human predicament. It is also the seat of God, if one can realise, as *Sītā* does, later.

नैषा पश्यति राक्षस्यः नैवपुष्पाफलद्रुमान् ।
एकस्थहृदया नूनं राममेवानुपश्यति ।। (*Sundara Kāṇḍa*)

She now is not tempted by the beauties of the flowers and fruits of this garden, but concentrates on *Rāma* whom she sees everywhere. That is *prāyaścitta*, expiation, self-imposed, rightly. She is now ready to be saved.

For His past, Lord *Rāma* sends out messengers, errand men in all directions, to find out the whereabouts of the missing queen. [Every lost soul is His Queen, in import philosophically !] But it is not everyone who can cross over the seas of sorrow, measuring a hundred leagues. Only a right preceptor can fly over it. That is the symbolic act of Hanumān skipping over the salty seas. Further He, the teacher, saves the self on the verge of self-annihilation (symbolically by avoiding *Sītā's* suicide) and presents the token of the Lord's vow to save it — *a signet Ring* — *Aṅguliyaka* — This is "granting immunity from fear", *Abhayapradāna,* God's initiation, the step of readiness to act to end the exile or imprisonment in darkness.

Sītā responds by offering her Great jewel — *Cūḍāmaṇi* — which symbolises the act of surrender, *namaskāra*, a literal bowing down of head !

Everything is ready now for redemption : the self is willing to be reclaimed; it has surrendered its eccentric 'Centre' of erroneous behaviour; the Lord has assured redemption. The preceptor returns to act as a bridge; the urge — *Saṅkalpa* — of the Lord, rises instantaneously. He moves on the seas, by installing a bridge of compassion, symbolised in the floating bridge on the salty seas; slays the demons of Egoism. Selfishness, lust, hatred etc, and redeems the Queen, and restore her back on His own seat in the Invincible city, called *Ayodhyā*, the celestial world of Eternity.

See therefore, the almost exact correspondence between the characters and incidents of the play and the Holy Epic, *Śrī Rāmāyaṇa*. Infact one can read this play as a kind of commentary on the *Rāmāyaṇa*. How *Deśika* sums up this correspondence in a single verse, is a marvel of marvels :

दर्पोदग्रदशेन्द्रियानन मनो नक्तं चराधिष्ठितम् । etc.

To hold a complex and comprehensive theme like this in a web of some ten acts, consisting in some forty characters and numerous symbolic episodes in a sustained attempt to unity edifying minor themes of *Vedānta* is no easy task.

Dr. (Smt.) R. Laxmi, has done a daring and marvellous job in highlighting and explicating the various aspects of this unique play, by her sustained study and analysis, going into great details.

I have read her work with great interest and pleasure, getting flashes of new meanings occasionally. The chapters on *Rasa* and *Alaṅkāras* are especially very illuminating and exhaustive. A lot of accessory materials are contained in the early chapters, introducing the play in its proper philosophical, poetic and dramatic perspective. The chapter on characterisation is of special interest, as it is central to the play. A chapter on its philosophical theme is added in all wisdom, deservingly, at the end, as the play intents the vindication of *Viśiṣṭādvaita* in a dramatic mould. A student attempting such a thesis must surely be well versed not only in poetics or Dramaturgy, but also in philosophy which it presupposes, both positively and negatively, by the maintainance of the work and the rejection of alternative views. Dr. (Smt.) Laxmi has demonstrated that she is not deferred by such a task. She deserves the commendations of all those interested in philosophy, poetry and dramatics.

To my best knowledge this is the first time a work is appearing on Śrī Deśika's *Saṅkalpasūryodaya*.

It now remains for me to pray that Dr. Laxmi shall be enabled to undertake other post-doctoral projects on the other master pieces of Deśika too, as she has made a successful entry into the *Deśika-vidyā-prapañca*, which is not normally easy. Śrī Deśika's works, (each, by itself) are worlds of grandeur, forts of beauty, impregnable to the uninitiated.

May the All-Merciful shower His choicest blessings on her and enable her to come out with more works of equal and better competance.

Mysore

Prof. K.S. Narayanacharya
Professor of English (Retd.)
Karnatak Arts College
Dharwad

Contents

Preface

Sanskrit language and literature is unequally rich and colourfully varied. It is the only language and literature which has been dispersing its own inner beauty and vitality to several countries of the world, observes rightly, Dr. D.N. Shanbhag. In this literature a novel branch of writing the dramas in an allegorical form came to light since the times of Aśvaghoṣa. The word 'Allegory' may be defined as "a systematic symbolism by which abstractions are represented as accurately as possible by concrete characters, plot and situations often with identifying tag names". Allegory, therefore is a new technique by which some dramatists went to the extent of writing dramas, building the plot from there imagination, thus treading a new path besides the Epics, the Purāṇas and the Folk tales. In course of time due to an advent of various philosophical systems many a dramatist used drama as a media to propagate their philosophical theories also. In this direction the *Saṅkalpasūryodaya*, the scholarly work of Vedānta Deśika, makes an interesting and useful study.

In the work an attempt is made to bring out the place of *Saṅkalpasūryodaya* in Sanskrit Literature from the point of a *Drama*. Besides, other aspects such as meaning of Allegory, significance of the drama, purpose of the dramatist, characterisation, *Rasa* delineation, *Alaṅkāras* and philisiphical doctorines reflected in the drama have also been dealt with. Finally conclusions from the study are also added.

In preparing this work, I have made use of original and secondary sources in Sanskrit and English, relevant Journals and Encyclopaedias, a list of which is given in Bibliography at the end.

However, the primary source studied is *Saṅkalpa-sūryodaya* itself and commentaries – the *Prabhāvilāsa* by Ahobila Śrī Śaila Tātārya and *Prabhāvaḷi* by M.M. Narasimhachariar thereon. I am much beholden to the authors of these works, in completing the work. On the basis of these two commentaries on this text, no attempt has been made so far in making a study from the point of aspects like characterisation, etc., and its contributions to Sanskrit literature and learning to modern times.

I am deeply indebted to Prof. K.S. Narayanacharya, (Retd.) Dept. of English, Karnatak College, Dharwad for penning a erudite *Foreword* to this work. He is a versatile scholar in English literature, Philosophy, Sanskrit, Physical Science and an author of several works in different languages too. His *Foreword* has undoubtedly enriched the value of this work.

In the preparation of this work, I took the guidance of Dr. K.B. Archak, Prof. & Chairman, Dept. of Studies in Sanskrit, Karnatak University, Dharwad. The suggestions given by him while going through the research script and its publication were of immense value to me for which I am very grateful to him. His sympathetic gesture while scrutinising the work is worthy of emulation.

I am in deep gratitude and obligation to Dr. D.N. Shanbhag, Prof. (Retd.), Dept. of Studies in Sanskrit, Karnatak University Dharwad, a recepient of President's Award and the President of Samskrita Shodha Samsthana

(Samshodhana), Sirsi, for his inspiring guidance from time to time in the research field.

I am grateful to Sharada Publishing House, Delhi, for having published this work in a magnificient manner.

I am thankful to the Management, Principal and Staff members of Smt. K.S.J. Arts and Dr. S.M.S. Commerce College for Women, Dharwad where I am working as a S.G. Lecturer & Head, Dept. of Sanskrit, for their Co-operation and appreciation.

My beloved thanks are due to Dr. C.V. Rangaswamy, M.A., Ph.D. Prof. (Retd.), Dept. of Studies in History & Archaeology, K.U.D. and other members of the family.

R. Laxmi

Chapter I

Date, Life and Works of the Author

1. INTRODUCTION

Vedānta Deśika *alias* Veṅkaṭanātha, a saint-philosopher who became very famous after Rāmānuja, (1017-1137 A.D.) by offering multi-faced contribution to the world of Viśiṣṭādvaita Vedānta and its literature, has authored an allegorical work — *Saṅkalpasūryodaya*. He is regarded as the unique and towering personality, for, we find in him a rare combination of the talents of a Poet, a Dramatist and a Philosopher. His scholasticity may be well witnessed by his epithets like Vedāntācārya, Karvitārkikasiṁha, and Sarvatantrasvatantra etc.

The generally accepted date of Vedānta Deśika, as far as ascertainable, would be 1268 to 1369 A.D. However, there are different opinions in this regard. The date of Vedānta Deśika's birth is Kali 4371, Śaka 1190 (1268 A.D.) as has been recorded in Vaḍagalai Guruparaṁparā.[1] This date has another support of an inscription of Coḷa Vijayagaṇḍa Gopāla Deva of Kāñcīpuram dated Śaka 1207 (1285 A.D.) found in Candramaulīśvara temple at Kāñcīpuram[2] which belongs to 1268 A.D. But, the date 1268 A.D. has not been accepted by Dr. Hultzsch[3] as the date of Vedānta Deśika. Because he is said to have lived as a centenarian; then it means, he should have died during 1369

A.D. Dasgupta opines that Vedānta Deśika died during 1371 A.D.[4] In his introduction to *Saṅkalpasūryodaya*, Dr. Veera Raghavacharya says that Vedānta Deśika flourished during 1268 to 1370.[5]

During the time of Vedānta Deśika, there persisted political unstability and religious crisis (1327 A.D.). Mohammadans marching towards the south, captured many South Indian kingdoms and destroyed religious places of worship. Along with the invasion, came the dreadful imposition of their religion on the local people. At the same time, there was utter confusion in the Hindu religion itself. Though Advaita Philosophy was very prominent in many parts, there were other systems of Philosophy like Sāṅkhya, Yoga, Vaiśeṣika and Pāśupata which started becoming popular. This led to religious fights and conflicts among the Protagonists. They started preaching their own religion with provocation and declaration of their religion as the supreme. Even in Viśiṣṭādvaita itself which was all along powerful, there arose two branches, one of which is, Vaḍagalai; while the other is called Teṅgaḷai. Great scholars like Śrīrāma Miśrā, Viṣṇucitta, Vātsya-Varadācārya, Sudarśanācārya and Ātreya Rāmānuja, all these Propounders of Vaḍagalai branch gave more importance to Rāmānuja's Philosophy. On the other side, Parāśarabhaṭṭa, Nañjīya Periyavācchan Pillai, Vadakku Tiruvidhi Pillai and Pillai Locācārya gave more importance to Dravida literature contributed by Āḷvārs. The former branch believed in continuing the old traditions, while the latter one believed in progress and reformation of the religion. Hence, a need to unite both the groups and to maintain peace was very much felt in the Śrīvaiṣṇavaite society itself. It was Vedānta Deśika who contributed to the successful unification and tolerance of the two off shoots.

Vedānta Deśika is considered to be a divine incarnation.

He lived as a Parama Bhāgavata, promoting the Rāmānuja Philosophy.

Vedānta Deśika himself gives the details of his lineage. To quote his words :

> अस्ति खलु समस्तलोकसंभावनीयस्य विश्वातिशायिनो विश्वा–
> मित्रगोत्रभूषणस्य विशुद्धविद्याविहार पुण्डरीकस्य पुडरीकाक्ष–
> सोमसुत्संभवस्यानन्तगुणशेवधेरनन्तसूरेरात्मसंभवः श्रीरङ्गराज–
> दिव्याज्ञालब्धवेदान्ताचार्यपदः कवितार्किकसिंह इति प्रख्यातगुण–
> समाख्यः छात्रजननिबद्धजैत्रध्वजप्रसाधितदशदिशासौधः सर्वतन्त्र–
> संकटप्रशमनविशङ्कटमतिः श्रीमद्वेंकटनाथो नाम कविः ।।[6]

Vedānta Deśika was born to parents Anantasūri, a great scholar and Totārammā or Totādryaṁbā. Anantasūri was the son of Ācārya Puṇḍarīkākṣa, the son of Ananta Somayājin. Anantasūri was one of the three chief Ācāryas of Śrīvaiṣṇavism and an immediate successor of Rāmānujācārya to the pontificial throne. His mother was the sister of Ātreya Rāmānuja, the author of Nyāyakulīśa and the immediate successor of Vātsya Varadācārya to the pontificial throne, instituted by the great Rāmānujācārya. They belonged to the Viśvāmitra Gotra and led a spiritual and pious life in Tuppil, a suburb of Kāñcīpuram.

In all probability, the birth place of Vedānta Deśika was Himavanam[7] near Kāñcīpuram. But he has not given any proof for his mention.

Regarding his life,[8] it is interesting to note that his birth is associated with the bell and its sound. His birth symbolizes the herald of a new age; as such, in the later period, Vedānta Deśika founded a new sect of Vaḍagalai doctrine in Śrīvaiṣṇavism. Like a bell, Vedānta Deśika proclaimed the Philosophy of Viśiṣṭādvaita in attending to the divine cause. Before the birth of Vedānta Deśika, once his parents saw two separate dreams. In them, his father had a holy vision of Śrī Veṅkaṭeśvara, the deity of Tirupati Temple. He received an advice that, if he worships the Lord at Tirupati, the Lord would bless him with a son. His mother too had a holy vision of Goddess Padmāvatī in dream and received similar advice. Being filled with joy, both of them visited Tirupati where Totārammā in a dream saw Lord Veṅkaṭeśvara standing before her in guise of a child. The Lord presented her with a bell and asked her to swallow it, and blessed her with a son. She felt that she had swallowed the bell according to Lord's desire. Next morning, the devotees in the temple found the bell having disappeared. They got firm faith that the bell itself is Vedānta Deśika incarnate.[9] This anecodote is recorded in the *Saṅkalpasūryodaya*.[10] Thus, Vedānta Deśika himself clearly indicates his divine incarnation. Therefore, Vedānta Deśika in his infancy was named as Vedānta Deśika to comme-morate this event.

2. EDUCATION AND SPIRITUAL ATTAINMENTS

Vedānta Deśika received his education under great scholars like Ātreya Rāmānuja, his maternal uncle and Anantasūri Somayājin his father, and also by Vatsya-varadācārya. Possessing inborn lustre of knowledge by the grace of Lord Veṅkaṭeśa, Vedānta Deśika had an ambition of teaching and propagating Rāmānuja's Philosophy.

In his early life, he became well-versed in all branches like *Nyāya, Mīmāṁsā, Vyākaraṇa, Alaṅkāra* and *Vedānta*. Vedānta Deśika's works like *Nyāyapariśuddhi* and *Śeśvaramīmāṁsā* testify to his deep insight and height of knowledge in different schools of Indian Philosophy.

Under the able guidance of his preceptor, Vedānta Deśika studied all works on the Philosophy of Viśiṣṭādvaita school, like the *Nyāyatattva* of Nāthamuni, the *Siddhitraya* of Yāmuna, the *Tattvaratnākara* of Parāśarabhaṭṭāraka, the *Tattvasāra* of Vātsyavaradācārya, the *Nyāyakulīśa* of

Ātreya and the works of Rāmānuja Nārāyaṇācārya and of Varadaviṣṇumiśra.

Vedānta Deśika was not only a Philosopher but a Poet and Dramatist too. On par with Kālidāsa's *Meghadūta*, he wrote a poetic work entitled *Haṁsa-sandeśa* depicting Rāma's message to Sītā through a Haṁsa, with all sublimity.

He used to sing mystic songs of Saint Nammāḷvār written in Tamil. He also summarised the Tamil Veda in his *Drāmiḍopaniṣatsāra* and *Drāmiḍopaniṣadratnāvalī*. Vedānta Deśika had also mastered the difficult *Mahādvidyā* – syllogisms of Kulārka, and was well acquainted with *Mahāvidyā* refutations of the Tārkikas such as Vādīndra (1225 A.D.) and others.[11]

3. VEDĀNTA DEŚIKA: AS A HOUSE-HOLDER

After completing his education, Vedānta Deśika married Tirumangai, belonging to a respected family. He had a son by name Kumāra-Varadanātha who later became a great scholar and a pioneer of his father's works. Vedānta Deśika was bestowed with the Garuḍa *Mantropadeśam*[12] by his preceptor, Ātreya Rāmānuja who passed away in 1295 A.D. Then Vedānta Deśika was crowned on the pontificial throne at Kāñcīpuram.

Sojourn at Kāñcīpuram and Tiruvahindrapuram

After having been crowned on the pontificial throne, Vedānta Deśika thought of performing his duties. He then started teaching *Śrībhāṣya* and propounded Śrīvaiṣṇava religion and its ethics to the public at large. In course of time, he became very famous. His popularity led to jealousy in the heart of the Teṅgalais. Therefore, Vedānta Deśika shifted his residence at Kāñcīpuram to Tiruvahindrapuram which was known for its peaceful environment. Here also, he started preaching the Philosophy of Śrīvaiṣṇavism. During his stay for fifteen years, Vedānta Deśika composed devotional hymns and poems in Sanskrit and Tamil. Seeing the height of his knowledge in all *Śāstras*, the people of Tiruvahīndrapuram conferred upon Vedānta Deśika the titles *Vedāntācārya* and *Sarvatantrasvatantra*.

In course of time, at the request of the people of Kāñcīpuram, Vedānta Deśika came back to Kāñcīpuram, and adorned the pontificial throne. Staying there, he wrote many works on Vedānta, including the commentaries on *Śrībhāṣya*. Because of Vedānta Deśika is ceaseless religious activities, Kāñcīpuram turned into a centre for education and religious activities.

He is said to have travelled both in northern and southern parts of India to propagate Rāmānuja's philosophy and religion.[13] During the course of his visits to different holy places, he had debates with the opponents and shone like Dhruva star in the field of philosophical schools. Such events gave him much force to write polemical and non-polemical works on the Viśiṣṭādvaita Vedānta.

4. WORKS

Vedānta Deśika is known as the most versatile and the most prolific writer in the field of Śrīvaiṣṇava literature. He had commanding intelligence in wielding his pen with equal felicity in the languages like Sanskrit, Tamil and in Maṇipravāḷa (Tamil cum Sanskrit). Such works of Vedānta Deśika are classified under the following *six* heads :

(a) *Manuals of Śrīvaiṣṇava Religion and Esotericism,*

(b) *Thesis on Śrīvaiṣṇava Theology and Ritualism,*

(c) *Devotional and Didactic Poetry,*

(d) *Literary Works,*

(e) *Original Philosophical Treatises, and*

(f) *Commentaries.*

The works of Vedānta Deśika coming under these heads are more than one hundred in number. Here is given in brief, the outlines of these works.[14]

(a) Manuals of Śrīvaiṣṇava Religion and Esotericism

Vedānta Deśika's manuals are marked with two objectives – spreading the ideas and ideals of Śrīvaiṣṇavism and preservation of Religion and Philosophy of the Āḷvārs and the Ācāryas.

(i) Nyāsadaśakaṃ : This is a short poem consisting of ten significant verses in *Anuṣṭub* metre dealing with the doctrine of *Prapatti* or self-surrender unto the Supreme Deity, Varadarāja of Kāñcī.

(ii) Nyāsaviṁśati : This is another work on *Nyāsa* or *Prapatti* which is a means to God realisation. It runs into twenty verses touching one after the other, upon pre-requisites, the essentials and the consummation of *Nyāsa* or *Prapatti*. This work is commented upon by himself, and Śrīnivāsa too. Another commentary upon it by Naḍādur Veṅkaṭarāmācārya in *Maṇipravāḷa* language is available.

(iii) Vairāgyapañcakaṃ : As the title of the work itself indicates, this work speaks of five kinds of complete indifferernce to the worldly objects. The five stanzas embodying this work give reply to the royal invitation from the Vijayanagara Court. Although lucid in expression, this poem is full of significance for Śrīvaiṣṇavism. An exposition of these five verses in Tamil by Veer Rāghavācārya is available.

(iv) ***Haridinatilakaṃ :*** This work of seventeen *Sragdharā* verses discusses the performance of *Ekādaśī* by Śrīvaiṣṇavas.

(v) Yajñopavītapratiṣṭhā : This small work of nine verses in *Sragdharā* metre explains the rituals of wearing the *Yajñopavīta* and the esotericism of the mantras accompanying it.

(vi) Vaiśvadevakārikā : Its nine *Sragdharā* verses represent the observance of the *Vaiśvadevayajña* in the scheme of the Śrīvaiṣṇava ethics of the *Pañcakālakṛtya.*

(vii) Śrīvaiṣṇavadinakārya : It is a work of ten verses written in Tamil. It summarises the details regarding daily religious duties of Śrīvaiṣṇavas in the spirit of the *Pāñcarātra Saṁhitās.*

(viii) Arthapañcakaṃ : This is a popular Tamil work in eleven verses. The author emphasizes here five spiritual disciplines of Śrīvaiṣṇava religion. Those are :

(a) the nature of Supreme Brahman,

(b) nature of *jīva,*

(c) the means of spiritual attainment,

(d) the results of spiritual attainment, and

(e) obstacles in the way of attaining the goal.

(ix) Pannirunāmaṃ : Consisting of thirteen verses, it discusses the significance of the twelve *puṇḍras* and the *nāma* on the body of a Śrīvaiṣṇavas.

(x) Āhāraniyamaṃ : As the very title indicates, in twenty one Tamil verses, this work prescribes the types of food for a Śrīvaiṣṇava, suitable for leading a life of religious discipline.

(xi) Tirumantracurukku

(xii) Dvayacurukku

(xiii) Caramaślokacurukku

} These small handbooks in Tamil, describe Śrīvaiṣṇava spiritualism, bringing out the significance of *Prapatti.*

(xiv) Tattvanavanītaṃ

(xv) Rahaśyanavanītaṃ

These two works are composed in *Maṇi-pravāḷa* style to expound important tenets of the Rāmānuja philosophy.

(xvi) Upakāra-saṅgrahaṃ **:** Written in Tamil, it explains the manifestations of Divine Providence in the life of man.

(xvii) Sāra-saṅgrahaṃ **:** It expounds the principles of Śrīvaiṣṇava ethics in Tamil verses.

(xviii) Munivāhanabhogaṃ **:** It is written in *Maṇi-pravāḷa* style. It is commented upon by Tiruppāṇāḷvārs, Amalanādippirān, expressing the mystic experiences of the ancient Tamil sage.

(xix) Madhurakavihṛdyaṃ **:** This work in *Maṇi-pravāḷa* style, is a commentary on Madhurakavi's *Kaṇṇi-numśiruttaṁbu.* It is not available at present.

(xx) Tattvatrayaculukaṃ and ***(xxi) Rahasyatraya-culukaṃ*** or ***Sārasaṅkṣepa*** **:** These are the short Tamil treatises written on the truths of Viśiṣṭādvaita philosophy and the ideals of Śrīvaiṣṇava religion respectively.

(xxii) Sāradipaṃ or ***Rahasyatrayasārdadīpaṃ*** **:** It is a Tamil work. It seems that it is a summary of the *Rahasyatrayasāraṁ* as referred to by Mahācārya.

(xxiii) Nigamaparimaḷaṃ and ***(xxiv) Stheya Virodhaṃ*** **:** These are the great expositions on the *prabandhas* but they are not available now.

(xxv) Guruparaṁparāsāraṃ **:** This is written in Tamil. It propagates the cult of the worship of the propounders of the Śrīvaiṣṇava religion.

(xxvi) Virodhaparihāraṃ **:** It is a rejoinder to the points of contraversy arising in the *Rahasyatrayasāraṃ* of Vedānta Deśika.

(xxvii–xxxiv) Tattvaśikhāmaṇi, Mummaṇikovai, Navaratnamālai, Punduppā, Kajalpā, Ammānepā, Uśalpā, Eśalpā : These works are not available now, yet they have been referred to by Mahācārya in his *Vaibhava-prakāśikā*. Hence, these works are believed to be composed by Vedānta Deśika.

(xxxv) Adaikāḷapaṭṭu : This is a devotional Tamil poem on *Prapatti* in eleven verses.

(xxxvi) Tiruchinnamālai : This is written in Tamil. It is on the bugle-song glorifying the Varadarāja procession at Kāñcī during the *Brahmotsava* festival.

(xxxvii) Añjalivaibhava : It is a *Śaraṇāgati* song in Tamil.

(xxxviii) Rahasya-śikhāmaṇi : This again is a work expounding the Śrīvaiṣṇava ideals of *Prapatti* in Maṇi-pravāḷa style.

(xxxix) Abhayapradānasāraṃ : This expounds the Śrīvaiṣṇava concept of Divine Providence.

(xl) Sārāsāraṃ : This work in Tamil embodies the principles of Śrīvaiṣṇava religion and philosophy.

(xli) Pradhānaśatakaṃ : This is a Tamil work on Śrīvaiṣṇavism.

(xlii–xlv) Rahasyaratnāvali-hṛdayaṃ, Rahasya-ratnāvalī, Tattvaratnāvali-pratipādyasaṅgrahaṃ : These are Tamil treatises on Śrīvaiṣṇava esotericism and mysticism.

(xlvi–xlviii) Rahasya-sandeśa-vivaraṇaṃ, Rahasya-sandeśaṃ and Tattva-sandeśaṃ : These are the three of the four famous treatises of Vedānta Deśika written with a view to initiating the prince, Sarvajña Siṅgappa into the idealism of the Śrīvaiṣṇava religion.

(xlix–xl) Rahasyamātṛkā and ***Tattvamātṛkā :*** These are short Tamil manuals of the Śrīvaiṣṇava *sādhana* of spiritualism.

(li–lii) Rahasyapadavī and ***Tattvapadavī :*** These two are written in Tamil to propagate the religion of Rāmānuja.

(liii) Saṁpradāyapariśuddhi : It is written in Maṇipravāḷa. This deals with the ideas and the ideals of *Munitraya-saṁpradāya*.

(liv) Ārādhanakārikā : As the very title indicates, in two simple verses it describes the method of worshipping the God.

(lv) Prabandhasāraṃ : In eighteen Tamil verses, it is in praise of twelve Āḷvārs the great seers of Śrīvaiṣṇavism.

(lvi) Hastigirimāhātmyaṃ : Written in Maṇipravāḷa, it describes the history of Kāñcīpuram in the style of the Paurāṇic texts. Lord Varadarāja of Kāñcī has been glorified herein.

(lvii) Paramapadasopānaṃ : Written in Maṇipravāḷa, it establishes the Śrīvaiṣṇava *sādhana* of *Prapatti* to the exclusion of the other means of the realisation of the Divine.

(b) Thesis on Śrīvaiṣṇava Theology and Ritualism

These traditional works characterise Vedānta Deśika as a teacher and a successor to the *Saṁpradāyapravartana*-seat of Rāmānuja, and hence aims at propounding the religion and philosophy of Śrīvaiṣṇavism. These works are:

(i) Nikṣeparakṣā **:** This is a thesis on *Nikṣepa* or *Prapatti* giving utmost importance to the cause of love and devotion to God. This work is considered to be Vedānta Deśika's literary genius at revealing the supreme secret of love for God, man and Nature.

(ii) Pāñcarātrarakṣā **:** It discusses at length, the self validity of the *Pāñcarātra-saṁhitās* and the universality of the Pāñcarātra religion and morality. It presupposes other works of its type like *Āgama-prāmāṇya* of Yāmunācārya and the works of Parāśara-bhaṭṭāraka, Kṛṣṇamuni and so on.

(iii) Saccāritrarakṣā **:** This is another work of Vedānta Deśika explaining the ritualism of initiation into Śrīvaiṣṇavism.

(iv) Drāmiḍopaniṣatsāra **:** It is one of major works of Vedānta Deśika, written in the *Sragdharā* and the *Śikhariṇī* metres. The *Drāmiḍopaniṣatsāra* expounds the majesty and the grace of the Supreme God. This is a Sanskrit version of the Gāthās or the Tamil songs of the saint Nammāḻvār.

(v) Drāmiḍopaniṣattātparya-ratnāvaḷī **:** It runs in one hundred and thirty *Sragdharā* verses divided into ten sub-sections. All these verses are based on the songs of the great Nammāḻvār and contain the essence of the doctrine of self-surrender.

(vi) Rahasyatraya-sāraṁ **:** It is magnum opus of Vedānta Deśika. It embodies the secrets of Śrīvaiṣṇava esotericism. It is considered to be the great *Prapatti śāstra* of the Vaḍagalai Śrīvaiṣṇavas.

(vii) Bhūgola-nirṇaya **:** Running into nine verses, it aims at describing all parts of the globe following the Purāṇas.

(viii) Śilpārthasāra **:** This is said to have been

written by Vedānta Deśika on the art of sculpture with special reference to Iconography. It contains the *'Ācārya Mudrā'* executed by him. This can be seen in the Deśika shrine at Tiruvahīndrapuram even today.

(c) Devotional and Didactic Poetry

A good number of devotional and didactic poems is credited to the academic genius of Vedānta Deśika. Poetic faculty and religious spirit of Vedānta Deśika are clearly reflected in his poems. Being inspired by the songs of the Āḷvārs, he wrote these poems which are as below :

(i) Hayagrīvastotra : It is a small poem containing thirty two verses in the *Upajāti* metre. It is written on Lord Hayagrīva, the Śrīvaiṣṇava deity of light and learning. This is sung by the Śrīvaiṣṇavas of Tiruvahīndrapuram during the Brahmotsavam festivals. The Vaḍagalai Śrīvaiṣṇavas have reverential regard for this hymn as they take it to be the poetic idealisation of the esotericism of Hayagrīva *mantra*. This poem is commented upon in Sanskrit by Velāmur Śrīnivāsācārya and Śrīśaila Tirumalai Nambi Rāghavārya. And Kurichi Gopāla Tātācārya and Gārgya Veṅkatācārya interpreted this poem in Tamil.

(ii) Daśavatārastotra : This hymn describes all images of the incarnations of Mahā Śrī Viṣṇu. It contains thirteen verses in the *Śārdūlavikrīḍita* metre. Most of the stanzas of this stotra have been repeated in Act VII of his drama, the *Saṅkalpasūryodaya*. It has three commentaries, of which, one in Sanskrit by Śrīśaila Tirumalai Nambi Rāghavārya; and two in Tamil, by Kurichi Gopāla Tatācārya and by Gārgya Veṅkatācārya.

(iii) Bhagavaddhyānasopāna : This devotional poem containing twelve *Mandākrānta* verses, speaks of poet's heart melting in Divine love. Describing the limbs of the images of Raṅganātha, this poem presents the sublime sense of *Prapatti*. It echoes forth the lofty ideas of the Tamil songs of Muni Vāhana, a great Tamil saint. This hymn is commented upon by –

(a) Anvil Veṅkaṭa Gopāladāsa,
(b) Śrīśaila Tirumalai Nambi Rāghavārya,
(c) Śrīśaila Vedānta Rāmānuja,
(d) Śrīśaila Sinnamu Raṅganathācārya (in Tamil)

and

(e) Gārgya Veṅkatācārya (in Tamil).

(iv) Gopālaviṁśati **:** Written in a variety of metres, this hymn containing twenty one verses deals with the faith and philosophical idealisation concerning Lord Kṛṣṇa. Some of fine stanzas are incorporated in the XV canto of the *Yādavābhyudaya*. Appayya Dīkṣita though a Advaita scholar, has appreciated Vedānta Deśika as the great Kṛṣṇa *bhakta*, capable of the highest flights of Kṛṣṇa-poetry. It has two commentaries, one in Sanskrit by Śrīśaila Tirumalai Naṁbi Rāghavārya and second in Tamil by Śrīśaila Sinnamu Raṅganāthācārya.

(v) Śrīstuti **:** Consisting of twenty six verses in the *Mandākrānta* metre, this hymn describes the glory of Goddess Lakṣmī. The *Śrīstuti* of Yāmunācārya is its main source of inspiration. This hymn is much honoured by Mahācārya, the celebrated commentator of the *Śatadūṣaṇī*. It has commentaries, one by Ātreya Varadācārya in Sanskrit and second by Kurichi Gopāla Tātācārya in Tamil.

(vi) Abhītistava **:** Consisting of twenty nine verses, this hymn expresses author's devotion on Śrī Raṅganātha of Śrīraṅgam. It gives some autobiographical touches and a clue to the chronological order of the works of Vedānta Deśika. It is commented upon by Śrīśaila Sinnamu Raṅganāthācārya in Tamil.

(vii) Varadarāja pañcāśata : Also called *Devarāja pañcāśata*, it is a hymn of fifty one stanzas on the deity Varadarāja of Kāñcīpuram describing the Brahmotsavam festivals and the glory of Varadarāja. It exposes the theology of Vaiṣṇavism with a special reference to the doctrine of *Prapatti*. Hence, it has been regarded as *śāstra* poem. It is commented upon by Karur Śrīśaila Śrīnivāsācārya.

(viii) Vegāsetustotraṃ : It is a hymn of ten stanzas on the deity enshrined in the Yathoktakārin temple at Kāñcī-puram. A story behind this, is that, once Lord Brahmā began the Aśvamedha sacrifice at Kāñcī in the absence of his spouse Sarasvatī. Enraged at this, Sarasvatī changed herself in the form of a river, Vegāvatī and started flowing towards the sacrificial field in order to extinguish the sacrificial fire. But, Viṣṇu the Yathoktakārin threw Himself across the stream and stopped the waters flowing towards the sacrificial altar. Since Yathotakārin became the *Vegāsetu* or the *setu* to the Vegāvati river, hymn composed on him, is called *Vegāsetu-stotra*. It has two commentaries, one by T.Ch.N.R.Tatācārya in Sanskrit and second by Śrīśaila Sinnamu Raṅganāthācārya in Tamil.

(ix) Aṣṭabhujāṣṭaka-stotra : It is a hymn of ten verses on Viṣṇu or Gajendravarada with eight hands enshrined in the Aṣṭabāhu temple adjacent to Yathoktakārina temple at Kāñcīpuram. This work is written by Vedānta Deśika during his early literary career.

(x) Kāmāsikāṣṭaka : A hymn of nine stanzas on Viṣṇu in the form of Narasiṁha, enshrined in the Kāmāsikā temple at Kāñcīpuram, it describes the glory of Lord Narasiṁha.

(xi) Paramārtha stuti : It is a hymn of ten verses on Viṣṇu in the form of Rāma or Vijayarāghava or Samara-puṅgava installed in the shrine near Tirupputkuḷi. It is commented upon by I.R. Sheshadryacar in Sanskrit and by Agnihotram Chakrapani Pattararya Dasa in Tamil.

(xii) Saraṇāgati-dīpikā : It is a hymn of sixty verses on the deity Dīpa Prakāśa consecrated in the Dīpa Prakāśa shrine at Kāñcīpuram. It shines like a lamp showing to us the inner recesses on the heart of Vedānta Deśika, a *śaraṇāgata*. It also explains the tenets of Rāmānuja Philosophy and Religion. It has three commentaries, of which, the first and the second by Śrīśaila Tirumalai Naṁbi Rāghavārya and by Gārgya Veṅkatārya are in Sanskrit and the third by K.M. Rājagopalācārya is in Tamil.

(xiii) Devanāyaka-pañcāśata : A hymn of fifty-three verses in *Vasanta-tilakā* metre is dedicated to Devanāyaka, the deity of Tiruvahīndrapuram. The ideas of the songs of great Tamil saint Ṇāmmāḷvār are reflected in this poem. It is commented upon by Śrīśaila Tirumalai Nambi Rāghavācārya in Sanskrit and by K.M. Rājagopālācārya in Tamil.

(xiv) Acyutaśataka : It is a devotional poem in Prākṛt containing one hundred and one Gāthās on Devanāyaka or Acyuta. Being the quintessence of Rāmānuja Philosophy, this work shows each and every facet of the saint Ṇāmmālvār. It has five commentaries such as:

(a) by T.Ch.N.R. Tātācārya (in Sanskrit)

(b) by T.V. Deśikācārya (Grammatical)

(c) by Śrī Śaila Sinnamu Raṅganāthācārya (in Tamil)

(d) by Taiylar Vangipuram Deśikācārya (in Tamil)

(e) by S.T.A.T. Kumāra Tātārya (in Sanskrit)

(xv) Dehalīśa-stuti : It is a devotional poem of twenty eight stanzas dedicated to Dehalīśa, the deity at Tirukkoilur. It consists of the story of the coming into being of Munitraya Sampradāya of Śrīvaiṣṇavism, to which Vedānta Deśika belongs. It has two Sanskrit commentaries one by T.Ch.N.R. Tātācārya and the other by Śrī Śaila Sinnamu Raṅganāthācārya. Also P.I. Lakṣmīnareshācārya wrote Tamil commentary on it.

(xvi) Nyāsa-tilakam **:** It is a hymn of thirty two stanzas on Śrī Raṅganātha of Śrīraṅgaṁ. As the name suggests this work deals with the *Nyāsa* or self-surrender. It has been commented upon in Sanskrit by Naināracārya, our poet's own son and by Śrībhāṣyam Śrīnivāsācārya. A Tamil commentary also by Kurichi Gopāla Tātācārya is available.

(xvii) Raghuvīragadya **:** It is a prose-poem on Śrī Rāma and closely resembles the *Raṅgagadya* of Rāmānuja. It is a beautiful poetic epitome of the *Rāmāyaṇa* of Vālmīki.

(xviii) Bhūstuti **:** It is a devotional poem of thirty three verses dedicated to Bhū or the Goddess Earth. It reads like a poem on the glory and the grandeur of Bhāratavarṣa also. It suggests poet's mystic speculations on the earth, a mode of the Divine. It has been commented upon by Śrī Śaila Tirumalai Naṁbi Rāghavārya in Sanskrit and by K.M. Rājagopālācārya in Tamil.

(xix) Ṣoḍaśāyudha-stotra **:** It is a hymn of eighteen stanzas in *Anuṣṭub* metre on the sixteen weapons accompanying the Sudarśana of Śrī Viṣṇu installed in the Śrīraṅgam temple. It is written on the lines of the Astrādhyāya of Viṣṇupurāṇa. It is commented upon by Tenbarai Rājagopālācārya in Sanskrit and by Kurichi Gopālatātācārya in Tamil.

(xx) Sudarśanāṣṭaka **:** It is a hymn of eight verses on Sudarśana or Viṣṇu's disc. It has Sanskrit commentary by Tenbarai Rājagopālācārya and by Kurichi Gopāla Tātācārya in Tamil.

(xxi) Garuḍa-daṇḍaka : It is a hymn on Garuḍa in the *Daṇḍaka* metre. The use of *Daṇḍaka* style is said to have been influenced by similar usage in the *Prabodha-candrodaya* of Kṛṣṇa Miśra. Vedānta Deśika is said to have invoked Garuḍa with this *Daṇḍaka* and defeated the snake charmer who had challenged Vedānta Deśika to show that he was *Sarvatantrasvatantra.* This work is incorporated in the X Act of his *Saṅkalpasūryodaya.* It has a Sanskrit commentary by Tenbarai Rājagopālācārya and Tamil one by K.M. Rājagopālācārya.

(xxii) Garuḍa-pañcāśata : A hymn written in *Sragdharā* metre is addressed to Garuḍa the presiding deity of wisdom and reason. The Śrīvaiṣṇavas regard it as the embodiment of the Garuḍa Mantra. This is included in the tenth Act of the *Saṅkalpasūryodaya.*

(xxiii) Yatirāja-saptati : A hymn of seventy four verses on Rāmānujācārya, the great founder of Śrīvaiṣṇava cult, expresses Vedānta Deśika's deep sense of devotion to his preceptor.

(xxiv) Dhāti-pañcaka : This is another work of five stanzas in honour of Rāmānujācārya. It glorifies the Ācārya as a great conquerer of rival religionists and the rival schools of philosophy.

(xxv) Divya-deśa-maṅgalāśāsana-pañcaka : It is a poem of five stanzas describing the holy places like Śrīraṅgam, Tirupati, Kāñcīpuram and Tirunārāyanapuram.

(xxvi) Pādukā-sahasra : It is a long hymn of one thousand and eight verses in thirty two *padyas* or sections on the Pādukās of the deity Raṅganātha of Śrīraṅgam. As depicted in the life sketch of Vedānta Deśika, this was written in a single night as a challenge to the *Padakamala-sahasra* of Teṅgalai scholar Aḷagiya Manavāḷa Perumaḷ Nainar. Since Vedānta Deśika won the competition, he was honoured with the title Kavitākikasiṁha. The Advaitic scholar Appayya Dīkṣita also is said to have commented upon it. Both the Vaḍagalai and Teṅgalai Śrīvaiṣṇavas adore it for its poetry and philosophy.

(xxvii) Subhāṣitānīvī : Vedānta Deśika is said to have composed this book of didactic poetry for Sarvajña Singappa Nāyaka of Rajmundry who sought moral and religious instruction from him. Some of the stanzas are found in the *Saṅkalpasūryodaya*. A Sanskrit commentary *viz.*, Ranapeṭīkā by Śrīnivāsa, is available.

(d) Literary Works of Epic, Drama and Lyric Type

(i) Yādavābhyudaya[15]

This is a *Mahākāvya* describing the Yadu race, Kṛṣṇa's birth, his childhood and the Govardhana episode, Rāsalīlā of Kṛṣṇa. Further, the scene of Kaṁsavadha, Kṛṣṇa's marriage with Rukmiṇī, Śyāmāntakamaṇi story, his marriage with Satyabhāmā, Śiśupālavadha, Narakāsuravadha, description of Nandana, Kṛṣṇa's aerial journey to Dvārakā, marriage of Aniruddha with Uṣa and Kṛṣṇa's conquest of Śoṇitapura, the incident of Gītā and Kṛṣṇa's *antaḥpura* scene — these details are well described in a variety of metres suggestive of a variety of ideas and imageries and emotions. This *Mahākāvya* is otherwise called *Yaduvaṁśa* or *Kṛṣṇābhyudaya*. From the introductory verses of Appayya Dīkṣita's excellent commentary (16th century A.D.) on the *Yādavābhyudaya*, readers come to know that, it was acclaimed as a *Mahākāvya*[16] even in the life time of the poet. A perusal of the 24 cantos of the *Mahākāvya* makes it emphatic that the *Bhāgavata-purāṇa* was the source of inspiration for Vedānta Deśika.

(ii) Saṅkalpasūryodaya

It is an allegorical play dramatising the Viśiṣṭādvaita philosophy and the Śrīvaiṣṇava religion. It runs into ten long acts which are more poetic than dramatic. The play depicts the toils and tribulations of the human soul on its way to God's realisation. It shows the saving power of divine grace at each and every step of the progress of the soul on the way to the conquest of ignorance. The characters of the play are formless representations or personification of higher virtues and spiritual values of a religious system and also the vice and the wicked feelings of a human being. It describes a battle scene in which the characters *Viveka* and *Moha*, the Hero and the Villain fight against each other, and the victory goes to the former. The human soul reaches its climax of achievement and obtains the Divine Grace.

The details of this play and its criticism are presented in the forthcoming chapters.

(iii) Haṁsa-sandeśa

It is a *Sandeśa Kāvya* written on the lines of the *Meghadūta* of Kālidāsa. It is divided into two parts and contains sixty stanzas in part I and fifty in part II.

The description of the lyric runs as follows. After learning from Hanumān, Śrī Rāma sends message to Sītā through a Swan whom he meets accidently. The swan found in Padmakāsāra resembled Sītā's royal pace, the purity of her apparels, the swan-like-sound of her anklets. And hence, Śrī Rāma choose Swan to be his messenger. Rāma sends a message that Sītā should be alive till she is rescued by him.

The places over which the Swan has to fly like Tirupati, Kāñcīpuram, Śrīraṅgam and Madhura have been described beautifully by the poet. It suggests the deep love of Rāma for Sītā or in other sense, the love of God for the human soul pinning away in separation from the Divine Lover and tortured by Rāvaṇa, representing the evil propensities of the mind. The description of the rivers that the Swan would see on the way, like Sarasvatī in Kāñcīpuram, Kāverī in Śrīraṅgam, Tāmraparṇī in the then Pāṇḍya Kingdom is very impressive. Śrī Rāma advises the swan to take the blessings of Śrī Veṅkaṭeśa, Śrī Raṅganātha and of Śrī Varadarājaswāmy, the main deities of Tirupati, Śrīraṅgam and of Kāñcīpuram respectively. The swan is instructed to stop Sītā under a Śiṁsupā tree amidst the security of Rāvaṇa. The swan tells Sītā that Śrī Rāma is keeping well and would come with the army, defeat Rāvaṇa and take her back.

(iv) Dayāśataka

It is a reflective lyric highlighting the aspects of Divine Love and Divine Providence. It contains one hundred and eight stanzas in various metres. One can see the inspiration of Kālīdāsa in this work also.

(v) Godāstuti

It is a lyric on Godā, the famous Āṇḍāl worshipped as a Goddess in the Śrīvaiṣṇava shrines. This *stuti* of twenty nine stanzas, suggests Vedānta Deśika's devotion to the Divine. It closely resembles the Tiruppāvai of Āṇḍāl. It is commented upon by Śrīśaila Tirumalai Rāghavācārya in Sanskrit and K.M. Rājagopālācārya in Tamil.

(vi) Yamaka-ratnākara

It is a voluminous work abounding in '*Yamaka*'. There is a dispute regarding its authorship of Vedānta Deśika. Nevertheless, the *Catalogus Catalogorum* mentions it as the work of Vedānta Deśika.[17] Also the Catalogue of Sanskrit Mss. in Mysore and Coorg, Rice ascribes it to Vedānta Deśika.

As Vedānta Deśika is an adept in *Yamaka* writing which is evident from his *Yādavābhyudaya*, it can be said that this work belongs to the authorship of Vedānta Deśika.

(vii) Samasyā-sāhasrī

It is a collection of one thousand and odd *Samasyās*. After the composition of this work, Vedānta Deśika was given the title — *Samasyā-sāhaśrī*, which Vedānta Deśika himself mentions this title in his *Stotra-ratna-bhāṣya.*

(e) Original Philosophical Treatises

Here, the most important philosophical works of Vedānta Deśika are taken note of. The originality of these works lies in their convincing presentation of the philosophical tenets of Rāmānuja. These are called Deśika Darśana or Deśika Tradition Works (Deśika *Saṁpradāya Granthas*) because these works show his profound knowledge, scholarship and the variety.

(i) Nyāyapariśuddhi

It is a successful attempt of Vedānta Deśika at the syncretisation of the ancient Nyāya-realism with Viśiṣṭā-dvaitic spiritualism and transcedantalism. As Vedānta Deśika himself suggests, his work was a great *'Paṇḍita-kṛtya'* meant to synthesize the divergent trends of the *Nyāya* with the Vedānta. This work is divided into five chapters. The first chapter introduces the *pramāṇas* accepted by Rāmānuja and outlines the types of knowledge and distinguishes right knowledge from wrong knowledge. The second chapter contains the exposition of Inference, and the third chapter has a discourse on *Śabda-prāmāṇya*. The fourth chapter points to present *Smṛti* as an independent means of knowledge. The fifth chapter deals with a *Prameyavicāra* of Rāmānuja Philosophy. This work is commented upon by

Śrīnivāsadāsa, under the title *'Nyāyasāra'*, which is available upto *Śabda-pramāṇa.*

(ii) Nyāyasiddhāñjana

This work, otherwise called *Tarka-siddhāñjana* is the continuation of the *Nyāyapariśudhi*. This work runs into six chapters or paricchedas. The first chapter contains the exposition of *Jaḍa Dravya*. The second chapter discusses the nature of the *Jīva*. The third chapter presents Īśvara as the Viśiṣṭādvaitic Absolute and indentifies it with Śrī Nārāyaṇa. The fourth chapter conceives of the Spiritual Matter and Its evolution resulting in the Vaikuṇṭha. The fifth chapter deals with epistemology of the Viśiṣṭādvaita school, and the philosophy of *Dharma-bhūtajñāna* subsisting with the *Jīva*. The sixth chapter defines and discusses ten *Ādravyas* or the *Guṇas* such as *Sattva, Rajas, Tamas, Śabda, Sparśa, Rūpa, Rasa, Gandha, Saṁyoga* and *Śakti*. Its commentary by Raṅga-Rāmānuja is an illuminating one.

(iii) Tattvamuktākalāpa

It is meant to be a necklace of five hundred pearls of *Sragdharā*-verses, wreathed into five strings. It is one of the most important and authoritative works of Vedānta Deśika. Mādhavācārya, Vidyāraṇya has referred to this text in his *Sarva-darśana-saṅgraha.*[18]

The First String or the *Jaḍa-dravyasāra* shows that matter and the material evolute as the *Śarīra* of the Indwelling Divine. *Prakṛti* is discussed as the Divine organism.

The Second String or the *Jīvasāra* reveals the *Jīva* or the self in its real essence of subservience to the Great Self. Influenced by Rāmānuja and Nammālvār, Vedānta Deśika has presented the self psychology to lead to the conclusions of the self-philosophy.

The Third String or the *Nāyakasāra* is the main string containing the essence of Viśiṣṭādvaitic philosophy. The God and Religion is equated, here, with the Absolute of philosophy, and the Kṛṣṇa of poetry is identified with the Śrīnivāsa of Śrīvaiṣṇavism.

The Fourth String or the *Buddhisāra* is meant for the presentation of the self-luminous consciousness as the inalienable adjunct of the finite self and the Supreme Self.

The Fifth String or the *Adravyasāra* is meant to show the '*Ādravyas*' as the states or the attributes or the energies or the functions of the *Tattvas* or the substances.

The comprehesive scheme of the *Tattvamuktā-kalāpa* entitles it to be the book of reference for Rāmānuja's philosophy. Its gloss called the *Ānanda-Dāyinī* of Nṛsiṁha Deva (16th or 17th century) has been published, in part along with its companion, the *Bhāva-prakāśa* of Śrī Parakāla Svāmin.

(iv) Sarvārthasiddhi

It is a gloss on the *Tattvamuktākalāpa* by Vedānta Deśika himself. It makes one understand *Tattvamuktā-kalāpa* easily. This work is testifies to the vast study, of the critical faculty and of the poetic bent of mind of Vedānta Deśika, the philosopher.

(v) Śatadūṣaṇī

It is a great dialectic work and attempts to refute the philosophy of Śaṅkara, Bhāskara and Yādavaprakāśa. The *Sapta-Vidhānupapattis* or the seven-fold incompatibilities or absurdities of the *Nirviśeṣādvaita* of Śaṅkara as pointed out by Rāmānuja have been amply magnified here. As its name suggests, it should contain one hundred and one refutations. But only sixty six refutations are available in the extant copy. Doḍḍayācārya has written a masterly commentary called the *'Caṇḍamāruta'*. He was called Mahācārya for this very commetary.

(vi) Śeśvaramīmāṁsā

It is an exhaustive exposition of the *Mīmāṁsā-sūtras* of Jaimini with a view to suggesting inherent relationship between *'Karma'* and *'Jñāna'* or *'Bhakti'*.

Vedānta Deśika's attempt in his *Śeśvaramīmāṁsā* is to equate the *'Apūrva'* (the power of action) to the *'Saṅkalpa'* or the will of God to save the Soul. The source of inspiration for Vedānta Deśika is the concept of *Pūrvottara-mīmāṁsaikakāṇṭhya* of Rāmānuja.

(vii) Mīmāṁsā-pāḍuka

It is of 173 stanzas in *Sragdharā* metre. Probably both *Mīmāṁsā-pāḍuka* and *Śeśvara-mīmāṁsā* were written from the inspiration that Vedānta Deśika got from his great teacher Ātreya Rāmānuja. This work proves that *Dharma* itself is the Brāhman the Eternal Absolute Reality. This work appears to be incomplete.

(viii) Adhikāraṇa-sārāvali

This is a metrical exposition of the various sections of the *Brahmasūtras*. It is not only a metrical summary of the *Śrībhāṣya* of Rāmānuja, but an original philosophical contribution to the Rāmānuja Philosophy. Vedānta Deśika's mastery over the intricacies of the *Sragdharā* verse as seen in the *Tattvamuktākalāpa* reaches its climax in the *Adhikāraṇa-sārāvali*.

Kumāra Vedāntācārya, Vedānta Deśika's son and successor, has written a commentary called *Adhikāraṇa-cintāmaṇi. Adhikāraṇa-kalpataru* of Attipattu Śatakopa Rāmānuja is another commentary available.

(ix) Paramata-bhaṅga

Written in *Maṇipravāḷa*, it has the same method of treatment as the *Sarvadarśana-saṅgraha* of Mādhava-Vidyāraṇya. It critically sums up the Indian philosophical systems and points to the greatness of *Rāmānuja Darśana* as the only practical philosophy conducive to the life of man forming a stage in Life Divine.

(x) Adhikāraṇa-darpaṇa

It is written on the lines of the *Adhikāraṇa-sārāvali* on the *Brahmasūtras.* It is not available now.

(xi) Vāditraya-khaṇḍana

This work appears to have been a brief criticism of the Philosophy of Śaṅkara, Bhāskara and Yādavaprakāśa.

(xii) Cakāra-samarthana

This is written by Vedānta Deśika with a view to proving the propriety of the occasional usages of 'm' in the *Śatadūṣaṇī*, which were probably charged with redundance by his critics. It is not available now.

The Commentaries of Vedānta Deśika form an important contributions to Viśiṣṭādvaitic literature. These works are faithful to the texts and yet critical to the core.

(f) Commentaries

(i) Tattva-ṭīkā : It is an exposition of the *Śrībhāṣya* of Rāmānuja, and it presents the outlines of the Viśiṣṭādvaitic metaphysics in all its details. It is the outcome of the twenty eight terms or sessions of the teachings on the Śrībhāṣya undertaken by Vedānta Deśika for the cause of the propagation and the preservation of the Rāmānuja Philosophy. It bares testimony on the vast scholarship and the versatile genius of the author. This commentary is decidedly the best of all commentaries on the *Śrībhāṣya.*

(ii) Tātparya-candrikā : It is a super commentary on the *Gīta-bhāṣya* of Rāmānuja. He has presented the view point of Rāmānuja on the highest philosophy of human life, *i.e. Prapatti.* It is as much constructive as critical. The Caramaśloka:

सर्वधर्मान् परित्यज्य मामेकं शरणं व्रज ।
अहं त्वा सर्वपापेभ्यो मोक्षयिष्यामि मा शुचः ॥ (XVIII.66)

is analysed to contain the quintessence of the *Gīta* which means deep, selfless love and devotion to God.

(iii) Gītārtha-saṅgraha-rakṣā : It is a commentary on the *'Gītārtha-saṅgraha'* of Yāmunācārya. It has eighteen chapters of the *Gītā.* It has made the *Gītā, Prapatti-śāstra* for the Śrīvaiṣṇavas. Vedānta Deśika has attempted a convincing synthesis of action and knowledge with love plus devotion. It is the nomenclature for the eighteen chapters of the *Gītā.* For example, the first chapter is named as *Śravaṇādhikārin*, the second as *Śravaṇādhikāri-mohaśamanam,* etc.

(iv) Gītārtha-saṅgraha-pattu : It is a Tamil treatise on the philosophy of the *Gītā* as explained by Yāmunācārya in his *Gītārtha-saṅgraha.*

(v) Catuśśloki-bhāṣya : It is a commentary on the *'Catuśśloki'* of Yāmunācārya. Here Vedānta Deśika presents his views on the significance of 'Śrī' in the concept of 'Śrī Viṣṇu'. Five view-points of 'Śrī' are mentioned and discussed :

(a) 'Śrī' as Divine Nature,

(b) 'Śrī' as Divine Essence or Energy,

(c) 'Śrī' as Divine Bliss,

(d) 'Śrī' as the 'Māyā' and

(e) 'Śrī' as the Supreme sense of Viśiṣṭādvaita.

(vii) Stotra-ratna-bhāṣya : It is an exhaustive exposition of the *'Stotra-ratna'* of Yāmunācārya, which has sixty five stanzas and is replete with the philosophy of Viśiṣṭādvaita. The *Stotra-ratna-bhāṣya* is similarly replete with the tenets of Viśiṣṭādvaita as taught by Yāmunācārya.

(viii) Rahasya-rakṣā or the ***Gadya-traya-bhāṣya :*** It is a fine commentary on the three *Gadyas viz.*, the *Śaraṇāgati-gadya,* the *Śrīraṅga-gadya* and the *Vaikuṇṭha-gadya* of Rāmānuja. It was written by Vedānta Deśika because the Teṅgaḷai teacher used to put their own interpretations on the *Gadyas*. Vedānta Deśika believes that the *Gadyas* of Rāmānuja contain the real essence of Viśiṣṭādvaita and Śrīvaiṣṇavism as the philosophy and religion of man.

According to Vedānta Deśika, the *Gadyas* are the text of the *prapatti-vidyā,* while the *Śrībhāṣya* is the text of the *Brahma-vidyā.*

(ix) Īśopaniṣad-bhāṣya : The *Īśopaniṣad* has been interpreted in accordance to the tenets of Viśiṣṭādvaita school of Thought. This *Upaniṣad* is considered to be in support of *Śaraṇāgati* doctrine of Rāmānuja.

Besides these works, there are other works too; but their authenticity is disputable. However, Vedānta Deśika's store-house of significant works speaks of his deep sense of duty to the Rāmānuja Philosophy, his great sense of satisfaction at the accomplishment of the duty and finally his God-intoxicated mind and heart.

REFERENCES

1. Dr. Satyavrata Singh, *Vedānta Deśika — His Life, Works and Philosophy - A Study,* Chowkhamba Sanskrit Series Office, Varanasi, 1958, p.3.

2. *Epigraphica Indica,* Vol. XIII, p.195.

3. *Epigraphica Indica* Vol.VI, p.323.

4. Surendranath Dasgupta, *A History of Indian Philosophy*, Vol. III, Motilal Banarasidass, Delhi, 1975, p.120.

5. Dr. Veera Raghavacharya, *Saṅkalpasūryodaya*, Sri Rama Press, Bangalore, 1954, p.1.

6. Krisnamacharya, V., *Saṅkalpasūryodaya*, Adyar Library, Madras, 1948, p.37.

7. Srinivasachari, S.M., *Advaita and Viśiṣṭādvaita*, Asia Publishing House, Adyar, Madras, p.6.

8. Biographical details of Veṅkaṭanātha given here, are mainly based on some original works published. They are :

   (1) सप्ततिरात्रोत्सवचम्पू of Bhayankaram Annan.
   (2) वैभवप्रकाशिका of Doddayacarya Swami.
   (3) परकालविजय चम्पू of कृष्णम्भ परकालस्वामि.

9. भाद्रपदमासगत विष्णु विमलर्क्ष्ये वेंकटमहीध्रपति तीर्थ दिनभूते।
   प्रादुरभवज्जगति दैत्यरिपु घण्टा हन्त कतिार्किक मृगेन्द्र गुरुमूर्त्या।।

   Saptatriratnamālikā of Bhayankaram Annan, D. Krishayyangar, *Śrī Vedānta Deśikaru*, Bangalore, 1964, p.21.

10. वित्रासिनी विबुधवैरिवरुथिनीनां पद्मासनेन परिचारविधौ प्रयुक्ता।
    उत्प्रेक्ष्यते बुधजनैरूपपत्तिभूम्ना घण्टा हरेः समजनिष्ट यदात्मनेति।।

    V. Krishnamacarya, *Saṅkalpasūryodaya,* I-14, p.40.

11. Vedānta Deśika, *Tattvamuktākalāpa*, IV.46-48, 9.

12. नमः पन्नगद्धाय वैकुण्ठवशवर्तिने।
    शृति सिन्धु सुधोत्पाद मन्दराय गरुत्मते।।

D. Krishnayyangar, *Śrī Vedānta Deśikaru* (Kannada), Bangalore, 1964, p.31.

13. For details — Dr. Satyavrata Singh, *Vedānta Deśika — His Life, Works and Philosophy — A Study,* Chowkhamba Sanskrit Series Office, Varanasi, 1958, pp.18-22.

14. Note : The details of each of the works have been taken from Satyavrata Singh's *Work, Vedānta Deśika — His Life Works and Philosophy — A Study.*

15. साहित्यगोष्ठीं सरसामातिष्ठन्नयमेकदा। यादवाभ्युदयं काव्यमश्रौषीद् विदुषां मुखात्।।
अव्याख्याततया पूर्वैरनभिव्यक्तभावकम्। अदृष्टभाव शिल्पज्ञैरभिजातं हरिन्मणिम्।।

D. Krishna Iyangar : *Śrī Vedānta Deśikaru* (Kannada), Bangalore, 1964, p.127.

16. तदाकर्णतः सम्यक् समुदञ्चत्कुतूहलः विदुषां पुरतस्तस्य विवृतौ मां न्यूयुजत्।।

Yādavābhyudaya : Ed. by Veera Raghavacarya, Ubhaya Vedanta Granthamala, Madras, 1969, p.1.

17. Theodor Aufrecht, *Catàlogus Catalogorum,* Part I, Franz Steiner Veriag Gmbh, Wiesbaden, 1962, p.472

18. तत्त्वमुक्ताकलापः श्री वेंकटनाथदेशिकविरचितो ।
विशिष्टाद्वैतमतानुसारी पञ्चसारात्मकः प्रकरण ग्रन्थः।।

Vasudevashastri Abhyankar, *Sarvadarśanasaṅgraha*, Bhandarkar Oriental Research Institute, Poona, 1978, p.104.

Chapter II

Place of Allegorical Dramas in Sanskrit Literature

1. INTRODUCTION

Vedānta Deśika rightly deserves the credit of being a dramatists for his allegorical drama *Saṅkalpasūryodaya*.

Rūpaka or Drama has occupied an important position in Sanskrit Literature. In the words of Vāmana, *Rūpaka* "is the blossom of poetry, the union of the epic and the lyric in the uninterrupted vivacity of an actual performance, developing itself in the spirit of the age to come."[1] Bharata, considered to be the founder of Sanskrit Dramaturgy, has said, "it is an imitation of actions and conducts of people, which is rich in various emotions, and which depicts different situations. This relates to actions of men, good, bad or indifferent and gives courage, amusement and happiness as well as counsel to them all."[2]

However, different theories both eastern and western have been prevalent regarding the origin of drama. In his *Nāṭyaśāstra*, Bharata gives a divine and mythical description about the origin of drama.[3] Yet, the fact remains that a drama is the imitation of the actions of particular characters which the dramatist thinks to have taken place against the background of certain incidents which may have taken place at a certain time or place. So, the story the dramatist, may be of various types with regard to its length, characters, situations, sentiments and so on. Bharata mentions ten types of the *Rūpaka*, *viz.*, *Nāṭaka*, *Prakaraṇa*, *Bhāṇa*, *Ihāmṛga*, *Vyāyoga*, *Aṅga*, *Vīthi*, *Prahasana*, *Ḍima* and *Samavakāra*.[4] Later on eighteen *Upa-rūpakas* were added to this list.[5]

It has been an usual tradition that dramas in Sanskrit, derive their themes from the epics, the *Purāṇa*s or the folk tales. Some dramatists even went to the extent of writing dramas building the plot from their own imagination. In course of time, due to an advent of various philosophical systems, many a dramatist used drama as a media to propagate their philosophical theories. This is how a new branch of writing the dramas in the allegorical form came into existance.

2. THE MEANING OF ALLEGORY

The word *Allegory* is derived from Latin word *Allegoria* which is borrowed from a Greek word. "*Allo*" means "something else", and *Agoreuein* means "to speak". It tends to say that an allegory of a story, poem, picture is that in which the characters and events are symbols of something else. Allegories usually point to some moral, religious or political aspect.[6] It is a story, or description, wherein the ideas such as patience, purity and truth are symbolised by persons who are characters in the story.[7] Thus, it refers to a form of art that conceals another meaning apart from the ordinary meaning. Hence, it may be said that an allegory is another type of matephor used.

According to the Reader's Encyclopedia "Allegory is a systematic symbolism by which abstractions are represented as accurately as possible by concrete characters, plots and situations often with identifying tag names".[8]

3. ORIGIN OF ALLEGORIES IN VEDIC LITERATURE

The origin of allegorical dramas in Sanskrit literature can be traced in the Vedic literature. Some hymns from *Ṛgveda* are the earliest examples of allegoric representation, where the seer supplies the personifications and figurative descriptions of the natural phenomena. The transformations of the natural phenomena into Gods and Goddesses such as *Sūrya* (Sun), *Soma* (Moon), *Agni* (Fire) etc. are seen in the *Ṛgveda*. Various emotions like *Moha, Krodha, Mātsarya, Kāma, Mada* and *Lobha* are represented as animals like pig, wolf, dog, wild-lizard, Garuḍa and vulture respectively.[9] In another hymn, the individual soul (*Jīva*) and the Supreme soul (*Brahman*) are described as two birds, one representing the *Jīvātman* and the other the *Paramātman*.[10] In the *Yajurveda*, the *manas* is personified and its various powers are explained equal to that of a human being.[11]

In the *Sāmaveda*, there is a reference, in which a thoughtful preceptor is said to be the father and faith as the mother of the worshipper.[12]

In the *Atharvaveda*, we come across a description of the marriage of *Manyu* (anger) with the daughter of *Saṅkalpa* (will or volition).[13]

The *Brāhmaṇas* are more advanced in the treatment of allegorical characterization. At that time, the sacrificial cult has attained perfection, and the philosophical thought had also shown considerable advancement. This provided an opportunity for a new interpretation of the old literature to make it fully applicable to this advanced cult. The interpreters invented new stories in support of their explanations. In the *Brāhmaṇas*, there are personifications of even the sense organs. The *Aitareya Brāhmaṇa*[14] and the *Śatapatha Brāhmaṇa*[15] are rich in such allegorical descriptions.

The personifications of sense-organs can also be seen in the Upaniṣads. In the *Chāndogyopaniṣad*, the superiority of *Prāṇa* over other senses has been often illustrated by dialogues and actions.[16]

In the *Nirukta*, *Vidyā* is personified. *Vidyā* went to a brahmin to seek refuge as it is his imperishable treasure.[17]

In the *Yogāvaśiṣṭha* is found, the personification of *Kāla* (time). It (time) is described there, as having a body, holding a sword and a nose, wearing a coat of mail, decorated with earrings and surrounded by a group of attendants.[18]

In the *Mahābhārata*, *Dharma* is personified as having ten wives – *viz. Kīrti*, *Lakṣmī*, *Dhṛti*, *Medhā*, *Puṣṭi*, *Śraddhā*, *Kriyā*, *Buddhi*, *Lajjā* and *Mati*.[19]

In the *Bhāgavata Purāṇa*, the story of king Purañjana can be taken as an allegoric representation. The story is being narrated by sage Nārada to king Prācinabarhis, that the king Purañjana being separated from his friends, deviates from his path of righteousness, experiences various sorrows and sufferings. At last, his friends take pity on him and lead him to the path of salvation through *Bhakti*. At the end of the narration, Nārada gives an allegorical interpretation of the whole story, its characters and places etc. Purañjana stands for *Jīva* or individual soul and his friend whom he forgets is the Supreme Soul. His wife Purañjani is said to be Buddhi.[20]

Also, in the stories of the *Pañcatantra* and of the *Hitopadeśa*, the animals and birds are humanised.

4. ORIGIN OF ALLEGORICAL DRAMAS IN CLASSICAL SANSKRIT

The allegorical interpretations in Vedic and Classical Literature inspired the later writers, and they began to introduce this technique in Sanskrit dramas too. Drama is a direct, objective and impersonal representation of life on the stage. And, the allegorical dramas convey a veiled moral meaning in which various qualities and virtues are personified.

Every dramatist has his own philosophy, and he imparts his message to the audience through this medium with a view to establishing some particular philosophy, which he believes, an author discusses all other philosophical thoughts on the stage. Normally, the study of philosophy is dull, abstruse and uninteresting. A drama simplifies and makes it presentable on the stage in a simple style, by which a common man can understand that philosophy without loosing interest in it.

It was Aśvaghoṣa who first brings out allegorical fragments like *Buddhi* (wisdom), *Kīrti* (fame) and *Dhṛti* (firmness) as characters in his drama *Śārīputraprakaraṇa*. These characters appear and converse on the stage as real human beings with all the features of a typical character.

Inspired by such personifications and representations, later writers started writing dramas with personified characters. Works like *Prabodhacandrodaya* of Kṛṣṇamiśra and the *Saṅkalpasūryodaya* of Vedānta Deśika, etc. are some examples of such dramas. The different types of imaginary characters in these dramas are brought on the stage in order to present certain philosophical, moral and social problems of that period.

In the series of such allegorical dramas, the *Āgama-ḍambara* or *Sanmatanāṭaka* of Jayanta Bhaṭṭa,[21] the author of *Nyāyamañjarī*, who flourished during tenth centruy A.D., can be said to be the first work of this kind.

This play consists of four acts. It presents the adherents of different schools of philosophy which were prevalant at the time of the poet.

The *Prabodhacandrodaya* of Kṛṣṇamiśra can be the first complete allegorical drama available to us. He was an ascetic, who lived in the later half of the eleventh century A.D. Being a follower of Śrī Śaṅkarācārya, Kṛṣṇamiśra propagated the Advaita Philosophy through this drama. Kṛṣṇa Miśra's play gives useful information about the fading phase of the Buddhistic and Jaina faiths. He shows considerable skill in giving human participation to his abstract theme.

Omkarnath, in his work[22] gives a list of forty-eight dramas of this type. Among them 16 plays have already been published. They are :

1. *Prabodhacandrodaya* of Kṛṣṇamiśra[23]
2. *Mohaparājaya* of Yaśaḥpāla[24]
3. *Saṅkalpasūryodaya* of Veṅkaṭanātha or Vedānta Deśika[25]
4. *Caitanya-candrodaya* of Kavikarṇapura[26]
5. *Amṛtodayam* of Gokulanātha[27]
6. *Vidyā-pariṇaya* of Ānandarāya Makhin[28]
7. *Jīvānandam* of Ānandarāya Makhin[29]
8. *Purañjana-caritam* of Śrī Krishna Datta[30]
9. *Jīvasaṁjīvaninā̄ṭaka* of Śrī Venkitaramanacarya[31]
10. *Dharma-vijaya* of Bhūdeva Śukla[32]
11. *Jīvanmukti-kalyāṇa* of Nalla Dīkṣita[33]
12. *Cittavṛtti-kalyāṇa* of Nalla Dīkṣita[34]
13. *Yatirāja-vijaya-nāṭaka* of Śrī Vātsya Varadācārya[35]
14. *Jñanasūryodayam* of Vādicandra Suri[36]
15. *Mithyājñānaviḍambanam* of Ravidāsa[37] and
16. *Municaturvijayam* authourship anonimous.[38]

The following dramas are those which are preserved in manuscript form in various libraries :

1. *Śārīputra-prakaraṇa* of Aśvaghoṣa[39]
2. *Muktipariṇaya* of Sundaradeva[40]
3. *Bhāvanāpuruṣottama* of Ratnakheṭa Śrīnivāsadīkṣita[41]
4. *Siddhāntabherināṭaka* of Sudarśanācārya[42]
5. *Viveka-vijaya* of Rāmānuja Kavi[43]
6. *Anumiti-pariṇaya* of Nṛsiṁhakavi[44]
7. *Bhaktivaibhava* of Jīvadeva[45]
8. *Mithyajñāna-khaṇḍana* of Ravidāsa[46]
9. *Pūrṇapuruṣārtha-Candrodaya* of Jātavedas[47]
10. *Prabodhodayam* of Śukleśvaranatha[48]
11. *Śivanārāyaṇabhañjamahodaya Nāṭikā* of Narasiṁhamiśra[49]
12. *Ṣatsaṅga-vijaya* of Vaijanātha[50]
13. *Svānubhūti* of Ananta Paṇḍita[51]
14. *Dharmodaya* of Dharmadeva Gosvāmi[52]
15. *Ṣaṇmata-nāṭaka* of Jayanta Bhaṭṭa[53]
16. *Tattvamudrābhadrodaya* of Triveṇī[54]
17. *Bhartṛharirājyatyāga* of Kṛṣṇabaladeva Varman[55]
18. *Citsūryaloka* of Nṛsimhadaivajña[56]
19. *Pāṣaṇḍadharma-khaṇḍana* of Dāmodarāśrama[57]
20. *Svātma-prakāśana* of Sundarashastri[58] and
21. *Kṛṣṇa-bhakti-candrikā* of Anandadeva[59]

The following dramas are known only by their names[60]:

1. *Māyāvijayam* of Anantanārāyaṇa Sūri
2. *Jñānacandrodaya* of Padmasundara
3. *Vijayarañjanam* of Indireshakavi
4. *Saubhāgyamahodaya* of Jagannātha Sikra Kavi
5. *Śivaliṅga-sūryodaya* of Mallanaraddya
6. *Śuddhasattvam* of Matamarṣi Veṅkaṭācārya

7. *Vidvān-manorañjinī* of Ciranjivi Bhattacarya
8. *Śivabhaktānanda* of anonymous authorship and
9. *Jñānamudranāṭaka* or *Arthapancaka Nāṭaka* of Śeṣa Rāmānuja.

In addition to the above mentioned dramas, Satnam Talwar[61] has referred to the following dramas. They are :

1. *Navagraha-carita* of Ghanaśyāma[62]
2. *Dhruvābhyudaya* of Kavi Śankarlal Singh[63]
3. *Caṇḍatāṇḍava* of Jivanyayatirtha Bhattacarya[64] and
4. *Vimukti* of Dr. V. Raghavan[65]

Besides these dramas, M. Krishnamacariar mentions certain other allegorical dramas[66]

1. *Śrīdamacarita* of Sri Somarāja Dīkṣita
2. *Prapanna-sapiṇḍīkaraṇa-nirāsa* of Ghattasisacarya
3. *Nāṭyapariśiṣṭa* of Kṛṣṇadeva Vacaspati
4. *Saralacitsukhīsāra* of Rameshacandra
5. *Śuddhasattva* of Madabhuri Veṅkaṭācārya
6. *Bhartṛharinirveda* of Harihara
7. *Brahma-vidyā* of Nārāyaṇa Shastri
8. *Śāntirasa* of Vaikunṭhapuri
9. *Vedānta-Vilāsa* of Varadācārya and
10. *Pramāṇādarśa* of Sukheśvara.

Dr. V. Raghavan in his "The Number of Rasas" mentions some other dramas.[67] They are :

1. *Mudrika-kumuda-candra* of Yeśaścandra
2. *Antarvyākaraṇa-nāṭya-pariśiṣṭa* of Kṛṣṇānanda Sarasvatī and
3. *Ihāmṛgī* or *Sarvavinoda* of Kṛṣṇāvadhūta.

Besides these, some other dramas are also found to be preserved for posterity. They are :

1. *Śrīnivāsāratha-vijaya-nāṭaka* of Narasimha[68]
2. *Dharmoddharaṇa* of Durgeswara[69] and
3. *Ubhayagrāsa-rāhūdaya* of Vijayindratirtha.[70]

In addition to these, some other allegorical works are available to us. They are :

1. *Bhartṛharinirveda* of Hariharopādhyāya[71]
2. *Pracaṇḍarāhūdaya* of Ghanaśyāma[72] and
3. *Vivekacandrodaya-nāṭaka* of Śivakavi.[73]

5. PLACE OF SAṄKALPASŪRYODAYA IN SANSKRIT LITERATURE

The *Saṅkalpasūryodaya* has been considered as a high ranking work among allegorical dramas. It is distinct in its own way as the sense of the theme is depicted indirectly through personified roles of the abstract human qualities. This drama is said to be written in a single night on a personal challenge to Kṛṣṇa Miśra, the author of *Prabhoda-candrodaya*.[74]

Even in earlier times, the science of dramaturgy was fully developed in our country. Ordinarily, Sanskrit plays were meant for staging. The dramas of Bhāsa and of others were popular in this regard. In course of time, the rules of dramaturgy and poetics came to be codified, and as a result of this, later writers gradually lost their stage mindedness. Dramas were written elaborately, hence were impossible of being staged. Though dramas were styled as *dṛśya-kāvyas*, practically they were reduced to the position of *śravya-kāvyas* or works meant for mere reading. The *Saṅkalpasūryodaya* belongs to this category of Sanskrit dramas. Unlike a normal drama of five to seven acts, this is composed in ten acts. As against the common usage of eight *rasas* like *Karuṇa*, *Śṛṅgāra*, *Vīra*, *Hāsya*, etc., Vedānta Deśika has selected *Śānta rasa* for his drama. As Bhāvabhūti has put in his *Uttararāmacarita* "एको रसः करुण एव" (III. 47) *Karuṇa rasa* is considered as superior to other rasas. In contrast with Bhāvabhūti Vedānta Deśika claims that *śānta* or emotive peacefulness is the possible and the appropriate *rasa* and all other *rasas* culminate in *śānta rasa*, and hence this *rasa* is predominant one according to Vedānta Deśika.[75]

The play is said to have been staged by Śrīvaiṣṇavas like the late M.M. Narasimhacariar and his pupils. Probably the drama is apt for the present day also. In this play, the metaphysical truths and philosophical concepts which are ordinarily beyond the reach of common man are brought home to the masses very artistically.

6. COMMENTARIES ON THE SAṄKALPASŪRYODAYA

It has been known from the commentorial literature of the Viśiṣṭādvaita Vedānta that there are six commentaries on the *Saṅkalpasūryodaya*. They are as below :

(a) *Prabhāvilāsa* by Ahobala of Ātreya family.

(b) *Prabhāvali* by Nṛsiṁharāja

(c) *Prabhāvali* (anonymous)

(d) *Vivaraṇa* by Śrīnivāsa of Kauśika family.

(e) *Vyākhyā* by Śrī Bhāṣya Nārāyaṇa of Śrīvatsa family, and

(f) *Vyākhyā* by Nārāyaṇa of Śrīvatsa family (different from the above).

Of these commentaries, the *Prabhāvilāsa* of Ahobala and the *Prabhāvali* of Nṛsiṁharāja are of great importance. These two commentaries have been published by Adyar

Library, Madras, in the year 1948. The earlier publication of Prabhāvalī was available upto five acts only. Also a Tamil rendering of this play by M.M. Narasimhacariar, Madras is available.

The commentary published in the Telugu edition of Kāñchipuram O.L. Institute is mixed up with the portions of two different commentaries leading to a confusion regarding their authorship. Acts six to ten are available in this commentary.

The commentary published in Devanāgarī edition of the Pandit Series, Benaras, is anonymous and breaks off in the fifth act. Commentaries on four to six are available only in fragments. The Grantha editions of Kāñchipuram contain a running gloss and not a regular commentary.

7. LATER ALLEGORICAL DRAMAS IN SANSKRIT LITERATURE

The tradition of composing allegorical dramas in Sanskrit Literature continued even after the 13th Century. Although such works are only a few with a little amount of certainty, we can say that the scholarly work of Vedānta Deśika, the *Saṅkalpasūryodaya* served as a model to later dramatists. We find some modifications in later allegorical dramas. For instance, we may note that instead of human characters as in the *Saṅkalpasūryodaya*, later authors have made use of natural or animal characters (probably on the line of *Pañcatantra*). We may make mention of later works themselves which were composed at Kerala.

Kamalinīrājahaṁsa[76] of Pūrṇasarasvatī is an allegorical play of Kerala. It is a play of five acts. The date of this play is not known. The characters of some of them are natural phenomena in which objects of nature are personified as endowed with human feelings and emotions.

The play deals with the love between Rājahaṁsa, the king of swan and Kamalinī, lotus of the Pampā lake and their subsequent marriage. Here, all the characters are natural phenomena.

Another allegorical play *Kamalinīkalahaṁsa*[77] is composed by Yoodalloor Nilakanthan Namboodripad. It is a play of six acts. It is on the model of *Kamalinirājahaṁsa*. The only difference is that the characters are not natural phenomena. In this play, all the characters belong to the animal world.

Subalavajratuṇḍa[78] of Śrīrāma is another play in five acts. In this play, Vajratuṇḍa, a rat is the hero and his beloved Subala is carried away by a snake Raktāṅga as its prey. The hero attacks him with an army of rats and rescued the heroine after killing this snake. Here, all the characters were taken from the animal world. Mice, serpent, lizard and chameleon are the characters which represent the human feelings and emotion.

Still another play is *Gīrvāṇavijaya*[79] of Rājarājavarma. It is a one act play. This play deals with the introduction of Sanskrit in Travancore. The main characters are the Pitāmaha, Saptarṣi, Bhāratī, Āṅgali, Kañcuki, Gairvāṇī. Here, Gairvāṇī and Āṅgali give an elaborate account of the merits and demerits of Sanskrit and English.

Besides these, *Kaivalyavallipariṇayam*[80] of Ilathur Ramaswamy Sastri, is another allegorical drama written on the model of *Prabodhacandrodaya*. The author of this drama lived in the 19th century A.D. However, the manuscripts are not available now.

Ekabhāratam[81] is a Sanskrit drama recently written by E.P. Bharata Pisharoti, in four acts. According to his own words, the plot of the drama is purely imaginary and is not based on any Paurāṇika story. All the characters in it are personifications of various naturally features of India like Himālaya, Gaṅgā, Oceans, Desert, Draught, Diseases and others.

Pūrṇapuruṣārthacandrodaya is the only typical allegorical drama with a philosophical theme found in Kerala. The plot of the drama is the attainment of salvation of the soul which is presented in an allegorical manner with the love story and marriage of King Daśāśva and Ānandapakvavalli. It is written almost on the line of Kṛṣṇa Miśra's *Prabodhacandrodaya*, and deals with all the philosophical systems through characters presented in the drama in the appealing manner. Prof M.S. Menon[82] assigns the date of the author to the 15th century A.D.

Still another work of the 17th century has been brought to light. It is an allegorical play under the title *Svarṇamukta-saṁvāda*[83] (or - *Vivāda*) composed by Maheśa Paṇḍita, a brahmin resident of Śrīnagar. A distinctive feature of the play is that the characters are inanimate objects like Gold, Silver and gems like pearl, diamond and coral excepting one. This character is a ruler (human being) named Balabhadra or Sāhi Bahadūr. As indicated in the title, the main theme is the dispute over the relative greatness and importance between Gold and Pearl, who are both patronised at the court of Balabhadra in Śrīnagar near the Himālayas. The disputes (metal objects) finally agree to the decision given by Balabhadra namely that they should give up their individual pride and stand united, although by the very nature of things, there will be difference and disparities.

REFERENCES

1. "तद्धि चित्रं चित्रपटवृद्धिशेषसाकल्यात् ।"

   Vāmana, *Kāvyālaṅkāra Sūtra*; I.3.31, Chowkhamba Sanskrit Samsthan, Varanasi, 1976, p.42.

2. नानाभावोपसंपन्नं नानावस्थान्तरात्मकं लोकवृत्तानुकरणं नाट्यमेतन्मया कृतम् ।
उत्तमाधर्ममध्यानां नराणां कर्म संश्रयं हितोपदेशजनं धृतिक्रीडासुखादिकृत ।।

Nāṭyaśāstra of Bharata, Vol. 1, I, 111-112, Oriental Institute, Baroda, 1934, pp.132-33.

3. ग्राम्यधर्मप्रवृत्ते तु कामलोभवशं गते । ईर्ष्याक्रोधादि सम्मूढे लोके सुखिदुःखिते ।।
सर्वशास्त्रार्थसम्पन्नं सर्वशिल्पप्रवर्तकम् । नाट्याख्यं पञ्चमं वेदं सेतिहासं करोम्यहम् ।। *Ibid.*, I. 9-15, pp.42-50.

4. नाटकं सप्रकरणम ङ्को व्यायोग एव च ।
भाणः समवकारश्च वीथी प्रहसनं डिमः ।
इहामृगश्च विज्ञेयो दशमो नाट्यलक्षणे । *Ibid.*, Vol.2, XVIII.2-3, p.407.

5. नाटिका त्रोटकं गोष्ठी सट्टकं नाट्यरासकम् । प्रस्थालोल्लाप्याकाव्यानि प्रेङ्खणं रासकं तथा ।।
संलापकं श्रीगदितं शिल्पकं च विलासिका । दुर्मल्लिका प्रकरणी हल्लीशो भाणिकेति च ।
अष्टादश प्राहुरूपरूपकाणि मनीषिणः ।।

Viśvanātha, *Sāhityadarpaṇa*, VI.4-6, Chowkhamba Sanskrit Series, Varanasi, 1989, p.388.

6. *Collins Compiled English Language Dictionary*, William Collins Sons and Co.Ltd., 1988, p.37.

7. *Oxford Advanced Learners' Dictionary of Current English*, Oxford University Press, New Delhi, 1982, p.23.

8. Bennet William Rose, *The Reader's Encyclopaedia*, Thomas, Y. Growell Company, New York, 1951, p.24.

9. उलूकयातुं शुशुलूकयातुं जहिश्वयातुमुत कोकयातुम् ।
सुपर्णयातुमुत गृध्रयातुं दृषदेव प्र मृण रक्ष इन्द्र ।। VII.104.22

Ṛgveda Saṁhitā, Volume 1, Maxmüller; The Honourable the East India Company, London, 1849, p.280.

10. द्वासुपर्णा सयुजा सखाय समानं वृक्षं परिषस्वजाते ।
तथोरन्यः पिप्पलं स्वाद्वृत्त्यनश्नन्नन्योऽभिचाकशीति ।। I.164.20 (R.V.)

Ibid., p.261; *Muṇḍakopaniṣat,* III.1.1.

11. सुषारथिरश्वानिव यन्मनुष्यान्नेनीयतेऽभीशुमिर्वाजिन ।
हृत्प्रतिष्टं यदाजिरं जवष्टिं तन्मे मनः इव । शिवसंकल्पमस्तु ।।

Śukla-Yajurveda (with Sanātana Bhāṣya) Sadguru Gangeshwara International Veda Mission, Bombay, XXXIV.6, p.397.

12. पिता यत्कश्यपस्याग्निः श्रद्धा मातामनुकवि ।।

Ed. S.V. Ganapati, *Sāmaveda, Āgneya Kāṇḍa* - IV, 10, Motilal Banarasidass, New Delhi, 1982, p.21.

13. अभीहि मन्यो तवसस्तदीयान् तपसा युजा विजहि शत्रून् ।
अमित्रहा वृत्रहा दस्युहा च विश्वा वसून्या भरा त्वं नः ।।

Ed. Pandit Sripada Damodara Satavalekar, *Atharvaveda Saṁhita*, VII.43, Swadhyaya Mandal Paradicity, Gujarat, (Noyan), p.74.

14. इन्द्रं वै वृत्रं जद्धिवासं नास्तुतेति मन्यमानाः सर्वा देवता अजुहस्तं मरुत् इव स्वपये नाजहु प्राणा वै मरुतः स्वप्नयः प्राणा हेवैन तत्राजहुः । तस्मादेवोऽच्युतः स्वपिमान् प्रगाधः शस्यते । अस्वापे स्वपिभिरित्यापि ह यद्यैन्द्रमेवात ऊर्ध्वे ध्वन्दः शस्यते । तद्ध सर्वं मरुत्वतीय भवत्येव चेदच्युतः स्वपिमान् प्रगाधः शस्यत अस्वापे स्वपिभिरिति ।।

Ed. Hari Narayana Apte, *Aitareya Brāmhaṇa* 3.12.5, Anandasrama, Poona, 1896, p.326.

15. अथातो मनसश्चैव वाचश्च । अहं भद्र उदितं मनश्च ह वै वाक् चारु भद्र उदति । तद्धे मन उवाच । अहमेव त्वच्छ्रेयोऽस्मि । न वै मया त्वं किञ्चनानाभिमतं वदासि । स यन्मम कृतानुकारवर्त्मास्यहमेव त्वच्छ्रेयोस्मीति । अथ ह वागुवाच । अहमेव त्वच्छ्रेययस्यमीति । यद्यै त्वं वेत्यहमेव तद्धितापयाम्यहमेव संज्ञापयामीति ।

Ed. N. Ganga Prasad Upadyaya, *Śatapata Brāhmaṇa,* Volume I, I-45.8.10. The Research Institute of Ancient Scientific Studies, New Delhi, 1962, p.92.

16. अथ ह प्राणाः अहं श्रेयसि व्युदिरेऽहं श्रेयानस्म्यहं श्रेयानमस्मीति । ते ह प्राणाः प्रजापतिं पितरमेत्योचुर्भगवन्को नः श्रेष्ठ इति तान्होवाच यस्मिन्व उत्क्रान्ते शरीरं पापिष्ठतरमिव दृश्येत् स वः श्रेष्ठ इति । सा ह वागुच्चक्राम सा संवस्तरं प्रोष्य पर्येत्योवाच कथमशकतर्ते मज्जीवितुमिती यथा कला अवदन्तः प्राणान्तः प्राणेन पश्यन्तश्चक्षुषा श्रृण्वन्तः श्रोत्रेण ध्यायन्तो मनसैवमिति प्रविवेश ह वाक् ।।

Chāndogyopanishad, Vol.1, 6-8, *Ten Principle Upaniṣads with Śaṅkara Bhāṣya*, Motilal Banarasidass, Delhi, 1964, pp.213-15.

17. विद्या ह वै ब्राह्मणमाजगाम । गोपाय माम् । शेवधिष्टऽहमस्मि ।।

L. Sarup, The *Nighaṇṭu* and *Nirukta*, II.4, Motilal Banarasidass, Delhi, 1967, p.46.

18. *Yogavasiṣṭham*, Volume. I, 23, 13-20 Chenkottukonam, Thiruvanantapuram, 1985, pp.510-12.

19. नमतो धर्मपत्न्यक्ताः कीर्त्यमाना निबोध मे । कर्तिर्लक्ष्मीर्धृतिर्मेधा पुष्टिः श्रद्धा क्रिया तथा ।
बुद्धिर्लज्जा मतिश्चैव पत्न्यो धर्मस्य ता दश । द्धाराप्तयेतानि धर्मस्य विहितानि स्वयं भुवा ।
Mahābhārata Ādiparva, 6613-14 Ed. (Malayalam Com.) Kannampuzha, S. Krishna Warior, Srimahabharata Publishing House, Annamande, Trichur, 1951, p.625.
20. *Bhāgavatapurāṇa*, Skandha IV, Adhyāyas 25-29. Gita Press, Gorakhpur, Vikrama Śaka 2020, pp.211-18.
21. *Āgamaḍambara* of Jayantabhaṭṭa, Ed. Dr. Raghavan, Mithila Institute Series, Darbhanga, 1964.
22. Omkaranath : (*Śodhaprabandha*) Sanskrit Vibhag, Prayaga, Viswavidyalaya, Prayag (Unpublished), 1967.
23. Chowkhamba Sanskrit Series, Varanasi, 1968.
24. Ed. Municaturvijaya Central Library, Baroda, 1918.
25. Ed. Pandit V. Krishnamacarya, The Adyar Library, Adyar, Madras, 1948.
26. Nirnaya Sagar Press, 23, Kolaphat lane, Bombay, 1917.
27. Chowkhamba Sanskrit Series, Com : by Acharya Ramachandra Misra, Varanasi, 1965.
28. Nirnaya Sagar Press, Kolaphat lane, Bombay, 1930.
29. Ed. Duraiswami Aiyangar, Adyar Library Series, 59, Adyar, 1947.
30. Vidarbha Samśodhana Mandala Granthamala No.16, Nagpur, 1961.
31. V.V. Subbayya and Sons Publishing House, Bangalore, 1945.
32. Vidya Vilasa Press, Gopalamandir lane, Varanasi, 1930.
33. Śrī Śankara Gurukula Series, No.10, Sri Vanivilasam Press, Srirangam, 1944.
34. Ed. Municaturvijaya Central Library, Baroda, 1935.
35. Tirupathi Devastanam, Tirupati, 1956.

36. Government Press, Nagpur, 1926.
37. Harischandra Kaviratnadwara Vidyaratna, Calcutta, 1894.
38. Gaekvad Oriental Series, Baroda, 1918.
39. An incomplete manuscript discovered by Lueders from Central Asia, Chinese Literature, 1956, Part III, p.149.
40. Tanjore New Catalogue, No. 4460, NW Province Catalogue pt., VII, p.46.
41. Srinivasa Diksit, Saraswati Mahal Library, Tanjore, No. 4427/979.
42. Catalogue of Sanskrit Manuscripts in Mysore and Coorg, p.286.
43. Government Orient Sanskrit Manuscripts Library, Madras, No. D.12683.
44. Descriptive Catalogue of the Madras Govt. Oriental Manuscripts Library, No. D.12463.
45. Triennial Catalogue Manuscripts collected from the Government Oriental Manuscripts Library, Madras, No. 3752; Descriptive Catalogue of Sanskrit Manuscripts in the Adyar Library Adyar, No. 1478.
46. (Bombay Branch, R.A.S. 1289-90, No. 10, 4200), 1951.
47. Descriptive Catalogue of the Sanskrit Manuscripts in the Government Oriental Manuscripts Library, Madras, No. 12540-41.
48. M. Hariprasad Sastri, Notices, 11 series, Vol. III, No. 190, p.12224.
49. The Asiatic Society Bengal, 1901, p.18 and M. Hariprasad Sastry, Report on Search for Sanskrit Manuscripts, 1805-1900.
50. Catalogue of Sanskrit Manuscripts in Private Library, Gujarat, No. 64, p.124.
51. Report of Manuscripts in Rajasthan and Centre India No.1904-6, p.4.

52. Journal of the Assam Research Society, Volume III-4, p.119.
53. Report of Operation in Search of Sanskrit Manuscripts in the Bombay Circle, by Peterson, Bombay, Volume V, No. 407, p.262.
54. Dr. M. Krisnamacarya, Sanskrit Poetesses, pp.62-63, Souvenir of Silver Jubilee of the Trivendrum Sanskrit Series.
55. Private Manuscripts, Lucknow, 1806, p.315.
56. List of Sanskrit Manuscripts in Private Libraries of Southern India by Gustave Oppest, Volume 1, Madras, 1906-28, p.437.
57. Catalogue of Sanskrit, Pali and Prakrit Books in the British Musium, Col.No. 316, London, 1906-29.
58. Private Manuscripts No.1037-38, Chidambaram, 1913.
59. Descriptive Catalogue of the Government Collections of Manuscripts deposited in the Bhandarkar Oriental Research Institute, Poona, 4, Volume XIV, 1937.
60. Oṃkarnath, *op. cit.*, p.18.
61. A Study of allegorical Sanskrit Dramas (unpublished thesis), Satnam Talwar, University of Delhi, 1967.
62. S. Gopal, Journal of the Tanjore Saraswati Mandir Library Tanjore, No. 3 (Volume - XV).
63. Ed. Limbadipura, First Ed., Samvat, 1968.
64. Acaryapanchanama Smritigranthalaya, No. 4.
65. Ed. in *Sanskrit Pratibha*, Sahitya Academy Publication, New Delhi, 1961.
66. Krishnamacariar, M., *History of Classical Sanskrit Literature*, Motilal Banarasidass, Delhi, 1974, pp.680-83.
67. Dr. V. Raghavan : *The Number of Rasas*, The Adyar Library, Adyar, 1940, pp.36-40.
68. *A Catalogue of the Sanskrit Manuscripts*, British Musium, Cecil Bendak, London, 1902.

69. Karnatak University Journal of Humanities, 1957.

70. A list of Sanskrit Manuscripts in Private Libraries of South India by Gustav, Madras, No. 2504.

71. Durgaprasad and Kasinath Pandurang Parab, Kavyamala, No. 29, The Nirnayasagar Press, Bombay, 1892.

72. Galgali Ramacarya, Satyadhyana Vidyapitha, Vidya Karyalaya, 1960.

73. K.V. Sarma, Vishveshvarananda Institute Series - 37, Vishveshvarananda Institute, Hoshiyarpur, 1966.

74. Dr. Satyavrata Singh, *Vedānta Deśika — His Life, Works and Philosophy — A Study*, Chowkhamba Sanskrit Series Office, Varanasi, 1958, p.68.

75. In his *Bhāratamañjarī,* Kṣamendra asserts that quality of Śama is very important faculty to restrain the mind.

    Thus, *Śanta Rasa* is upheld as predominant one.

    Quoting an example of Duryodhana's plight, Kṣamendra in his *Bhāratamañjarī* illustrates thus :

    रत्नोदार चतुः समुद्ररशनां भुक्त्वा भुवं कौरवो
    भग्नोरुः पतितः स निष्परिजनो जीवन्वृकैर्भक्षितः ।
    गोपैर्विश्वजयी जितः स विजयः कंसैः क्षिता वृष्णाय–
    स्तस्मात्सर्वमिदं विचार्य सुचिरं शान्त्यै मनो दीयताम् ।।

    Kṣamendra : *Bhāratamañjarī,* Ed. Mahāmahopādhyaya Paṇḍit Śivadatta and Kashinath Pandurang Parab, Motilal Banarasidass, 1965, p.851.

76. *Ibid.*, p.218.

77. Ullur S. Parameswara Iyyer, Kerala Sahitya Caritram, Volume III, University of Kerala, 1963, pp.64-65.

78. Rajarajavarma (Vadakkumkur) Kerala Sanskrit Caritam, Volume VI, National Book Stall, Kottayam, 1965, p.34.

79. Ullur S. Parameswara Iyyar, Vijnanadeepika, Volume III, Pub. R.T. Pillai and sons, chalai Trivendrum, No. 1122, p.314.

80. E.P. Bharata Pisharoti, Ekabharatam, Kamadhenu Publication, P.O. Eranallur, Trichur.

81. *Subhadraharaṇa*, Brahmadatta Nạrayana, Dept. of Sanskrit, University of Calicut, 1983, p.131.

82. Janaki, S.S., *Svarṇamukta-saṁvāda* (or – *Vivāda*), Prof. Kuppuswami Sastri Birth Centenary volume.

Chapter III

Summary of Saṅkalpasūryodaya

1. SIGNIFICANCE OF THE TITLE

A general survey of the Dramatic Literature in Sanskrit, reflects an idea that the titles of varied Sanskrit dramas can be grouped into two sections, one being the *varṇātmaka* or descriptive titles and the other *dhvanyātmaka* or suggestive titles. It is the descriptive title, which on hearing directly makes the reader or audience understand the theme of the drama; whereas it is the suggestive title that implies the theme of the drama, and the fuller meaning thereof will be revealed after reading the important scene, to which the title is connected, occuring elsewhere in the drama, either in the beginning or in the middle or at the end. Thus, the titles like *Abhijñāna-Śākuntalaṃ*, *Vikramorvaśīyaṃ* are the examples of descriptive type; and the titles like *Pratimānāṭakaṃ, Ūru-bhaṅgaṃ, Mudrārākṣasaṃ* etc. are the instances of suggestive type.

In this vien, any reader of the *Saṅkalpasūryodaya* should know that the title thereof is a *suggestive* one. Because, the title of the drama *Saṅkalpasūryodaya,* consists of two words *Saṅkalpa* and *Sūryodaya,* which collectively means '*Dawn of Divine will* '. It also means '*The Sunrise of God's Resolve*' (to save man). In this connection, the commentator Ahobala explains the term *Saṅkalpa* as *prasādarūpa icchāviśeṣaḥ* which means Divine will of the Blissful form of the Lord. Further, the commentator substantiates this meaning quoting a scriptural statement from *Śvetāśvatara Upaniṣad* (III.20).

> अणोरणीयान् महतो महीयान्
> आत्मा गुहायां निहितोऽस्य जन्तोः ।
> तमक्रतुं पश्यति वीतशोको
> धातुः प्रसादान्महिमानमीशम् ।।[1]

Being subtler than the subtle and vaster than the vast, He resides in the cave of the heart of this *jīva*, being its director. When one sees that Supreme, who is free from the taint of Karma and who is a superbly glorious ruler one becomes freed from grief on account of the grace of that Supporter. It may be explained that the dark night of *Saṁsāra* is dispelled by the will of the Lord, which is equated with the rise of the Sun.[2] In spite of supplying such explanation, readers might not get clearly the theme of the drama in all its perspectives. But, the comprehensiveness of the title "*Saṅkalpasūryodaya*" would become emphatic gradually through the connected scenes of the drama.

In fact, the *Prayojana* or the purpose of the drama is made clear by the author himself. "This play, rich with a variety of interests representing as it does, the spirit of warlike heroism in the person of the accomplished Viveka, revealing the heroism of grace and mercy, while treating of the dealings of the Supreme Being with His creation, and embodying the spirit of tranquil, resignation associated with the self or *jīva* who has attained illumination, is sure to be welcomed even by those who experience the pleasures of *Saṁsāra*.[3] Yet, the comprehensiveness of the title '*Saṅkalpasūryodaya*' can be seen emphasized in the tenth act of the drama.

Thus, one can arrive at conclusion that the title *Saṅkalpasūryodaya* is suggestive and never descriptive.

Saṅkalpasūryodaya throughout its narration, prominently develops *Śāntarasa* and lays much emphasis on proclaiming the cardinal doctrines of Viśiṣṭādvaita philosophy. This play portrays the task of achieving salvation by a man who is put into several kinds of adversities, and explains how he ultimately wins the same by the *Saṅkalpa* or Grace of God.

In the drama, the *Prakṛti* with her power of illusion binds Puruṣa (or *Jīvātma*) in the chain of births and deaths. And, this Puruṣa has given birth to Viveka and Mahāmoha along with their followers. Viveka is the *Nāyaka* or hero of the play, whereas Mahāmoha plays the role of *Pratināyaka* or villian. With the help of his followers, Mahāmoha makes efforts to win over Viveka, the hero. But, at last Viveka becomes victorious with the help of his assistants of *sattva* quality, through the *Saṅkalpa* or Grace of the Lord. Thus, having shattered all bonds of *Saṁsāra*, Puruṣa is liberated and remains in *Kaiṅkarya* at the feet of Lord Nārāyaṇa. In this context, *Rise of God's Grace* on the 'Individual Soul' is termed here as *Saṅkalpasūryodaya*.

Precisely in the play, Viveka and Sumati are portrayed as king and queen. It is needless to say that they are working for good; Vyavasāya the human effort, is the Commander-in-chief of Viveka. Vedānta Deśika has provided a very prominent place to Vyavasāya in the play. For the successful realisation of the purpose of human effort, Divine Grace is very much required. It is true that the final goal can be attained by the Divine Grace only, still the factor of human effort cannot be neglected. On the contrary, Mahāmoha and Durmati work for evil. Puruṣa represents the warring element, and the final victory of Viveka will bring him good.

After the victory of the good over evil, God's Grace is bestowed upon the individual soul to save himself from the cycle of births and deaths. This is the final stage of *Sādhana* where man attains salvation.

As is made clear, in the drama, *Saṅkalpa* is represented as Divine Will or Grace. Infact, this is the crux of the entire drama. Vedānta Deśika has taken great pains to portray the characters of *Saṅkalpa* or Divine Will, which is quite necessary to attain salvation. Hence, he is not merely a dramatist but a philosopher too. Without *Saṅkalpa*, human effort is futile. This is the doctrine of *Prapatti*. *Prapatti* also denotes *sāttvikatyāga* by which the person makes a continuous realisation of the presence of God in everything and act accordingly. No doubt, *Prapatti* in Viṣṇubhakti is essential to achieve the goal; but as Vedānta Deśika makes it explicit, the *Saṅkalpa* is indispensable.

Human effort promoted by *Saṅkalpa* is thus necessary for the attainment of salvation. In this way *Saṅkalpa* is like a golden thread woven round the drama. In fine, the title *Saṅkalpasūryodaya* is all significant.

2. ACT-WISE SUMMARY

ACT I

The first Act of *Saṅkalpasūryodaya* establishes the important doctrines of Viśiṣṭādvaita of Rāmānuja. Therefore, as remarked by Nṛsiṁharāja in his Commentary *Prabhāvali*, this Act may be designated as 'A clear Exposition of Right Doctrine'.[4] This is further highlighted by N. Krishnamacharya in his *Upodghāta* or Introduction to the drama.[5]

The theme of the first Act of the drama is divided into three sections such as –

(a) Prastāvanā or Prologue,

(b) Miśra-Viṣkambhaka and

(c) Narration of the main theme.

(a) Prastāvanā

As usual, the *Prastāvanā*[6] section opens with two benedictory verses in praise of Lord Nārāyaṇa :

"May Śrīman Nārāyaṇa (Nārāyaṇa with His consort Śrī) be pleased to convey me over all the ills (of life) — Nārāyaṇa whose *will* like Sunrise dispels at once the night of *saṁsāra* (or the recurring cycle of births and deaths), who is capable of being seen by the *Jīva* (or embodied soul) when its deep devotion has attained to the state of the dawn of day — Nārāyaṇa whose supremacy is self-dependent and eternal, arising, as it does, from His missiles and ornaments which are symbolic of the various *tattvas* or 'reals' of the Universe !"[7]

"May Lakṣmī's beloved Consort, Who is the ocean of the milk of mercy, bless you with happiness – the Lord on Whose chest shines luminous, the gem *Kaustubha* symbolic of the *Jīva* which, like a feathered arrrow aimed at by strong man, has been discharged at that target from the bow of *praṇava*, by those rich in quality of *sattva* or holiness, who are ever absorbed in the contemplation of the Lord's attributes revealed in the Vedas and forming, as it were, the string of that bow !"[8]

Then, the *Sūtradhāra* or Stage Manager enters the stage and announces that he brings to light the established doctrines of Rāmānuja Philosophy, through a media of enacting the drama called *Saṅkalpasūryodaya* wherein Viveka is the hero.

The *Sūtradhāra* further calls *Naṭī*[9] and converses with her regarding the qualities of the drama. He also brings out the place of *Śāntarasa* in the drama. The *Sūtradhāra* then declares that the characteristics and sentiments of the drama appeals to gifted audience. And he convincingly says to *Naṭi* that she should not be hesitant about the comprehensiveness of the play.

And, further he proclaims that this drama is staged in the holy Śrīraṅgam, the place of learned scholars who can appraise the qualitative aspect of the drama.

Finally *Sūtradhāra* concludes his conversation with *Naṭi* proclaiming that the audience who were similar to sages Parāśara, Vyāsa and others in status would not scorn the staging of the play.

Besides, *Sūtradhāra* appeals to them to bestow their attention on this most interesting play providing the path to salvation. He also expresses that this drama consists of five divisions such as *Mukha, Pratimukha, Garbha, Vimarśa* and *Nirvahaṇam.*[10]

After the conversation is over, both *Sūtradhāra* and *Naṭi* retired to the background and proclaim certain generalisations that the virtues are capable of dispelling the darkness. Again behind the curtain, *Sūtradhāra* and *Naṭi* challenge king Mahāmoha and his queen Durmati and particularly addressing Kāma, as, how they would succeed in foiling the efforts of the virtuous people graced by the Supreme Brahman. Recalling the episode of Maheśvara, Ķāma and Rati, the author lets the audience to observe the coming one after the other in a significant manner. Thus, ends the *Prastāvanā*.

(b) Miśra-Viṣkambhaka

Miśra-Viṣkambhaka is the second section of the first Act of the drama. Here, it is proper to know the technical meaning of *Viṣkambhaka*. It is a scene which shows in a few words, the relation between the parts of the story past and to follow by means of a conversation among the characters other than the chief ones. It is *Śuddha-viṣkambhaka* when the conversation is carried on by minor characters in Sanskrit; and it is *Miśra-Viṣkambhaka* or *Saṅkīrṇa* wherein, conversation takes place between two or more minor characters in Sanskrit and Prākṛt medium.[11]

However, the *Miśra-Viṣkambhaka* part of the first Act reveals in a nut-shell the stratagies made by Kāma and Vasanta to defeat Viveka. Verily, this subject is brought to light through a conversation between Kāma (Commander-in-chief of Mahāmoha), Vasanta (friend of Kāma) and Rati (wife of Kāma). Both Kāma and Vasanta converse in sanskrit, while Rati speaks in Prākṛt. The gist of this *Miśra-Viṣkambhaka* follows thus :

In the beginning, Kāma assertively professes, that he is finding stratagies to get success in making Viveka flee away. Responding to Kāma, Vasanta assures that he will certainly assist him by inaugurating Vasanta's festival resulting to the glory of their king Mahāmoha and frightening away Viveka.

Accelerating the desire of Vasanta, Kāma tells that inauguration of the festival has taken place on the banks of the Kāveri wherein the pleasure grows or more fasinating than that of the heaven. Therefore, this festivity indicates the victory of Mahāmoha and the defeat of wretched Viveka. Thus, he considers the occasion of festivity as a good omen for the victory of his king.

On the otherhand, Rati being clouded with anxiety regarding an adverse and irresestible destiny of a king Mahāmoha, expresses that Viveka is by nature a invincible foe. Kāma who is confident of his capacity, does not like praising Viveka. He thinks that Rati must have been misled by young adherents of enemies party who are not aware of Mahāmoha's prowess and glory. According to Kāma, Mahāmoha is invincible even to the gods. In this manner, Kāma's speech highlights the strength of Mahāmoha.

Being curious, Rati asks the reason of the enemity that exists between Viveka and Mahāmoha. In reply to Rati's question, Kāma answers thus : *Jīva* endowed with the qualities *sattva, rajas* and *tamas*, has Buddhi as his consort. This devoted wife Buddhi gives birth to three families, of which *Sattvakula* is the first. This *Sattvakula* consists of members like Viveka being the chief and his followers. They are averse to the pleasures of mundane life. The second family is predominant in *Rajoguṇa*, and the third being predominant in *Tamoguṇa*. These two have joined their forces together.[12] The group of second and third families is headed by Mahāmoha. Thus, Viveka and Mahāmoha have been kings crowned by their respective subjects of similar character. Sumati ever considering the sensual pleasures as evil, is the wife of Viveka ; and Durmati who is always in the habit of looking upon *Mokṣa* as an evil, is the wife of Mahāmoha.[13]

Since *Rāga* and others who are characterised by *Rajas* are helping Mahāmoha and his followers, the latter's party is growing stronger. And, the race of Viveka has a few allies, and therefore not strong enough. Yet, Viveka and his followers are making attempts to destroy Mahāmoha and his groups. Therefore, Mahāmoha led by his followers, has given up brotherly feelings towards the wicked fellows of Viveka, and now planning to slay them all. Since then, Mahāmoha and his assistants are pursuing the policy of *Pravṛtti*; while Viveka and his assistants are pursuing the policy of *Nivṛtti*. However, the race of Viveka is put into the shade by Mahāmoha like the light of fire-flies by the Sun's rays.

Rati then asks whether there is any prospect of ending the dreadful state of enmity between Mahāmoha and Viveka; but Kāma rules out the possibility of peace between them. Further, he betrays the counsels and plans of the enemies of Mahāmoha. As Kāma being one of the assistants of Mahāmoha does not like the goodness of Viveka; and so he calls Viveka and his followers as the cruel persons. He says that *Parābhakti* which rises by practising the *Nivṛtti-dharmā*, is *Brahma-rākṣasī*. This *Parābhakti* leads then to obtaining grace of Lord Janārdana. This itself is *Saṅkalpasūryodaya* which, as Vasanta says may uproot the existence of Mahāmoha and his group.[14] Towards the close of *Miśra-Viṣkambhaka*, it is reported behind the curtain, that Viveka and his followers are to enter the stage. Kāma, Vasanta and Rati have no support of their allies. Therefore, they thought that it is not proper on their part to remain in the presence of their enemies. Hence, they left that place. Thus, ends the *Miśra-Viṣkamabhaka*.

(c) Narration of the Main Theme

In the beginning, Viveka the king and Sumati his wife enter the stage, and the dialogue between these two characters forms the main scene and latter portion of the first Act of the drama.

However, Viveka knows the stratagies planned by Vasanta and Kāma, who are influenced by Mahāmoha. Therefore, Viveka explains to Sumati that due to the application of the ointment of delusion to the eyes, persons find faults with others, which really do not exist; but they do not see the merits of others which really exist. In reverse, they consider themselves as possessing the virtues which are verily absent.[15] As Sumati remarks, ugly persons attribute the ugliness of their own face to the mirror though it is very clear.

Being compassionate at Jīvātma, Viveka explores that Jīvātma is in a pitiable condition. He says, he is making efforts to liberate *Jīva* from the clutches of Mahāmoha etc. by driving out both the inner and the outer enemies. Viveka is confident that he will get success in this endevour by grace of Lord Nārāyaṇa.[16]

Sumati expresses a doubt as to what could be the cause of *avidyā* in which *Jīva* is drowned. Clarifying the doubt, Viveka tells that owing to the taint of *Karma*, *Jīva* gives up his essential nature and gets into the cycle of *Saṁsāra*. He will resume his original and true nature when the bond of *Karma* completely disappears, and hence *Jīva* gets liberation from this beginningless cycle. Thus, though *Jīva* is indeed Śuddha, he gets into the cycle of *Saṁsāra*.[17]

Like Sītā imprisoned in Laṅkā, *Jīva* is bound in *Saṁsāra*. His embodiment itself is Laṅkā. The mind swayed by the ten sense-organs, is Rāvaṇa. Like Laṅkā sorrounded on all sides by the ocean, the embodiment is sorrounded by the ocean of *Saṁsāra*. Like Sītā, *Jīva* too is in a pitiable condition. As Hanumān unfolds the auspicious qualities of Rāma, the Spiritual master guides the *Jīva* and explains his true nature.[18]

When being bound, *Jīva* remains in the mundane world, his intellect (*buddhi*) though self-luminous, treads, but not the right path. Just as, when the Sun remains in a far off distance, the lotus-lake gets its beauty contracted, the intellect (*Jīva*'s wife) retires from functioning towards right path. When her husband, *Jīva* remains in a distant place being associated with *Prakṛti*. The intellect attains a similar state of night, when the moon has suffered an eclipse owing to the shadow cast by Rāhu. Thus, in all respects, intellect becomes incapable of awakening her husband — *Jīva* from delusion.[19]

Thus, like a child which is possessed by many evil spirits, the *Jīva* is gripped by lust (*kāma*), hatred (*krodha*) and conceit (*ahaṅkāra*). And just as a royal magician makes the evil spirit disappear and brings back the child to previous state, a competent teacher destroys lust and hatred. of the embodied *Jīva* and brings on the right path of salvation.[20] When he treads the path shown by his preceptor, the virtues like pure knowledge etc. arise in him.[21] And, gradually he becomes eligible for liberation.[22]

However, by the advice of the preceptor, the intellect of the embodied soul becomes pure. The fruit of meritorious deeds helps him to procure the grace of the Supreme Lord. Being supported by the grace of the Lord, he follows the path of *Prapatti* which opens the door of the Realm of the Lord.[23]

In this way, this night constituted of the three *guṇas* of *Prakṛti*, which keeps the sentient being in troubled and beginningless sleep, will disappear by the *Saṅkalpasūryodaya* that is rise of the Will of the Effulgent Sun, the Supreme Lord.[24]

At the end of the first act, Viveka concludes that so far, the *Siddhānta* view has been established; and indicates that overthrowing his enemies' forces, *i.e.* refutation of rival systems will be done in forth-coming portion.[25]

ACT II

As implied by Vedānta Deśika at the end of the previous act, this act is entitled as *Parapakṣapratikṣepa* or the Refutation of the views of Rival Systems, and deals with the same subject-matter.

This Act commences with *Praveśaka* or Prologue wherein the dialogue between Śraddhā and Vicāraṇā (friends of Sumati) takes place. Through their dialogue, audience comes to know that Viveka has made all preparations for defeating the rival systems. To make Viveka victorious, his wife – Sumati seeks divine favour; as such she is engaged in worshipping Goddess Lakṣmī on Ratna Parvata near Pramadavana. For, Śraddhā says, she is going to collect lotuses.

Similarly, Vicāraṇā says, on hearing of the military arrangements made by king Viveka with assistance of Vyavasāya the Commander-in-chief, Mahāmoha becomes angry and orders his deceitful disputants to establish the doctrines of Jaina, Buddha and of perverse heritics. Still Vicāraṇā opines that Mahāmoha's attempt of getting victory over Viveka is as foolish as resorting to a rock when crossing the vast ocean. Being commanded by Sumati, Vicāraṇā says, she is approaching Vyavasāya to inform the arrival of Mahāmoha together with his deceitful disputants.

Thus both the characters – Śraddhā and Vicāraṇā inform the audience, that now the scene presents the refutation of the rival systems by Viveka and his alliance, and exit from the stage. Here ends *Praveśaka*.[26]

The main theme of the second Act can be brought under two scenes. In the first scene, both the king Viveka and his Commander-in-chief Vyavasāya enter the stage. Thereafter, Viveka declares his determination, *i.e.* since Puruṣa has been restrained by strong bonds of past *Karma*, his activities are becoming fruitless. He is engulfed in delusion. Therefore, Viveka says, he has taken a vow of making Puruṣa free from the clutches of *Saṁsāra*. And for this, proper time has arrived now. To take into consideration that has been done so far in the direction of his salvation and all that is yet to be done. Therefore, Viveka determines the things to be executed.

After pondering over himself for a while he says with

much affliction that in this Universe, dull-witted persons display an unaccountable hatred of innocent people and invent diverse systems to promote hostility among mankind. They teach fallacious doctrines to the people at large. As a result many persons have been deceived.[27]

In order to lift the society from danger, Viveka seeks favour of Supreme Nārāyaṇa. Addressing to Vyavasāya, Viveka assures that different systems of thought preaching fallacious doctrines cannot stand the test of *Pramāṇas*. Therefore, they can delude the mankind in the absence of the sunlike-true-systems of thought. Thus, they are like darkness bound to disappear at the rise of the Sun.[28] With a view to destroying these elephants like disputants, a *Vādisiṁha* is required. He should possess five sharp claws of logical reasoning (*ātmāśraya, anyonyāśraya, cakrāśraya, anavasthā* and *aniṣṭaprasaṅga*). He has to have two teeth of *svapakṣasādhana* or justification of right doctrine and *parapakṣopalambha* or refutation of false doctrine. Such a man of wisdom can drive away the disputants easily. In this manner, Viveka is engaged in planning for the victory over Mahāmoha.

At this juncture, two characters, Guru or preceptor and Śiṣya or disciple enter the stage. The dialogue between them begins. The preceptor here is Rāmānuja and the disciple is Vedānta Deśika himself. Vedānta Siddhānta and vāda are here disguised as preceptor and disciple. Preceptor says that he wishes to win over the rival systems through his disciple just as Viśvāmitra drove the demons away through Rāma.[29] Then the preceptor instructs the method of debating and winning over the opponents. He says, when discussions are held with people belonging to one's own school of Vedānta, one should argue accepting the authority of *Śāstrās* held in common by both. When a debate is with the people holding the views oppose to one's own school, one should take one's own stand on the system of Viśiṣṭādvaita following the path shown by great teachers like Parāśara, Vyāsa, Śaunaka, Bodhāyana, etc.

Bearing all these things in the mind and having the support of valid proofs one should argue and would appeal to the hearts of the audience. Further, the Preceptor pinpoints that one should defeat the opponents following the path of contrary to the *Pramāṇas* by the application of Sthālīpulākanyāya.[30]

Meanwhile an announcement is made that the boastful disputants would be considered not even as a cotton, the blade of grass or broken husk. This announcement suggests the victory of Viveka over Mahāmoha. The disciple confidently says that he has studied all schools of thought as such it is easy for him to find out their weakness and to defeat them. By direction of the preceptor, the disciple begins refuting all opponents' views. Those who believe the Sāṅkhya systems of thought built by the sages such as Kapila, Āsuri, Pañcaśikhā etc. maintain that *Prakṛti* is different from *Puruṣa*. But they are sinful-minded as they don't admit the existence of Supreme Being.[31] It is refuted thus :

If under the influence of *Prakṛti*, you are prepared to accept only *Prakṛti* (matter) and *Puruṣa* (the individual selves), in what way has the Supreme Being, who shines like the crest jewel of the Upaniṣads, offended you ? If the Supreme Person is rejected by you with minds hardened by hundreds of perverse arguments, there will arise robbers who will deprive you of even these two in which you have faith.[32]

Similarly Yoga system of thought is suggestively refuted as below.

"These men hold the false doctrine of Yoga prate of

Bhagavān's Lordship and Glory as being of the nature of the reflection (in a mirror). The Upaniṣads which declare hosts of qualities like *Jñāna*, *Vīrya* and strength as being natural to Īśvara are an irresistible reply to these (thinkers)."[33]

Vaiśeṣika view then is taken for refutation as follows:

Your Majesty's commands will be obeyed. Here – This system assumes the creation of new objects which did not exist before (as pots from mud). In other respects, too, it rejects the doctrines of the *Śrutis*. This tall talk indulged in by Kaṇāda is said to have begun from the teaching of Ulūka (the owl) and, at present, it survives only in name.[34]

In the like manner, Mādhyamikā's Śūnyavāda is refuted in the following manner.

The Mādhyamika who indulges in captious argument (*vitaṇḍā*) refutes himself as his speech defines all propriety by the arguments in his armoury contradicting one another. What is there left for us ? To point out any fallacy in his argument is like the trouble taken in beating down with a hammer a man who is already dead.[35]

So, also Jain's view of *Sapthabhaṅgi* is refuted by indication.

Not so, These Jain ascetics covered with dirt have mingled feelings of joy at the defeat of the Buddhists and of sorrow as well, and while admitting the validity of sense — perception and inference, find great difficulty in the exposition of their dialectic based on "*Saptabhaṅgi*" which has lost its influence over mens' minds and thus made them feel depressed and they are now deceiving the ignorant by twirling round peacock feathers.[36]

They hold at the same breath that a thing perhaps does not exist and that perhaps it does exist. So, also they maintain that a thing perhaps exists while saying that it may not exist. So, what further refutation is needed except the inconsistency of their own words ?

Then, the disciple proceeds to show the weak points of the Advaita school of thought as under.

These men (the Advaitins) say that, owing to the powerful influence of *avidyā*, the world is superimposed on Brahman. And this world can neither be called sentient, nor in-sentient thing, like the cloud-city seen in the sky. Thus, the world is *anirvacaniya* or inexplicable. (In maintaining this doctrine) they have to face contradictions, which far from being unreal, are stronger than even the Vindhya mountains. They are, therefore, to be classed among the heralds who sing the praise of monarchs born of barren women.[37] And in the light of Viśiṣṭādvaita Vedānta, "the 'I' is revealed as the knower, underlying all his knowledge; the doer, underlying all his deeds and the enjoyer, underlying all his enjoyment. Neither is the 'I' the momentary stream of consciousness nor is it the eternal universal consciousness. The 'I' is essentially the conscious being with the power of his consciousness revealed in the intellectual, the emotional and the volitional spheres. The 'I' is, therefore, not to be proved from the 'I' experiences of desire, aversion, volition, pleasure, pain and knowledge as is done by the Nyāya-Vaiśeṣika-Philosophy. The 'I' is the self-proved, self-conscious entity which can be realised in our common objective experiences, our subjective states, our intense discrimination of the subject from the object and to crown all, in the transcendental realisation of its real being."[38]

Let those who are free from hatred (due to bias) ponder over this :– The truth that Brahman is full of auspicious qualities and free from all blemishes and short comings, and is (therefore) worthy of (our) worship, is accepted at first by these disputants, who (afterwards) deny all attributes and qualities in Brahman. If this is the only course left open to us from the nature of the case, the contention, arising from the desire to maintain the theory of a Brahman free from all distinguishing features and qualities which is opposed to all *Pramāṇās* like sense-perception, is impossible of being sustained.[39]

Like Indrajīt who disappeared mysteriously from the sight of all men with the help of some magic power given to him by Śaṅkara, who moved about freely in darkness and caused a great deal of suffering to those who stood in front of him as enemies, these students of Brahma-Mīmāṁsā, who are characteristic of *Kali-Yuga*, explain the existence of world illusion owing to a principle called *Māyā* postulated by Śaṅkara, and create much confusion by their interpretation of the texts denoting opposition in the *Śrutis*, such as "That Thou Art", and are always engaged in objectionable activities being spotted by nature. It is therefore in the fitness of things that Lakṣmaṇācārya, (*i.e.*, Śrī Rāmānuja), appeared in the world for their overthrow (even like Lakṣmaṇa to overthrow Indrajīt). Like Pauṇḍraka who declared I am Vāsudeva these Advaitins declare I am Brahman and there is nothing but Brahman, and their doctrine of the Self being eternally free, secures for them eternal freedom from fitness for discussion.

The purpose of bringing in the analogies or Indrajīt and Pauṇḍraka by Vedānta Deśika in the context of Advaita is two-fold : (i) to show like Indrajīt (Meghanāda), Advaitins cannot face genuine Vedantic questions by the opponents, and hide themselves under clouds and have recourse to indirect attacks from invisible positions. (ii) Like Pauṇḍraka, they claim to the nature of Supreme God-Head; while the Lord is otherwise elsewhere differently. In otherwords, it is an attack of untenable explaination of texts *ahaṁ brahmasmi*.

The Advaitin tries to create an additional and unique *Mokṣa* to the released Soul who is eternal and is characterised in his essential nature by an absence of distinguishing features. In doing so, he will surely be able to create a new sweetness to the taste of the honey on the flower seen in a dream.[40]

Thus, in the presence of king Viveka and his Marshall–Vyavasāya, both the Preceptor and the Disciple are shown as refuting the representatives of rival schools of thought and putting them to shame. Thus, the end of second Act.

ACT III

The third Act is entitled as '*Muktyupāyārambhaḥ*' or Commencement of the Adoption of the means for *Mokṣa*. This Act begins with the entrance of Rāga and Dveṣa.

Addressing his friend – Dveṣa, Rāga express his full confidence in achieving Mahāmoha's purpose. To this, Dveṣa replies that he feels delight in joining Rāga (as ordered by his master) in resisting the efforts of Viveka. Rāga wishes to convey to Dveṣa something of his own. He adds that on account of success of Viveka so far, the only means left to him is to drive the poor Virakti, and that he should take advantage in removing Viṣṇubhakti. Thus, making the poor, leads to evil-ways. He continues in support of his scheme to attract the poor towards the good things of *Svarga* and the evils of *Mokṣa*. Dveṣa agrees. Rāga adds further that the followers of Pūrvamīmāṁsā adhere to the Vedas, and they could be easily allured to the Nirīśvara Vāda and strengthen his doctrine by some convinient arguments. Dveṣa supports-Rāga's plan.

The argument that Rāga wishes to putforth is that a person who desires the perishing pleasures of this life and of *Svarga*, is animated by desire. And if so, how can one who desires bliss of *Mokṣa* be regarded as free from desire and to have Virakti Rāga makes use of a dilemma in interpreting *Mokṣa*.

"If bliss means the attainment of one's self, it is false (because we are already in the attainment of our self); if on the other hand, bliss means the attainment of something other (than one's own self), then since it is the desire for something else, there cannot be a *Puruṣārtha* called *Mokṣa* other than Kāma which is desire. Therefore, *Svarga* which results from our own desire and which dances (before our eyes) as a treasure of good experiences should itself be called *Mokṣa*, as stated by the atheistic mīmāṁsakas whom we hold in high esteem." [41]

Expressing joy, Dveṣa gives support to Rāga saying that Mahāmoha's doctrine Nirīśvaravāda is the Supreme to which a large multitude could be easily make to fall a prey. He continues to convey his own interpretation of *Mokṣa* in an argumentive style.

"If it is held in accordance with Viśiṣṭādvaita that *Mokṣa* is the attainment of Supreme splendour (called Brahman), which has for its body this world of *cit* and *acit*, then this attainment will not be the cessation of pain or suffering, for all the ills of *cit* and *ahit* (which would cling to Brahman owing to that body will be ours. If, on the other hand, the Advaitin's view is accepted that *Mokṣa* is being Brahman without any attribute or distinguishing feature, then it cannot be enjoyable. So, the Upaniṣads (the head of the Vedas) can remain only as a subject of study without any practical use." [42]

Rāga agrees with the argument of Dveṣa and continues that Viṣṇubhakti can be made to flee, that Viveka's reasoning capacity can be made clowdy as not to guide house-holders in the attainment of *Mokṣa* and that any one can be attracted by the charms of young women. To this, Dveṣa draws the attention of Rāga to difference of opinion among scholars in marrying celestial woman (which is regarded as *Mokṣa*) supported by Vātsyāyana and his associates. He proclaims that even the Supreme Brahman is subject to certain desires. Rāga regrets that Vedantins consider charming women as mere form of flesh and blood, while the fact is that they are imbude with honey.

"These (Vedāntins) consider as mere flesh the breasts of beautiful women which are as charming as golden goblets full of honey; and they deceive the ignorant like evil spirits."[43]

Looking up, he adds that it is difficult to convince blind persons that water is clear and transparent. Under this situation, Dveṣa bemoans the attitude of Vedāntins who are guided by Viveka. He further calls the followers of Viveka as demons and expresses surprise. Similarly, he points out that 'the notes of the quail, have no charm for the ears of the deaf' and again reminds their ultimate aim, *i.e.* Viveka is to be conquered. He further tells that the conquest of Viveka will mean the conquest of scholars, just as the creepers fall off when the supporting tree is cut off. Rāga expresses delight. Dveṣa rediculously says that Viveka is drowned in the doctrines of Upaniṣads and cannot establish the existance of God.

After this conversation, a voice is heard behind the curtain as to 'who are there ?' It is learnt, the voice is that of Viveka's followers. So, at once Rāga and Dveṣa anticipate some trouble and feel diffident in carrying out their master's mission. Both realise that Virakti and Viṣṇubhakti have joined Viveka. They are overpowered at the sight of Viveka coming with his queen Sumati; and the joy felt by Virakti and Viṣṇubhakti at the turn of situation. They become disheartened and express as to how they can defeat Viveka and his followers who are right now attending to release of Puruṣa from the bonds of *Saṁsāra*. Here, ends *Śuddha-Viṣkambhaka* of the third Act.

Next, Viveka and Sumati enter the stage. Sumati is frightened at the scheming but ignorant conversation of Rāga and Dveṣa. However, king Viveka tends courage to the queen, and asks her to be comforted. Because, Viveka and Viṣṇubhakti have joined them, in the presence of whom, Rāga and Dveṣa have no place. In spite of this, the queen expresses a doubt regarding success in their efforts. Because, she feels the presence of Rāga and Dveṣa somewhere around, and waiting for an apportunity to produce their evil efforts. Observing the queen's timidity, Viveka proclaims the truth that Rāga and Dveṣa would not even stand before his presence who is supreme. He cites the instance of Lord Kṛṣṇa offering protection to Arjuna; and God's grace is enough to take care of suppliants lịke him and the queen. Still Sumati is uneasy. She says that the *jīva* is in a pitiable condition because of *Svarga* and in *Naraka* suffering misery in the painful states of waking, dreaming, dreamless sleep, swoon and death. She continues to say that fate governs the life of each man, and he is subject to Lord's sport and is being tossed to and fro in this world full of sins, which enjoyment of a youth and which passes away quickly, and with the terrors of oldage and death. To this note of sorrow, Viveka replies that a new situation in which Puruṣa is placed, is different, that as a result of his virtuous action, he desires to climb up the path, where from there is no return. Puruṣa has become tired of *Svarga* because of his longing for the Supreme Being. This longing is to be strengthened by his power of meditation.

"Puruṣa's understanding, which has lost its longing for life in *Svarga* on a consideration of the fear, that it, too, must end some time or other, has now acquired a boundless thirst for the Supreme Being. This thirst for *Mokṣa*, though wavering on account of the weakness of the intellect, is strengthened by the thought mentioned before. So, his power of meditation on the Supreme Being will be established on a firm basis."[44]

He acquires real *bhakti* to the Supreme Being. He understands the difference between several forms of meditation and becomes as it were, a bee drinking the honey of the feet of the Supreme Being. The Puruṣa has been got rid of by the cycle of *Saṁsāra* that he is to be made to understand the qualities of meditation in every *Vidyā*. Then he explains to Sumati the manner of removing the confusion in the mind of the Puruṣa : If *Mukti* means the same kind of experience for all, there need not be a diversity of *Vidyās* ; if *Mukti* means different experiences for different individuals, it would be like *Svarga* with different forms of enjoyment, as favoured by certain schools of thought. These schools ignore strength of the *Pramāṇās* and weaken Puruṣa's intellectual power, where as the Śrutis clearly say that the released soul will have perfect resemblance to the Lord.[45]

So, he wants that such doubts should be removed as they keep Puruṣa in confusion.

Then, Sumati puts on courage and is convinced of the *Pramāṇās* given by Viveka. Admiring Viveka in a panygeric manner, she agrees with him because *Pramāṇas* are to all intellectuals. She adds that the *Vidyās* mentioned in the Upaniṣads for meditation are very clear and sweet. If Puruṣa adopts any one of these, he would get liberation by giving up his delusion arising out of this world. Viveka, then with full confidence says that such delusion is already removed from Puruṣa because of his acquiring detachment from the bond of *Saṁsāra*. And this *Vairāgya* that has been cultivated, will certainly take him to the path of *Mukti*. He adds that yoga which he is practicing, now has made him give up all rites as suggested by the scriptures which are not necessary for meditation. He adds that Puruṣa has realised the superfluity of *Nitya Naimittika-Karma*, that he has set his mind with concentration on Supreme Being (Nectar). He further adds that *Jīva* on account of *Vairāgya*, has realised that all sensual pleasures are illusory. And with the help of Viveka, he will certainly abandon all mental confusion and attains the status of an 'exclusive devotee of the Lord which will help him to overcome *Saṁsāra*.'

"The *Jīvātmā*, now in the body, sees with fellings of shame in his mind that the praise of the sweetness of sense-pleasures is as illusory as the city of Gandharvas (cloud-city). When I have given him a helping hand, he will get over his mental confusion and having soon attained the state of an exclusive devotee of the Lord (with single-minded *bhakti* to the Lord) he will leap over the ocean of *Saṁsāra* as if it were a mere puddle (caused by the feet of a cow)."[46]

At this, Sumati expresses surprise and feels ashamed even sages have fallen a victim of sensual pleasures like a fish in the fish hooks. Viveka again informs Sumati not to feel timid and fall into different moods. He calls the attention of Sumati and says that the wise men do not give importance to external pleasures and he will fix his mind on *Ātmānubhūti*. Very soon he will acquire a desire to get rid of *Saṁsāra* and will become eager to enjoy the boundless bliss of realising Brahman.[47] He further says that when righteous path of learned men is enough to realise Brahman, then it is certain that persons who know Brahman, do attain *Mukti*. Being convinced of the efficacy of Viveka's speech, Sumati replies that with his assistance Puruṣa can surely conquer the bondage of *Saṁsāra*. He then tells that Sumati is eager to consider a person about to get deliverance from *Saṁsāra* as though he is already liberated. Viveka adds that in the case of others, they are to be guided by right descrimination what is to be feared and what is not to be feared — in order to obtain the grace of God. Because, one who practises Brahma Vidyā, need not fear anything. And he is sure to attain *Mokṣa*. To this reply, sumati questions Viveka as to how a person can contemplate on Brahman fearlessly as most of the activities are the source of fear ? Appraising this question, Viveka explains the path of practising the secret of Brahma Vidyā. In fact, Sumati is aware of this but at present appears to be unable to recaptulate the same. Viveka further gives clarification to Sumati in a more effective manner. In otherwords, he gives prominence to compassion of the Lord again and again, without which a man cannot do anything. Without His Compassion, a person cannot achieve anything, and his efforts will be in vain. His faith in Lord's compassion makes him successful in his practice and ultimately he gets liberation from the bondage of *Saṁsāra*. Still Sumati entertains a doubt and wishes to know from Viveka the reason of even persons of renounced everything and possess knowledge of the Supreme Brahman, do not get success immediately. Viveka, giving further clarification to Sumati's doubt, replies that he would elaborate the secret which is known and practised by sages like Sanaka, Sanatkumāra and others. The secret centres round *Karma* – may be a small one or a big one. However, Viveka adds by way of caution, that no one should harm a man of wisdom. The period which determines the attainment of *Mokṣa*, depends on the intensity of *Karma*. The period also depends on the manner of gratitude shown by a person for a good act to the one who is the source of good action. Never one should be ungrateful to a devotee; because, it is the worst of all sins. Expressing her satisfaction to this reply, Sumati further questions him whether there is any solution to get rid of sinful deeds. Viveka replies that there is only one way, *i.e.* to beg pardon from virtuous people to whom sinful deeds have been done. This truth is supported by Viveka by the instance of 'fish out of water'.

The creature called fish suffers when taken out of the water and is restored to normal life when brought gradually into the water again. In the same way, the individual who has fallen into darkness by insulting the great will obtain a vision of the supreme truth again, only by seeking their protection.[48]

He continues to explain the significance of meditation which is possible for persons who have done good deeds only. This is also possible for persons who cultivate *Parābhakti* as it helps the person to cross the 'sea of *Saṁsāra*'. But, Sumati thinks over meditation and *Parābhakti* as a means to attiain *Mokṣa* ; and points out that the obstacles might come in the way of persons, eager to attain liberation. Agreeing with this thoughtful comment, Viveka emphasizes the need for prevention of the origin of such hindrances than by attempts to get rid off them after their occurrence.

Just then, Saṁvṛtti Satya comes on the stage and greets king Viveka. He is the personification of relative truth which is different from Absolute Truth. He says to the king Viveka that he is the envoy of king Mahāmoha, and that he is always in his company. His appearance causes perplexion to Viveka. He wants to know the purpose of his coming on the stage and exhorts him to give up evil ways. Instantly he takes out a palm leaf from his head and shows it to Viveka. The letter is the order of the emperor Mahāmoha. He adds that the order was prepared by the accountant Lobha and now presented to Viveka. The contents of the order should not on no account, be disobeyed.

King Viveka expresses his indifference and asks him to read the letter in privacy. The messenger agrees to read the letter. Evidently the letter of king Mahāmoha, the esteemed friend of Kāma and others, strikes a note of difference between the attainment of *Svarga* and attainment of *Mokṣa*. Viveka with a contemptuous smile, enquires Sumati whether they too are to obey the orders of Mahāmoha. Viveka makes an analysis of the order, and suggests that he should use the method contained in the letter. He adds futher that the message is similar to the story of a begger stretching his foot and claims the house as his own. He concludes on the letter that it (his remarks) suits king Mahāmoha only and has no appeal to the virtuous. Sumati is in agreement with the act of king Viveka. The messenger continues to read the letter and threatens king Viveka not to disobey the order and face the attack by Krodha and Moha. He adds further that the prowess of Krodha and Kāma is to be taken note of by king Viveka. But, king Viveka does not see in this any harm, because Śiva's third eye is sure to foil the attempts of Krodha and Kāma.[49] He points out the truth of the *Śrutis* that the Supreme Being first created the world, maintains it and destroys it by mere will. And thus no one is free from Kāma. At this juncture, Sumati says to Viveka that Manmatha is not invincible, and why he should feel proud of his power. To this, Viveka replies that pratings of Moha is covered by illusion and his power need not be taken very seriously. He shows his willingness to listen, entirely to the letter. Just then the envoy announces that one who is angry with anger, then one does not get over-anger. On the otherhand, how can one who is not angry with *krodha*, conquer *krodha*? Thus it is, as it were, a rope with a noose on either side. Sumati adds that it is mere difficult to conquer Kāma than Krodha. And for the conquest of Kāma, Krodha is required. Making a descrimination between bad temper raises anger, Viveka says that the latter is not a sin and that it is necessary to conquer Kāma and others. Now, Viveka thinks of sending a reply to King Mahāmoha through that envoy. His reply is contained in the following verse :

"The world will (soon) show the greatest regard to Viveka who will kill Mahāmoha, defy Manmatha, and shake off Krodha with contempt."[50]

The envoy decides to get back. For in his estimation it is difficult to conquer Viveka and Sumati who are ever eager to awaken those who are asleep, promotes the welfare of the world. He feels unhappy over the errand for which his master sent him. Proclaiming a proverb that for the sake of a family an individual is to be deserted.[51]

Sumati strikes a note of appreciation at Viveka's efforts to take men on the right path; if he does not succeed, all his efforts will be in vain. However, she is confident of Viveka's success in his efforts. Viveka lends courage to Sumati and points out that according to the Upaniṣads, Puruṣa is aware of the means for *Mukti* along with their respective accessories. He will advance towards *Mokṣa* by cool path of *Arcis* free from the thick mire of mental confusion mingled with sharp thorns of Kāma and Krodha.

At this juncture, a voice of proclamation by two heralds behind the curtain is heard, hailing Viveka as a Victor. Addressing Sumati, Viveka says that the proclamation of the heralds has to be regarded as the beginning of a new phenomena, *i.e.* the end of darkness and the beginning of sunrise. In otherwords, the herald signifies the defeat of Kāma and others who are the source of evil acts on account of their wicked nature. Just then, Viveka makes a reference to the lighting of lamps for performing *Ārati* in the evening (an auspicious function sponteneously). Now, relieved of the evil forces he feels pleasure in performing the evening lights with pleasure. At this happy ending both retire from the stage. Thus, ends the third Act.

ACT IV

The fourth Act is entitiled as '*Kāmādivyūhabhedaḥ*' or 'The break up of the military array of Kāma etc.' At the outset, Kāma and Vasanta enter the stage. Here Vedānta Deśika vividly brings out the evil forces of Kāma, Vasanta, Krodha and others, and their logical results by which several ordinary persons succumb and get defeated. His purpose in introducing these characters is evidently to strike a note of caution in the mind of Puruṣa in his goal to attain Brahman.

In the beginning Kāma proclaims before Vasanta expressing his prowess with which, he could make an attempt to conquer Śiva. A conversation between Kāma and Vasanta follows complimenting each other. It is explicit that when Kāma is provided with weapons and missiles and thus be assisted by Vasanta, the entire world can be deluded. Vasanta replies that virtuous persons do certain acts forbidden by Kāma. After doing such acts, they throw the blame on Kāma and Krodha and thus loose their right vision. He further admires Kāma and his jurisdiction over which, he exerts his power. Immediately, Kāma reciprocates Vasanta hailing him as the king of seasons, source of all kinds of flowers, his friend and assistant and that his strength is in no way inferior.

After a long talk of mutual praise, both Kāma and Vasanta suddenly remember the work for which they have been sent by king Mahāmoha. They become busy themselves to attend to their assigned duties. Their mission is to create disturbance in the minds of persons, confuse their knowledge of discrimination and create an atmosphere to which they fall a prey and give up meditation (particularly if they are timid and weak). Kāma says that a Puruṣa engaged in meditation (but without firmness) can be easily diverted by his power, to an enchanting women. In his eyes, a woman is a symbolic creation. He says, he would confer bliss on man (evidently transitory bliss or happiness).[52] Vasanta then declares that even sages fall a victim to the charms of a young women and to her enticing dance and words. If this is the reality, in the opinion of Vasanta, Puruṣa's down fall is certain. This is corroborated by an example of sage Soubhari :

"If Viveka grown arrogant by his association with Vyavasaya continues his efforts (to lead Puruṣa towards *Samādhi*), in disregard of me, he will then be himself the cause of creating in Puruṣa the condition of Soubhari (who was lured by a hundered women)."[53]

Vasanta reiterates the prowess of Kāma that there is no need for Vasanta to stain himself in his errand. However, Kāma is aware of his limitations; and therefore he says that both Vasanta and himself should spare no efforts in causing disturbance to Puruṣa because their enemy (Viveka and others are strong). Recaptulating the environment capable of being created by Kāma, where man looses senses, Vasanta makes Kāma remember his prowess and says thus :

"Puruṣa now dreads the great fears of *Saṁsāra* ; at the same time, he longs also for the home (and other pleasures); he is eager to attain Brahman and, at the same time, has an eye for the prosperity (of *Saṁsāra*). He has a passion for the pleasures of the senses and, at the same time, is ashamed of them. So, his contemplation of the Supreme Brahman is both manifest and unmanifest, and is therefore in sure peril."[54]

Then, observing incompletion of Puruṣa's Yoga, Kāma decides to make a night-attack using all his missiles.

Agreeing with Kāma and also witnessing the period appropriate for use of evil powers, Vasanta suggests to Kāma to use his weapons in his military headquarters to divert Puruṣa from meditation, particularly to the company of women and their dalliance. Kāma underestimates Viveka saying that he is attracted by a desire to obtain *Samādhi*; but it is not very easy for him to get *Samādhi*. Because, he suffers from ills of the body and the mind. He is not aware of the hurdles which lies before him.

Puruṣa is still not free from the excitement caused by the eagerness to enjoy life and is inebriated with draughts of the liquor of sense-pleasures. In trying to secure deliverance for him, Viveka seems to be unaware of the joyful experience of the dalliances of celestial women, which is like a sweet drink consisting of nectar mixed with the juice of the grape."[55]

Symbolising his prowess in the form of a noose, Kāma makes a statement of a dilemma ; *i.e.* if the person engaged in *Dhyāna*, becomes angry due to Mahamoha's evil power, Puruṣa cannot attain Brahman. According to Kāma, such person seems to be making a foolish attempt to attain *Samādhi*, because he is sure that Puruṣa cannot easily escape from his clutches.

Next, Krodha enters the stage with a dreadful face, and admires Kāma who is according to him, capable of defeating Viveka. He goes round the stage and makes a big laughter. He also reposes confidence in Kāma's prowess in defeating Viveka. Kāma welcomes Krodha and expresses compliments to him as a powerful member of the military array. He further speaks even if Dambha, Moha and himself were to fail in the master's task, Krodha is one who cannot be overpowered. (He is sure to win a victory for the master). Then, Vasanta intervenes and hails Kāma and Krodha, who like wind and fire fight in the battle. In this case, *i.e.* when a favourable set of circumstances have been created why should there be delay in taking the offensive. He is eager to begin the battle.

"Let the celestial women (*apsarās*) bent with the weight of their beautiful breasts which are as attractive as the bunches of flowers in the gem — like creepers nurtured by the ladies attendant on Manmatha — let these celestial woman with tremulous eyes resembling the bees which form the bow - string of Manmatha, attended on Puruṣa, who now regards *Vairāgya* as his great weath."[56]

As per the plan of Kāma, Krodha and Vasanta begin their march in which, Vasanta wishes to make a night-attack. Just then admiring Vasanta, Krodha expresses that proper atmosphere has been set to pursue the battle. Kāma gives a description of the moon light which is again suited to continue the battle. Kāma then gives a beautiful description of the natural setting with the waters of the Gaṅges and moonlihgt which is conducive to the evil forces to win a victory over Viveka.[57] However, Krodha is in full support of Kāma and Vasanta. Instantly Kāma suggests that there need not be any delay in foiling Puruṣa's efforts who is already engaged in meditation. At this juncture, Vasanta sees Puruṣa who is disinterested in external objects and who is in the grip of Viveka. He comes out with the attainment of Puruṣa in the midst of books and above to win his object. In his opinion, Puruṣa is in two minds - whether to proceed further in meditation or withdraw. However, he is a little diffident in fulfiling his errand. But Kāma and Krodha do not entertain any wishful thinking as Vasanta entertains.

Then Vasanta directs Krodha to enter the mind of *Jīva* (Puruṣa). There is also another thing to be borne in mind by both of you who are the dread of your enemies. Even to one who has shrunk from all contact with external desires, the desire for honour or renown is a great obstacle — to meditation. That is why, — remembering the words of Brahma — Saṁvarta, Bharata (Jaḍa Bharatha), Vidura and others courted the contempt of the world and pretended to be mad men, because they thought it would cut off all sins. So, before Puruṣa seeks contemptuous treatment from others, Krodha should enter by force into him by inducing in him pain at the thought of losing his reputation and the like. He continues that if Krodha does not influence Puruṣa, he would take interest in listening to stories of the Lord; there by he becomes so strong that he could not be made fall from his righteous duties. He finds in Puruṣa a firm determination to renounce all allurable objects that come in the way of spiritualism. However, Kāma does not agree with Vasanta's comments and chides him not to be afraid of the battle that has begun. Again Kāma warns Vasanta not to act like a coward on the battle field. Kāma further says that he is capable of controlling gods, men and beasts. While Krodha by his cruel nature could not put up with any harm to them. They therefore, decide to function together.

Krodha then demands that Kāma and Vasanta should join him in giving effect to his plan and in order to achieve the goal. He cites the examples from mythology relating to Jamadagni and Rāvaṇa.[58] Vasanta categorically remarks that though he agrees with the plans of Kāma, he expresses a doubt regarding their, success. Because, Puruṣa has no interest in worldly desires. Still Krodha declares that though Puruṣa is unattached, he would cause havoc in his environment namely stealing and hiding of articles, like rags of cloth, grass seat and *Kamaṇḍala*, mental excitement, mental delusion and thus brings about the loss of *Samādhi*.[59] He quotes the example of Śiva and justifies the strength of action. Kāma looking at Vasanta, gives his support to Krodha. He explains about his plans. "Who is there that has the strength to withstand the *tamas* (ignorance) caused by Krodha, the like of which cannot be found in sleep, swoon or death, which causes all differences of high and low to disappear, in which all distinctions of caste are forgotten and which spreads on all sides as black as the waves of the river Yamunā over-flowing its banks on account of the heavy downpour of rain at the end of a kalpa ?"[60] He continues that even sages are not free from his prowess and cites the instance of Vālmīki and other Paurāṇika personalities. Appraising Kāma, Vasanta encourages Krodha to pursue his course of action. Kāma replies that all his actions are abated by Vasanta. In turn Vasanta admires Kāma. Still Vasanta entertains a doubt regarding their success.

At this time, another character, Lobha accompanied by his mistress Tṛṣṇā enter the stage. Vedānta Deśika has brought in this character of Lobha to show that it is capable of cutting at the root of *dharma*, nips in the bud the 'sprout of serenity and self control'. He is another assistant of king Mahāmoha in creating obstacles in Puruṣa's meditation. On the arrival of Lobha, Kāma and Krodha feel delighted. Vasanta now regains the hope of victory, because Lobha is capable of filling in the minds of persons delusion, nay, even the entire world. Kāma and Krodha also feel jubilant at Vasanta's suggestion. As a logical sequence, he welcomes Lobha and Krodha also joins him. Feeling elated, Lobha replies that he has been accompanied by his wife Tṛṣṇā, and no offering can possibly satisfy them. In Jubilance, he embraces his spouse, and says that all the gold and silver offerings fail to satisfy Tṛṣṇā. Lobha with pride proclaims that even the gods, kinnaras, demons, sages men and beasts have been over-powered by him. As such diverting Puruṣa from meditation is a small work. Tṛṣṇā is confident of his strength to defeat Puruṣa because they know, their strength has been firmly established in the three worlds. Declaring that his presence and support are now required to Kāma and Krodha, Lobha pointing to his wife, shows his eagerness to join his friends. Tṛṣṇā also joins her husband. Kāma and Krodha bless Lobha and Tṛṣṇā.

Vasanta feels extremely happy at this, and says that the combination is similar to that of wind, rain and fire. Therefore, their master Mahāmoha, need not have any doubt of success. Meanwhile, the spouses of Krodha and Lobha also join together and embrace each other indicating complete cordiality in their errand. Kāma enquires Lobha whether his functioning yields fruit. Lobha shares his favours with Kāma. Admiring Lobha, Krodha compliments that his attempts are always successful. Lobha replies that with their support (they being the *Puruṣārthas*) he is always successful. Lobha makes a generalisation as to how greed gives rise to further greed and knows no end. Vasanta agrees with Lobha who joined with Tṛṣṇā can do anything. He asserts that realisation of *Puruṣārthas* is possible by Lobha alone. He points out the importance of wealth to men and also the study of *Arthaśāstra* to kings. He adds that acquistion and security of wealth is possible with the help of Lobha only. He continues to say it is time now to decide how Puruṣa safeguarded by Viveka can be defeated.

Then Vedānta Deśika portrays how the concerned characters arrange their military array to defeat Puruṣa. Kāma comes out with the proclamation that he proceeds first; and then Tṛṣṇā in the centre, and Lobha to follow him. Krodha and Lobha are to be on both sides safe-guarding the array. This invincible array is to proceed further to destroy Puruṣa's objective. Then they march five to six paces. Kāma is already prepared with piercing strings of sharp and soft bows and arrows to disturb Puruṣa's penance. Puruṣa is all the while engaged in penance, who now apprehends some outside disturbance.

Therefore, he sits firmly controlling his breath and giving up all attachments and showing his firm determination to reach the goal. Making a keen observation of this situation, Vasanta takes it for granted that Puruṣa is lifted by Viveka from the ocean of *Prakṛti* and eager to place him in Vaikuṇṭha being far removed by *rajas* and *tamas*. Viveka is seen by Vasanta to plan a further strategy for Puruṣa with the help of Sumati. Kāma now appears to have an upper hand because since the time in memorial, he has been a powerful force in devouring mediation. He finds Puruṣa being now surrounded by hunger, thirst, delusion, grief and fishing in the sea of sins; so it is easy for him to defeat Puruṣa just as the fisherman picks up a fish from the hook.[61] In his eyes Puruṣa, though doing penance is under the affliction of love and the pretext of mental serenity. He repeats the Veda of love. However, Vasanta thwarts the ambition of Kāma and hints caution. Just then Lobha is upset by the mental restlessness of his spouse Tṛṣṇā. Still he asks her to remain comfortable as the entire array is with her. She too, now gets courage and express the security when she is amidst other warriors who are the friends of Lobha. But in surprise and terror, Kāma observes that Viveka without loosing good sense is fortified by patience and contentment. He is seated in the chariot of *praṇava*. Hence, though approached by military array of Kāma, Krodha and others, Puruṣa breaks their military array.

The result of the first attack on Viveka is expressed by Vasanta. He says to his friends that moment the news of defeat is conveyed to Mahāmoha, he will give up his life. So, he asks his friends to retreat from Viveka. Lobha says that they should not fight in the absence of their King Mahāmoha. Krodha feels regret for having given up the combat which would show their ungratefulness to the king. Lobha thinks that there is no use in wasting time but think off protecting themselves and from future dangers. Kāma supports Lobha and his words. Kāma anticipating danger, asks his friends to remain move cautiously. Because he finds Viveka, symbolising the yawning gulf, warns his friends not o fall into yawning gulf. He asks his friends to flee in different directions and to love their life. Their present decision and to save their life. Their present decision to flee is similar to a wise saying that (*ātmārthe'pṛthiviṁ tyajet*) to save one's life even the whole earth may be sacrificed.

Act four comes to a close with the exit of Kāma, Krodha, Lobha, Tṛṣṇā and Vasanta.

ACT V

The fifth Act is entitled as 'दम्भाद्युपालम्भो नाम पञ्चमोऽङ्कः' in the colophon by Ahobala, as it describes mutual recrimination of Dambha and others.[62] King Mahāmoha having known the defeat of Kāma, Krodha and Lobha, orders Dambha and Darpa to poison the mind of Puruṣa. Thus, Dambha, Kuhanā and others enter the stage. These characters are the personifications of vices. The act is full of powerful satire.

In the beginning, Dambha seeks Kuhanā's support in carrying out their master's order. He admires Kuhanā's fidility. To this, Kuhanā reproaches her husband while she is expecting higher compliments from him. But again, Dambha praises Kuhanā recalling her services on the occasion of Yajñas. He further recalls the help given by Kuhanā at the time of offering *Darśapūrṇamāsa* and *Śrāddhas*. Dambha again recalls the favour done by Kuhanā for performing the vedic rites rigidly, and her service on *ekādaśī* and *dvādaśī* days, makes repeated appeals not to leave him alone, particularly in the Kali age. He adds that he has been instructed by Durmati to destroy Viveka as he is capable of it. He further boasts of himself that he has begun initial *dharma* of worshipping the god of unrighteousness. This God is the personification of six men of vices, such as (1) the person who has committed arson, (2) the prisoners, (3) the one who comes with a sword to kill, (4) the one who has deprived one of one's wealth, (5) or one's land and (6) the person who has abducted one's wife.[63]

For, he asks Kuhanā to fetch the flowers. To this, Kuhanā replies hesitatingly that it is not easy to destroy Viveka, who is well protected by Śāma, Dama etc. But Dambha calls Kuhanā as a foolish woman and asks her not to under estimate his prowess. True to his nature, Dambha proclaims his profound scholarship and his successful performance of a number of sacrifices. He appeals to Kuhanā to have confidence in his strength and his ability to do a *Yajña* to bewitch Viveka who is trying to foil the attempt of king Mahāmoha.

Kuhanā, now wants to know from Dambha the nature of *śyenayāga* which is going to be performed against Viveka. Dambha assures Kuhanā, that the *Yajña* he is going to perform against is not *Śyenayāga* and appeals to her again to have confidence in his strength. He adds that another *Yāga* is going to be performed, which is meant to destroy Viveka. Kuhanā feeling comforted, supports Dambha's plan and expects showing to the preceptor who had suggested the performance of this *Yāga*. Dambha expressing laughter at Kuhanā's question, says that he himself is a perfect scholar in all the rites, and he does not need any other preceptor. Even then, he says that he has invited one of his disciples. Garva or Darpa remains present during the course of *Yāga* because he is a very able assistant of king Mahāmoha. He sits in a proper posture to perform the *Yāga*.

Kuhanā has nothing but all praise to Dambha in his attempt. With great satisfaction Kuhanā praises Dambha for his appropriate arrangements for the *Yāga*. Then Dambha, a believer in omens now experiences a good one, *i.e.* throbbing of the right eye indicative of success in the work undertaken. Instantly Dambha notices Darpa's arrival to his hermitage.

Darpa approaches the hermitage holding a banner advertising his greatness. Dambha now observes Darpa proclaiming the purpose of his visit. Before this, Darpa announces the strength of his prowess. He tells the purpose of his arrival. He, being sent by Mahāmoha, carries out the mission of vilify good and great men. He further says that he has descended from Satyaloka after being worshipped by Gods with valuable gifts. He admires himself that he is considered as the thirteenth Sūrya, the twelfth Rudra or ninth Vasu. He says, since his ancestors could not find a befitting priest to conduct *Yāga* on their behalf, his family has been renowned as *anadhvarakula*.[64] He further says that he has composed the treatises on forty-eight varieties of Buddhist doctrine, and he has brought down the pride of the followers of Vedic religion.[65]

He further says, he enjoys a great joy in seeing the quarrel between the exponents of different Schools of thought, as these exponents are initiated into particular School of thought by himself. He expresses that these exponents are his relatives. All the religious activities he says, have been performed for gaining popularity.

The rest of the long speech of Darpa consists of laughing at *Saṁnyāsins*, condemnation of malpractice among brahmins in *agrahara*, misinterpretation of Gāyatrī *Mantra* and *Sandhyopāsanā* and those who perform it, men taking to *Vairāgya* due to the influence of Kali extols *Agnihotra* among young couples makes fun of certain practices among brahmins and pontiffs of *Maṭhas*, rediculing persons wearing *Yajñopavīta*, *Japa* and *Mantra,* condemning hypocritical practices of *Yogis* or saints only in name of meditation, makes fun of performers of *Yajñas* and *Yāgas*, redicules *Vairāgya* and collection of wealth by *Saṁnyāsins* for erecting *Maṭhas*. He bemoans that on account of these increasing hypocrates, Viveka has no sacred place in a region like Gaṅges and Yamunā. At last he finds a hermitage for which he has all but praise because he finds delight and happiness. In the hermitage, he seems to find the son of Sūrya or some one of his lineage. He approaches the *Yogi* when his right eye throbs. He also feels happiness perhaps in meeting his spouse there.

Just then, Asūyā enters as a female ascetic on the stage. As she proclaims, her purpose is to carryout the behest of the queen Durmati, *i.e.*, to impart confidence in the beginning but later only to beguile the scholarship of learned men. She says that she has travelled throughout the fourteen worlds, and she is approaching the hermitage where *Kulapati* Bhagavān Dharmadhvaja dwells. There also she acts as a spy, in order to attribute the faults of virtuous men. She takes pride in saying that if she were awake and vigilant, even Lord Śiva or Rāma would be subject to false comments. She walks a few steps forward and tries to know about the persons doing penance in the area or whether they are just pretending. Further, she gives a description of the *Yogis* who have given up Vedic religion and makes fun of them. In her estimation, they are those who perform *Yajñas* to secure a good reputation in society. The Supreme Brahman that they know is the Brahman of the six *rasas*; the only deity in whom they have exclusive faith is Kāma and their devoted service is to the cowry (*i.e.*, money). They are the *Śiṣyas* of the cat, the cock and the crane and the *Śāstra* they follow is that of Cārvāka (atheists and materialists).[66]

Just then Darpa is seen by Asūyā in the hermitage. Addressing her, Darpa says that she looks like the presiding deity of the *saṁnyāsa āśrama* and like Sulabha,[67] she is proficient in Yoga. Asūyā chides him (Darpa) and says that he should not ask questions, of which answers should not be told by the *Saṁnyāsins*. However, both express their superior status and there is no point in one asking the other to offer respect. To this, Asuyā replies that it is better to seek the advice of the *yogin* in the hermitage who is well-versed in *Dharmaśāstra*. Darpa answers that he has now become aware of her powers but could not identify her (because she was in the garb of a *Saṁnyāsinī*). Still Asūyā does not give up her superior status and says that she too has seen him earlier; but she demands expiatory act as he did not respect her before. Darpa does not readily agree to her words and wishes to consult the *yogin* and enter the hermitage.

In this context, Dambha and Kuhanā are seen entering the hermitage. Noticing the presence of Darpa and Asūyā in the hermitage, Dambha makes a sign to his wife Kuhanā probably indicating the arrival of Darpa and Asūyā. Kuhanā says to Darpa and Asūyā that they have travelled too much and are not pure and they should not approach her master. To this, Darpa does not agree. He replies that they have taken bath already in the sacred rivers and that they are pure. Dambha has put on a show of *Tapas* and learning that instead of respecting them, she is failing in her duty. Evidently Dambha will have heard this which was enough to break his silence. Suddenly, Kuhanā approaches Dambha and asks him to break his silence and offer respect to the newly arrived revered guests. But, Dambha is not prepared to offer respect to Darpa and Asūyā and refuses to do so. To this, Darpa replies that having come from Toṇḍamandalam with a respectable lineage. His purpose was not to disrespect Dambha; but on the other hand, he should make it a point to recognise his superior status. The prose portion which follows this reply and the verse number thirty seven shows how Darpa further substantiates his great status and how he even went to the extent of abandoning his virtuous mother on the ground, that she conversed with a old woman who was alleged to be bad.[68] All these indicate the climax of Darpa's characteristic feature *viz.* uncompromising nature and demanding reverence from one and all. Dambha is equally self-conscious of his nature. Replying to Darpa, he says that if he were so great, he should respect the holy *Saṁnyāsinī*, *i.e.* Kuhanā and even prostrate before her. This reply is indicative of how Dambha elevates his spouse and his hypocratical nature. Further, it brings out his arrogant nature and how he even makes use of vile vocabulary and how he is in no way superior to Prajāpati, Brahmā, Paśupati who are well-known to him, and therefore demands recognition of his position. He also curses him that he would go to hell after his death for having disrespected him.

Kuhanā next joins her hands with Dambha and endorsing his reply to Darpa, says to Asūyā that Darpa is nothing but a wicked brahmin who would meet with destruction. Because, he has not shown respect to the sage, *i.e.* Dambha. Addressing Kuhanā, Asūyā comments that she happens to be the wife of a religious person and still fails to recognise both of them as of the same status and even calls Darpa as a noble soul. Dambha becomes angry and addressing Darpa says that he abuses only to show off his superior status that he has wandered too much like a good person thrown out by his community or like an animal sent out of the house (which eats only filth material) and that he has no shame in condemning him. Claps his hands, Darpa questions why Dambha gets angry like a monkey with him. He states that he speaks only what is true. To this, Dambha replies Darpa that he has grown like a pillar without acquiring wordly knowledge, and that is why, he does not know, how to behave with him. He continues to assert his superiority saying that many persons who committed sins are rid of the sin by sprinkling his *Pādodaka* on their head.[69] Naturally Kuhanā lends support to what Dambha says.

Darpa says to himself that Kuhanā and Dambha belong to his category only and they are boasting of themselves in great height. A little later, with reverence to Kuhanā, Darpa speaks out saying that he is all-knowing (*sarvajña*). He says that he would suggest something of his own decision. Evidently Darpa's answer brooks satire. He takes the view that no decision could be taken in the company of deceitful Dambha and Kuhanā who do selfish acts and get benefit for themselves. For instance, when doing *Yāga*, Asūyā endorses his view. Listening to this, Dambha rebukes Darpa as one vilifying those who are superior to others and attributes the same to Asūyā who has (hypocratically) put on the dress of a *Saṁnyāsini*.

Suddenly a voice in the air is heard and chaos begins behind the curtain. The voice from the air is to the effect that both the householder *i.e.*, Dharmadhvaja and his guests are one and the same standing true to their statements they hail from Gauḍa and Lāṭa countries respectively. This aerial voice is enough to bring about reconciliation between Darpa and Dambha. Darpa accepting the aerial voice as entire truth, both reciprocate respect mutually and also pardon each other. The result is that Darpa, Dambha, Kuhanā and Asūyā rejoice themselves and greet with warm affection. They all decide to meet their king Mahāmoha.

Then, there enter king Mahāmoha with his queen

Durmati. Addressing his queen, Mahāmoha says that he made an attempt to destroy Viveka who is helping Puruṣa to attain *samādhi* by sending Kāma, Krodha together. He continues that they have failed in their purpose and taken to fast unto death. So, he is now sending their wives to comfort them. Durmati replies that she has already attended to this work. The king appreciates her fore-thought in attending to her husband's errand. He suggests to his queen that his associates should be asked to come back at the time of the battle. She agrees. The king reminds his queen of their ultimate object, viz., defeating the attempt of Viveka in helping Puruṣa to attain *Samādhi*. He continues that he has already made the *asuras* bear his orders on their heads and take to action at the proper time. In a tone of superiority and glorification he further continues to say that all those who are in *Svarga* are under his control, and that he has confined the triolords — Brahmā, Viṣṇu and Maheśvara to the lotus, the ocean, and the mountain respectively. As such, he has no doubt in achieving success in the battle. Then he himself thinks that Viveka who has somehow getting on success should be conquerred. Looking at Durmati, he gives his plan to achieve success on Viveka by means of spreading diverse system of doctrines. Again because of the flowers of Upaniṣads have over shadowed them; realises failure on the part of Kāma and others in conquerring Viveka, create further confusion in the minds of men by making them believe in Bhedābheda thought. So, that ego or 'I' in them, may result in conceit; thus loosing right thinking and in upholding the doctrine that what is visible is the supreme end of life. Thus, Mahāmoha plans to establish *Pūrvapakṣa* view and stultify the efforts of Viveka.

He further continues that earth, water, fire and air— these are 'reals' (the only *tattvas*) and from their combination with one another arises consciousness, in the same way as the power of intoxication arises when certain substances are mixed together; misinterpret idea of the soul. He further proclaims his view by way of a reply to Durmati that the doctrines of the Upaniṣads vary from time to time. He now intends to establish firmly the fact that the Vedāntins are under his influence. He even goes to the extent of saying that doctrines of Bṛhaspati are nothing but his own doctrines which appeal to hearts of men, while others doctrines oppose to their own stand. He says that he would make men believe in the things that are perceptible. Durmati then asks Mahāmoha regarding the nature of *Mukti*, *Sukha* and of the deity to be worshipped according to the opinion of Bṛhaspati. Mahāmoha replies that the fall of the body is *Mokṣa*, *Sukha* or heavenly bliss on earth is the sexual pleasure and young ladies giving such pleasure are the deities to be worshipped.[70] Mahāmoha then adds that in his battle with Viveka these young ladies, the perce-ptible deities are the main source of victory over Viveka.

Durmati then asks Mahāmoha that how he could win over Viveka with the instrumentality of young ladies. Mahāmoha explains how even men engrossed in deep meditation become weak before young ladies. "Even the students of the Upaniṣads declare that one who has attained the Supreme Being by giving up all the pleasures of sense objects has (in Paramapada) (the pleasure of) eating and the enjoyment of the company of women who have unending delight in sex pleasures. This is indeed intriguing. Those who run away from fear of scorpions, should not fall into the mouth of (venomous) serpents."[71] For, the influence of Manmatha is very effective continuing the same trend. He cites examples of certain divine personalities like Garuḍa, and even the highest Lord Nārāyaṇa conferring *Mukti* who are attracted by the element of 'lady'. He further says that it is impossible to refute the doctrines of Cārvāka in the face of celestial beings who are no exception to the influence of the powerful instinct of love. Durmati tells that all ladies are her maids, and hence she can get Mahāmoha the victory over Viveka through these ladies who know this art very well. By this means the followers of Viveka who believe in the doctrine of reality can be distracted and can be made to believe in a doctrine of enjoyment. Mahāmoha further explains how other Schools of Philosophy have come to light.[72] Ignoring the creed enunciated by Bṛhaspati which imposes no strain nor any painful rites, men become keenly interested in the interminable disputes of various thinkers, indulging in fallacious arguments such as Kapila (*Sāṅkhya*), Hiraṇyagarbha (*Yoga*), Kaṇabhojana (*Vaiśeṣika* logical system), Buddha and Jina (Jainism). He even goes to the extent of saying that the cause and effect theory is baseless and that events happen by chance. For the betterment of the world, the secret of *Asuropaniṣad* was brought to light by Brahmā through Virocana who had served the former for long period.[73]

The older School of Cārvākas held that *Mukti* consisted in the disintegration of the body and the senses. Mahāmoha declares that he has added a corrective to it in his *Vārttika,* because he thinks that their view is wrong.[74]

In her praise to Mahāmoha, Durmati proclaims that he has been trying to protect the world of *jīvas*, while the followers of diverse systems welcome different hostile systems and create hurdles in his path of Mahāmoha. To this Mahāmoha replies in a tone of confidence that no one can change the nature of 'thieves', (or the wicked followers of different systems). Becoming alert of his duty, Mahāmoha calls his associates to assist him in his future plan.

Accordingly Dambha and Darpa come forward and approach Mahāmoha. The latter welcomes the two praising that they are his well wishers. Both are now ready to bring the plan into action as directed by Mahāmoha and seek his instructions.

Firstly, King Mahāmoha enquires Dambha and Darpa about the whereabouts of Kāma an others. Dambha responds to Mahāmoha and says that he is aware of the plight of Kāma and Lobha. He informs that Kāma has suffered a rereat in a night — attack and being put to shame has concealed himself. He conveys further that even Lobha has suffered a defeat on account of devices planned by Viveka and not able to divert Puruṣa. Further Darpa informs him of the pitiable condition of Krodha who has failed in his duty due to the influence of *Vairāgya* on him.

Under this circumstance, Mahāmoha has no way but to laugh bitterly. He attributes his disappointment to Viveka. He now comes out with his purpose *viz.*, to spread *adharma* to the extent that Viveka would become quite unable to take revolt against it intends to protect his race of *adharma.* Mahāmoha declares, that which *adharma* is itself *dharma* for them. Thus, if vices are substituted for virtues invincible Viveka can easily be defeated. He hopes to win a victory over Viveka with his battle array as a knife cuts green leaves. In spite of his earlier disappointment, Mahāmoha speaks proudly to his wife about his keeping up the promise to put his plan to action. As he is aware of the inability of Kāma and others to assist him, he declares thus :

"Whether Kāma and his friends, Krodha and Lobha, are despondent, or whether they come to my aid at the proper time, I wil display the stand taken by Rāma in his battle with the Rākṣasas (*i.e.*, fight single — handed with Viveka). Let this *Kaliyuga* be my chariot now, and you, my Durmati, will be my charioteer. Dambha will blow the trumpet at my victory and likewise Darpa will be my armour."[75] Dambha agrees with Mahāmoha and says that he himself is enough to win a victory. On behalf of others Dambha assures all support and co-operation to Mahāmoha in his plan of action against Viveka.

After getting assurance, Mahāmoha gives instructions to his agents to pursue their course of action. Dambha is to go to the holy banks of Ganges to pursue his duty, while Darpa is to dwell in the hearts of sages who are engaged in performing *Tapas*. Dambha and Darpa once again give assurance about carrying out the orders of Mahāmoha and exit with their wives from the stage.

Now, Mahāmoha thinks of the first step to his action to win over his enemies, and wishes to perform *Prāṇāgnihotra* by offering four kinds of food (eatable, suckable, lickable, and drinkable) as oblation in *Jaṭharāgni*.[76]

The Act closes with Mahāmoha's observation of the voice of Vaitālikas for the worship of the deities representing *Prāṇa* and makes his exit to his private appartment *i.e.*, together with his wife, Durmati.

ACT VI

The Sixth Act is entitled as "स्थानविशेषसंग्रहो नाम षष्ठोऽङ्कः" as it deals with Viveka's search for a suitable place for meditation and communion. In the beginning of the Act, the scene of *Śuddhaviṣkambhaka* is brought in, which opens with entrance of Kañcuki or chamberlin.

The chamberlin introduces himself as being the son of Darpa, and door-keeper of king Mahāmoha, and his duty is to put obstacles in the way of good and virtuous men. He feels disgusted as he is to serve a cruel master and to do what all is expected of an efficient servant. He is awaiting the arrival of the spy in order to convey the news to his master king Mahāmoha. Mahāmoha has already sent Vighna to create disturbance to Viveka and to his followers who are engaged in meditation. The chamberlin reports that this Vighna has travelled all through the five *sthānas* (places) — *Yama, Niyama, Āsana, Prāṇāyāma* and *Pratyāhara.*[77] But, finding his way barred everywhere by righteous observances, he has returned after seeing Viveka flying in the aerial car, from distance. At last, the Chamberlin indicates the entrance of Viveka thus : "Viveka is approaching here, seated in his chariot of *Manoratha* (wish) driven by the charioteer – Tarka (reason) to find a suitable place for meditation." [78]

In the beginning of the main scene of the Act, Viveka together with his charioteer, Tarka enter the stage. This entire scene runs through the dialogue between Viveka and Tarka, describing more than twenty holy places through which they have travelled. In course of his entourege, Viveka firstly visits the mountain Meru, observes it and describes thus :

(i) Meru Mountain : "This is a place suitable for the rest and repose of those who, in their pursuit of pleasurable ends, go about to and fro, weary and fatigued, in the wilderness of *Prakṛti* and finding no happiness anywhere. The mountain of gold (Meru) shines like the pericarp of the lotus-like earth supported on the stalk of *Ādiśeṣa* and the smaller mountains surrounding are like the filaments of that lotus (the earth)." [79]

(ii) Kailāsa : "Though occupied by the Lord who overthrew Manmatha, Mount Kailāsa is no fit place for uninterrupted meditation. The juice flowing from the mountain like cheeks of Vināyaka and bubbling like the (dark) waves of the Yamunā covers the whole place as with black paint." [80]

(iii) Gandhamādana : "This excellent mountain enchants the minds of all beings. It is like the bulbous root from which the future *Svarga* will be created."[81] Viveka finds this place unsuitable for his meditation. Because here, (in Gandhamādana) "blow breezes which bring with them the essense of the odour of the flowery arrows of Manmatha blossoming on the braid of the hair of loving Śabara (hunter) women is *Svarga* walking along (with their lovers). This breeze is wet with the thick spray of juice flowing from the pan-like temples of herds of elephants in rut."[82]

(iv) Himālaya : "This Himālaya is the father of the mountain Maināka; he is, as it were, the calf of the cow named Earth; he is the son-in-law of Meru and the father-in-law of Śiva."[83]

(v) Gaṅgā : "This is the river Gaṅgā, whose waters are irretrievably muddy owing to hordes of wild buffaloes butting the banks with their horns ! The river Gaṅgā, (on the other hand) is beautiful with the sandal paste washed down from the breasts of the women in Indra's Zenana playing in her waters with gentle movements of their limbs. It stands to reason that the Gaṅgā does not like being compared with the other streams."[84] This Himavān, where live many sages doing penance, is not a fit abode for those who want to cultivate control of the senses, for the mountain with its forests and caves is always reverberating with the roar of the waterfalls of the Gaṅgā (who starts from the feet of Hari).

(vi) Region of Vindhya Mountains : This region is abounding in holy places and sacred groves of various kinds. Here are found large numbers of pilgrims travelling together in groups and having the satisfaction of doing a righteous thing. The sight of these pilgrims is a feast to my eyes which have been fasting long. Owing to their joy at the acquisition of invaluable *dharma*, they go from place to place as if they are riding on proud elephants. This place also is found unsuitable as therein three legs (*tapas*, *dāna* and truthfulness) of *dharma* have become broken.

(vii) Ayodhyā : "The city of Ayodhyā is really *Paramapada*; the river Sarayū which flows here is really the river Virajā in *Vaikuṇṭha-loka*; these sacrificial posts that we see here are the very posts to which the animals were tried in accordance with the rules when the Lord (Śrī Rāma) performed *Aśvamedha* sacrifice; when Śrī Rāma rose to His own abode (*Vaikuṇṭha*) at the appointed time, He took with Him all beings in Ayodhyā, those that moved and those that could not move, without any exception, for His all-powerful independence could not be withstood by anyone."[85]

(viii) Mathurā : "In order to lighten the burden of the earth, here, indeed, was born Vāsudeva along with His bed of *Ādiśeṣa* (Balarāma). Let the words 'I bow' be used by us in connection with the Lord who appeared in the false guise of a cowhered and saved these worlds by His wonderful, varied, and multitudinous actions of the Lord who enjoyed Himself on the banks of the Yamunā, and who danced fearlessly and alternately, this side and that, on the many stage - like hoods of the serpent Kāliya, brilliant with gems."[86]

Well, driver ! this city of Mathurā now bears witness to the story of the *gopis* in whoose company the Lord enjoyed Himself. In the same way as the city of Dvārakā was enveloped by the sea, this city, too is enveloped by *Adharma.* I do not therefore consider it suitable for acquiring the wealth of Yoga. What is there that does not undergo a change in its nature in the process of time ?[87]

(ix) Śālagrāma : "Śālagrāma is the place sacred to Śri Viṣṇu, wherein time of yore, sages like Puṇḍarīka who were afraid of re-birth lived for a long time. If one should plunge even once into this pure *Cakratīrtha*, one will rise soon out of the depths of the sea of *Saṁsāra*."[88] "This country is now haunted by thievish hunters who covet the little gold that could be obtained from within the *Śālagrāma* stones; and those who aspire to *Mukti*, who long eagerly for the ocean of nectar consisting in the vision of the supreme Brahman with His manifold attributes and who encounter frequent obstacles, avoid the place." [89]

(x) Vāraṇāsi : "This is the holy city of Vāraṇāsī, where great sages are observing their spiritual exercises in surroundings, washed by the waves of the Gaṅgā, and whose neighbourhood is surrounded by the two rivers, Vara and Nasi (or Vārāṇa and Asi) — this holy city is like an ornament to the earth." [90] Viveka does not think that it is a fit place from which to ascend to the top of the mansion of *Samādhi* by the steps of *dharma* and *dhyāna*. For the place which is not to the liking of the minds of those who taste the nectar of the stories of Nārāyaṇa.

(xi) Region of Sahyādri Mountains : "The Gaṅgā of South India with its sweet water now inhabited on all sides by thieves is like Brahma Vidyā vitiated by (the interpretation of) perverse thinkers." [91] Therefore, Viveka thinks this place unfit for his meditation.

(xii) Yādavācala (Melukote) : "This place is so called because of its reputed excellence in having been favoured as an abode of the Lord, the most noble scion of the race of the Yadus. It is inhabited by men superior in intelligence even to Bṛhaspati, the priest of Indra by wise men whose minds are like bees settled at the lotus feet of the Primeval Person." [92] Though Viveka finds this holy place fit for his meditation, being curious to visit other suitable places, he moves to the next holy place of Paraśurāma.

(xiii) Paraśurāmakṣetra : "Neither I nor my son (Śiva) nor the gods nor any of the multitudes of sages with minds ever absorbed in meditation — none of us know the essential nature of Viṣṇu. Listening to this speech of the child (Brahmā) lying on the lotus of His navel, Śrī Padmanābha is reclining with Lakṣmī on His bed, the Prince of serpents."[93]

"Men who are flattered by hungry beggers for virtues not found in them who are *Saṁnyāsins* only in name, deride noble souls who aspire to *mukti* with harsh words (of ridicule) which are as turbid as deadly poison (Kālakūṭa) arising from minds filled with ignorance due to the intoxication of conceit in the possession of the little wealth which they have acquired by foul means."[94]

(xiv) Malaya Mountain : "Here dwells the sage Agastya, the son of Brahmā, shining like one who has already obtained *Mukti*; his greatness was exhibited in his putting a stop to the further growth in height of the Vindhya mountain; he sipped off all waters of the ocean; the fire of his stomach digested the Asura's flesh swallowed by him as a morsel; his might was so resistless that he turned into a serpent Nahuṣa who had become the king of the gods."[95] Therefore, this is, indeed, *Svarga* on earth inhabited by men. But it is wonderful that, on this lovely spot, sages averse from Kāma move about. Thus, Viveka rejects this place too.

(xv) Pāṇḍya Country : "Tarka says that, this is the land of Pāṇḍyas whose glory is enhanced by the large number of saints who are travelling to and fro with the desire to see the bridge (across the sea) built by Nala." Viveka remains silent regarding its suitability which indicates its being unfit.[96]

(xvi) Vṛṣācala : This is "the best of all mountains, which bears the spring called Nūpuranandi and which has the great sacredness of the Gaṅgā. The wind carries with it the fragrance of the sandalwood trees dancing on the hill and is ever tossing to and fro the branches of the forest trees growing on the top of the hill and these branches striking against the moon, nectar flows down from the sphere of the moon and increases the volume of water in the Nūpuragaṅgā."[97] In this place the ears of men are deafened with the roar of the waves of the southern ocean dashing against the many peaks of mountains of which Nala's bridge is built. So, he does not think *Samādhi* is possible here. Contemplating thus Viveka goes further.

(xvii) Coḷa Country : As soon as Viveka sees this country, he thinks it unfit because here are poets who steal (deceive) the minds of ignorant men with the flow of their verses which, with their charms, remind us of the (jingling) sound made by the anklets of Brahmā's wife (Sarasvatī) when she happens to walk fast.

(xvii) Śrīraṅgam : Reaching this holy place, Viveka with his folded hands, prays earnestly the Supreme God Śrīraṅgarāja, for his favour : "O ! Lord of Śrīraṅgam, with the full approval of my mind dancing (with joy), I will ever render service at Thy feet. I will not allow my eyes to look with shame on the dreaded face of some covetous rich man with closed eyes and knitted brows, and often uttering discourteous words."[98] Viveka approves this place to be fit for his meditation. Yet, he is eager to see other such places. Hence, he goes to the next place, *i.e.*, Tuṇḍīramaṇḍala.

(xix) Tuṇḍīramaṇḍala : "This place is worthy of being the crest-jewel of the whole world. Here is a holy place called Satyavrata held in reverence by the leaders of the gods and capable of mitigating the fear of *Saṁsāra*. In this place, when His son, Brahmā, performed an *Aśvamedha* sacrifice, the Supreme Lord manifested Himself for wiping out all the stains of the earth."[99]

(xx) Veṅkaṭācala : "In its great forest where dwell

many good men, and which looks wonderful owing to the successive falls of water from the Ākāśagaṅgā which takes its risk from the feet of the Primeval Person (Lord Nārāyaṇa) in the middle of the hill — in this great forest, men who have the ripe wisdom to distinguish between what is high and what is low and even animals live happily without any enmity and have a *darśana* of the Supreme Reality."[100] (Śrī Śrīnivāsa).

Then Viveka rejects all these holy places which is informed to us by the following verse :

Tarka then continues, "Śrīraṅgam, Vṛṣabhācala (Tirupati), Hastigiri (Kāñchipuram) — these places, my lord, have been seen by you. In the land of the Dramidas, these and certain other shrines, adored by Brahmā shine (with glory). In any one of these places, which are all capable of destroying the confusions created by the dreadful *Kaliyuga*, that has just began, let Puruṣa who has now renounced *dharma, artha* and *kāma* be settled in *Samādhi.*"[101]

To this Viveka replies "of what avail are these places outside ourselves which are full of varied obstacles, and which have become famous owing to their having grown high in the estimation of men by the accidental fulfilment of *siddhi* ? I will now fix up Puruṣa for *dhyāna* in an inner seat of contemplation suited to *yogins*, *i.e.* in *daharākāśa* in the heart which is absolutely free from all evils and is full of excellent qualities."[102]

Therefore, the lotus of the heart which is free from all stains, is regarded by Viveka as suitable place for his meditation. On the contrary, that place which (*divyadeśa*) is disliked by the person engrossed in tasting the nector-like divine-story of Lord Nārāyaṇa, is not suitable for meditation to a *prapanna*, whether it be Kāśī, or Ayodhyā or Avantī or Kāñci or Mathurā. This is one of the ideals of

Vedānta Deśika for the welfare of the society of devotees of Viṣṇu.[103] Thus, thinking Viveka desires to create in Puruṣa a clear realisation of the steps in the fulfilment of *yoga*. Then both Viveka and his charioteer Tarka exit. Thus, the end of sixth Act.

ACT VII

The seventh Act is called "शुभाश्रयनिर्धारणं नाम सप्तमोऽङ्कः" – as it deals with the determination of Pure and auspicious form for Puruṣa's meditation.

This Act commences with the *Śuddha-Viṣkambhaka* wherein *Saṁskāra* enters the stage, and introduces himself as the son of Anubhava. His duty here is to assist Viveka in his own way. When Mahāmoha's assistants are seen fleeing in different directions and make a search for a resting place, Viveka becomes desirous of seeing the picture of the Universe. So, he sends his orders to *Saṁskāra* through the commander-in-chief, Vyavasāya. Accordingly, *Saṁskāra* is ready to carry out the orders.

As such, *Saṁskāra* has turned the mind of Puruṣa who pursues Brahmavidyā into the wall of *Antaḥkaraṇa*, and painted thereon the picture of whole universe which can be divided into — the pure and the impure.[104] He further describes the picture as follows :

"The picture — gallery containing paintings which will put to shame the skill of even Viśvakarmā who can please all beings with his artistic work — this picture gallery will be an ornament even to the Lord who dwells within the heart. The brilliant rays which issue from the pillars set with gems will look like windows in the middle of staircase and in the ridge of the roof, as it were, a new painting executed there." [105]

At the end of this *Viṣkambhaka*, *Saṁskāra* suggests

the arrival of Viveka together with Sumati, and Vyavasāya, then exits.

Having dealt with in the previous Act, the choice of a suitable locality for Puruṣa's meditation, it is said that the forms of the deities like Brahmā and Śiva; who are subject to *Karma,* are not fit for meditation. Therefore, for felicitating Puruṣa's meditation, Viveka asks *Saṁskāra* to draw the picture of the Universe on the wall of *Antaḥkaraṇa.* Accordingly, he has carried out the orders. Viveka goes on seeing the pictures and describes one by one. The pictures that are drawn, are the Universe and ten *Avatāras* of the Supreme Being.

This picture — gallery, though limited in space, represents the boundless Universe (in the form of artistic work) and affords a good illustration of the Divine Person called *Dahara-ākāśa* who the Upaniṣad says, lives in the lotus of the heart.[106]

The first picture which is seen by the king is Lord's *nityavibhūti* (which is constituted of *pure sattva*). Lord's *nityavibhūti* includes his varied forms like *Para Vāsudeva,* the *Vyūhas* (Vāsudeva, Saṅkarṣaṇa, Aniruddha and Pradyumna) and supplimentary *Vyūhas* like Keśava, Nārāyaṇa, Mādhava etc. These are the *vibhavas* or *avatāras* wherein the Lord assumes the likeness of gods, men and beasts.

Vyavasāya reommends that "the Lord is seen in the forms of Matsya, Kūrma and the Haṁsa and the like giving succour to His creation by sight, by thought, by touch and the like, (so that they may attain salvation by looking at His incarnations, by meditating on them and by actual contact with them)."[107]

"The divine activities of the Lord, the wielder of cakra, follow one another in every *Kalpa* in succession, like a regular stream for the protection of these worlds and they are prompted by His compassion."[108]

Here follows the description of the picture of *Matsyāvatāra* as described by Vyavasāya. In this picture is seen Lord's form as a Matsya : "By His eyes which are eagerly searching for the Vedas, which has been completely sunk in the ocean, the great Fish is creating, in the interior of the waters of the ocean, a forest, as it were, of lotuses and it delights in mounting the swing raised by the incessant waves of water dashing freely against one another."[109]

Then follows the description of *Kūrmāvatāra* due to which Indra obtained freedom from old age and death, that Śiva obtained a beautiful ornament for his head, and that the ocean became a favourite residence of the Lord himself.[110]

"May the waves of the breath of the Supreme Form of the Kūrma which went to sleep owing to the lulling effect of the scratching of its back by the mountain Mandāra moving incessantly — may these waves protect the three worlds ! By the rolling of the waves of the ocean caused by this inhalation and exhalation, the Lord enjoys Himself with goddess Lakṣmī with great delight as on a swinging couch."[111]

At the time of the churning of the Milky ocean with the great help of Kūrma, many valuable things "like *Ucchaiśravas*, *Airāvata*, Candra, *Amṛtakalaśa* and others have been produced from the milky ocean. And this view has been well painted. Further Vyavasāya shows another picture of milky ocean. This has the mine for the production of the gem *Kaustubha*; it served as a place for tying the *Airāvata*; it is the artist who shaped a pleasant ornament (the Moon) for the head of Śiva, the destroyer of the three cities; it is the tavern which provided Varuṇa with Vāruṇī : likewise, it is the ancient nursery for the growth of the *Kalpaka* tree. To the gods, it is the kitchen that supplies the food most desired by them (nectar) and to the Lord it is the couch in the harem."[112]

Then is seen the picture of goddess Lakṣmī, as being seated in the bloomed lotus and as being casted her gracious glance at the world. "Goddess Lakṣmī is the divine wealth of Viṣṇu, who is the celestial cow that yields whatever is asked for by the world, who is the fullest treasure of all lovely and auspicious things, who is the extreme limit of compassion and who is the eternally fragrant garland on the head of the Vedas."[113]

Then Vyavasāya describes *Varāha* form of the Lord, "that bears goddess earth, on whose tusk the goddess of the earth clings to it in joy that looks like a streak of mud."[114]

Then follows the picture of *Narasiṁha avatāra*, who protected his devotee Prahlāda and destroyed the demon Hiraṇyakaśipu. "The wondrous roars of Narasiṁha, who killed His foe by the play of His claws sharp as a sword, which made Prahlāda rejoice, which brought delight into the lives of the gods who worshipped Him with devotion, which belittled the loudness of the thundering sounds of the terrible multitudes of clouds at the time of *Praḷaya* and which convulsed the Seven seas."[115]

Then continues the description of *Vāmanāvatāra*. "The foot step of Trivikrama makes Śiva's head pure an standing like a soldier in the vanguard of the army of the fame of the generous *asura* who was ashamed at being asked to give only three feet of land. The Gaṅgā, the river of the gods, with her many tributary streams, proclaims His glory on the top of the mansions of the eight quarters, as with waving banners raised aloft to prove it."[116]

Then follows the description of three Rāmas born respectively of the races of Bṛghu, Raghu and Yadu, who protected the three worlds by the destruction of wicked men.

They are by name Paraśurāma, Raghurāma and Balarāma. The description of all these incarnations with their valourous deeds runs at length.

Further, follows the description of *Kṛṣṇāvatāra* who is renowned as the Ācārya of the Bhagavad Gītā. In this context, the glorious deeds in Kṛṣṇa's life have been drawn effectively.

At last the enumeration of the pictures relating to the *avatāras* of Lord Nārāyaṇa ends with the description of the *Kalki avatāra*. King Viveka observes the form of *Kalki* and praise thus :

"May the future incarnation of the Lord as *Kalki*, the son of *Viṣṇuvyaśas*, who will put an end without any exception to all the convulsions caused by *Kali* serve to put end to our *Saṁsāra* ! With this sword, He will surely root out all the thorns (enemies) of the earth and cause the *dharma* of *Kṛta Yuga* to sprout again, like a cloud which, its showers, helps useful plants to sprout on the earth after the thorns have been rooted out."[117]

Thus, Lord Nārāyaṇa incarnated as *Matsya,* to favour the Universe to gladden the Universe as *Kūrma*, to uphold the earth as *Varāha*, to show His being All-Indweller as *Narasiṁha*; to protect the gods surerendered unto Him as *Vāmana*; to exhibit the peak of wrath as *Paraśurāma*, to protect the entire mankind, with utter compassion as *Raghurāma,* to weild playfully the plough as a weapon against demons as *Balarāma*, to display divine sports gladdening the entire *Gokula* as *Kṛṣṇa*, and to protect the Universe from the evil spirits. Lord appeared in the form of *Kalki* riding on the horse having a copper skin, white hairs and tail.

At last, king Viveka choosing one of the pure forms of Lord's incarnation proceeds to impell Puruṣa to engage in meditation. The seventh Act ends with Viveka's declaration as to take follow up action against the powerful enemy Mahāmoha.

ACT VIII

The eighth Act is entitled as "*Mohādiparājayaḥ*" for it deals with the defeat of Mahāmoha and others. It begins with the Miśra-Viṣkambhaka, where in Abhiniveśa enters and introduces himself as being the treasurer of Mahāmoha. However, he is described as being addicted to the evil practices. Admiring himself, Abhiniveśa conveys to the audiance that under his influence, men resort to seven kinds of addiction[118] namely, sexual indulgance, gambling, drinking, hunting, harsh-speech, cruel-punishment of offenders, idle-talk.[119]

As a brother of Lobha, he is all-in-all with the support of Mahāmoha, who gains his objectives with his brotherly assistance. In spite of the evil power with which Abhiniveśa boasts of, he expresses diffidence in his fight with Viveka. Because he has learnt that Puruṣa is taught the lessons on Vedānta. This Supreme Knowledge enables Puruṣa to realise Brahman without any obstacle. He finds Puruṣa realising the futility of various systems of philosophy and religion. He has found out that Kāma and Krodha have practically no influence on Puruṣa. Almost he finds himself lost as he finds Puruṣa getting engaged in firm meditation.

With a long sigh, Abhiniveśa expresses that Kāma and Krodha are defeated by women themselves. As Viveka is growing more powerful, Abhiniveśa becomes doubtful as to whether Mahāmoha gets victory over Viveka. Therefore, he desires to help his lord, Mahāmoha, and as such Abhiniveśa asks his wife Durvāsanā to make efforts in his endevour. Being afraid of Viveks's strength, Durvāsanā tells that there is no doubt that generally women can easily defeat men by means of their attractive glance, yet in case of Puruṣa who is boosted up by Viveka, here effort might go in vain. She gives the analogy of night-moths which perish themselves by approaching the lamp unknowing the result. Still Abhiniveśa tries to fill confidence in her by slightly modifying the analogy. There is also a possibility of the moths falling on the lamp itself, and thus extinguishing it. He desires to change his name to Samādhayabhiniveśa; and asks his wife to change her name to Suvāsanā, which Durvāsanā readily accepts. Being disguised so, Abhiniveśa thinks that he and his wife can remain closer to Viveka, influence him, spoil his meditation and finally can win over Viveka.

At this time, Abhiniveśa perceives Nārada and Tumburu coming in his way, He sees Nārada as a white crow entering the capital. He considers this as a bad omen. He thinks, this omen is an indication of defeat of king Mahāmoha. He is terribly upset became, "coming events casting their shadows before".

Further, there enter on the stage, king Mahāmoha, Durmati and Nārada. Addressing Nārada, king Mahāmoha expresses his delight at the grand arrangements made in his capital Māyā to which the divine sage made his entry. Evidently he is overcome with joy at the apparent decoration of the capital (as is usual with demonish forces). Nārada is too eager to appreciate the decoration and praise king Mahāmoha. Instantly king Mahāmoha suggests his spouse to pay homage to sage Nārada. Accordingly Durmati offers the sacred articles of worship to him. But Nārada refuses to accept any offering, as it is the day of *Ekādaśī*. Yet king Mahāmoha praises sage Nārada : "Your gait has the charm of movements in dancing. Your Vīṇā with its many strings is extremely sweet to hear. Your body lights up the light of the moon. You have therefore come here to heighten our enjoyment. Though Nārada praises the powers of Mahāmoha, he inwardly considers him as a fool."[120]

At this juncture, Dṛṣṭapratyaya, an envoy of king Viveka, approaches Mahāmoha and conveys Viveka's message of peace treaty. Further, he tells that if the peace treaty is accepted then all of them will remain within the limits of the territory agreed upon. If war is to follow, then king Viveka will dispel Kāma, Krodha, Lobha, Moha; destroy Kuhanā, Dambha, Darpa, Abhimāna, bring down Īrṣā, Asūyā, Mada and terminate Mātsarya, Stambha, Jāḍya; then he will establish the predominance of *sattva* in the world.[121] But, Nārada by all possible means prevents this treaty between Viveka and Mahāmoha. Mahāmoha too did not become ready to conclude peace with Viveka. Also, Mahāmoha gets angry and orders to kill the envoy. But Nārada avoids Mahāmoha from doing so by saying that an envoy should not be killed as per the code of polity. After envoy exits, Nārada too departs therefrom, under the pretext of performing the *Sandhyopāsanā* at the time of sunset.

Then, Mahāmoha being moved by beautiful evening twilight entertains a desire for sexual embrace with his wife Durmati. But, the latter tries to awaken him from indulging in love affair as powerful enemies — Viveka and others, are making the preparations for war. Yet, as Mahāmoha is over-confident of his strength, does not listen to wife's suggestion, and expresses his desire to enjoy his heart's content in wife's company. Then he exists with his wife.

Now, come on the stage, Nārada and Tumburu playing on the musical instrument. Nārada expresses optimism for the bright day has dawned for Viveka. This day begins with the Sun-rise, dispelling the darkness, Vedic chanting and disapprearance of ignorance. Tumburu joins with Nārada at the beginning of bright day. Both anticipate the battle in which Viveka gets Victory. Nārada again expresses a glorious day for Viveka as the Sun's rays begin to spread sharply. Nārada reminds the audiance about battle between Rāma and Rāvaṇa and again speaks of ultimate victory for Viveka in his fight against Mahāmoha. He adds that Viveka is sure to win a victory being assured by Brahman at whose realisation, Mahāmoha is destroyed. Tumburu showing a little diffidence wants to know from Nārada how he is sure of Viveka's victory because in a battle always an element of luck is present. Nārada reposes confidence again. At this juncture, a loud voice is heard behind the curtain. Then Nārada and Tumburu feel delighted. He compares a noise to a sumptuous feast to the ear. To him the noise is all divine music leading to breaking open the doors of *Svarga*. Tumburu shares the feelings of Nārada. The conversation between them gives a description of the battle. Nārada conveys to the audiance, the fight between them is fierceful as weapons are discharged against one another in large number. In charging against one another, both the armies of Viveka and Mahāmoha seem to have become one. "In this exciting scene of the battle of the two armies which display, respectively, the prowess of Viveka and Moha, the goddess of victory enjoys, as it were, the pleasure of being seated on a swing, for it is difficult to guess on which side she will turn."[122]

"I bow to Lord Viveka, who, in battle, kills his angry foes and whose image is seen in full reflection like the Sun in the fresh pool of blood which is as sweet as honey."[123]

Then Nārada informs that Lobha, armed with the weapon of *Viparīta buddhi* which makes the enemies fall senseless, is rushing like Ekalavya. But he is then swallowed up by *tuṣṭi* possessing five faces in the form of five *jñānendriyas*.

Then Kāma enters who is advancing bow in his hand with an army consisting of young lovely women. "He has arrows of different colours tipped with honey given to him by his esteemed friend, Vasanta; Kokilās are the healds who sing his praise and swarms of bees form his twanging bow-string. He is allied with the breeze blowing from the mountain Malaya and has the shark as his banner."[124]

Then Kāma marches against Viveka. "This Manmatha, armed with his bow of flowers and displaying his banner with the emblem of the shark is coming to the fight being delighted with the array of his lovely women in military formations resembling chariots, elephants and horses in order to please Rati with his heroism."[125] At the same time Viveka, the conqueror of the world, is discharging a counter - missile in the form of woman, namely Virakti to overthrow Kāma.

"Having learnt, with great concern, that his friend, Lobha, whose loyalty had been proved to be sound by provocative tests in the form of bribes of three kinds (*dharma*, *artha* and *kāma*) — having heard that this true friend, Lobha, had been consumed in the great digestive fire of contentment, Manmatha entered into the fire of the broad vision of Virakti who was like the deity presiding over the battle field and he became deprived of his body once again."[126]

After Kāma is burnt to ashes, the demon, Krodha is approaching the battle-field. "This raging fire called Krodha is known to be very powerful and if roused, he will consume not only the entire army of his enemies but also all the mountains, the oceans and the earth itself."[127] Viveka directs Kṣānti whose rise could not be prevented by any one to put down Krodha. "Krodha's threats, and vile abuse and other such activities were cruel and arrogant ; the three worlds slept or kept awake as he closed or opened his eyes ; but having bound him hand and foot, Kṣānti is now slaying Krodha whose strong arms reveled in the sport of causing violent injuries not sanctioned in the Vedas."[128] (such as injuries for sacrifices and the like). Ultimately Krodha is reduced to the position of the short-lived lightning by Kṣānti, who is superior to all other virtues.

Then Mahāmoha sends his minister, Darpa. "He, though only one, soared high as if he were many, by virtue of his good birth, wealth, learning, conduct, skill and the like. But on looking at the superior glory of Viveka, he was quickly made to lie dead on the warrior's bed (in the battle-field) by the lady Atidṛṣṭi."[129]

Unable to endure the death of Darpa, the demoness Asūyā approaches Viveka. But in no time, she is forced by fate to go sleep from which there is no awakening.

Thus, by the decree of fate, the valiant fighters Darpa and others, in close embrace with their beloved wives Īrṣā and others are lying on the ground in endless sleep.

Further, finding his ministers, killed without exception by Viveka, king Mahāmoha appears on the battle-field like Rāvaṇa. Viveka too with his wonderful power attacks him. After tumultous fight between them, Mahāmoha like the poison-tree falls down due to the force of Viveka, like thunderbolt.

Though regaining consciousness, Mahāmoha attacks Viveka, the former falls down being struck down by the irresistible Viveka. As Mahāmoha has been slain by Viveka, the Dharmas of *Kṛtayuga* have won; Śama, Dama and others have triumphed. Thus, like Śrī Rāma, who slew the Rākṣasa chiefs that had arisen to cause suffering to good men, Viveka, too, shines like the Sun, has now displayed his prowess in putting down Moha, an act which would please the *ṛṣis.*[130]

At last Tumburu declares that all gods are much delighted at the victory of Viveka. In this manner, king Viveka has made the ocean Mahāmoha dry up having quickly drunk it with his might and on his head bowed with modesty, now falls a shower of celestial flowers as fragrant as the refutation of those that speak ill of the eternal bliss of mystic meditation of the Supreme Being.[131] Here ends the eighth Act.

ACT IX

The nineth Act has been entitiled as "समाधिसम्भवो नाम नवमोऽङ्कः" for it describes Puruṣa's getting engaged in *Samādhi*.

In the beginning under Cūlikā,[132] the dramatist informs that Viveka who has destroyed Mahāmoha, who shines as the lamp of knowledge, enters the stage. This verse runs as below :

"The spotless Viveka who swallowed up the ocean called Moha and is the sprout of the creeper named *Mokṣa*, is coming at a distance — Viveka who shines like a unique lamp in the mansion of wisdom, who has the force of a storm that drives away the discourses of rival systems of thought, as if they were mere puffs of cotton, who is a strong bolt, as it were, that keeps the door to suffering shut, and who is like a shower of nectar in quenching the fire of the cruel Krodha." [133]

Addressing Vyavasāya, Viveka offers congratulation for having assisted him in vanquishing Mahāmoha. To this, Vyavasāya very modestly answers that he is only an instrument and it is Viveka who played the main role in the battle. He further refers to the real nature and stature of Viveka while fighting. For instance, Viveka's eye-brows were calm and corners of his eyes never turned red. In otherwords, he was bereft of anger and wickedness even when fighting against Mahāmoha. On the otherhand, Mahāmoha was full of *tamas* and devoid of lustre when he approached Viveka. The defeat and death of Mahāmoha led to his women in the palace abandoning all articles of decoration and beauty. Viveka befitting to his nature, woes everything to the Lord's will.

The existence of all things mentioned below and other similar things, their continuance and their activities are entirely dependent on the Lord's will and it is by the encircling waves of His *Līlā* that the wind blows strong, the stars move fast in the sky, the fire burns, the ocean does not cause the earth to shake, and the earth shows herself fit to bear things that move not and beings that move.[134]

He further says that the Lord offers to everyone, the rewards according to their acts of charity, in *Yajñas*, worship, *Bharanyāsa* and *Bhakti*.[135] Commenting on the final result of the battle, Vyavasāya says that by his heroic efforts, all the obstacles in the path of *Mokṣa*, have been removed. Hence, this is the time for the installation of Viveka. Viveka replies that his achievement is still incomplete because Puruṣa is still to get on meditation to attain *Samādhi*. He referes to the commencement of Puruṣa's *Samādhi* to secure knowledge of Brahman. He adds that without a proper support, Puruṣa cannot attain Samādhi and its final goal. Suddenly, he becomes thoughtful because he is aware of the hard task to be followed by Puruṣa in order to attain Samādhi, *i.e.* the Puruṣa has to struggle hard to achieve the progressive vanishing of the *Ahaṁ* in him. He still to obtain deep faith and identify himself with the Divine. Viveka very eagerly replies as to how the task before the Puruṣa is hard when he has given up the false notion in regard to his own body.

Further, Viveka says, "Puruṣa would not be deluded by words like *so'haṁ, ahaṁ saḥ*, etc., if he has realised Brahman as Indeweller of himself."[136]

Viveka then says that though success has been achieved by Puruṣa, it is incomplete. Puruṣa's *sādhana* has to be fulfiled yet. It is that, *Karma* has its own impact on the Puruṣa though Kāma, Lobha and others have been conquered. To be precise, *sañcitakarma* is something like a thick forest which continue to influence Puruṣa for a number of years.

Further follows a detailed description of Puruṣa's conquering the effects of evil *Karma*, and finally achieving the goal.

"Due to the effects of evil *Karma* mind is distracted and as a result attainment of Samādhi is weakened."[137]

"Moreover, with the support of the favour of Brahman, one should ever be careful to avoid pit-falls."[138]

"Though one's knowledge is powerful, Puruṣa finds it difficult to restrain the fickle mind wandering about in the forest of external objects."[139]

"Such mind becomes as powerful as an elephant. Therefore how can a thin thread spun wide the spider fetters the feet of the elephant, which is very much in the excitement at the sport of knocking at the banks of mud."[140]

"Though mighty Kāma and others have been destroyed still there is *avidyā* in the form of *Karma* which can restore them to life."[141]

"But this great forest of *Karma*'s will be perished by the Lord's grace which would grow in volume and intensity."[142]

"As Vyavasāya suggests Puruṣa avoids all worldly honours like deadly poison, Young women like corpses, the assembly of the learned like a serpent and the court of the kings like the hell known as *Kumbhīpāka*."[143]

"Further Puruṣa follows the path laid down in the *Śāstrās* until his release from bondage. He has laid down the entire responsibility of his protection on Supreme Brahman."[144]

"Having performed the religious duties in accordance with his *Varṇa*, Puruṣa gets great delight in serving the feet of the Lord. Being embraced by *Vairāgya*, he now enters the main path to *Mokṣa* which is free from all sufferings."[145]

"In addition to this, Viṣṇubhakti who restores to a higher spiritual life, those who have attained *Vairāgya*, who is well-known to be the origin of righteousness, who is extolled by learned men, who is divide of defects is now entering the heart of Puruṣa as holy Ganges mingles with the ocean."[146]

"Thus, Puruṣa has resorted to the sentiment of Śānta. This Viṣṇubhakti caused disgust in the body of the Puruṣa. Also she has caused laughter and redicule in sense enjoyment, anger at sleep, grief at non-fulfilment of Samādhi dread of cruel speech to others, astonishment at the ripening of the fruit, streanuous efforts for getting rid of sinfulness and love for Brahman."[147]

"Thus Puruṣa now finds delight in the great *Mantras* which are like echos of the sound heard when the door to *Mokṣa* is opened wide."[148]

"King Viveka has got rid of the fear due to Kāma, and has exercised the demon of greed for wealth. Thus, being fearless as sandals for stepping out of the prison house of *Saṁsāra*."[149]

All such experience is due to the effects of past deeds. As there is an interval between states of sleep and waking, there is interval between *Bhoga* and *Mokṣa*. The learned persons having realised their nature and effects follows the path of *Jñāna*, *Bhakti* and *Prapatti*, and pass the rest of their life.

Such being the case, there is no scope for anxiety in Puruṣa's accomplishment of his goal.

"Śrī, the imperial spouse of the Lord is the only media to free the Puruṣa from the bondage of *Saṁsāra*. Besides this, Puruṣa also requires the guidance of a *Sadguru* who has acquired *Brahmajñāna*. Viveka seeks the grace of Lord Nārāyaṇa on the Puruṣa, by which alone attainment of *Mukti* is possible. Goddess 'Śrī' is ever willing to aid the Puruṣa on the path of *Mukti*. But the only one thing which Puruṣa has to possess, to gain the compassion of the Goddess 'Śrī'. In order to acquires this, Puruṣa has to follow the path shown by Ācāryas who are far from being engaged in vain activities and who have carefully reflected on the teachings of *Śuka*, *Śaunaka* and others.[150]

It is the tenets of Viśiṣṭādvaita philosophy which have been expressed through dialogue between Viveka and Vyavasāya. Towards the close of their dialogue, they say that they approaching Puruṣa to make him delightful with the joyful news of the auspicious event which is soon put to a place.

In the next scene Sumati makes an entrance on the stage knowing this Viveka feels very happy considering her arrival as a good omen in the achievement of Puruṣa. In course of his efforts to achieve the goal, Vyavasāya wants to get him suitable preceptor. Viveka, in his characteristic way adds that even the guidance of an Ācārya is possible by the grace of the Lord. As though their efforts would succeed, Sumati sees the bright light similar to that of *Pūrṇodaya*. Evidently removing the doubts of Viveka that the bright light is due to some conjure. Vyavasāya answers that the bright light is caused by the lustre of Nārada, the divine ministrel, who is arriving. As Nārada is arriving, he contemplates that Viveka by his own *sāttvika* nature has got rid of the bands of enemies both external and internal and has created in Puruṣa superior mental condition.

"Puruṣa, the muni, now bears with patience the pairs of opposites (like pleasure and pain, heat and cold) ; he has become quick to grasp (the truth of things). He eats only what happens by mere chance to come to him without any effort of his and gives up what should be abandoned. Like the bee he has a taste now for imbibing the true essence of things. He is grateful (for the good done to him) and is firm in the pursuit of the supreme goal (of life). He delights in solitude and aspiring to *Mukti*, fixes his mind on Brahman without being distracted."[151]

Yet, Nārada makes Viveka aware of the things which should not be neglected.

"Like a bullock grazing in the pastures on the shore of the sea whose neck is raised above to receive the yoke, man is afflicted with the desire to enjoy the pleasures of the senses owing to bad impressions left by past experiences in this world of Prakṛti (with its three *guṇas*) and is busily engaged in satisfying these desires in every *Yuga*. As the bullock is tied by means of strong ropes to the water — wheel and is made to go round and round (by the farmer), so also, Time who is an independent agent, tied man to his wheel with the ropes of past *Karma* and forces him to go round and round in the water-well of *Saṁsāra*. However, there is something here to consider."[152]

Further, Viveka requests Nārada to protect Puruṣa. As such he beseeches thus :

"By those who have lost their eye-sight and have not

found a *guru* to show them the way, neither the path of worldly life here nor the path indicated in the Veda can be (safely) trodden. Therefore, Holy Sir, be pleased to protect Puruṣa, who is under my guidance, with the *mantra* just as, formerly you did Puṇḍarīka."[153]

Nārada of course readily agrees to favour Puruṣa and makes his exist. Now Viveka, finds Puruṣa as being favoured by the Lord. Because :

"Ignored by the common run of men who are intoxicated with the liquor of sense — pleasure, in some place suitable for meditation and in times fit for it, Puruṣa now fixes his vision inward so as to behold the Supreme splendour that is within, with perfect control of his senses, and with inner joy, after subduing his vital breaths."[154]

"With his hair standing straight on his strong limbs and with eyes overflowing with tears of joy, Puruṣa now enjoys the sweetness of *Samādhi* with his vision turned inward. It is certain that his progress to the (full) attainment of his aim which consists in the supreme glory of enjoying the great bliss called Brahman will hereafter meet with no impediments."[155]

Thus, it is taken for granted that Puruṣa's Samādhi is fructified. As Vyavasāya proclaims – "His Samādhi which is the means for the attainment of *Mokṣa*, the desired fruit, is now almost equal to the fruit itself, (namely, the bliss of *Mokṣa*) and only makes us ask whether the means is short of, or equal to, or superior to, the end."[156]

At the close of the Act, Viveka expresses that the ivine Viṣṇubhakti is entering the pure mansion of Sumati (*i.e.* the mind) :

"She is Viṣṇubhakti who is like a branch of the Kalpaka tree in granting all our prayers for obtaining what we desire and is adored by hosts of *Siddhas* whose minds are pure and who cherish no other interests than the attainment of the Lord. She illumines all the quarters up to their extreme limits with the abundance of her radiance and is now entering the pure mansion of Sumati (the mind).[157]

This indicates that Puruṣa has almost completed the adoption of the Upāyas and is closer to win his goal. Lastly, saying that he could carefully observe the code of conduct required for Puruṣa's attainment of *Mokṣa*, Viveka makes his exit. Thus, the end of ninth Act.

ACT X

The tenth Act has been entitled as "निःश्रेयसलाभो नाम दशमोऽङ्कः" since it deals with the Attainment of Eternal Bliss.

At the outset Viṣṇubhakti enters. She introduces herself as follows :

"I entertain myself with the graceful dance of service to the Lord with the proud and exalted dance of removing all sins."[158]

"My mother is the spotless understanding of Puruṣa ; my father is Puruṣa who is ever bent on *dharma*. Contentment is my sister, forbearance is my consort and righteous conduct is my servant, who ever does my bidding. I am myself Vidyā (being *Bhakti* or *Upāsanā*) and my sport consists in destroying the sins of the world. I am Viṣṇubhakti and live chageless, and I feel sure that *Saṁsāra* will come to an end."[159]

Viṣṇubhakti says, "devotion rises in that person who observes the code of conduct prescribed in the three Vedas, when he has controlled by sheer strength of mind the different vital breaths and the senses, meditated on the *Kuṇḍalinī Nāḍī* and has counted his veins, tissues, the vital centres and the like ! It is only if he is well established in me that he is sure to obtain release form *Saṁsāra*.[160] This itself is the essence of *Bhagavad Gītā*, she declares."

When *Nivṛtti* Dharma and Yoga follow Viṣṇubhakti, then only they yield the fruit. As such it is declared :

"When the aspiration for *Mukti* is strong and when the delusions of the mind have disappeared, *Samādhi* with the Lord arises, and it brings in cessation of all sins. What the wise man to whom rebirth is repugnant performs after that stage, it is difficult and vain to discuss whether it is a means to *Mokṣa* or *Mokṣa* itself, whether we should call it a means for a further fruit or gain or whether it is the fruit itself."[161]

Viṣṇubhakti thinks that "Puruṣa who is attacked by enemies like senses, body, son, housewives due to remnants of *Karma* — shall be made free by herself."[162]

However, Viveka the doctor curing the disease of *Saṁsāra*, has already destroyed all blemishes pertaining to the body. Viṣṇubhakti further indicates that Puruṣa is fully and seriously engaged in deep meditation.

"Like the moon who rises in the sky on the first night after the new moon with one-sixteenth part of his disc and is bowed to by the whole world and who afterwards increases day after day in size and whiteness, Puruṣa, too, rising in spiritual glory as a result of his *Vidyā* or meditation, has now become an object of reverence to the whole world and grows to spiritual perfection, day after day, pure of nature and with deep devotion to the feet of the Lord."[163]

Puruṣa is now bathing, Viṣṇubhakti tells, in the ocean of knowledge and bliss.

"Puruṣa issuing from the initial stage of *Samādhi* which is associated with uninterrupted and constant meditation or *dhyāna*, which, like the flood of the Gaṅgā, is by its very nature, pure, steady and sweet, is now bathing in the immense ocean of conciousness and bliss (called Brahman), which is full of invaluable and auspicious gem—like attributes and qualities. Having bathed there, he will no longer have to sink in the ocean of *Saṁsāra*."[164]

Thus, Puruṣa has reached that higher stage where there is no taint of *Āgāmi Karma* and *Sañcita Karma*.

Behind the curtain, it is suggested that the rising time of *Saṅkalpa Sūrya* (or *will of Lord*) is being very closer.

"The world - lotus was formerly all closed in darkness, and now the sun rising on the eastern mountain has dispelled the darkness. In the sky free from darkness we see, at a great distance, the first splendour of the rising Sun as if it were his banner."[165]

Viṣṇubhakti exhibits her own experience that "the three worlds have now become serene and untroubled, meditation is undistrubed: the intelligence has become as clear as the spreading waves of nectar. My left eye is frequently throbbing and it indicates that, very soon, we shall have success in our endeavour."[166]

"Then, with the help of the Lord's divine compassion, I will prompt *Saṅkalpa Sūrya* to take the necessary action for the salvation of Puruṣa, for He is always beneficient and disposed to grant my desires."[167]

Viṣṇubhakti tells that the devotion bears fruit only when the grace of Lord is obtained. Thus the dawn of *Bhagavatkṛpā* is awaited. Power of *Kṛpā* or *will of Lord* is thus described : "The Gods of *Svarga*, Indra and others, enjoy their respective positions because of having been seen by Thee once : so also you voachsafe, to the kings of this world, all desirable enjoyments far beyond their own expectations. Further, you became ashamed at the helplessness of men and became gracious to them and create in them such boons as freedom from desires and (in course of time) the different steps to the attainment of the bliss of mokṣa."[168]

Then arrives God Garuḍa whom Viṣṇubhakti extols thus:

"May you ever triumph, O Garuḍa of beautiful wings, you feed on hooded serpents and snatched away nectar from the king of the gods. You bear on your body, like an ornament, the scar left by the edge of Indra's *Vajra*. You strike every one with astonishment, when you rise resembling the tempest at the end of a *Kalpa* in great valour. Your glory is well understood from your occupying the victorious banner of Viṣṇu, the enemy of the Asuras, on high; you are, indeed, Saṅkarṣaṇa, O Garuḍa, and are the deity presiding over, and directing, the five vital breaths. (*Prāṇa*, *Apāna*, *Vyāna*, *Udāna* and *Samāna*) and assume five forms – *Satya, Suparṇa, Vijaya, Tārkṣya* and *Vihageśvara*. There is none equal to you and I bow to you again and yet again."[169]

"I bow to you who are ever the object of adoration. By the force of the gale caused by the successive flapping of your wings, the ocean overflows and its waves strike against the deeps of *Pātāla* as with out-stretched hands, raising a loud sound resembling '*bhaṅg*'. At that sound great serpents of the lower world become wrathful and you attack them with the rows of your talons which look like hooks of steel."[170]

In the *Pāñcarātra Āgamas*, "it is declared that the equipment (*Sannāha*) and resolve (Saṅkalpa) of Hari the saviour of the world, appear as visible manifestations in the form of Garuḍa and Sudarśana respectively."[171]

Just then there arrives *Saṅkalpa* of Lord. *Saṅkalpa* itself speaks of its strength. Thus,

"I am the Lord's *Saṅkalpasūryodaya* (the sunrise of His Resolve to save man). When there is the slightest manifestation of me, whose glory is of astonishing greatness, this world, pure and impure, attains, all at once, *Mokṣa* and *Svarga*. All sentient beings are in sound slumber in the great night of Māyā (*prakṛti*) and are in such a state that they can be said merely to exist, and this night of Māyā is not like the night which comes at the end of the day, for it is continuous and has no break or interval and it is I who am capable of waking them up from that (death like) sleep."[172]

"Now *Saṅkalpa* awakens Puruṣa with endless magnificient wisdom by wiping off within a second beginningless sleep (of *Avidyā*)."[173]

In next scene, both Viṣṇubhakti and *Saṅkalpa* meet each other. Viṣṇubhakti is overwhelmed with joy to see *Saṅkalpa*. And, through the dialogue between them, it becomes clear that Viṣṇubhakti is under the command of *Saṅkalpa*. Yet, the latter gives her due honour and describes her greatness :

"You are cherished by those who are endowed with spiritual serenity and the source of the ripe fruit of creeper of Knowledge. You are indeed, the perfect development of the Śrutis and the abiding place of purity. You are the guarantee of heavenly bliss and the dawn that dispels the fear of *Saṁsāra*. You are the lamp that illumines the truths concerning all things, high and low, O revered Lady of devotion to Hari, you are like a divine ornament to the Ātma or self."[174]

Viṣṇubhakti then conveys to *Saṅkalpa* to favour

Puruṣa. Because "the Yoga begun by Puruṣa based on *karma* and *jñāna* and adorned by his sole and exclusive devotion to the Lord without any other interests in life, — this *yoga* will now confer on him the clear vision of the Supreme Being which will give him the great joy of looking at a concealed treasure."[175]

"The embodied being is deluded with the dance of Māyā or Prakṛti ; and the Supreme Brahman, who is the Lord of everything and whose greatness is unequalled, is besides Himself with compassion, which is bent on saving him and with the snow of the worship of His feet (Śaraṇāgati) quenches the fires of his suffering and cancels his sins."[176]

"The Supreme Brahman in the Upaniṣads to be Himself she means *Upāya* of attaining Him. The ways of *Bhakti* and *Prapatti* are indicated for winning His grace. The adoption of these ways is the result of the great ripening of meritorious deeds (done in the past) and, even for this, the Lord, who has the ability to create everything is Himself the cause."[177]

"When the mind is clouded by bile, when the throat is choked with phlegm, when the limbs have become swollen with wind, when the mouth has become delirious, when the senses have fled from their functioning, when life is about to depart, when the strength is all lost and when relatives are all mad with grief, who is there capable of protecting this creature (man) except the Lord who wields the cakra and who is moved by compassion."[178]

"The Jīvātmā on whom has fallen the gracious look of the Lord of Lakṣmī has all his sufferings like sin driven away to a great distance. Though he sleeps in the life of *Saṁsāra* he will soon attain, with the help of his unimpeded desire for *Mukti*, a state of awakening after which he will never close his eyes (in the sleep of *Māyā*)."[179]

When *Saṅkalpa* doubts Puruṣa's eligibility to attain *Mokṣa*, Viṣṇubhakti professes that she herself has witnessed Puruṣa's desire to attain *Mokṣa*.

"Puruṣa now sees that even Brahmā has to suffer helplessly from the inroads caused by such *asuras* as Madhu and Kaiṭabha. Since Puruṣa is now aware of all these evils, he will entertain no liking at all for *svarga*, which is only one of the varieties of hell."[180]

"The bird (Cātaka), when thirsty, remembers the dark rain cloud shedding water and does not seek the pond or the ocean. So also the Brahmin (Brahmavit) remembers that only Śrī Kṛṣṇa can, like the darks, cloud, confer the eternal bliss of *Mokṣa* and does not seek either the *loka* of Indra or even the *loka* of Brahmā."[181]

Therefore Viṣṇubhakti says, Puruṣa is fit for attaining *Mokṣa*.

Then Saṅkalpa however observes Puruṣa's state, and gives his favourable opinion that "He is now extremely fortunate and happy and shines like the very embodiment of the sentiment *Śānta*, having passed beyond the reach of the objects of *Śṛṅgāra, Vīra, Karuṇa, Adbhuta, Bhayānaka, Bībhatsa* and *Raudra* and has all the accessories and accompanishments of *Śāntarasa*."[182]

"Over his limbs, the hair frequently stands on end, His mind is tuned inward to the Supreme Being within. His meditation is sweet like syrup ; and cool tears of joy come out of his eyes. I think therefore that seated on the chariot of his mind, he is rapidly journeying on the high road to Vaikuṇṭha indicated in its different stages by that inscrutable charioteer who sang the Upaniṣad called the Gītā."[183]

Still he keeps an observation on Puruṣa to read his mental state.

Puruṣa then enters together with Śraddhā, and tells thus :

"Thoughts of the body and other wordly objects familiar for a long time still continue to linger in the mind as consequence of *Karma* and these toss my soul about as in a swing. I am indeed possessed of very little light and am like the tiny firefly. How many more days have I still to spend, weak and helpless !"[184]

"I am not now a *Mukta* such as I shall be in the future, nor am I a *Baddha* or soul in bondage as in the past. O how weak I am ! I do not know what I should do or what I should refrain from."[185]

"I am now without sins done deliberately and endowed with such virtues as Samā (mental serenity) which display a high degree of *Sattva* and which keep me off from improper ways. I spend my time in such Yajñas, as the meditation of the Supreme Being, singing hymns in His praise and prostrating before Him and avoid all vain activities. In this manner, I am awaiting eagerly the time of fruition."[186]

"While the Supreme Brahman, who is ready to grant everything desired by those that have sought His protection even once, who has all things, sentient and non-sentient, for His body, and who is declared in the Upaniṣads, to be our great good fortune when the Lord is ever ready to help us, my vain desires sullied by thoughts of sense-pleasures never turn back from delusion. Alas ! how wretched I am."[187]

"What a man desirous of good should do when he knows for certain that he will die today — that he should always do even when he does not know the time when death will come."[188]

"We become exhausted by frequent ascent to *Svarga*

and desent back to the earth along the path of the *Pitṛs* like the water-pot going up and down the well by the rotation of the water-wheel. (We become exhausted like-wise) by incessant journeys, to and fro, along the route to hell. (So) Hari makes the various deities (on the shining path of archis) entertain us who are so exhausted and at length confers bliss on us by keeping us, as it were, under His shade, which is like the (cool) shade of a sandal-tree)."[189]

Through these words of Puruṣa, *Saṅkalpa* is convinced of Puruṣa's state. That is why he says :

"Puruṣa is now untouched in his understanding by false knowledge and the like, which have been destroyed by Viveka. He has leaped over the slush of the desire for enjoyment connected with *cit* and *acit*, whose evil nature he has now realised; he has seen the bliss of *Mokṣa* reflected in the steady mirror of meditation and is now eager to reach the shore beyond the sea of *Saṁsāra*."[190]

"As he now sees the real truth, concerning all things, high and low, he has become noble in conduct and turns with aversion from activities that are unwholesome. Being free from mental affliction, he is ashamed to see the demons of temptations (like sex, gambling etc.) which allure the minds of men from weak and wretched understanding."[191]

"The servants of Yama tremble before him and even Time which destroys all (not excepting Indra and Brahmā) is in dread of him. The gods of *Svarga* are afraid that he might displace them from their seats. *Rākṣasas, Asuras, Yakṣas, Guhyakas* and others flee in fear to a great distance. And all this is the result of his having surrendered his self at the two lotus - feet of the Lord of Lakṣmī."[192]

Hence, *Saṅkalpa* approaches Puruṣa and addresses him thus :

"Most noble Sir ! I am, indeed, the Resolve or will of the Supreme Person (to save man). You are the foremost of those who are solely and exclusively devoted to the Brahman. By the Lord's compassion who is His beloved Spouse, and who is always full of affection towards the weak and helpless, I have been ordered to see that you are released from the two kinds of endless fetters, called, *Puṇya* and *Pāpa* and to enrich you with the wealth arising from ripe and perfect *bhakti* extending up to the service of the Supreme Person who adorns the heavenly couch (in *Paramapada*). I have long been eager to see your honoured self and am now come to you. Therefore be free from all fears and doubts concerning the treasure of *Mokṣa* which is close at hand."[193]

In ecstacy, Puruṣa says "When Brahman who does everything in the company of His spouses, Lakṣmī and Bhūmi, who abides in the three Vedas, who like the gem, *Cintāmaṇi*, grants whatever is desired, and who is in the thought of the devotee when He is gracious, *Samādhi* gives joy and soon makes the self feel as if it is one with the Lord."[194]

Saṅkalpa then favours Puruṣa :

"You are like the parrot the redness of whose beak can never disappear, whose wings are ever green in colour and which is in a cage made of strings. In order to make you fit to go to the world from which there is no return, I will now set you free from the cage of Prakṛti with its three *guṇās* as I set free the sage Śuka ; for your love is immovably fixed on the Supreme : you maintain the doctrine that the Real called Hari is the Supreme Reality."[195]

"The (black) ointment of Prakṛti with its three *gūṇas* will be washed off your soul. Owing to your adoration of Brahman with auspicious qualities, you will manifest the possession of the eight qualities (sinlessness and the rest) and attain Supreme resemblance to Brahman but will never lose sight of the marks of difference between the Supreme self and your own self. And finally you will be vouchsafed the privilege of being a servant to the Lord, even like Ādiśeṣa and others as long as you exist, (*i.e.* for ever and for ever)."[196]

"When you are about to enter *Paramapada* at the end of this life, the fruits of the *Puṇya* which have been given up by you will be taken over by your friends, and those of the *Pāpa* done by you will be taken by your enemies."[197]

"Led by his guides (*Archis* and others) to the Lord of Lakṣmī who is possessed of varied glories, in the region beyond *tamas* (*i.e.* Prakṛti) and having attained Him, the *Mukta* has his essential nature in full manifestation and realises his inseperable connection with the Supreme Brahman, and as a consequence, acquires the eight attributes (of freedom from sin and like) and, without any question of his returning again (to *Saṁsāra*), he attains in regard to the enjoyment of bliss, perfect resemblance to the Lord. So, if I deserve to be told about it, I beg of you to disclose it to me."[198]

Saṅkalpa describes that this tradition, has to be continued ceaselessly. Therefore, addressing the entire universe he declares as follows :

"The highsouled Puruṣa, who has surrendered his self to the Lord, the Treasure of the Śrutis, is now on the face of the earth, He sees all things (at a single glance). Therefore, let those men of wide intelligence who would like to be his disciples learn all truths form him with care and attention by putting questions to him just as they please."[199]

After this, Puruṣa shows his desire to see Viveka and Viṣṇubhakti, as they two have blessed him to reach the goal. He feels that he is closer to *Mokṣa*. Therefore, he approaches Viveka and Viṣṇubhakti who are performing *Dvādaśī* residing in *Tulasivana*.

In the next scene, Viveka, Sumati and Viṣṇubhakti enter the stage, and speak about Puruṣa's achieving the goal. Viṣṇubhakti glorifies king Viveka. Thus :

"Your heart is, indeed, pure being *Sāttvika* generous, firm, sweet and exaulted. You are lofty in nature by virtue of your compassion and enthusiastic endeavour, grateful and easily accessible to those who are your friends. Like the ocean you are deep in your knowledge of the scripture, in your intelligence, in your power of mental concentration and in your retentive memory. Your conduct is always noble and exalted. You are the only one who can win the appreciation of the Śrutis and the Smṛtis."[200]

"Among literary heroes of the type called *dhīrodātta* possessed of the greatness of beneficent and noble qualities, you stand foremost and your wedded wife, and help-mate, Sumati, is ever devoted to you and loved by you. Your efforts to secure the attainment of eternal bliss for your master, Puruṣa have been crowned with success. So, in all the three worlds, only Śrī Rāma and you are of unassailable prowess in the field of battle which is like a playing field to you."[201]

In the meantime Viveka says that Puruṣa is not freed form Prakṛti "Agni, Day-time, Śuklapakṣa, Uttarāyaṇa, the year, the intervening Vāyu, Sūrya, Candra, Lightning Varuṇa, the king of the Devas (Indra) and Prajāpati (or Brahmā), — having traversed this path in the order given above, the soul crosses the river Virajā ; then follows the wonder that defies all description in words."[202]

"Like an invaluable gem with inner brilliance whose lustre is rendered dim by contact with unclean objects which have reduced it to a state of uncleanness, the soul of man has an inner splendour or brilliance which has been rendered dim as a consequence of past *Karma* which acts as a hindrance to its light and it is placed in the group of non-sentient objects by the deity called Māyā."[203] To this, Viṣṇubhakti replies that :

"This is not the time for your majesty to feel depressed. Today Puruṣa's sea of sins of which only the *Karma* that had begun to yield its fruit in this birth remained, has been made to dry up by the Lord's *Saṅkalpa* as by the fire at the end of a *Kalpa*. *Prakṛti*, too, like the serpant's slough, will be cast off by Puruṣa who will then become as pure as Ādiśeṣa and this shedding of Prakṛti will take place at the end of this life and in the region beyond *Tamas*, (*i.e.*) in *Paramapada*."[204]

Viṣṇubhakti further says, this view is endorsed by the sound of divine drum, just heard behind the curtain.

"The *ḍinḍimās* of the gods are beaten (jubilantly) stifling the taste for the first three objects of life, *dharma, artha* and *Kāma* and proclaiming thus : Puruṣa, who is now a Vidvān and who has accomplished what ought to be done is now free of all stain in his understanding. His sense organs, both those of knowledge and those of action, are under his perfect control. All the bonds of his *Karma* have been cut off by his meditation of the Supreme Being and he is now rapidly entering on the path leading to the wonder of *Mokṣa*."[205]

Then Viveka sees Puruṣa approaching them all. Therefore, they go closer to him.

Puruṣa recalls the efforts made by all of them to lift him up from the ocean of *Saṁsāra*. He pays them homage and earnestly asks them :

"You, Viveka, whose essential nature consists in knowing the truth concerning the three 'reals' (*Acit, Cit,* and *Īśvara)* and their differences from one another, you, Sumati, who are good at suggesting the means for overthrowing the evils of the sea of *Saṁsāra* and you Viṣṇubhakti, who are of the nature of the love of the Supreme Being; You three should never leave me even in the region beyond *tamas* and even after I have cast off Prakṛti with its three *guṇas*."[206]

Viṣṇubhakti directs Puruṣa's attention towards the *Arcirādi* path. *i.e.* "The blast of the celestial *dundubhi* is heard in all directions again and again. The chants of the *Sāma Veda* by the gods Hāvu Hāvu are heard like waves of sound beating against the sky. *Arcis* and others who obey the commands of the Lord of Lakṣmī and who are to be the escorts (of Puruṣa) have begun decorating the high road to *Paramapada* in an artistic manner and by these escorts the path to be taken by Puruṣa is indicated."[207]

Puruṣa filled with joy, asks their permission to follow this divine path. He says — "Let there be no further delay. If so, I whose object has been fulfilled take leave of you who have done all that you had to do. I am awaiting the last day. To you who have all along been my wellwishers farewell ! good bye !"[208]

At this juncture, Viveka, Sumati and Viṣṇubhakti make their exit.

Now Viṣṇubhakti proclaims that "having passed the stage of indebtedness to the gods, the *ṛṣis*, animals, *pitṛs* and mankind, and having been granted freedom from fear by the Lord's compassion, with firm and deep devotion to the Lord, he will soon reach the Supreme Abode of the Brahman which has already been occupied by our *Gurus*."[209]

"The sin committed without deliberation in the course of this life by this devotee who is sunk in the sea of Mukunda's compassion will not, like the fire lit in the tail of

Hanumān, burn him and it will burn only those to whom it is transferred."[210]

At last, king Viveka glorifies the fulfilment of Puruṣa's goal.

"Moha, born of Prakṛti, has been felled down to the earth, never to rise again and you, Viṣṇubhakti, ever full of happiness, shine in the fulness of your glory without suffering any obstruction. Puruṣa, purified of all his sins, has taken the route to *Paramapada* from which he will never return. What more do we want ? The fruition of our desires is now dancing before our eyes. What more can I pray from you ?"[211]

"Let men of unclouded intelligence ever pursue the study of Vedānta. Let the *dharma* of renunciation characteristic of the first *Yuga*, which is beyond all other blessings, prevail on earth. May Vāsudeva, the Lord of Śrī, the boundless ocean of compassion, who is the author, the audience and the subject of this composition be gracious (to all) !"[212]

The drama *Saṅkalpasūryodaya* ends with the uttering of *Bharatavākya* :

"Let the world gather together to praise or to ensure our composition or to tolerate it. It is of no concern at all to us who are steeped in the blissful enjoyment of meditating on the Supreme Being. Those to whom we are *śiṣyas* trained in the study of Vedānta and those who are our *śiṣyas* – to them this treatise is sure to give delight. Of what avail is the clamour of others ?"[213]

REFERENCES

1. *Mahānārāyaṇa Upaniṣad*, 12-1; *Kaṭhopaniṣad,* 2.20.
2. Rajagopala Iyengar, *Saṅkalpasūryodaya,* Madras, 1977, p.xxii.

3. विवेकप्रागल्भ्यस्फुरितरणवीरव्यतिकरः परब्रह्मोदन्तप्रकटितदयावीरविभवः ।
प्रबुद्धक्षेत्रज्ञस्थितिघटितशान्ताकृतिरभूत प्रयोगश्चित्रोऽयं भवरसभुजामप्यभिमतः ।।
S.S., I-9, p.32.

4. तत्र प्रथमेऽङ्के स्वसिद्धान्तस्थापनम् ।
V. Krishnamacharya, *Saṅkalpasūryodaya* of Veṅkaṭa-nātha (with two Sanskrit commentaries) Adyar Library, Madras, 1948, p.6.

5. तत्र स्वपक्षप्रकाशो नाम प्रथमोऽङ्कः । *Ibid., Upodghāta,* p.14.

6. चित्रैर्वाक्यैः स्वकार्योत्थैः प्रस्तुताक्षेपिभिर्मिथः
आमुखं तत्तु विज्ञेयं नाम्ना प्रस्तावनापि सा ।। (VI-32).
Viśvanātha, *Sāhitya Darpaṇa,* Krishnadas Academy, Varanasi, 1989, p.403.

7. यद्भक्तिप्रचयात्मके दिनमुखे दृष्टिक्षमः क्षेत्रिणः
क्षिप्रं संसृतिशर्वरीं क्षिपति यत्संकल्पसूर्योदयः ।
तत्त्वैरस्त्रविभूषणैरधिगतः स्वाधीननित्योन्नतिः
श्रीमानस्तु स मे समस्तविपदुत्ताराय नारायणः ।।
Saṅkalpasūryodaya (*S.S.*), I-1, p.1.

8. लक्ष्ये यत्र श्रुतिमितगुणाकृष्टिलब्धावधानैः प्रत्यग्बाणः प्रणवधनुषा सत्त्ववद्भिः प्रयुक्तः ।
मध्येवक्षः स्फुरति महसा पत्रलः कौस्तुभात्मा पद्माकान्तः स भवतु दयादुग्धसिन्धुः
श्रियै वः ।। *S.S.*, I-2.

9. सूत्रधारो नटीं ब्रूते मारिषं वा विदूषकम् ।
स्वकार्य प्रस्तुताक्षेपि चित्रोक्त्या यत्तदामुखम् ।। *Ibid.*, I-7, p.26.
This statement is quoted by Ahobala in his *Prabhāvilāsa*, p.27.

10. मुखं प्रतिमुखं गर्भो विमर्शो उपसंहतिः ।
इति पञ्चास्य भेदाः स्युः क्रमाल्लक्षणमुच्यते ।।
Viśvanātha, *Sāhitya Darpaṇa,* VI-75, p.430.

11. वृत्तवर्तिष्यमाणानां कथांशानां निदर्शकः । संक्षेपार्थस्तु विष्कम्भो मध्यपात्रप्रयोजितः ।। 19 ।।
स द्विविधः । शुद्ध संकीर्णश्चेति । केवल संस्कृत प्रायः शुद्धः । संस्कृत-प्राकृत मिश्रितः संकीर्णः ।
Pratāparudrīya of Vidyānātha, The Sanskrit Education Society, Madras.

12. त्रिगुणघाटितादभोक्तुर्बुद्धिः सती तदनुव्रता समयनियतोच्छ्रायं त्रेधा कुलं समजीजनत् ।
प्रथममिह तद्योगद्वेष्यं विवेकपुरः सरं द्वितयमितरज्जुष्टं रागप्रमोहमुखं मिथः ।।
S.S., I-46, p.96.

13. मोहस्य धर्मपत्नी दुर्मतिरपवर्गदोषदृष्टिमयी ।
विषयरसदोषदृष्टिः सुमतिरनन्या विवेकस्य ।। *S.S.*, I-47, p.98.

14. जनितवलयभङ्गे दत्तहारावमर्दे मुषितनिखिलखेदे मोहसंतोषहेतौ ।
सचकितपरिरम्भे साम्प्रतं कातराक्ष्यास्त्यजति युगलचिन्तामङ्गयोरत्नरात्मा ।।
S.S., I-54, p.112.

15. निर्धूतनिखिलदोषा निरवधिपुरुषार्थलम्भनप्रवणा ।
सत्कविभणितिरिव त्वं सगुणालंकारभावरसजुष्टा ।। *S.S.*, I-64, p.129.

16. स्वतः प्राप्तं रूपं यदिह किल भावेषु तदपि त्यजन्तस्ते दृष्टा नियतिर्घाटितोपाधिवशतः।
प्रकृत्या तिष्ठन्ति ह्युपधिविगमे ते च तदसावनादिः संसारः पुरुषमुपरुन्द्धे गलति च।। *S.S.*, I-66, p.136.

17. मिथः कलहकल्पनाविषमवृत्तिलीलादया परिग्रहणकौतुकप्रथितपारवश्यः प्रभुः ।
स्वलक्षितसमुद्गमे सुकृतलक्षणे कुत्रचित् घुणक्षतलिपिक्रमादुपनिपातिनः पाति नः।।
S.S., I-67, p.138.

18. बहुलदुरितद्वारे ब्राह्मे पुरे परसंमतस्वमतिघटितस्वातन्त्र्यत्वादयन्त्रितचेष्टितः ।
विषमसचिवः स्वे स्वे कार्ये विगृह्य विकृष्यते नरपतिरिव क्षीवो नानाविधैरयमिन्द्रियैः।।
S.S., I-72, p.146.

19. दुरासेधस्थेम्ना दुरितपरिपाकेन भविनः प्रमाथी संसारः प्रशमरहितोऽयं प्रभवति ।
निरोधे तस्यैका निरूपाधिककारुण्यघटितस्वतन्त्रेच्छाशक्तिः स्वयमुपधिमाधाय रमते।।
S.S., I-75, p.151.

20. अनघदेशिकदृष्टिसुधाप्लवे विधिवशादुपसेदुषि देहिनः ।
विमलबोधमुखा विविधा गुणाः परिणमन्त्यपवर्गदशाङ्कुराः।।
S.S., I-77, p.154.

21. स्वाधीनेतरपातभीतिपरुषस्वर्वासदुर्वासनापाशाकर्षणयन्त्रणाभिरभितः क्षिप्तात्मनः क्षेत्रिणः।
निष्प्रत्यूहविजृम्भमाणकरुणादुग्धार्णवे निर्भरा भक्तिः सेत्स्यति भागधेयवशतः प्राप्ये परे ब्रह्मणि।। *S.S.*, I-78, p.155.

22. मदनमत्सरमानमयः पुमान् बहुपिशाचगृहीत इवार्भकः ।
निगमसिद्धनरेन्द्रनिरीक्षणान्निपुणपद्धतिमभ्यवपद्यते।। *S.S.*, I-76, p.153.

23. निरपायदेशिकनिदर्शितामिमां कमलासहायकरुणाधिरोहणीम् ।
क्रमशोऽधिरुह्य कृतिनः समिन्धते परिशुद्धसत्त्वपरिकर्मिते पदे।।
S.S., I-81, p.162.

24. आबध्नती विगतशान्तिमनादिनिद्रां चेतस्विनस्त्रिगुणशक्तिमयी त्रियामा ।
नाथस्य केवलमसौ नरकान्तकर्तुः संकल्पसूर्यविभवेनसमापनीया।।
S.S., I-87, p.175.

25. अस्मद्विजयसन्नाहसन्धुक्षकैरमरपतिभिरयमभिहन्यते दुन्दुभिः ।
तदिह स्थापितस्वपक्षैरस्माभिः। परपक्षप्रतिक्षेपे प्रयतितव्यम् ॥
S.S., pp.193-94.

26. प्रवेशकोऽनुदात्तोक्त्या नीचपात्रप्रयोजितः अङ्कद्वयान्तविज्ञेयः शेषं विष्कम्भके यथा ॥
Viśvanātha, *Sāhitya Darpaṇa*, Krishnadas Sanskrit Series, Varanasi, 1989, VI-57, p.419.

27. जडमतिबहुलेऽस्मिन्दैवकोपाज्ञनित्वा जगति निरपराधे जातनिर्व्याजवैराः ।
कति कति कलहार्थं क्लृप्तसिद्धान्तभेदाः प्रलपनमुखभेदान् पाठयन्ति प्रबन्धान् ॥
S.S., II-5, p.209.

28. असुरादिमोहनविधौ विहिताः प्रमितावतीतसमयाः समयाः ।
तपनापनेयतिमिरक्रमतः प्रचरन्ति हन्त जगदन्तरतः ॥ *S.S.*, II-12, p.217.

29. तदहमिदानीं परिगृहीतनियमानुगुणं स्वयं विपक्षनिरसनमकुर्वाणः
कौशिक इव राघवं त्वां पुरस्कृत्य कुदृष्टीन् बाह्यांश्च निराचिकीर्षामि ।
Prabhāvilāsa, Commentary, p.225.

30. प्रमाणपथ विभ्रष्टप्रधानार्थविमर्दनैः स्थालीपुलाकनीत्यैव निवर्त्याः प्रतिवादिनः ॥
S.S., II-40, p.253.

एकस्मिन् पुलाके पक्वे सर्वमन्नं पक्वमिति स्थालीपुलाकन्यायः ।
Prabhāvilāsa Commentary p.253.

31. कपिलासुरिपञ्चशिखादिमुनिप्रतिपादिनः सांख्यमतप्रवणाः ।
प्रकृतिं पुरुषं च विभज्य परं पुरुषं न पठन्त्यघरुद्धधियः ॥
S.S., II-64, p.282.

32. प्रधानपुरुषौ यदि प्रकृतियान्त्रितैरादृतौ परः किमपराध्यति श्रुतिसहस्रचूडामणिः ।
कुतर्कशतकर्कशौर्यदि विभुः प्रतिक्षिप्यते भवत्परिगृहीतमप्यपहरन्तु पाटच्चराः॥
S.S., II-66, p.284.

33. य एते योगाख्ये कतिचिदपतन्त्रे पठितिनः प्रजल्पन्त्यैश्वर्यं प्रतिफलनकल्पं भगवतः।
स्यतः सिद्धान् बोधप्रशककबलादीन् गुणगणान् गुणन्तस्त्रय्यन्ताः प्रतिभणितिरेषामवितथा॥
S.S., II-68, p.286.

34. असद्द्रव्यसृष्टिप्रभृत्यर्थक्लृप्त्या श्रुतिप्रक्रियाणामधिक्षेपतश्च ।
उलूकोपदेशापदेशप्रवृत्तः कथाशेषितोऽसौ कणादप्रणादः॥
S.S., II-70, p.288.

35. परस्परविघट्टनत्रुटिततर्कशस्त्रच्छटा तिरस्कृतचमत्कृतिः स्वयमखण्डि वैतण्डिकः।
किमत्र परिशिष्यते किमपि दूषणोद्भावनं स्वतो निहतमुद्गरप्रहरणप्रयासायते ॥
S.S., II-75, p.294.

36. शिथिलोदयसप्तभङ्गिशिक्षा विषमोपन्यसनव्यथाविलक्षाः।
मलिनास्त इमे मयूरपिञ्छ-भ्रमणैरेव विलोभयन्ति मन्दान् ॥
प्रतिक्षिप्तं विदधतां विहितं प्रतिषेधताम् ।
क इवान्यः प्रतिक्षेपः कार्यः स्ववचनादृते ॥

S.S., II-76-77, p.296.

37. अविद्यामाहात्म्यादनहमिदमर्थे जगदिदं गुणन्त्येते भातं गगन इव गन्धर्वनगरम् ।
अवन्ध्यैर्व्याघातैरतिपतितविन्ध्यद्रढिमभि र्निबन्ध्यास्ते वन्ध्यासुतनृपतिवैतालिकगणे॥
S.S., II-90, p.314.

38. Dr. Satyavrata Singh, *Vedānta Deśika – His Life, Works and Philosophy — A Study*, Chowkhamba Sanskrit Series Office, Varanasi, 1958, pp. 335-36

39. निध्यायन्त्वसूयवः शुभगुणं निर्दोषमाराध्यमित्यध्वा
विश्वविशेष शून्यकथकैरप्यादितः स्वीकृतः ।
यद्यर्थस्थितिरेतदेकशरणा सप्रत्यवायो
भवत्यध्यक्षादिविरुद्धनिर्गुणकथानिर्वाहगर्वाहवः॥ *S.S.*, II-91, p.315.

40. मुक्तस्य नित्यमविशिष्टतनोरपूर्वां मुक्तिं प्रकल्पयितुमात्तविचारयत्नः ।
स्वप्नप्रसूनमकरन्दरसस्य मन्ये स्वादुत्वमन्यदुपपादयितुं क्षमेत ॥
S.S., II-92, p.319.

41. स्वस्यावाप्तिः सुखमिति मृषा स्वेतरस्यानुभूतौ
कामादन्यः क इव घटते मोक्षनामा पुमर्थः।
तस्मादस्मद्बहुमतनिरध्यक्षमीमांसकोक्त्या
स्वेच्छानृत्यद्बहुगुणनिधिः स्वर्ग एवापवर्गः॥

S.S., III-3, p.338.

42. प्रपञ्चकृतकञ्चुकं यदि परं महः प्राप्यते
न दुःखमपहस्तितं भवति नैकधोपप्लवात् ।
अथैकमखिलोज्झितं न खलु भोग्यतामेति
तत् ततो निगममस्तकैर्निगदमात्रशेषः स्थितम् ॥ *S.S.*, III-4, p.339.

43. मधुभरितहेमकुम्भीमधुरिमधुर्यौ पयोधरौ सुदृशाम् ।
पिशितमिति भावयन्तः पिशाचकल्पाः प्रलोभयन्ति जडान्॥
S.S., III-8, p.344.

44. पातत्रासनिरीक्षणप्रशमितस्वर्वासदुर्वासना पुंसः
संप्रति शेमुषी निरवधिं पुष्णाति तृष्णां परे।
अर्थित्वे मतिकश्मलप्रचलितेऽप्येवं प्रतिष्ठापिते
सामर्थ्ये च समाधिसीम्नि नियतावस्थं व्यवस्थाप्यते॥

S.S., III-17, p.355.

45. समाना मुक्तिश्चेन्न खलु घटते साधनभिदा
न चेत्स्वर्गन्यायस्तरतमतयान्याभिमतया ।
प्रमाणप्रागल्भ्याप्रणिधिमवधूय प्रलपतामिति
क्षीबः क्षोभः स्वमतिविहतेरेव निहतः ॥ *S.S.*, III-20, p.358.

46. विलक्षोपक्षिप्तं विषयरसगन्धर्वनगरप्रशंसायाथार्थ्यं प्रणिदधति चित्तेऽपि तनुभृत् ।
मया दत्ते हस्ते मतिकलुषमुल्ल्य तरसा परब्रह्मैकान्ती भवजलनिधिं गोष्पदयति ॥
S.S., III-24, p.363.

47. विषमधु बहिष्कुर्वन्धीरो बहिर्विषयात्मकं परिमितरसस्वात्मप्राप्तिप्रयासपराङ्मुखः ।
निरवधिमहानन्दब्रह्मानुभूतिकुतूहली जगति भविता दैवात्कश्चिज्जिहासितसंसृतिः ॥
S.S., III-25, p.365.

48. तोयोज्झनेन परितापमुपेत्य जन्तुस्तोयेन जीवति पुनः क्रमयोजितेन ।
तद्वन्महत्त्यजनतस्तमसि प्रविष्टस्तत्संश्रयेण भजते परमार्थदृष्टिम् ॥
S.S., III-34, p.378.

49. विश्वाधिको विलयमेष्यति कस्य भूम्ना वीरः प्रसिद्धमहिमा विबुधेषु कामः ।
क्रोधोदितं यदनुभाववशेन शम्भोः श्रृङ्गारशीतलमभून्नयनं तृतीयम् ॥
S.S., III-39, p.386.

50. अप्राणितमहामोहमनङ्गीकृतमन्मथम् ।
विधूतप्रतिधं लोको विवेकं बहु मंस्यते ॥ *S.S.*, III-42, p.388.

51. त्यजेदेकं कुलस्यार्थे ग्रामस्यार्थे कुलं त्यजेत् ।
ग्रामं जनपदस्यार्थे आत्मार्थे पृथिवीं त्यजेत् ।
Prabhāvilāsa Commentary, p.390.

52. परमानन्ददायिन्यः प्रजानां सृष्टिहेतवः ।
ब्रह्मलक्षणलक्षण्या न कथं ब्रह्म योषितः ॥ *S.S.*, IV-8, p.401.

53. यदि मामवमत्य संयतेत व्यवसायान्वयदर्पितो विवेकः ।
वनिताशतवञ्चितस्य पुंसः स्वयमाधास्यति सौभरेरवस्थाम् ॥ *S.S.*, IV-12, p.405.

54. स्मरति महतामातङ्कानां मनस्कुरुते गृहान् प्रसजति परब्रह्मप्राप्तौ समृद्धिमपेक्षते ।
अभिनिविशते भोगोदन्वत्यपत्रपते पुनः प्रणिधिरधुना सिद्धापायः सितासितपद्धतिः ॥
S.S., IV-17, p.408.

55. पुरुषमजहदभोगश्रद्धापुरस्कृतसंभ्रमं विषयमदिरास्वादक्षीबं विमोचयितुं स्थितः ।
अमृतमिलितद्राक्षावल्लीफलद्रवसंपदाममरतरुणीबिब्बोकानामवैति न वैभवम् ॥
S.S., IV-22, p.412.

56. रतिपरिवारयोषिदनुपालितरत्नलतास्तबकविलोभनीयललितस्तनभारनताः ।
अमरमृगेक्षणाः परिचरन्तु विरक्तिधनंमदनधनुर्गुणभ्रमरमन्थरतारदृशः ॥
S.S., IV-26, p.416.

57. पदे विष्णोरेषा प्रभवमधिगम्य प्रसृमरा स्फुरत्ताराफेनस्तबकपरिपाटिपरिगता ।
क्षरन्ती पूर्वाद्रेरमरतटिनीसंप्लवसखी तमिस्राकालिन्दीं शबलयति चन्द्रांशुपटली ॥
S.S., IV-31, p.420.

58. जमदग्निमुखान् परित्यजन् परिगृह्णन् दशकंधरादिकान् ।
विनिपातितवानुपायतः पुरुषानद्भुतपौरुषानहम् ॥ *S.S.*, IV-40, p.428.

59. पुंसस्त्यक्तपरिग्रहस्य विषयग्राहोज्झितस्याप्यहं
कन्थाविष्टरकुण्डिकादिहरणप्रच्छादनाद्याश्रयः ।
अन्तःक्षोभमलीकजल्पमसदारोपस्पृहां पैशुनं
संमोहादि च संमुखय्य सहसा दास्ये समाधिक्षयम् ॥
S.S., IV-41, p.428.

60. निद्रामुग्धिनिमीलितेष्वसुलभं निर्धूतनिम्नोन्नतं
निद्राणाखिलवर्णभेदनियमं विष्वक्प्रवृत्तोदयम् ।
कः क्रोधोद्भवमुत्सहेत तरितुं कल्पान्तकादम्बिनी-
कालोद्वेलकलिन्दशैलतनयाकल्लोलकालं तमः ॥
S.S., IV-43, p.430.

61. अनघसमाधिसंपदुदरंभरिरात्मभवः प्रबलमहोर्मिजालभरिते दुरिताम्बुनिधौ ।
जडमति जन्तुजातमुपजातविहारमसौ सुखबडिशावकृष्टमुपदंशदशां नयति ॥
S.S., IV-56, p.441.

62. *Prabhāvilāsa* Commentry, p.528.

63. "अग्निदो गरदश्चैव शस्त्रपाणिर्धनापहः" इत्याद्युक्तेष्वाततायिषु प्रकृते क्षेत्रहारित्व-
मभिप्रेतम् । *Prabhāvilāsa*, Commentary, p.452.

64. मद्वंशोद्भवयाजनार्हपुरुषालाभादमुष्मिन्
जगत्या गोत्रप्रथमादनध्वरतया प्रख्यातमस्मत्कुलम् ।
अप्रत्यक्षमनक्षपीडनविधि प्राबल्यतः स्थापितं
विष्वग्वृत्ति तपः परं किमपि मे विश्वाधिकं के विदुः ॥
S.S., V-7, p.462.

65. अष्टाचत्वारिंशतं बौद्धभेदान्नीचोक्त्याहं भाषया निर्मिमाणः ।
अध्यासीनो बोधिवृक्षस्य मूलं विद्यादर्पं वैदिकानामहार्षम् ॥ *S.S.*, V-11, p.465.

66. श्रद्धायाजी षड्रसब्रह्मवादी कामैकान्ती काकिणीनिष्कदासः ।
मार्जाराणां कुक्कुटानां बकानां छात्रा एते सिद्धयार्वाकतन्त्राः ॥
S.S., V-33, p.484.

67. Sulabha is a *Saṁnyāsini*, who has a long philosophical discussion with king Janaka (*Mahābhārata, Śāntiparva*, Chapter 325).

68. रथ्यावादविशङ्क्यमानजरठासंबन्धिसंभाषणात्
त्यक्ता हन्त पतिव्रता गुणनिधिः सत्रासमम्बा मया ।
विद्यातश्च विवाहतश्च विदितादाचारतश्च क्षितौ
कूटस्थाभ्यधिकस्य मे किमधिकः को वा समः कथ्यते ॥

S.S., V-37, p.492.

69. कति कतीह पुरातनतापसाः कमलसंभववंशसमुद्भवाः ।
अतितरन्ति महान्त्यपि पातकान्यहह मामकपादजलाप्लुताः ॥

S.S., V-41, p.496.

70. शरीरप्रलयो मुक्तिर्भोगस्तु रतिरुत्तमा ।
देवतास्तत्प्रदायिन्यः स्त्रियस्तारुण्यभूषणाः ॥ *S.S.*, V-49, p.505.

71. अपि तपसि रतानामप्यधीतागमानामपि यमनियमाद्यैरन्वहं शिक्षितानाम् ।
शिथिलयति समाधिं शिल्पिहस्तानपेक्षं वरतनुमयचित्रं वासनाभित्तिलग्नम् ॥

S.S., V-50, p.506.

72. अमरगुरुप्रणीतमनपायमपोह्य मतं विविधकुतर्कजालकलहायितकौतुकिनः ।
कपिलहिरण्यगर्भकणभोजनबुद्धजिनप्रमुखसमर्थितेषु समयेषु भजन्ति रतिम् ॥

S.S., V-55, p.511.

73. चिरसेवनतोषितेन धात्रा निपुणस्थानविदा निवेदितार्थः ।
असुरोपनिषद्रहस्यमग्र्यं प्रथयामास विरोचनः प्रजानाम् ॥ *S.S.*, V-58, p.514.

74. करणविलयरूपा मुक्तिरित्युक्तमाद्यैर्वितथमिति मयान्यद्वार्तिके विन्यवेशि ।
स्तनयुगलबृहत्वस्थापनीयस्वभूम्ना बहुगुणविभवेन ब्रह्मणा भोगसाम्यम् ॥

S.S., V-59, p.514.

75. कामस्ताम्यतु कोपलोभसहितः काले समभ्येतु वा रक्षः
संयति राघवस्थितिमहं व्यङ्क्ता विवेकाहवे ।
कालस्त्वेष रथो भवत्विह कलिस्त्वं सारथिर्दुर्मते दम्भः
संप्रति जैत्रदुन्दुभिरसौ दर्पस्तथा कङ्कटः ॥

S.S., V-64, p.519.

76. चतुर्विधम् — भक्ष्यभोज्यलेह्यचोष्यरूपम् ।

Prabhāvilāsa Commentary, p.521.

77. सत्त्वरं यथा तथा परिक्रान्तयमनियमासनप्राणायामप्रत्याहाराख्यस्थानपञ्चकः ।

Prabhāvali Commentary, pp.533-34.

78. मनोरथरथारूढो विवेकस्तर्कसारथिः दिदृक्षुः संयमस्थानमितः समभिवर्तते ।

S.S., VI-5, p.534.

79. भुजगपतिनालविधृते भूपद्मे कर्णिकारूपः ।
विलसति केसरभूधर परिवृततनुरत्र काञ्चनक्ष्माभृत् ॥ *S.S.*, VI-8, p.538.

80. विजितमनोभवेन विभुनाधिगतोऽपि सदा निरुपधिसंयमस्य न पदं कलधौतगिरिः ।
गजमुखगण्डशैलघनदान कलिन्दसुतालहरिझलंझलाबहलकज्जलकम्बलितः ॥
S.S., VI-12, p.542.

81. एतं गिरिवरं सूत मन्ये विश्वमनोहरम्।
आगमिस्वर्गसृष्टीनामादिकन्दमिव स्थितम्॥ *S.S.*, VI-13, p.543.

82. सहचरभव्यदिव्यशबरीकबरीविकसन्मदनमहेषुजालमधुसौरभसारभृतः ।
इह मरुतो वहन्ति मददन्तुरदन्तिघटाकरटकटाहवाहिघनशीकरशीभरिताः ॥
S.S., VI-14, p.543.

83. एष मैनाकजनको धरणीधेनुतर्णकः ।
त्रिदशाचलजामाता त्र्यम्बकश्वशुरो गिरिः ॥ *S.S.*, VI-21, p.551.

84. वाहिन्यः कति सन्ति वन्यमहिषश्रेणीविषाणाहतिक्षुभ्यद्
दुर्दमकर्दमाङ्कपयसस्तत्संमितिं क्षाम्यति।
वारिक्रीडितवल्गिताङ्गवलभिच्छुद्धान्तसीमन्तिनी
वक्षोजक्षरदङ्गरागसुभगोत्सङ्गा न गङ्गापगा॥
S.S., VI-22, p.552.

85. अयोध्या दिव्येयं वहति सरयूरत्र विरजा विभोरेते यूपा विधिनियमनिर्मुक्तपशवः ।
अकुण्ठस्वातन्त्र्यः स्वपदमधिरोहन्नवसरे सहानैषीदत्र स्थिरचरमशेषं रघुपतिः ॥
S.S., VI-26, p.555.

86. नाथायैव नमः पदं भवतु नाश्चित्रैश्चरित्रक्रमैर्भूयोभिर्भुवनान्यमूनि कुहनागोपाय गोपायते।
कालिन्दीरसिकाय कालियमणिस्फारस्फटावाटिकारङ्गोत्सङ्गविशङ्क-
चङ्क्रमधुरापर्यायचर्या यते ॥
S.S., VI-30, p.558.

87. इमामधर्मिण विभाव्य संप्लुतामुदन्वता द्वारवतीमिवाधुना।
न भावये संयमसंपदास्पदं न कालतः कस्य गुणव्यतिक्रमः॥
S.S., VI-33, p.561.

88. पुनरुपजनिभीतैः पुण्डरीकादिभिस्तैश्चिरपरिचितपूर्वं श्रीहरिक्षेत्रमेतत् ।
सकृदपि विमलेऽस्मिन्मज्जतश्चक्रतीर्थे भवजलनिधिगर्तात्क्षिप्रमुन्मज्जनं स्यात् ॥
S.S., VI-34, p.562.

89. अयमुपहतः सालग्रामोपलान्तरवस्थितद्रविणकणिकालुब्धैर्देशो मलिम्लुचलुब्धकैः ।
बहुगुणपरब्रह्मप्रेक्षासुधाब्धिमनोरथैर्मुहुरुपनतप्रत्यासेधैर्मुमुक्षुभिरुज्झितः ॥
S.S., VI-35, p.562.

90. लब्ध्वापि मूर्तिमधरीकृतपूर्वरूपां रत्या समेत्य च रथाङ्गभृतः प्रसादात् ।
धर्मोपरोधमिह नेच्छति पुष्पधन्वा त्र्यम्बकात्प्रचकितो नयनात्तृतीयात् ॥
S.S., VI-36, p.563.

91. इमां मधुरपानीयां दक्षिणापथजाह्नवीम् ।
चोरैः परिवृतां मन्ये विद्यां कुमतिविप्लुताम् ।। *S.S.*, VI-47, p.572.

92. कपर्दिमतकर्दमं कपिलकल्पनावागुरां दुरत्ययमतीत्य तद् द्रुहिणतन्त्रयन्त्रोदरम् ।
कुदृष्टिकुहनामुखे निपततः परब्रह्मणः करग्रहविचक्षणो जयति लक्ष्मणोऽयं मुनिः ।।
S.S., VI-49, p.574.

93. नाहं नापि च मत्सुतो न च सुराः सर्वे न चामी
सदा ध्यानारोपितचेतसो मुनिगणा जानन्ति विष्णोः पदम् ।
इत्थं नाभिसरोजशायिपृथुकव्याहारमाकर्णयञ्शेते
पन्नगसार्वभौमशयने श्रीपद्मनाभः श्रिया ।। *S.S.*, VI-53, p.577.

94. बुभुक्षाभिक्षाकब्रुवपठितमिथ्यागुणगणा मुमुक्षूनक्षुद्रानिह मुहुरुपघ्नन्ति परुषैः ।
कदध्वोपानीत द्रविणकणदुर्मानमदिरागुणक्षैब्य क्षुभ्यन्मतिकलहकाकोलकलुषैः ।।
S.S., VI-55, p.579.

95. विन्ध्यस्तम्भ प्रकटमहिमा विष्वगाचान्तसिन्धुः कुम्भीसूनुर्दनुजकबलग्रासदीप्तोदराग्निः।
नाकधीशन्नहुषभुजगीकारदुर्वार शक्तिर्ब्रह्मापत्यं मुनिरिह वसन्भ्राजते मुक्तकल्पः।।
S.S., VI-56, p.579.

96. सारः सारस्वतानां शठरिपुभणितिः शान्तिशुद्धान्तसीमा मायामायामिनीभिः
स्वगुणविततिभिर्बन्धयन्तीं धयन्ती ।पारं पारंपरीतो भवजलधिभवन्मज्जनानां जनानां
प्रत्यक्प्रत्यक्षयेन्नः प्रतिनियतरमासंनिधानं निधानम् ।। *S.S.*, VI-61, p.583.

97. अग्रे पश्य वृषाचलं क्षितिभृतामग्र्यं यदग्रे
हरेर्मञ्जीरोदकमाबिभर्ति महतीं मन्दाकिनीसंपदम्।
नृत्यच्चन्दनगन्धवाहनियतव्यालोलचूडाटवीशाखाता-
डीतचन्द्रमश्च्युतसुधाधाराभिसंवर्धितम्।।

S.S., VI-63, p.585.

98. दास्यं लास्यवतानुमत्य मनसा रङ्गेश्वर त्वत्पदे नित्यं किंकरवाण्यहं न तु पुनः
कुर्यां कदार्याश्रयाम् ।मीलच्चक्षुषि वेल्लितभ्रुणि मुहुर्दत्तावमानाक्षरे भीमे कस्यचिदाढ्यकस्य
वदने भिक्षाविलक्षां दृशम् ।। *S.S.*, VI-69, p.590.

99. किमपि विबुधमुख्यः सेवितं क्षेत्रमेतद्भवभयशमनार्हं भाति सत्यव्रताख्यम् ।
निजसुतहयमेधे यत्र दिव्येन पुंसा क्षितिकलुषमशेषं क्षेप्तुमाविर्बभूवे ।।
S.S., VI-70, p.592.

100. पारेशृङ्गमिहादिपूरुषपदप्रस्यन्दिपाथस्विनीपाथः पातपरंपराद्भुतमहारण्ये शरण्ये
सताम्। पारावर्य विवेक पक्त्रिमधियः सत्त्वाश्च तत्त्वं परं पश्यन्तः प्रचरन्ति हन्त
सुखिनः सर्वेऽपि निर्वैरतः।। *S.S.*, VI-75, p.598.

101. श्रीरङ्गं वृषभाचलः करिगिरिर्दृष्टानि देव त्वया दीव्यन्ति द्रमिडेष्वमी च कतिचिद्देशाः
प्रदेशार्चिताः। प्रत्यग्रोदितघोरपश्चिमयुगप्रक्षोभ विक्षोभकेष्वेतेषु क्वचिदस्तु
संयमविधिस्वास्थ्यं त्रिवर्गत्यजः।। *S.S.*, VI-78, p.601.

102. बहिर्भूतैरेतैर्विविधविनिपातस्थपुटितैर्यदृच्छासंवादप्रचितगुणविख्यातिभिरलम् ।
प्रतिक्षिप्तावद्यं प्रवरगुणभूयिष्ठमधुना नियच्छाम्यन्तःस्थं किमपि यमिनः संयमपदम् ।।
S.S., VI-80, p.603.

103 (i) सा काशीति न चाकशीति भुवि सा अयोध्येति नाधास्यते
साऽवन्तीति न कल्मषादवति सा काञ्चीति नोदञ्चते।
धत्ते सा मथुरेति नोत्तमधुरं नान्याऽपि मान्या पुरी
या वैकुण्ठकथा-सुधारसभुजां रोचेत नो चेतसे ।। *S.S.*, VI-38.

(ii) यत्रैकाग्र्यं भवति भगवत्पादसेवार्चनादेः
यत्रैकान्त्य व्यवसितधियः यस्यकस्यापि लाभः।
वासस्थानं तदिह कृतिनां भाति वैकुण्ठकल्पं
प्रायो देशाः मुनिभिरुदिताः प्रायिकैचित्यवन्तः ।।
Śrī Vedānta Deśika *Rahasyatraya Sāra* Ed. S. Rangachar, Sri Tillasthanam Swamy Kainkaryasabha, Jayanagar, Bangalore-41 and Sanskrit Sahitya Sadana, Mysore-4, 1990, p.145.

104. विदुषश्चिन्तनां शक्त्या चित्रभित्तिं वितन्वता ।
शुद्धाशुद्ध विभागार्हं विश्वं विलिखितं मया ।। *S.S.*, VII-1, p.609.

105. विश्वप्रीणनविश्वकर्मरचनाचातुर्यकातर्यदैः शिल्पः कल्पयतीव मण्डनमसौ चेतः
स्थितेर्मण्डपः। रत्नस्तम्भ भुवोऽपि रश्मय इमे सोपानगोपानसीमध्यं यत्र
गवाक्षयन्ति विहित प्रत्यग्रचित्रक्रमाः ।। *S.S.* VII-3, p.612.

106. परिमितमपरिमितानामास्पदमेतत्प्रपञ्चचित्राणाम् ।
दहरगगनाभिधानं दिव्यं पुरुषं निदर्शयति ।। *S.S.*, VII-6, p.615.

107. ईक्षणध्यानसंस्पर्शप्रमुखैः पोषयन्प्रजाः ।मत्स्यकूर्मविहंगादिविग्रहः प्रेक्ष्यते प्रभुः ।।
S.S., VII-12, p.620.

108. त्रातुं जगन्ति कृपया कल्पे कल्पे भवन्ति दिव्यानि ।
चरितानि चक्रपाणेः प्रवाहवृत्त्या परस्परप्राञ्चि ।। *S.S.*, VII-15, p.622.

109. निर्मग्नश्रुतिजालमार्गणदशादत्तक्षणैर्वीक्षणैरन्तरतन्वदिवारविन्दगहनान्यौदन्वतीनामपाम्।
निष्प्रत्यूहतरङ्गरिङ्गणमिथः प्रत्यूढपाथश्छटाडोलारोहसदोहलं भगवतो मात्स्यं
वपुर्दृश्यते।। *S.S.*, VII-17, p.624.

110. आखण्डलीयमजरामरमाधिराज्यं त्र्यम्बकं सुभगशेखरमुत्तमाङ्गम् ।
औदन्वतं प्रियतरं स्वगृहं यतोऽभूत स्वाधार एष कमठो विधृताद्रिमन्थः ।।
S.S., VII-18, p.625.

111. अव्यासुर्भुवनत्रयीमनिभृतं कण्डूयनैरद्रिणा
निद्राणस्य परस्य कूर्मवपुषो निश्वासवातोर्मयः।

यद्विक्षेपणसंस्कृतोदधिपयः प्रौलपर्यङ्किका
नित्यारोहणनिर्वृतो विहरते देवः सहैव श्रिया ॥ *S.S.*, VII-19, p.626.

112. आरादाकर एष कौस्तुभमणेर्वारी मरुद्दन्तिनः
क्रीडाशेखरशिल्पकृत्पुरभिदो गुञ्जागृहं पाशिनः।
प्राचीनाङ्कुरपालिका सुरतरोरालक्ष्यतामद्भुतः
स्वैराहारमहानसः सुमनसां शुद्धान्तशय्या हरेः ॥ *S.S.*, VII-21, p.629.

113. कल्याणानामविकलनिधिः कापि कारुण्यसीमा
नित्यामोदा विगमवचसां मौलिमन्दारमाला।
संपद्दिव्या मधुविजयिनः संनिधत्तां सदा मे
सैषा दैवी सकलभुवनप्रार्थनाकामधेनुः ॥ *S.S.*, VII-24, p.631.

114. प्रवर्धमानात्प्रलयाम्बुराशेराविर्भवन्नादिवराह एषः ।
दंष्ट्रानुषक्तां धरणीं दधानो जम्बालरेखामिव केलिलग्नाम् ॥ *S.S.*, VII-28, p.635.

115. प्रह्लादह्लादनानि प्रणतसुरगणप्राणन प्रीणनानि
प्रत्यूढस्थेमभीमप्रलयघनघटाघोषणाडम्बराणि।
क्षुभ्यत्सप्ताम्बुधीनि क्षुरपरुषनखक्रीडितक्षुण्णशत्रोरस्मद्भीति
व्यपोहं विदधतु नृहरेरट्टहासाद्भुतानि ॥ *S.S.*, VII-40, p.643.

116. व्रीडाविद्धवदान्यदानवयशोनासीरधाटीभटस्त्रैयक्षं
मकुटं पुनर्नवतु नस्त्रैविक्रमो विक्रमः।
यत्प्रस्तावसमुच्छ्रितध्वजपटीवृत्तान्तसिद्धान्तिभिः स्रोतोभिः
सुरसिन्धुरष्टसु दिशासौधेषु दोधूयते ॥ *S.S.*, VII-42, p.646.

117. भाविन्या दशया भवन्निह भवध्वंसाय नः कल्पतां
कल्की विष्णुयशःसुतः कलिकथाकालुष्यकूलंकषः।
निःशेषक्षतकण्टके क्षितितले धाराजलौघैर्ध्रुवं
धर्मं कार्तयुगं प्ररोहयति यन्निस्त्रिंशधाराधरः ॥ *S.S.*, VII-48, p.658.

118. हृष्यन्ति व्यसनेषु सप्तसु मुधारब्धेषु मत्प्रेरिताः प्रारब्धं
न परित्यजान्ति च मुहुः प्रत्यूहवात्याहताः ।
नानादुःखभयानकेऽपि न जहत्यर्थे पुमर्थे रतिं
मोहस्याभिनिवेश एकदृगहं कोशाधिकारे स्थितः ॥ *S.S.*, VIII-1, p.664.

119. स्त्रीद्यूतमृगयामद्यवाक्पारुष्योग्रदण्डताः ।
अनुपायव्ययंश्चेति राज्ञां व्यसनसप्तकम् ॥ *Prabhāvilāsa* - śloka p.664.

120. लास्यान्विता चं ललिता च गतिस्त्वदीया मञ्जुस्वना बहुगुणा च विभाति वीणा ।
देहश्च दर्शयति चान्द्रमसीमभिख्यां प्राप्तोऽसि नस्त्वमिह भोगसमृद्धिहेतुः ॥
S.S., VIII-8, p.676.

121. निष्कामक्रोधलोभं निपतितकुहनादम्भदर्पाभिमानं
निर्धूतेर्ष्याभ्यसूयामदविह्वति जहन्मत्सरस्तम्भजाड्यम् ।
अद्य श्वो वा विदध्यादपि चरमयुगे विश्वमक्षुद्रसत्त्वं
वेलातीत प्रसर्पन्मधुमथनदयादत्तसेको विवेकः ॥ *S.S.*, VIII-15, p.684.

122. एतस्य संभृतविवेकविमोहभूम्नः सेनायुगस्य समराङ्गणसंभ्रमेण ।
प्रायेण संप्रति विकल्पितया स्ववृत्त्या दोलाधिरोहणरसं लभते जयश्रीः ॥
S.S., VIII-35, p.701.

123. प्रणमामि विवेकदेवं प्रकुपितप्रतिपक्षप्रतिमथनप्रधनम् ।
शोणितनवमधुप्रवाहे सूर्यमिव समग्रलग्नप्रतिमानम् ॥ *S.S.*, VIII-37, p.703.

124. महितमधुप्रदिष्टमधुदिग्धविचित्रशरः परभृतवन्दिमान् भ्रमरसंहतिगीतगुणः ।
मलयमरुत्सखो मकरलक्षणकेतुरसौ धृतधनुरभ्युपैति मदनः प्रमदापृतनः ॥
S.S., VIII-48, p.710.

125. रथवारणवाजिभिः प्रहृष्यन्माहिलारत्नसमूहनेन सिद्धैः ।
मकरध्वज एष पुष्पधन्वा रणमभ्येति रतिप्रियापदानः ॥
S.S., VIII-56, p.718.

126. स्वमित्रमुपधात्रयप्रथितशुद्धि लोभात्मकं झटित्यलघुतुष्टिकुक्ष्यनलदग्धमित्याकुलः ।
विरक्तिरणदेवताविपुलदृष्टिवैश्वानरं प्रविश्य मकरध्वजः पुनरनङ्गतामागतः ॥
S.S., VIII-60, p.721.

127. अपि वैरिवरूथिनीमशेषामपि शैलानपि सागरानपि क्ष्माम् ।
ग्रसितुं प्रभवत्ययं प्रदीप्तः प्रथितः कोपतनूनपादनूनः ॥ *S.S.*, VIII-68, p.726.

128. यस्य त्रासनतर्जनप्रभृतयः क्रूरोद्धता वृत्तयो
यस्योन्मेषनिमेषयोस्त्रिभुवनं निद्राति जागर्ति च।
आबध्यैनमवैधहिंसनमहा संरम्भसंभावितक्रीडोड्डामर-
बाहुदण्डलडहं क्रोधं निहन्ति क्षमा ॥ *S.S.*, VIII-76, p.729.

129. अभिजनधनविद्यावृत्तदाक्ष्यादिरूपै रुपधिभिरयमेकोऽनेकधा जृम्भमाणः ।
पृथुमहिमविवेकप्रेक्षणादुत्पतन्त्या प्रसभमधिकदृष्ट्या प्रापितो वीरशय्याम् ॥
S.S., VIII-86, p.734.

130. दिनकर इव दीव्यन्दृष्टशक्तिस्तथासौ मुनिपरिषदभीष्टे मोहभङ्गे विवेकः ।
समतनुत यथैकः साधुपीडोद्यतानां रजनिचरपतीनां राघवो दीर्घानिद्राम् ॥
S.S., VIII-102, p.743.

131. हतजीवजीवितेशां विषादमूर्च्छादिलुप्तनिश्वासाम् ।
तृष्णादयः सकुल्या दुर्मतिमभितो निपत्य विलपन्ति ॥
S.S., VIII-105, p.745.

132. "अन्तर्जवनिकासंस्थैः सूचनार्थस्य चूलिका"।
"It is *Cūlikā,* when something is suggested behind the curtain."
Viśvanātha, *Sāhitya Darpaṇa,* (VI-58) p.419.

133. मोहकूपारकुक्षिंभिरिरयमनघो मुक्तिवीरूत्प्रोहः प्रज्ञासौधैकदीपः प्रतिसमयकथा-तूलवातूलवेगः। दुःखद्धारोपरोधास्थिरतरपरिघो दूरतः प्रत्युपैति क्रूरक्रोधा-शुशुक्षण्युपशमनसुधा सारसेको विवेकः॥ *S.S.,* IX-1, p.748.

134. वायुर्दोधूयते यद्यदयमुडुगणो बंभ्रमिति द्रुतं खे तेजो
जाज्वल्यते यद्यदपि न जलधिर्माधवीं दोधवीति ।
भूर्यद्वा बोभवीति स्थिरचरधृतये तच्चतादृक् च
सर्वं स्वायत्ताशेषसत्तास्थितियतनपरब्रह्म लीलोर्मिचक्रम् ॥ *S.S.,* IX-5, p.751.

135. यथाधिकरणं प्रभुर्यजनदान होमार्चनाभरन्यासनभावनाप्रभृतिभिः समाराधितः ।
फलं दिशति देहिनामिति हि संप्रदायस्थितिः श्रुतिस्मृतिगुरूक्तिभिर्नयवतीभिराभाति नः॥
S.S., IX-6, p.752.

136. सत्त्वोदग्रसमग्रनन्दथुभुवः सालम्बनध्यानतः शुद्धे
चेतसि यद्यपि प्रभुरिहादृश्यो दरीदृष्यते ।
प्रत्यग्वस्तु विशेष्यवर्ष्मणि पुनस्तस्मिन्दृढप्रेक्षिते नाथः
सोऽहमहं स इत्यापि गिरो नाध्यासमध्यासताम् ॥ *S.S.,* IX-12, p.755.

137. तत्त्वज्ञाने विशुद्धे शमयति दुरितारम्भमात्मावधाने
व्यक्ताकृष्टेतराक्षे विरमति च मरोवानरं चापलात्स्वात् ।
भस्मच्छन्नाग्निकल्पः परपरिभवनाद्यागमे दीप्यमानः श्लक्ष्णः
संस्कार सारस्तरलयति शनैरुज्झिहानं समाधीम् ॥ *S.S.,* IX-13, p.757.

138. क्रमपक्त्रिमकर्मजागरूकस्थिरसंस्कारनिरूध्यमानचित्तः ।
स्मरति प्रणिधातुमेकतानो बहिरर्थान्विवशः पितामहोऽपि ॥
S.S., IX-14, p.758.

139. बहुरपि लघुः प्रत्यक्चिन्ता बहिर्विषयाटवीविहृतिचटुलं चेतो रोद्धुं कथं प्रभविष्यति ।
अनिभृततटक्रीडोत्कण्ठाविजृम्भितसंभ्रमे कलभचरणे लूतातन्तुः कथं निगलायते ॥
S.S., IX-15, p.759.

140. स्वयमिह विपदो वा स्वप्नवत्संपदो वा नियतिविपरिवृत्तौ नेमिवृत्त्था भवन्त्याम् ।
शतमपि विशयानां शस्त्रवच्छातयन्ती नयनिगमसमीची न व्यतिस्ते मतिस्ते ॥
S.S., IX-16, p.760.

141. अपि निर्मुक्तजीवानां कामादीनां बलीयसाम् ।
अविद्या कर्मसंज्ञा तु मृतसंजीवनी स्थिता ॥ *S.S.,* IX-17, p.760.

142. दहति निरवशेषं देवसंभूतिरेनां।
युगपदिह समिद्धो योगकल्पान्तवह्निः ॥ *S.S.,* IX-18, p.761.

143. सत्कारकालकूटं तरुणीकुणपं सभाभुजंगीं च ।
परिहरति राजधानीकुम्भीपाकं च गुप्तमाहात्म्युः ॥ *S.S.*, IX-19, p.762.

144. मुकुन्दे निक्षिप्य स्वभरमनघो मुक्तवदसौ स्वतन्त्राज्ञासिद्धां स्वयमविदितस्वामि हृदयुः।
परित्यागे सद्युः स्वपरविविधानर्थजननादलङ्घ्यामा मोक्षादनुसरति शास्त्रीयसरणिम्॥
S.S., IX-20, p.762.

145. अनघमतिरनुज्ञान्नाश्रमादिव्यवस्थां हरिचरणसपर्यास्वादतुष्टो मनीषी ।
अवतरति विरक्त्या गाढमालिङ्गितोऽसौ मुषितनिखिलखेदे मुक्तिघण्टापथेऽस्मिन् ॥
S.S., IX-21, p.763.

146. संसाराख्यज्वलनभसितीभूतसंजीवनार्हा धर्मोत्पत्तिप्रथितविभवा धार्यमाणा गिरीशैः ।
गम्भीरत्वादकलुषगतिर्गम्यतीर्थोपपन्ना गङ्गेवान्या पुरुषजलधिं गाहते विष्णुभक्तिः ॥
S.S., IX-22, p.764.

147. जुगुप्सां देहादौ विषयरसभोगेषु हसनं प्रकोपं निद्रादौ परपुरुषवादादिषु भयम् ।
शुचं योगालाभे फलपरिणतौ विस्मयमपि प्रयच्छत्युत्साहं दुरितविरतौ ब्रह्मणि रतिम्॥
S.S., IX-23, p.765.

148. प्रत्यक्तत्त्वसतत्त्ववेदनसुखप्रत्यूहसिद्धिप्रदैः क्षुद्रैः केवलकालयापनपरैरन्यैरनाकृष्टधीः।
मुक्तिद्वारकवाटिकाविघटनध्वानप्रतिश्रुन्निभैरध्यक्षीकृतसत्पथैर्मुनिरसौ मन्त्रैर्धृतिं विन्दति॥
S.S., IX-25, p.767.

149. कामातङ्कमतीत्य कोपदहनं निर्वाप्य वित्तस्पृहावेतालीं
व्यवधूय बान्धवकथागर्तं समुत्तीर्य च।
सङ्गोत्तंसितवासनासहचरः संसारकाराकुटीनिष्क्रान्ति
क्रमपादुकां तनुमनुद्विग्नो मुनिः क्षाम्यति ॥ *S.S.*, IX-26, p.768.

150. विमुक्तिपथदेशिकैर्वितथावृत्तिवैदेशिकैर्विमुष्टशुकशौनक प्रभृतिभाषितैरुज्झितम् ।
भिषज्यति भवं प्रभौ पितरि शेषिणि श्रीपतावपथ्यविनिवर्तकं किमपि भद्रमभ्यर्थये ॥
S.S., IX-29, p.770.

151. तितिक्षुर्द्वन्द्वानि द्रुतमतिरयत्नोपनतभुक्परित्याज्यत्यागी भ्रमर इव सारग्रहरुचिः ।
कृतज्ञः प्राप्तव्ये नियतधृतिरेकान्तरसिको मुमुक्षुः संधत्ते मुनिरनिभृतं ब्रह्मणि मनः ॥
S.S., IX-35, p.778.

152. त्रैगुण्याम्भोधिवेलावनतृणविषयग्रासदुर्वासनोद्यदभोगैदं
पर्यपर्याकुलितमनुयुगोत्कण्ठितो-दग्रवृत्तिम्।
भूयो भूयः स्वचक्रे भ्रमयति नृपशुं गाढबन्धोपरुद्धं
कालोऽसौ कर्ममालाघटित-भवघटीयन्त्रतन्त्रस्वतन्त्रः ॥ *S.S.*, IX-40, p.781.

153. लुप्तदृष्टिभिरलब्धदेशिकैर्लोकवेदपदवी दुरत्यया ।
तत्प्रसीद भगवन्मदीक्षितं पुण्डरीकमिव पाहि मन्त्रतः ॥ *S.S.*, IX-42, p.783.

154. विषयमदिरामुग्धैरत्यक्तः स एष पृथग्जनैः क्वचन समये यत्रैकाग्र्यं क्वचिच्च तथास्पदे।
निभृतकरणग्रामस्तृप्यन्निरुद्धमरुद्गणः परमिहपरि धाम्नि प्रत्यङ्मुखः प्रतितिष्ठति ॥
S.S., IX-45, p.788.

155. पुलकमुकुलोत्तुङ्गैरङ्गैरुदश्रुभिरीक्षणैरथमनुभवत्यन्तर्दृष्टिः समाधिरसं पुमान्।
ध्रुवमिह महानन्दब्रह्मोपलम्भनलक्षणे महति विभवे निष्प्रत्यूहा मनोरथपद्धतिः ॥
S.S., IX-46, p.789.

156. स्वफलेन तुलारूढः समाधिर्मुक्तिसाधकः ।
न्यूनाधिकसमत्वेषु विकल्पायैव कल्पते ॥ *S.S.*, IX-49, p.791.

157. इयमखिलपुमर्थप्रार्थनाकल्पवल्ली सितमतिभिरनन्यैः सेविता सिद्धबृन्दैः ।
द्युतिभिरविरलाभिर्द्योतयन्ती दिगन्तान् विशति सुमतिसौधं विष्णुभक्तिर्विशुद्धम् ॥
S.S., IX-52, p.793.

158. अहं वैकुण्ठदास्यैकलास्यलीलाविनोदिनी ।
विश्वकिल्बिषसंहार विभ्रमारभटीनटी ॥ *S.S.*, X-1, p.795.

159. अम्बा मे पुरुषस्य बुद्धिरनघा तातः स धर्मोत्तरः
संतुष्टिः सहजा क्षमा प्रियसखी सद्वृत्तिराज्ञाकरी।
विद्यैव स्वयमस्मि विश्ववृजिनप्रध्वंसनं क्रीडितं साहं
प्राणिमि विष्णुभक्तिरचला संतिष्ठते संसृतिः ॥ *S.S.*, X-2, p.796.

160. निरुध्य तरसा मरुत्करणमण्डलीं कुण्डलीं
विचिन्त्य विगणय्य वा धमनिधातुमर्मादिकम् ।
किमत्र निगमत्रयस्थितिमतापि लालभ्यते मयि
स्थितिरवस्थिता यदि किमुच्यते मुच्यते॥ *S.S.*, X-3, p.797.

161. मुमुक्षुत्वे सिद्धे मुषितमतिमोहस्य मुरभित्समाधिः संरोहन्नुपहरति सर्वाघविरतिम् ।
परस्तादास्थेयं यदिह विदुषानिष्टजनुषा फलार्थं तत्किं वा फलमिति वितर्कः श्रमफलः॥
S.S., X-4, p.798.

162. अघपरिणमितैरमित्रभेदैः करण कलेबरपुत्रदारिकाद्यैः ।
ग्रहिल इह मयैव मोचनीयो मुरभिदनुग्रहलीलयां मुमुक्षुः ॥ *S.S.*, X-5, p.799.

163. कलया विहितोदयः कयाचित्प्रतिपच्चन्द्र इवैष विश्ववन्द्यः ।
उपयाति दिने दिने समृद्धिं पुरुषो विष्णुपदाश्रितः सितात्मा ॥
S.S., X-8, p.802.

164. स्वतः सिद्धस्वच्छस्थिरमधुर चिन्तासुरसरित्प्रवाहोपाश्लेष्टात्प्रणिधिमुखभागादवनरन् ।
चिदानन्दोदन्वत्यनघगुणरत्नौघ भरिते निमज्जत्यन्यस्मिन्नयमपुनरुन्मज्जनमिह ॥
S.S., X-9, p.802.

165. लुलितभुवनपद्मां लुम्पतो वासतेयीमुदयशिखरिमध्यादुज्जिहानस्य भानोः ।
अपतमसि पदेऽस्मिन् वैष्णवे दृश्यमारादिह भवति पताकास्थानकं धाम पूर्वम् ॥
S.S., X-10, p.803.

166. त्रिभुवनमिदं शान्तक्षोभं समाधिरनाकुलः
प्रसृमरसुधाधाराकारा प्रसीदति शेमुषी ।
स्फुरति च मुहुर्दृष्टिः सौव्या तदप्युपरि स्फुटं
तदिह महतीं सिद्धिं मन्ये झटित्युपतस्थुषीम् ।। *S.S.*, X-11, p.804.

167. वैकुण्ठकृपया देव्या मदभीष्टे व्यवस्थितम् ।प्राध्वं संकल्पमार्ताण्डं प्रवर्तयितुमुत्सहे ।।
S.S., X-12, p.805.

168. त्वददृष्ट्या सकृदीक्षिता दिविषदः स्वं स्वं पदं भुञ्जते
भोगानत्र च भूभुजामभिमतान् पुष्णासि तृष्णाधिकम् ।
किंचोदञ्चदनुग्रहा कृपणतामालक्ष्य वैलक्ष्यतो
नैराश्यप्रमुखानि सौति भवति निर्वाणपर्वाण्यपि ।। *S.S.*, X-15, p.806.

169. जय गरुड सुपर्ण दर्वीकराहार देवाधिपाहारहारिन्
दिवौकस्पतिक्षिप्तदम्भोलिधाराकिणाकल्प कल्पान्तवातूलकल्पोदयानल्प-
वीरायितोद्यच्चमत्कार दैत्यारिजैत्रध्वजारोहनिर्धारितोत्कर्ष संकर्षणात्मन् गरुत्मन्
मरुत्पञ्चकाधीशसत्यादिमूर्ते न कश्चित्समस्ते नमस्ते पुनस्ते नमः ।।
S.S., X, p.810.

170. नम इदमजहत्सपर्याय पर्यायनिर्यातपक्षानिलास्फालनोद्वेलपाथोधिवीचीचपेटाहतागाध-
पातालभांकारसंक्रुद्धनागेन्द्रपीडासृणीभावभास्वन्नखश्रेणये चण्डतुण्डाय नृत्यद्भुजङ्गभ्रुवे
वज्रिणे दंष्ट्रया तुभ्यमध्यात्मविद्या विधेया विधेया भवद्दास्यमापादयेथा दयेथाश्च मे ।
S.S., X, p.811.

171. व्यक्तौ सन्नाहसंकल्पौ विश्वगोप्तुरिमौ हरेः ।
प्रथितावागमग्रामि पक्षीश्वरसुदर्शनौ ।। *S.S.*, X-19, p.813.

172. यस्मिन्विस्मयनीयभूमनि मनागुन्मीलिते नैकधा सिध्यन्त्यस्य सितासितस्य जगतः
स्वर्गापवर्गादयः।ऐशः सोऽहमवासरात्ययभवन्मायामहायामिनीसत्ताशेषसुषुप्त बोधनपटुः
संकल्पसूर्योदयः।। *S.S.*, X-20, p.813.

173. अनिदं प्रथमां निद्रामपावर्त्य क्षणादहम् ।
अनिदंपश्चिमां पुंसो जनयिष्यामि जागराम्।। *S.S.*, X-22, p.815.

174. शमधननिधिः संविद्वल्लीसमग्र फलोदयः श्रुतपरिणतिः शुद्धिस्थेमा सुखप्रतिभूरसि ।
भवभयतमः प्रातः संध्या परावरदीपिका भगवति हरौ भक्तिर्दिव्या परिष्कृतिरात्मनः।।
S.S., X-26, p.818.

175. प्रकृतः क्रियया धिया च योगैः परमैकान्त्यपरिष्कृतस्य पुंसः ।
निधिदर्शनवन्निरूढहर्षं प्रणिधत्ते विशदं परप्रकाशम् ।। *S.S.*, X-28, p.819.

176. स्वमायाशैलूषीविहरणपरिभ्रान्ततनुभृत्परित्राणोद्योगप्रवणकरुणावेशविवशः ।
प्रतिक्षेप्तुं तापान् प्रभुरयमपर्यन्तमहिमा हिमानीमानीय स्वपदनतिमेनः प्रणुदति ।।
S.S., X-30, p.820.

177. उपायः स्वप्राप्तेरुपनिषदधीतः स भगवान् प्रसत्त्यै तस्योक्ते प्रपदननिदिध्यासनगती ।
तदारोहः पुंसः सुकृतपरिपाकेन महता निदानं तत्रापि स्वयमखिलनिर्माणनिपुणः ॥
S.S., X-31, p.821.

178. ग्रस्ते पित्तेन चित्ते गलकुहरमुखे संनिरुद्धे कफेन व्याप्ते वातेन गात्रे विलपति लपने कांदिशीके हृषीके । जाले जीवितांशे जिगमिषति बले जन्तुमुद्भ्रान्तबन्धुं कस्त्रातुं चक्रहस्तादपर इह दयादत्त दृष्टिः क्षमेत ॥ *S.S.,* X-32, p.821.

179. कालोपयातकमलापतिदृष्टिपाताद् दूरापनीतदुरितादिपरिप्लवोऽसौ ।
सुप्तोऽपि जागरमुपैत्यपुनर्निमेषं स्वान्तेन निष्प्रतिघमुक्तिमनोरथेन ॥
S.S., X-33, p.822.

180. अपि पद्मयोनिरवशो भजते मधुकैटभादिजनिता विपदः ।
इति दृष्टदोषनिवहः पुरुषो न वहेन नाकनरकेषु रतिम् ॥ *S.S.,* X-36, p.825.

181. अमृतस्यन्दिनं कश्चित्कृष्णमेधं द्विजः स्मरन् ।
उदन्यया न वेशन्तमुदन्वन्तं च वीक्षते ॥ *S.S.,* X-37, p.825.

182. शृङ्गारवीरकरुणाद्भुतहास्यभीतिबीभत्सरौद्रविषयानतिवर्तमानः ।
तत्त्वावलोकनविभावसमेधितात्मा शान्तो रसः स्फुरति मूर्त इवैष धन्यः ॥
S.S., X-38, p.828.

183. अङ्गान्यस्य मुहुर्मुहुः पुलकितान्यन्तर्मुखं मानसं
चिन्ता च द्रुतशर्कराप्रतिनिधिः शीताश्रुणी लोचने ।
मायासारथिगीतयोपनिषदा दृष्टक्रमं द्रागसौ मन्ये
याति मनोरथेन पुरुषो वैकुण्ठघण्टापथम् ॥ *S.S.,* X-39, p.828.

184. चिरपरिचितदेहाद्यर्थचिन्तानुवृत्त्या नियतिमनुसरन्त्या नित्यडोलायितात्मा ।
अयमहमिह मन्दोद्द्योतखद्योतकल्पः कति कति दिवसानि क्षीणशक्तिः क्षिपेयम् ॥
S.S., X-40, p.830.

185. न मुक्तो न च बद्धोऽहं यथा पश्चाद्यथा पुरा ।
कृपणः किं करिष्यामि न करिष्यामि वा स्वयम् ॥ *S.S.,* X-41, p.830.

186. अमतिविहितैरंहःस्तोमैर्झटित्यहमुज्झितः शमितविपथैः सत्त्वोदग्रैः शमादिभिराश्रितः ।
परमपुरुषध्यानस्तोत्रप्रणाममुखैर्मखैः परिहृतमुधाकालक्षेपः फलोदयमाद्रिये ॥
S.S., X-42, p.831.

187. सकृदपि विनतानां सर्वदे सर्वदेहिन्युपनिषदभिधेये भागधेये विधेये ।
विरमति न कदाचिन्मोहतो हा हतोऽहं विषम विषयचिन्तामेदुरा मे दुराशा ॥
S.S., X-43, p.832.

188. मृत्युराद्येति विदुषा यत्कर्तव्यं हितैषिणा ।
तदेव नित्यं कर्तव्यमनिर्धास्तिमृत्युना ॥ *S.S.,* X-44, p.833.

189. पितृपथघटीयन्त्रारोहावरोहपरिभ्रमैर्निरयपदवीयातायातक्रमैश्च निरन्तरैः ।
अधिगतपरिश्रान्तीनाञ्चाधरैरतिवाह्यनः सुखयति निजच्छायादायी स्वयं हरिचन्दनः ।।
S.S., X-45, p.835.

190. मिथ्यादृष्टिमुखैर्विवेकमुषितैरस्पृष्टधीः कश्मलैरु-
त्तीर्य प्रतिरुद्धदोषचिदचिद्भोगस्पृहाकर्दमात् ।
निध्यानस्थिरदर्पणप्रतिफलन्नैः श्रेयस
श्रीरसावद्य प्रत्यवपत्तुमिच्छति भवाकूपारपारस्थलीम् ।। *S.S.*, X-46, p.836.

191. प्रगुणवृत्तिरपथ्यपराङ्मुखः कृपणचित्तहरैर्व्यसनग्रहैः ।
अयमपत्रपते निरुपप्लवः परगतैरपि दृष्टपरावरः ।। *S.S.*, X-47, p.837.

192. कम्पन्ते यमकिंकराः स्वयमसौ कालश्च सर्वकर्षः
शङ्कन्ते किल निर्जरा निजपदावष्टम्भनं पाक्षिकम् ।
रक्षोदानवयक्षगुह्यकमुखा धावन्त्यतो दूरतः
पद्मावल्लभपादपद्मयुगल-प्रत्यर्पितस्वात्मनः ।। *S.S.*, X-48, p.837.

193. संकल्पः – महाभाग, अहं किल परमपुरुषसंकल्पः परमैकान्ति परिषदग्रगण्य-
यमनन्तसुकृतदुष्कृतनिगलयुगलविगलनपूर्विकया परमपदपर्यङ्क परिष्कारब्रह्मसेवा
पर्यन्तया भक्तिपरिपाकसंपदा संघटयितुं तदेकवल्लभया कृपणजनविषयकृतपक्षपातया
कृपया नियुक्तश्चिरप्रार्थितदर्शनं भवन्तमुपगच्छामि। तदिह निकटवर्तिन्यां निःश्रेय-
ससंपदि निर्विशङ्केन भवता भवितव्यम् ।।

S.S., X, pp.841-42.

194. निरूढनिगमत्रये निखिललोकचिन्तामणौ प्रसत्तिमधिजग्मुषि प्रणिदधानभावास्पदे ।
रतिं भजति भावना लयमिवोपयाति द्रुतं रमावसुमतीसहाचरितधर्मणि ब्रह्मणि ।।
S.S., X-54, p.844.

195. निरुपायमुख्यरागं निजपक्षनिविष्टनित्यहरितत्वम् ।
गुणपञ्चरस्थितं त्वां शुकमिव मोक्ष्यामि दिव्यगतियोग्यम् ।।*S.S.*, X-58, p.847.

196. निर्णिक्तत्रिगुणाञ्जनस्य परब्रह्मोपसंपत्तितः
प्रादुर्भूतगुणाष्टकस्य च परं साधर्म्यमभ्येयुषः ।
पारावर्यविभागलक्षणपरित्यागप्रसङ्गोज्झिता
शेषादेरिव शेषवृत्तिरपि ते सत्तावधिः सेत्स्यति ।। *S.S.*, X-59, p.848.

197. सुहृदस्तवादीरन् सुकृतफलं यत्त्वा परित्यक्तम् ।
दुष्कृत फलं द्विषन्तः प्रारब्धान्ते परं पदं विशतः ।। *S.S.*, X-60, p.849.

198. वितमसि पदे लक्ष्मीकान्तं विचित्रविभूतिकं
सचिवगमितः संपद्याविर्भवत्सहजाकृतिः ।
स्फुटतदपृथक्सिद्धिः सिध्यद्गुणाष्टकतत्फलो
भजति परमं साम्यं भोगे निवृत्तिकथोज्झितम् ।। *S.S.*, X-61, p.850.

199. भगवति निहितात्मा भागधेये श्रुतीनां पुरुष इह महात्मा वर्तते भूतधात्र्याम् ।
तदयमवदधानैः सर्वमन्ते वसद्भिः पृथुमतिभिरभीष्टं पृच्छयतां विश्वदर्शी ।।
S.S., X-65, p.853.

200. महासत्त्वोदारस्थिरमधुरगम्भीरहृदयः कृपोत्साहोत्तुङ्गः कृतविदभिगम्यः प्रणयिनाम् ।
श्रुतप्रज्ञामेधास्मृतिजलधिरक्षुद्रचरितस्त्वमेकः सर्वासामनघभणितीनामभिमतः ।।
S.S., X-70, p.859.

201. धीरोदात्तानुकूलोत्तमगुणमहिमा नायकेष्वग्रणीस्त्वं
स्वाधीनत्वत्सनाथा सुमतिरभिमता धर्मपत्नी तवासौ ।
स्वायत्ता चाद्य सिद्धिः समजनि भवतः स्वामिनिःश्रेयसार्था
रामस्त्वं च त्रिलोक्यां रणविहृतिमुखैरप्रधृष्यानुभावौ ।। *S.S.,* X-71, p.859.

202. ज्वलनदिवसज्योत्स्नापक्षोत्तरायणवत्सरान् पवनतपनप्रालेयांशून्क्रमादचिरद्युतिम् ।
जलचरपतिं देवाधीशं प्रजापतिमागतस्तरति विरजां दूरे वाचस्ततः परमद्भुतम् ।।
S.S., X-72, p.861.

203. मलिनिमदशामातन्वानैर्मलीमसवस्तुभिर्मणिरिव महानन्तर्ज्योतिर्निरुद्धनिजप्रभः ।
शुभतररुचिप्रत्यासेधस्वकर्मफलच्छलाज्जडपरिषदि न्यस्तो दैव्या न दीव्यति मायया ।।
S.S., X-73, p.863.

204. नासौ महाराजस्य निर्वेदावसरः । अद्य हि परसंकल्पकल्पान्तपावकेन प्रारब्ध-
कर्मलेशपरिशेष उपशोषितः पुरुषस्य दुरितार्णवः । प्रकृतिरपि निर्मोककल्पा
शेषपरिशुद्धस्वभावं पुरुषमायुषः पारे तमसः पारे निर्मोक्ष्यति ।।*S.S.,* X, p.865.

205. निवृत्तमतिकश्मलो निभृतबुद्ध्यबुद्धीन्द्रियः परप्रणिधिवैभवत्रुटितकर्मबन्धः कृती ।
विमुक्तिपथमद्भुतं द्रुतमुपैति विद्वानिति त्रिवर्गरसघस्मरस्त्रिदशडिण्डिमस्ताड्यते ।।
S.S., X-78, p.868.

206. विवेकोऽयं तत्त्वेष्ववितथविशेषग्रहतनुर्भवोदन्
वद्दोषप्रतिगमनिकात्मा च सुमतिः ।
परप्रेमाकारा त्वमिति समवेतास्त्रय इमे तमः
पारे त्यक्तत्रिगुणमपि च त्यक्ष्यथ न माम्।। *S.S.,* X-81, p.871.

207. दिव्यः संप्रति दुन्दुभिर्दिशि दिशि ध्वानैर्मुहुः श्रूयते
देवानामपि हावुहावुलहरी विक्षोभयत्यम्बरम् ।
आरब्धप्रतिसंस्कृतैः कृतमुखैरर्चिर्मुखैः श्रीपतेराज्ञाधा
रिभिराति-वाहिकगणैरादिश्यते पद्धतिः।। *S.S.,* X-82, p.873.

208. अलं कालप्रहाणेन प्रतीक्षे पश्चिमं दिनम् ।
अस्मदेक हितैषिभ्यः स्वस्ति वः साधयाम्यहम् ।। *S.S.,* X-83, p.873.

209. देवर्षिभूतपितृमर्त्यऋणातिलङ्घी दत्ताभयस्य कृपया दृढभक्तिशाली ।
पत्युः समस्तजगतां परमं पदं तत् प्राप्स्यत्यसौ गुरुजनैः प्रथमाधिरूढम् ।।
S.S., X-91, p.881.

210. कृतमिह दुरितं प्रमादवृत्त्या किमपि मुकुन्दकृपानिमग्नमेनम् ।
पवनतनयवालवह्निनीत्या न दहति धक्ष्यति योजितं परेषु ।।
S.S., X-92, p.882.

211. अपुनरुदयो मायामोहः स्थलीमधिशायितः
स्फुरति मुरभिद्भक्तिर्भव्या भवत्यनुपप्लवा।
सरणिमपुनः प्रत्यावृत्तिं भजत्यनघः पुमान्
किमिह बहुभिः क्रीडत्यग्रे समीहितमद्य नः।। *S.S.*, X-96, p.886.

212. अङ्गीकुर्वन्त्वकलुषधियो नित्यमध्यात्मविद्यामाद्यो धर्मः स्पृशतु वसुधामाशिषः पारवर्ती।
देवः श्रीमान्निरवधिदया सिन्धुरस्मिन्प्रबन्धे वक्ता श्रोता वचनविषयः प्रीयतां वासुदेवः।।
S.S., X-97, p.888.

213. स्तोतुं निन्दितुमस्मदुक्तमथवा सोढुं समूढं जगत् किं
नश्छिन्नमनन्त चिन्तचिन्तनरसे सुस्थे सुखं तस्थुषाम् ।
शिष्याः शिक्षितबुद्धयः श्रुतिपथे येषां वयं ये च
नस्तत्संतोषसमर्पणक्षममिदं साडम्बरः किं परैः ।। *S.S.*, X-98, p.889.

Chapter IV

Literary Analysis of the Drama

1. CHARACTERISATION

Characterisation occupies a position of supreme importance not only in English dramas, but also in Sanskrit dramas. Writers on rhetoric and dramaturgy make elaborate divisions of Nāyakas and Nāyikās, carefully lay down the various characteristics that belong to them and accurate definitions of almost every character that figures in a drama. All this elaboration creates the impression that the task of dramatist is more or less mechanical and little scope is left for the poet's ingenuity. But actually poets have freely excerised their powers and though characterisation as such does not occupy a position of commanding importance in the science of dramaturgy, we find in Sanskrit drama characterisation of a very high order.

"Characterisation is of two types either to portray highly individualised characters or to present pictures of highly typical men and women. This was a time in England when dramas like Ben Jonson's *Volpone* or *Every man in his Humour*, which depict types of character without much plot in them, could please the people. The dramatist's skill however, lies in portraying characters that are both individual and universal, characters that are sufficiently individualised, but have a permanent interest for all time."[1]

In this vein, the *Saṅkalpasūryodaya* too, though an allegorical drama, is a unique one in so far as the portrayal of different characters. This drama imbibes many more characters like Viveka, Mahāmoha etc. which of course are symbolical ones. There are more than forty characters including both male and female in the drama. Of these, some twenty characters are grouped under the leadership of the king Viveka, the Nāyaka of the drama. And similarly other characters belong to the king Mahāmoha, the *Pratināyaka*. These characters are appropriately chosen here.

In all, forty four characters are portayed in the *Saṅkalpasūryodaya*. They are as below :

1.	Sūtradhāra	—	The Stage Director
2.	Viveka	—	The King
3.	Puruṣa	—	Father of Viveka and Mahāmoha
4.	Sumati	—	Queen of Viveka
5.	Buddhi	—	Wife of Puruṣa
6.	Śraddhā	—	Friend of Sumati
7.	Vicāraṇā	—	Friend of Sumati
8.	Vyavasāya	—	A commander of Viveka
9.	Vedānta Siddhānta	—	Preceptor of Viveka (Guru)
10.	Vāda	—	Disciple of Vedānta Siddhānta
11.	Tarka	—	Viveka's charioteer
12.	Saṁskāra	—	Viveka's artist
13.	Viṣṇubhakti	—	Devotion to Viṣṇu

14. Puṣṭi — Servant to Sumati
15. Virakti — do
16. Kṣānti — Servant to Sumati
17. Dṛṣṭapratyaya — Messenger of Viveka
18. Nārada — Divine Sage
19. Tumburu — Divine Sage
20. *Saṅkalpa* — God's Will
21. Śama and Dama — Ministers of Viveka
22. Mahāmoha — The Great Delusion
23. Durmati — Wife of Mahāmoha
24. Kāma — Leader of the army of Mahāmoha
25. Rati — Wife of Kāma
26. Vasanta — Comrade of Kāma
27. Rāga — Friend of Kāma
28. Dveṣa — Mahāmoha's minister
29. Saṁvṛti Satya — Messenger of Mahāmoha
30. Krodha — Leader of the army of Mahāmoha
31. Lobha — Minister of Mahāmoha
32. Dambha — Mahāmoha's follower
33. Tarka — Viveka's charioteer
34. Jighāṁsā — Wife of Krodha
35. Tṛṣṇā — Wife of Lobha
36. Kuhanā — Wife of Dambha

37. Īrṣā — Wife of Darpa
38. Asūyā — do
39. Stambha — Mahāmoha's follower
40. Abhiniveśa — Mahāmoha's Treasurer
41. Durvāsanā — Abhiniveśa's Wife
42. Śṛṅgāra — Kāma's follower
43. Kali — Mahāmoha's follower
44. Bhrama — Mahāmoha's friend

In the succeeding pages, a critical estimate of all main characters has been taken into consideration. King Viveka is the leader of the characters promoting the fulfilment of the dawn of *Saṅkalpasūry*a, while Mahāmoha is the leader of the characters obstructing the path of Puruṣa's attainment of the Final Bliss.

Major Characters

Viveka

(The Hero of the Drama)

First of all, it should be understood that King Viveka is portrayed as *Dhīrodātta* type of hero in the drama. This point however is suggested by the dramatist himself in the beginning and at the end of the drama.[2] *Dhīrodātta* or the hero of sublime qualities, is one who is *Mahāsattva* or one whose mind does not get disturbed by grief, anger, greed lust etc.), *Atigambhīra* (very sincere boasting), *Kṣmāvān* (Patient), *Avikatthana* (not given to boasting), *Sthira* (of firm resolve), *Nigudhā-haṅkāra* (whose self-conceit is concealed due to his modesty), *Dṛdhavrata* (one who accomplishes the work undertaken.)[3] The Hero thus equipped may take into his service, ministers of state and others who can help in the accomplishment of the goal.

In the present context, the role of the King Viveka is portrayed, showing to have possessed all these qualities of *Dhīrodātta* type of hero. The dramatist gives more prominence to the role of Viveka, because all stratagies and the actions thereof relating to the goal, *i.e.* the rise of the will of the Lord, find directly or indirectly the place in him. Therefore, all the scenes in the play centre round King Viveka. There could be some obstacles brought about by the rival hero, Mahāmoha and his supporters, still they see the end in miserable failure, due to the irresistible force of Viveka and Saṅkalpa.

So far as Viveka's geneology is concerned, the drama expresses that Buddhi, the devoted wife of Puruṣa (Individual Self) endowed with the three qualities *Sattva, Rajas* and *Tamas,* gave birth to three families each at a time. When one or other of Puruṣa's three qualities was predominant in him. The first family consisted of Viveka and others who are averse to his pleasures and pains in life, and the other two of and Rāga and Mahāmoha who have joined their forces together being associated respectively with *Rajas* and *Tamas.*[4]

As Rati tells, Viveka is invincible foe of Mahāmoha. He is entrenched in the strong and rugged fortress *Vairāgya,* and is guarded by his ever-watchful ministers like Śama, Dama etc. He is a warrior that needs no ally and is possessed of infallible darling.[5]

As Kāma remarks, Viveka is free from all doubts, has studied the Vedānta Philosophy thoughtfully and reads about those observances leading to *Mokṣa.* He has cultivated the virtues like self-control, and guards his policies from being known to others (practising in secret the repetition of *Aṣṭākṣara*), and is always trying to understand the Gītā with unstinted devotion. Like the Sun who having just risen, is endowed with brilliant deep-red colour, and proceeding westwards with his light in the sky, dispels the mist, Viveka too, cultivating the bright virtue of introspection in the form of Sumati and entertaining the deepest and staunchest love of God though in prosperity, keeps *Ahaṅkāra* under perfect control and seeks the feet of the Lord.[6]

Viveka is characterised as a man of pure wisdom. Sumati asks Viveka about the means of Liberation. In response to this, Viveka gives a clear picture of the philosophy of Viśiṣṭādvaita in essence : "Like a child possessed by many evil spirits, Puruṣa, who is in the grip of lust, hatred and conceit, seeks the path trodden by the wise, when the Lord, the royal magician indicated in the Vidyās casts His glance on him. When Puruṣa bathes in the ambrosial stream of the glances of Guru of spotless character, various virtues like pure knowledge will ripen in him as sprouts for the state of release from *Saṁsāra*. And in Puruṣa who is dragged to and fro by the bonds of evil impressions, and longings for the pleasures of *Svarga* which are mingled with pains owing to the thought that (at some time or other) there must be a fall from there independently of his own will — in the individual self, *Bhakti* will appear by good luck towards his goal, namely the Supreme Being, who is, in the manifestation of His resistless compassion, like the ocean of milk."[7] "From Brahmā down to the blade of grass, it is only staunch devotion to the Supreme Person, the creator and Sustainer of Puruṣa, that will produce the end of all suffering. The seeker after *Mukti* who adores other deities, is like a fool who wants to quench his thirst, with drops of dew. Then, the night constituted of the three *guṇas* of *Prakṛti,* which keeps the Puruṣa in troubled and beginningless sleep, will disappear only by the splendour of the Sun, *i.e.* the will of the Lord, who slew the demon *Naraka.*"[8] Further, in the sacrifice of *Bhakti*, Puruṣa should give away all the wealth possessed by him as *Dakṣiṇā*. In this *Yajña,* Viveka together with his wife is *Yajamāna,* the great virtues — Śama, Dama and the rest are the *Ṛtviks* performing the priestly duties. The *Havis* is the *Jīva.* The Lord Himself is the *Devatā.* Thereby, the animal bound for the sacrifice (*i.e. Jīva*) will be freed from the fetters of *karma* and attain salvation."

"When Puruṣa performs this *Yajña, i.e. Prapatti,* which is of the nature of surrendering one's own protection to God, the Supreme Lord destroys all his sin so that it may not sprout again. Being well instructed by Guru he ascends the ladder of Lord's compassion. After complete working out the *Prārabdha karmas*, *Puruṣa* who has completely surrendered unto the Lord, attains liberation which is of pure *Śuddhasattva.*"[9]

King Viveka has such a grip over Viśiṣṭādvaita philosophy as to refute all rival schools. In the Second act, we find king Viveka entering into deputation with the votaries of Bauddha, Sāṅkhya, Yoga, Pāśupata, Vaiśeṣika, Nyāya schools and the Advaitins. With the able assistance of his marshall, king Viveka succeeds in putting all the rival schools to silence.

Viveka is pictured as *Jitakrodha* or as having won anger. Though Viveka is condemned as decietful, sinner etc. by Kāma and Vasanta, he does not get angry. Rather he says that — because of the effect of the ointment of delusion, in others men mind faults which do not exist even, and cannot see the good in them although it does exist. Just as the reverse is their perception concerning themselves.[10]

In the *third act,* an envoy of Mahāmoha approaches Viveka and reads out the message of his lord : "If you should disobey the orders, you will be attacked by your wrathful foes, Krodha, and others, who will rush against you at the dance-like knitting of our brow, and you will then cease to be."[11] Listening to these words, Viveka quietly says that "this is indeed a blessing to us for having been ever devoted to our *dharma*."[12] Here Viveka's capacity of finding a merit on others' demerit is really remarkable. At the same time he shows another face of anger saying that — Righteous indignation is not a sin, for it is praised by those who know the real truth, as being necessary for winning Krodha."[13]

Viveka being a king possesses right thinking power for future. In the sixth Act, Viveka explains the glory of all holy places like Meru, Kailāsa, Gandhamādana, Himālaya, Vindhyā mountain, Ayodhyā, Mathurā, Vāraṇāsī, Yādavācala, Nārāyanādri, Malaya mountain, Pāṇḍya country, Coḷa country, Śrīraṅgam and Veṅkaṭācalam. He observes these places whether they are fit places for meditation. But at last for one or the other reason, he regarded those places not suitable for Puruṣa's firm meditation. This indicates Viveka's far-sighted thought.

When Puruṣa is attacked by the evil forces, he falls into a pitiable condition. Seeing this, Sumati sometimes expresses her doubt as to whether they could liberate Puruṣa from the clutches of *Saṁsāra*. In such contexts also, Viveka remains patient and asks Sumati the same, filling courage in her heart.[14]

Viveka appears in the drama throughout as *Sthira* or steady in his accomplishments. He does not yield to any evil influence of Mahāmoha and his assistant. Rather he makes his assistants like Sumati firm in carrying out their duties.

Viveka as a valiant hero-king, applies stratagies of Polity like *Sāma, Dāma, Bheda* and *Daṇḍa,* but does not jump at drastic action. In this vein there is a reference to Viveka sending the envoy called *Dṛṣṭapratyaya* with peace-treaty to Mahāmoha. It runs thus : "From his residence in his pleasure-resort in *Śvetadvīpa,* King Viveka, whose conduct is extolled even by the gods, greets king Mahāmoha and informs him thus : The low are fond of quarrels but the good always desire peace. Surrender to us all the people living in the Southern Regions until the end of *Kaliyuga*. Enjoy without any interference from us all the rest consisting of plants and animals. In this way, by your accepting these terms, let there be peace between us, so that our race may not perish. Our words are ever true and our intentions honourable."[15] This scroll points to Viveka's being righteous and firm.

Though Viveka becomes victorious over Mahāmoha finally by his own power, he entertains no egotism, but expresses his sense of modesty. Thus speaks : "The origin of all the world, its maintenance, its dissolution — these proceed in the form of a regular stream and form the *Līlā* of the Lord. Like a blade of *Kuśa* grass discharged with the utterance of the respective mantra so as to make it a missile, I was only an instrument in the Lord's hands for causing the distruction of those who had to be slain by me."[16] Listening to this, Vyavasāya extols that the greatness of his modesty excels even his prowess. Thus it characterises Viveka as *Niguḍhāhaṅkārī* or free from egotism.

Viveka, the hero of valour possesses exclusive power to destroy Kāma, Krodha etc. In the fourth and fifth acts, readers can see Viveka taking up a brave fight with the evil forces of Mahāmoha, and ultimately they are defeated. Viveka marches ahead in the battle against Mahāmoha. He displays his excellance in archery by discharging appropriate weapons against those of Mahāmoha. This is clear from the closing part of the eighth act.[17]

Even doing the fight against Mahāmoha, Viveka did not get hesitated; but with all enthusiasm and courage without loosing self-reliance, he fights with Mahāmoha and becomes victorious. This shows his being *dṛḍhavrata* or confident of his work undertaken.

Even after getting victory, Viveka does not sit idle. He goes on making efforts till Puruṣa gets liberation. After choosing the right place for Puruṣa's meditation Viveka provides proper guidance to him for getting himself engrossed in *Sāmadhi.*

He prescribes consorted and assidious efforts that Puruṣa practises cultivation of intense Viṣṇubhakti which would lead to the attainment of *Sāmadhi.* Thus, Viveka remains always wakeful till Puruṣa attains liberation.

In this manner, the essential qualities of a *Dhīrodātta* hero are seen in Viveka. So, that he may be crowned as the hero of the drama.

Sumati

Sumati is the *Nāyikā* or the Heroine of this drama. Heroine must be possessed of the qualities similar to that of the Hero. She is of three kinds. They are I. *Nāyikā* : 1. *Svakīya,* 2. *Parakīya* and 3. *Sādhāraṇa.* Of these three *Svakīya* type of Heroine is the wife of hero and possesses the qualities like *vinaya, ārjava* and *pātivratya* etc. The heroine of this drama Sumati can be said as possessive all such qualities and that is why she may be said to be the first type of heroine.[18]

Sumati represents right thinking or understanding. This virtue is essential for acquiring *vairāgya* leading to *sāmadhi.* In the drama, she is portrayed as ably and timely assisting king Viveka in his attacking king Mahāmoha and his followers and winning a victory over them.

Queen Sumati is firm in her conviction. She does not sustain to know the condemnation of Viveka by Vasanta,

Kāma and Rati. For instance, Kāma condemns Viveka. "That prince of fools, Viveka, has suggested a path or *dharma* called *Nivṛtti* which has been followed by some cruel persons who live in the swamps of the Upaniṣads, and who want to practise the wiles of black magic against our race. This path or *dharma* called renunciation is supported by many perverse thoughts such as saying to oneself, "I am not the author of these actions of mine." We hear that a person who follows this path falls into a painful state in regard to such things as looking into other's faults, like one who is blind, deaf, impotent, lame and dumb."[19]

To this Sumati wisely responds that ugly persons attribute the ugliness of their own face to mirrors, clear though they are.[20] In fact Viveka is a little despondent as a result of these harsh words spoken about him. It is at this appropriate time that Sumati displays her courage of conviction. She points out to Viveka the line of right understanding. Viveka having realised the value of Sumati's words, comes out spontaneously with the priceless attributes of Sumati : '*Yathārthadarśanī, Yathārthavādinī.*'[21] "What you say is quite true, my dear, You see the truth always, and speak of just what you have seen well :

"Like the composition of a good poet, faultless in words and grammar, and capable of representing the different aims of life, which is beautiful with stylistic qualities like lucidity and sublimity, with figures of speech like similes and metaphors, with depth of emotions and the sentiments (or *rasas*) arising from a description of them, like good poetry, you are spotless and ever bent on attaining the supreme end of life, and like it, you too possess noble qualities and ornaments and display noble emotions."

In another context, Sumati expresses pity on Puruṣa who is likely to fall a prey to king Mahāmoha's forces.

"How was Puruṣa who, in his essential nature, is eternal, supremely blissful, spotless, and radiant, thrown by Mahāmoha, Conceit, Pride, Hatred and others into the ocean of sorrow, dreadful owing to the impact against one another of the great waves of sin mingled with resistless arrogance."[22]

Viveka, speaks the virtues of Sumati stating that: My keen-eyed queen ! How can we reject what is actually perceived ? How can we disbelieve what is said in the Śāstras ?[23]

On the contrary sometimes Sumati expresses a doubt regarding Puruṣa's attainment of Salvation. "I am troubled at heart, my lord, with misgivings. In the beginningless past, *Mokṣa* was never attained before. How and by whom, then can it be attained in the future which too, is endless"? [24]

Though imbude with right understanding, Sumati being Sumati (knowing *Paramārtha*) looses hope on Puruṣa's progress in attaining *samādhi.* But this apprehension is only baseless. Because she represents womanhood or *Prakṛti tattva.* On such occasions she is made to realise her role in the path of realisation, by her spouse. Sumati has sheer sympathy for Puruṣa's pitiable condition. She therefore wants to make him free from the clutches of *saṁsāra.* Therefore, she asks Viveka the way of realisation. Responding to this king Viveka says :

"My dear ! You are always desirous of seeing others happy. I will explain clearly the reason for all this, In doing so, I shall only be reminding you of what you already know."

"This cycle of births and deaths called *Saṁsāra* arises from the fruition of sinful deeds done in the past and is of resistless and firmness. It afflicts the *Jīvātma* and cannot be easily put down, being all powerful. There is only one thing that can stop its flow and that is the might of *Īśvara*'s independent resolve, combined with His natural compassion and this satisfies itself by finding a pretext of *vyāja* (for the *Jīva*'s deliverance)."[25]

Sumati is confident of winning success in the fight between her spouse and Mahāmoha. Addressing Viveka she assures :

"My Lord, just as the Great Boar lifted the earth sunk in the waters of the ocean during *Pralaya*, so too, you, my lord, have to lift Puruṣa sunk in the sea of *Saṁsāra*. I should like to say this also. I am eager to see your skill in battle similar to that of the Great Boar whose snout rang with the sound of the stream of thick blood flowing from the chest of Hiraṇyākṣa torn by His tusk as from a rugged doorway."[26] Vyavasāya endorses Sumati's opinion : देवि, सेत्स्यति खलु मङ्गल्यनिधेर्भवत्या मान्यं समीहितं — "Surely your noble desire will (soon) be fulfilled."

Sumati contributes to Puruṣa's dedicated pursuit of *Samādhi*. She boosts up concerted and assidius efforts on the part of Puruṣa. Nārada points out this. That is "Viveka, the emperor, held in the highest esteem by Sumati, has himself, by his own *Sāttvika* nature, got rid of the bands of enemies, both external and internal. He knows how to distinguish between what is smooth (and proper) and what is uneven (and improper) and has created in Puruṣa superior mental condition."[27]

With Viveka, Sumati is equally responsible in achieving the goal. Sumati makes Viveka realise his responsibility of lifting Puruṣa up from sins and evil forces.

She adds "To a Yogī who is a man, there would be a natural attraction to something that resembles a man. My lord, just as the Lord saves the Vedas which had sunk in the ocean, you have lifted them up from the darkness of ignorance into which they had sunk. Are there other forms of the lord similar to this ?"[28]

Thus, Sumati plays her role till the emergence of Viveka to assist Puruṣa to obtain *Saṅkalpa*. She feels superme delight in the victory gained by her spouse, in the fight with Mahāmoha. Infact, she shares Supreme happiness on account of *Vivekodaya* and rise of *Saṅkalpa* in Puruṣa. When Viveka finds the completion of all preparations for *Samādhi,* he goes forward to see the place where Puruṣa is to take to *samādhi*. He happily says, thus : "This is Sumati's mansion, the mind of pure *sattva* from whose heights we can judge the strength of the texts in the Upaniṣads. Its glory is proclaimed by many authoritative passages and it is free from *Rajas* and *Tamas*."[29]

Puruṣa

Like Viveka, the role of Puruṣa too occupies a prominant place in the drama. Because the entire theme of the drama depends on Puruṣa's achievement of the goal. However, Puruṣa is personified as an Individual Soul.

Puruṣa is said to be the father of both Viveka and Mahāmoha. This relation of Puruṣa is expressed by Kāma– जनकश्चास्माकं क्षेत्रज्ञः स्वयं मध्यस्थस्वभावोऽपि सहधर्मचारिण्या देव्या बुद्ध्या सहाद्य यावदस्मासु बहुलं दत्तदृष्टिः । (I - p.99) Buddhi is the devoted wife of Puruṣa endowed with *Sattva, Rajas* and *Tamo guṇas.* She gave birth to three families each at a time, when one or the other of his three qualities, *Sattva, Rajas* and *Tamas* was predominant in him. Of these three families, *Sattva* family is the first family which consisted of Viveka and others, who are averse to pleasures and pains in life. And other two families dominating in *Rajoguṇa* and *Tamoguṇa* have joined their forces together, having the Mahāmoha as the leader.[30]

Being the son, Viveka always thinks good for his father

Puruṣa. That is why, Viveka makes all efforts to lift him up to the Salvation. But Mahāmoha possessing apposite nature to that of Viveka does not bear the activities of Viveka. Therefore, Kāma, one of the assistants to Mahāmoha considers Viveka's efforts as defective and as tormenting to Puruṣa. He says "Puruṣa will be like one born blind to the faults of others, supremely dumb in speaking ill of others, and in regard to listening to scandal, he will be like a great incarnation of deafness. He will be like a woman in the matter of seeking the wives of other men and in avoiding the reduction of women. He will avoid even looking at them like one bereft of the organs of sense."[31]

Virtually Puruṣa enjoys bliss by surrendering completely to the Lord.[32] But being by the fetters of *Saṁsāra* Puruṣa has to experience various sufferings brought upon by Mahāmoha etc. Somehow he should be made from these sufferings and should get him emancipation. This is however possible by *Samādhi* only. Naturally, these are many internal and external enemies obstructing Puruṣa's meditation. Puruṣa is very much deluded by the attractions of mundane world. As a result he has no much interest in meditation. Therefore Viveka says, his delusion should first be removed. Then internal enemies should be made flee away. Such a great work can be completed only by the grace of the Lord.[33]

Puruṣa in his essential nature, is eternal, Supremely blissful, spotless and self-effulgent. Yet being thrown by Mahāmoha, Mada and Matsara etc. into the ocean of sorrow. This is clear from the following statement of Viveka: "We often see the true and essential nature of objects given up by them owing to some circumstances brought about by fate when those circumstances disappear, they resume once again their original and true nature. So, this endless cycle of births and deaths called *Saṁsāra* obscures the true nature of

Puruṣa and (when the proper time comes) it will glide away also."[34]

It is further elaborated thus : "like a child possessed by many evil spirits, Puruṣa who is now in the grip of lust, hatred and conceit, will seek the path trodden by the wise, when the Lord, the royal magician indicated in the Vedas, casts His glance on him."[35]

Going a step ahead Viveka says as below : "Fortunate, indeed, are they who climb up the ladder of compassion placed (at their disposal) by the Lord of Lakṣmī and pointed out to them by Ācāryas as an unfailing means. Step by step they ascend and at last enjoy the bliss of that region which is built of pure *Śuddhasattva.*[36]

"This is certain that, for the attainment (by Puruṣa) of the boundless bliss (of *Mokṣa*) the Lord's unshakable compassion will arise either now (in the case of the *Prapanna*) or some time hence (in the case of the Bhakta) taking away the Lord's *Līlā* consisting in the desire to punish the *Jīva* for his sins and suggesting the means for that attainment, namely, *Prapatti* or *Bhakti*, which is delightful and wholesome."[37]

On the path of attaining the highest goal Puruṣa, has to execute the religious duties contributing to the pure knowledge of Brahman. Gradually, he has to perform his duties to please the Lord. Thereby devotion to the Lord makes its appearance in him. Then through the path of *Bhakti* Puruṣa is expected to meditate upon Brahman.[38]

Such Puruṣa considers the sweetness of sensual pleasures as illusory as the city of *Gandharvas* (cloud city). Gradually, he gets over his mental confusion and attains the state of an exclusive devotee of the Lord. He then leaps over the ocean of *Saṁsāra,* as if it were a near puddle caused by the feet of a cow.[39]

In spite of Puruṣa's unstinted devotion, he dreads the great fears of *Saṁsāra*; at the same time, he longs also for the home (and other pleasures); he is eager to attain Brahman and at the same time, has an eye for the prosperity (of *Saṁsāra*). He has a passion for the pleasures of the senses and is equally ashamed of them. So, his contemplation on the Supreme Brahman is both manifest and unmanifest, and is therefore in sure peril.[40]

Therefore, Puruṣa studies the treatises which deal with the causes of fear and also sleeps frequently; he has often a vision of his own self (apart from the body) and also satisfies his body duly. He desires the disappearance of the sea of sorrow and at the same time longs for the pleasures of life. Thus, my friend, being in conflict with two ideal Puruṣa is now sadly tossed to and fro as a swing.[41]

Being boosted up by the triumphs of Viveka "Puruṣa has now learnt to have a vision of his self as the result of a special form of meditation; he is unshakable owing to his control of the senses and other members of his body; he has (good) control of his breath and having given up all attachment to the things of the world, is practising the *dharma* of renunciation."[42]

Such Puruṣa is portrayed as bearing with patience, the pairs of opposites (like pleasure and pain, heat and cold); he has become quick to grasp (the truth of things). He sustains only what happens by mere chance to come to him without any effort of his and gives up what should be abandoned. Like the bee he has a taste now for imbibing the true essence of things. He is grateful (for the good done to him) and is firm in the pursuit of the supreme goal (of life). He delights in solitude and aspires for to *Mukti* and fixes his mind on Brahman without being distracted."[43]

Describing the picture of Puruṣa engrossed in

samādhi, Viveka says thus : "Ignored by the common run of men who are intoxicated with the liquor of sense-pleasures, in some place suitable for meditation and in times fit for it, Puruṣa now fixes his vision inward so as to behold the Supreme splendour that is within, with perfect control of his senses, and with inner joy, after subduing his vital breaths."[44] He adds further :

"With his hair standing straight on his body and with eyes overflowing with tears of joy, Puruṣa now enjoys the sweatness of *Samādhi* with his vision turned inward. It is certain that his progress to the (full) attainment of his aim which consists in the supreme glory of enjoying the great bliss called Brahman will hereafter meet with no impediments."[45]

Thus Puruṣa's aspiring for *Mokṣa* has become very strong. Due to the progressive development of *Samādhi* all sins ceased to exist. And whatever he performs being engrossed in *Samādhi*, all such activities yield the fruit of communion with the Lord.[46]

Even at this stage, attainment of *Mokṣa* gets impeded. It is due to the *Prarabdha karmas* yet to be got over by Puruṣa. Therefore, "the Puruṣa who was fettered in his movements by the undesirable chains called wives, sons, brothers and the like who are relatives in his imagination and who cannot be easily put away, has now placed the responsibility for his protection on the Lord who is by nature, his true well-wisher and (as a result of it) calmly awaits whatever happens to him, good or bad, as a blessing."[47]

All these details of Puruṣa's efforts to ascend the ladder of salvation have been explained through the roles like Viveka, Sumati, Viṣṇubhakti etc. Besides being intellectually backed up, Puruṣa actually enters the stage in the last scene of the Xth Act.

As he enters the stage, he broodes over his helpless condition, *i.e.*, he is nor a *Mukta* nor a *Baddha*. He does not know what he should do or he should refrain from?[48]

Puruṣa himself says that he is now without sins and endowed with virtues like Śama and Dama he spends his time in such *yajñas* as the meditation on the Supreme Being. Thus he is eagerly awaiting the time of fruition.[49]

As Puruṣa is endowed with deep *Śraddhā* or faith he is described as having a dialogue with the role named *Śraddhā*. Through their dialogue Puruṣa comes to know that he should approach Viṣṇubhakti. (another female character), who can lead him to *Mokṣa*.

At this juncture, *Saṅkalpa* describes the position of Puruṣa who possesses more love for devotees than for the highest Puruṣa. Therefore, he is asking the favour of devotees in the foregoing manner : "With our words which emit a fragrance that would be eagerly desired by the lotus which sprouted in the pond of the Lord's navel; we will not beg of the Lord the trifling pleasures of this world and of *Svarga* nor *Kaivalya*, nor even *Mokṣa*. We only pray that we should have the grace of the pure and firm-minded *Bhāgavatas*, who are like the chaste wives of the royal harem; for their grace is like the dawn which heralds the day of the splendour of *Mokṣa*"[50]

Keenly observing the status of Puruṣa *Saṅkalpa* says as follows :

"You are like the parrot the redness of whose beak can never disappear, whose wings are ever green in colour and which is in a cage made of strings. In order to make you fit to go to the world from which there is no return. I will now set you free from the cage of *Prakṛti* with its three *guṇas* as I set free the sage suka; for your love is immovably fixed on the Supreme. You maintain the doctrine that the Real called Hari is the Supreme Reality."[51]

Then Puruṣa approaches Viṣṇubhakti along with Viveka and Sumati. Viṣṇubhakti informs him, that after passing through *Prārabha karmas* Puruṣa leaves of his subtle body in the *virajā* river. Then he will attain the realm of Lord Viṣṇu. Puruṣa feels very much blessed by Viṣṇubhakti and others. He expresses his gratefulness to Viveka, Sumati and Viṣṇubhakti. He then follows his final journey to *vaikuṇṭha.*

Viṣṇubhakti then informs the audiance that "In one of the holy places where the Lord has Himself revealed His presence or in a wilderness, whether it be in a holy place or an impure spot, wherever the *Prapannas* have cast off their body in accordance with the decree of fate, Mukunda whose glory is proclaimed in the Vedānta will lift up these pure *Prapannas* and lead them to the security of His own abode."[52] She says further : "And now the Lord, who has the whole universe for His body and who is absolutely free from all that is impure, has decided to lead the saintly Puruṣa along the road to His own city from which there is no return to *Saṁsāra.*"[53]

At last, Viveka expresses his joy to see Puruṣa, who is free from all stain like the moon freed from Rāhu. Puruṣa being purified of all his sins, has taken the route to *Paramapada* from which there is no return.

The nature of this *Paramapada* is thus described : "The (black) ointment of *Prakṛti* with its three *guṇas* will be washed off your soul. Owing to Puruṣa's adoration of Brahman with auspicious qualities, he will manifest the possession of the eight qualities (sinless and the rest) and attains supreme resemblance to Brahman but will never lose sight of the marks of difference between the Supreme self and his own self. And finally Puruṣa becomes vouchsafed the privilege of being a servant to the Lord, even like Ādiśeṣa and others as long as Puruṣa exist for ever."[54]

This is the fruition of Puruṣa's deeds prompted by Viveka and others. In this way, in the whole of the drama, Puruṣa's role finds scope in each and every scene. He is portrayed as a predominant character.

Vyavasāya

(Commander-in-chief of Viveka)

The character of Vyavasāyain the drama is portrayed by Vedānta Deśika as the commander-in-chief of king Viveka. Vyavasāya's duty is to maintain discipline and to keep up the determination of the mind of Puruṣa in order to make him reach the goal. Though Vyavasāya appears in second, seventh and ninth Acts of the drama, the effects of his systematic plans have spread all over the drama.

For the first time Vyavasāya appears on the stage in the second Act. Puruṣa is found as being fettered by the noose of *karma*. As a result all his activities render fruitless. He is wielded by Mahāmoha. Observing this condition of Puruṣa, Viveka has made on oath to make him free from the bondage of *Saṁsāra*. Viveka feels Vyavasāya's help necessary in fulfilling his oath. Therefore, he asks Vyavasāya his help. At this juncture, Vyavasāya makes a remark seeing the condition of Puruṣa. It is that however Viveka has blessed Puruṣa with the knowledge of Vedānta. But due to the surrounding atmosphere of other systems of philosophy, Puruṣa's faith in the knowledge of Vedānta is shaken of. Therefore, Vyavasāya suggests to the king that the renewal of Puruṣa's want of faith should be done.[55]

Viveka feels happy to see Vyavasāya's insight to find out the lacicites.

However Vyavasāya follows Viveka in all his activities just like a shadow. He does not entertain any kind of self-respect. He says, he is simply an instrument for use against the enemies like weapons. This shows his modesty.

Vyavasāya is an adept in Vedānta Philosophy. He is confident of getting victory in philosophical discussions. He ably assists Viveka in choosing right Guru and Śiṣya for *Saṁvāda*; because he is aware of propriety in this circumstance. He receives the due compliment from the Guru which may be cited below :

"Vyavasāya, the worthy Commander-in-chief of Viveka, stands here with wise and learned men revealing himself to those who are on his side."[56]

Vyavasāya considers ego (I) as condemnable. Therefore, he avoids such scenes where ego is reflected.

"Enough of these vain and false boasts which would be approved of only by immature minds intoxicated with each other's praise but which would be condemned by an assembly of spotless renown. Your activities are sure to be crippled if you should attempt to follow in the foot steps of eminent disputants."[57]

With his efficiency in putting down the rival shools, he upholds Viśiṣṭādvaita :

"The tip of the Ācārya's tongue shines bright — being the throne on which is seated Hayagrīva. So, we do not consider any deity higher than the Ācārya. Even Nārāyaṇa plays the part of the Ācārya without ever giving up His Supreme greatness in order to save those who are sunk in the sea of *Saṁsāra*."[58]

Vyavasāya possesses firm faith in the Guru. Therefore, he emphatically declares thus :

"What a man obtains from a single glance or two of the Ācārya cannot be obtained from any one ele's three or eight or even a thousand eyes."[59]

Vyavasāya always keeps his eye on the philosophical discussions and makes a significant remark causing awareness in the mind of Viveka. It can be witnessed by his words as below :

"Like the Jains, they, too, being unable to endure the words of our friend are trying to promote faith in their system by some deceitful trick like causing rains out of season."[60]

In the seventh act, As per the command of Viveka, Vyavasāya asks *Saṁskāra* to draw the picture of the Universe on the wall of the mind. The painting seen in this picturescroll, of the past and future, appear to us without exception just like present events. Because they have been depicted with full faith in authorities or *Pramāṇas* like the Vedas and *Purāṇas.*

Vyavasāya remarks that such picture should not be seen by Puruṣa. Because he is expected to concentrate his mind on the *Vibhūtis* of the Lord. It is clear from his words as below :

"This ocean of *Prakṛti* with its three *guṇas* (*Sattva, rajas* and *tamas)* is not fit to be seen by those who aspire to yoga, for it is inhabited by foolish creatures like the tortoise, the shark and the crocodile which live in a state of incessant change going into and coming out of the islands of various objects of sense, and which live in constant fear of one another."[61]

Thus, Vyavasāya awakens Puruṣa at times wherever necessary.

In some other context, Vyavasāya is portrayed as knowing the secret of Vedānta. Therefore, seeing the picturescroll he reproduces the gist of the *Bhagavad-gītā*, *i.e.* "the Supreme Being whose teaching is authoritative says in the Bhagavad-Gītā that those who understand the secret of Lords incarnations will attain the Supreme and will not be born again."

Vyavasāya possesses an unique quality of glorifying others merits, which is of course regarded as one of the virtues of a gentle man.[62]

Here his glorification of the ability of Saṁskāra is noteworthy :

"Neither Māyā nor Viśvakarmā, nor any other, nor even Brahmā, the mighty creator of the universe, can, by his skill paint this picture (of *Nityavibhūti* or *Paramapada*). It is the Lord Himself, the consort of Lakṣmī, the first architect of the boundless Brahmāṇḍa that has painted this picture of what belongs to Himself."[63]

In the similar manner, Viveka describes different forms of the Lord's incarnations like *Kūrma, Matsya, Varāha* etc. He gives here the significance of each of the *avatāras* thereby highlights the importance of respective incarnations of the Lord. It clearly indicates Vyavasāya's depth of knowledge in *Purāṇas.* Finally, towards the end of the seventh Act, Vyavasāya suggests to the king that Puruṣa can take up his meditation in any one of these forms of incarnations. So, that his meditation definitely yields the desired fruit.

Vyavasāya in the ninth Act, is shown to be submissive though quite competent to do everything independently in favour of Viveka.

After Viveka's victory Vyavasāya remarks that he and

others are merely instruments in Viveka's hands like the vehicles Viveka rides in each and every aspect of victory, the principle part is played by his master.[64]

Vyavasāya sets the ground well prepared for action to be taken up by Viveka. He again enters the stage in the ninth Act in order to provide greater confidence to his master in the ensuing combat with Mahāmoha. He says emphatically that '*Avidyā*' has no place in the presence of Viveka and that successful yoga graced by *Saṅkalpa* is sure to make Puruṣa attain *Samādhi.*

In short, Vyavasāya graced by *Saṅkalpa* is indispensable for attainment of success and salvation. However, there is also sufficient truth in the brief that "Divine grace will alight only on him who has by his meritorious life and sustained effort, qualified himself and deserved it." It may be mentioned again that this is like a golden thread through which the entire play is woven. This aspect is evident by use of the epithet Vāsudeva at the end of the play by the author.

Thus, it is evident that whenever Puruṣa being commonly bound by the noose of *karma*. He loses right understanding and so he suffers a lot. It is in this context that Vyavasāya plays his role. He kindles in the Puruṣa an inclination to acquire right understanding, which ultimately makes him realise the Lord. With his penetration into mental furniture of the Puruṣa, the forces of king Mahāmoha gradually falls out. Thus, he assures king Viveka winning the final victory in the fight with king Mahāmoha and his forces. In fine, on the path of Puruṣa's realisation of Highest Truth, Vyavasāya stands out as a torch-bearer.

Saṅkalpa

The role of Saṅkalpa is the crest of all characters;

because in the absence of which the drama becomes insignificant. In general terms, *Saṅkalpa* means Resolve; but in the play, it has a significant meaning of God's grace or resolve which is sure to shower result. This is the most indispensable principle and doctrine inculcated in the drama. Divine grace is essential to obtain salvation which has been very graphically broughtout in the play. In any undertaking, human effort is necessary. But without Divine grace, such effort cannot be fruitful. The doctrine of *Saṅkalpa* is the central norm of *Prapatti* or self-surrender. This is the consequence of the final *Sāttvikatyāga*.

The very title of the play has the prefix '*Saṅkalpa*', which brings out the importance of the character. The emergence of *Saṅkalpa* is very essential to wipe out the ignorance just as the rise of the Sun dispels the darkness. The following *Nāndi* verse brings out this import.

"May Śrīman Nārāyaṇa (Nārāyaṇa with His Consort Śrī) be pleased to convey me over all the ills (of life) — Nārāyaṇa whose will like sunrise dispels at once the night of *Saṁsāra* (or the recurring cycle of births and deaths), who is capable of being seen by the *Jīva* (or embodied soul) when its deep devotion has attained to the state of the dawn of day — Nārāyaṇa whose supremacy is self-dependent and eternal, arising, as it does, from His missiles and ornaments which are symbolic of the various *tattvas* or 'reals' of the Universe."[65]

In other words, human effort and attainment of requisite eligibility from the stage to the other, are necessary for ultimate success. But they can be acquired by God's *Saṅkalpa*. The two factors — Human effort and Divine grace are interdependent. They are not also related as cause and effect. In reality, the inscrutable divine grace emerges in the case of a Puruṣa who is fit to receive it by his meritorious life and sustained effort which qualify him to attain salvation. That is why this character is depicted as the golden thread throughout the drama, though he appears on the stage in the last act of the play. Thus, *Saṅkalpa* is required at every step to Liberation. Hence, the character of *Saṅkalpa* moves unseen upto the tenth Act, and appears on the stage in the tenth Act where it is necessary.

Saṅkalpa is necessary not only for salvation but fruitful for everything. This is not a belief in fatalistic doctrine, but in life in general, it is often cited that not even grass moves without *Saṅkalpa*. (तेन विना तृणमपि न चलति।) Therefore, the wise persons say one's efforts bear the fruit by God's *Saṅkalpa* itself.

The play commences with the Keynote character, *i.e.* *Saṅkalpa*; and concludes with the epithet of Nārāyaṇa, Vāsudeva, whose *Saṅkalpa* is absolutely necessary for the attainment of salvation. The dramatist has meaningfully used this term to indicate the fullest satisfaction in achieving the goal and also blessing with good, both the listners and reciters.

The beneficial impact of *Saṅkalpa* is declared by Viṣṇubhakti. To quote :

"How wonderful ! all the quarters of the world and all the intermediate quarters shine with a brilliant light. It looks as if *Saṅkalpa* of the Lord, who is the lover of compassion is approaching."[66]

Infact he stands for the mental activity. "In the *Pañcarātra-Āgamas*, it is declared that the equipment *(Sannāha)* and resolve (*Saṅkalpa*) of Hari the saviour of the world, appear as visible manifestations in the form of Garuḍa and Sudarśana respectively."[67]

Another verse cited below describes the resultant benefit of Saṅkalpa by the efforts of Viṣṇubhakti.

"With the help of the Lord's divine Compassion, I will prompt *Saṅkalpasūrya* (the Lord's resolve or Will) to take the necessary action for the salvation of Puruṣa, for He is always beneficient and disposed to grant my desires."[68] Because she is everything when joined by *Saṅkalpa* while she is effete in His absence.

The following verse is an evidence to this aspect of *Saṅkalpa*.

"I am the Lord's *Saṅkalpasūryodaya* (the Sunrise of His resolve to save man). When there is the slightest manifestation of me, whose glory is of astonishing greatness, this world, pure and impure, attains, all at once, *Mokṣa* and *Svarga*. All sentient beings are in sound slumber in the great night of *Māyā* (*Prakṛti*) and are in such a state that they can be said merely to exist, and this night of *Māyā* is not like the night which comes at the end of the day, for it is continuous and has no break or interval and it is I who am capable of waking them up from that (death - like) sleep."[69]

Saṅkalpa is secured as a result of pure meditation of the Supreme Being. In support of this aspect of *saṅkalpa*, the prose portion is worth citing here :

"By the Goddess Lord's compassion, whose favour was won by the practice of pure meditation of the Supreme Being who is pleased to reward Puruṣa and who is attended upon by other noble qualities, I have been ordered : Puruṣa has now become glorious as a result of the endeavours of Viveka, the conqueror of Moha and others, whose activities receive their guidance from me."[70]

The prowess of *Saṅkalpa* is remarkable. Among many of his accomplishments, mention may be made of vanguishing Madhu and Kaiṭabha, and saving the heaven and earth from Hiraṇyākṣa and Hiraṅyakaśipu.[71]

"I will now instantly wake up Puruṣa from the sleep (ignorance) which had no beginning, and create in him a state of awakening (knowledge) which will have no end."[72]

But the most relevant exploit of His is to awaken Puruṣa from deep sleep (adhyāsa) to self-realisation.

Saṅkalpa is capable of releasing Puruṣa from the bondage of *Saṁsāra*. "Puruṣa has placed his burden on Him with full faith (*Bharanyāsa*) and dedication, and has now steadily fixed his mind on the middle path, namely, that of performing *nitya* and *naimittika karmas,* without any desire for the fruits thereof. He has turned back from the performance of those *Kāmya karmas* which are sinful and hence dangerous. By his glory resulting from the compassion of the Lord, he has got rid of his sins. I will therefore deliver him (from *Saṁsāra*).[73]

Saṅkalpa has respect for Viṣṇubhakti when she prostrates. *Saṅkalpa* lifts her up with all affection and regard. He is an object of adoration to her.

Saṅkalpa carries sometimes his own doubts about Puruṣa's eligibility to attain *Mokṣa.* Because he is aware that Puruṣa is involved in obtaining wordly pleasures which is a common trait from the birth of the Universe, i.e. *Saṅkalpa* desires to put Puruṣa to test before finally conferring the blessing on him. However, Viṣṇubhakti suggests to *Saṅkalpa* not to entertain such doubts about Puruṣa. Further Viṣṇubhakti makes it clear that Puruṣa has abandoned all pleasures and happiness of heaven and has surrendered completely to Nārāyaṇa. He is therefore considered as worthy of *Saṅkalpa's* boon.

After carefully putting this Puruṣa to observation, *Saṅkalpa* is convinced of his eligibility to receive the boon from him. This causes confidence in Viṣṇubhakti.

Lord Nārāyaṇa is symbolised in the character of *Saṅkalpa*:

"Most noble sir, I am, indeed, the resolve or will of the Supreme Person (to save man). You are the foremost of those who are solely and exclusively devoted to the Lord. By the Lord's compassion who is His beloved spouse, and who is always full of affection towards the weak and helpless, I have been ordered to see that you are released from the two kinds of endless fetters, called, *Puṇya* and *Pāpa,* and to enrich you with the wealth arising from ripe and perfect *bhakti* extending up to the service of the Supreme Person who adorns the heavenly couch (in *Paramapada*). I have long been eager to see your honoured self and am now come to you. Therefore, be free from all fears and doubts concerning the treasure of *Mokṣa* which is close at hand."[74]

To such a Puruṣa, *Saṅkalpa* has all admiration and eagerly assures him of the salvation. In turn Puruṣa is grateful to *Saṅkalpa*.

Conferring the boon of salvation on Puruṣa in present context is not a mere concern of *Saṅkalpa*. He also symbolises perennial keeping up of traditional set up by such a Puruṣa, before and after. So, he makes an open declaration almost at the end of the play that this tradition is to suffer no break at all in the future :

"The high-souled Puruṣa, who has surrendered his self to the Lord, the treasure of the *Śrutis,* is now on the face of the earth, He sees all things (at a single glance).

Therefore, let those men of wide intelligence who would like to be his disciples learn all truths from him with care and attention by putting questions to him just as they please."[75]

Viṣṇubhakti

Viṣṇubhakti is also one of the important characters in the play. Devotion to Lord Viṣṇu is here personified as Viṣṇubhakti. Viṣṇubhakti's entrance on the stage is suggested by king Viveka in the concluding portion of the ninth Act. Due to Viṣṇubhakti's arrival, resplendant rays of her are spread over everywhere. Gazing this king Viveka eagerly says that she has the loveliness of a flood of pure nectar, and appears to be the deity of *Śvetadvīpa* as it were. As king describes her glory :

"She is Viṣṇubhakti who is like a branch of the Kalpaka tree in granting all our prayers for obtaining what we desire and is adored by hosts of *Siddhas* whose minds are pure and who cherish no other interests than the attainment of the Lord. She illumines all the quarters up to their extremest limits with the abundance of her radiance and is now entering the pure mansion of Sumati (the mind)."[76]

The tenth Act, however begins with the entrance of Viṣṇubhakti herself. As Viṣṇubhakti enters the stage she introduces herself in the following manner :

"I entertain myself with the graceful dance of service to the Lord and with the proud and exalted dance of removing all sins."[77]

"My mother is the spotless understanding of Puruṣa; my father is Puruṣa who is ever bent on *dharma*. Contentment is my sister, forbearance is my consort and righteous conduct is my servant, who ever does my bidding. I am myself Vidyā (being *Bhakti* or *Upāsanā*) and my sport consists in destroying the sins of the world. I am Viṣṇubhakti and live changeless and I feel sure that *Saṁsāra* will come to an end."[78]

She also says that she declares a truth that has been

stated by great sages who have gained direct vision of the Lord.

Further Viṣṇubhakti referred to as one who helps Puruṣa in getting rid of all sins and makes himself eligible for liberation.

"Puruṣa, who is eagerly thirsty for *Mukti*, and who is in the grip of such classes of enemies as the senses, the body, sons, wives and the like, which are in reality the products of sins, should be released (from these bonds) by me alone, for I am the *Līlā* of Lord's grace."[79] She gives her opinion that when, with the help of Divine compassion, she would prompt *Saṅkalpasūrya* to take the necessary action for the salvation of Puruṣa.

It is here clear that without the support of Lord's compassion, Viṣṇubhakti cannot get Puruṣa anything else.[80]

Viṣṇubhakti has high regard for Garuḍa, the chariot of Lord Nārāyaṇa. She glorifies earnestly Garuḍa at length. An example of Garuḍa's praise will be given here :

"May the gambols of the Lord of Birds in his childhood which consisted in sportive flights in the interior of Brahmāṇḍa from the nether world, pātāla, upwards to the top of the mansion of Brahmā, may these gambols help to remove our suffering ! (When he played as a child in this manner) the mountains were broken to pieces, the four oceans were convulsed and his wings were wet with their water. The stars in the sky looking like garlands were split and scattered and the abodes of the gods were turned topsy-turvy."[81]

As *Saṅkalpa* observes Viṣṇubhakti is cherished by those. "Viṣṇubhakti, shines as white in complexion as the wave of nectar. Her hair always stands on end (owing to her deep devotion) and she sheds copious tears of joy. She has given up all attachment (to worldly things) and is ever singing hymns with falttering accents. In the excessive joy (of her devotion) she dances and is absolutely free from the fear of hell."[82]

"She is here seated in the chariot of her mind with full control of her senses that are like horses and with *Śānti* or spiritual serinity."[83]

Saṅkalpa expresses his joy to see greatness of Viṣṇubhakti. He says that "She is cherished by those who are endowed with spiritual serenity and the source of the ripe fruit of the creeper of knowledge. She is indeed, the perfect development of the *Śrutis* and the abiding place of purity. She is the guarantee of heavenly bliss and the dawn that dispels the fear of *Saṁsāra*. She is also the lamps that illumines the truths concerning all things, high and low. Addressing her as revered Lady of devotion to Hari he exclaims that she is like a divine ornament to the *Ātmā* or self.[84]

Though Puruṣa is qualified for attaining *Mokṣa, Saṅkalpa* doubts about his efficiency. In this context, Viṣṇubhakti says that whatever has happened in the past and is to happen in the future, remains as a witness. Therefore, she is eager to cut off the knot of *Saṁsāra* of Puruṣa. Viṣṇubhakti says, she will now perform *Abhigamana* and other daily rites and take with me the eight flowers and proceed in the company of Viveka who is solely devoted to you. By *Saṅkalpa's* prowess, all his past sins have been destroyed and his future transgressions will not stain him. He now worships the lords and no other and meditates on no one but the Lord. He is now exceedingly glad to know that efforts are being made for his attainment of external bliss."[85]

Viṣṇubhakti knows Puruṣa's merits and his efforts to

attain liberation. Therefore, whenever Viveka becomes anxious to see Puruṣa's condition, Viṣṇubhakti gives him a support and tells something convincingly in favour of Puruṣa, *i.e.*

"This is not the time for your majesty to feel depressed. Today Puruṣa's sea of sins of which only the *karma* that had begun to yield its fruit in this birth remained, has been made to dry up by the Lord's *Saṅkalpa* as by the fire at the end of a *kalpa. Prakṛti,* too, like the serpent's slough, will be cast off by Puruṣa who will then become as pure as Ādiśeṣa and this shedding of *Prakṛti* will take place at the end of this life and in the region beyond *Tamas*, *i.e.* in *Paramapada*".[86]

Towards the end of the tenth Act, contemplating something on herself, Viṣṇubhakti suggests that Puruṣa is following the path; from which there is no return to *Saṁsāra*, *i.e.* "Having passed the stage of indebtedness to the gods, the *ṛṣis*, animals, *pitṛs*, and mankind, and having been granted freedom from fear by the Lord's compassion, with firm and deep devotion to the Lord, he will soon reach the supreme Abode of the Lord which has already been occupied by our *Gurus*."[87]

Thus, the role of Viṣṇubhakti is the ultimate stage of Puruṣa's attainment is seen very important. It is she who lifts Puruṣa up to lead the path to Lord's realm of *Vaikuṇṭha*. Though appears to be a minor character, Viṣṇubhakti carries her responsibility of making Puruṣa reach the point of culmination — in the last moment. Hence, Viṣṇubhakti is not necessarily a minor character in the drama.

Minor Characters
(Supporters of Viveka)

There are some other minor characters who help and support at appropriate time to Puruṣa, Viveka and to Sumati.

They are Śraddhā and Vicāraṇā, Vedānta Siddhānta (Guru) and Vāda (Śiṣya), Tarka, Saṁskāra, Śama, Dṛṣṭapratyaya, Nārada and Tumburu.

Śraddhā and Vicāraṇā

Śraddhā and Vicāraṇā are the female assistants to Sumati. The conversation between these two characters form the *Praveśaka* of the second Act. In the beginning Vicāraṇā asks Śraddhā as to why she is in a hurry. She replies that king Viveka has concentrated his mind on the doctrines of Upaniṣads; but he is obstructed by Mahāmoha. Sumati is engaged in an *pūjā* to propitiate goddess Lakṣmī, desiring victory over Mahāmoha. Therefore she said, she is ordered by Sumati to bring golden lotuses for *pūjā* from the banks of Gaṅges. Thus Śraddhā is rushing to that place. Similarly Śraddhā too asks Vicāraṇā for 'what have you come for' ? Vicāraṇā replies that she is to see Vyavasāya and to request him to watch the movements of enemies representing rival schools of thought, sent by Mahāmoha to destroy the efforts of Viveka and his military arrangements. Thus, the dialogue between these two characters suggests the scene of philosophical discussion to take place.

In the tenth Act, Śraddhā again appears to give courage and support to Puruṣa in his attainment of *samādhi*. In turn, Puruṣa seeks the help of Śraddhā and asks her to convey to Viṣṇubhakti his eagerness and to attain liberation.

It should be noted here that Śraddhā in the tenth Act, may be considered as different from that who is seen in the second Act. Because, so far as the context and force in the tenth Act is concerned, Śraddhā may be portrayed as the Personification of faith. As such she awakens Puruṣa and Puruṣa too asks her help in his endevour. Further, Puruṣa addresses Śraddhā as '*Bhadre*' which indeed conveys a little higher status of her. But, Śraddhā in the second Act, has no other important responsibility than to convey, the message of king Viveka to Vyavasāya. Thus, Śraddhā in the second Act is simply a female attendant.

Vedānta Siddhānta and Vāda

Vedānta Siddhānta and Vāda are personified as Guru and Śiṣya respectively, and they appear in the second Act to hold a philosophical discussion.[88]

These two characters play their roles effectively in the discourse arranged by Viveka. Evidently, the discourse is on the futility of rival schools of thought and the utility of Viśiṣṭādvaita Doctrine. They engage in philosophical discussions on the systems of Cārvāka, Sāṅkhya, Naiyāyika, Bauddha, Jaina, Vaiśeṣika and Advaita Vedānta.

Finally, it is declared that these rival schools of thought are defeated. Also, Guru shows the superiority of Viśiṣṭādvaita Vedānta.

Later the Śiṣya declares that Śrī Rāmānuja took his birth in order to refute the Advaita Vedānta an end in the Kali age, and to establish the superiority of Śrīvaiṣṇava doctrine and of *Pāñcarātra Āgama* doctrines as well. Śiṣya proclaims that they have succeeded in elevating the Yatindra doctrine, *i.e.* Viśiṣṭādvaita Vedānta. At this point, Vyavasāya suggests to the king to distribute the prize, to the winner (Śiṣya) in the discourse. Śiṣya is so unassuming and proclaims that the reward is already given to him. The reason for this is evident from the following verse :

"I have already been honoured by the grace of my great *guru* by the kind glance of his majesty and so also by the delight which you have (expressed in what I have) done."[89]

Both Viveka and Vyavasāya appraise Śiṣya for his scholarship, humility and *Gurubhakti*. The king declares that the Śiṣya has been able to establish the doctrines of Viśiṣṭādvaita firmly. The king offers Śiṣya an anklet. Śiṣya receives it as he feels that he should not disobey king's words.

Saṁskāra

Saṁskāra is another interesting and significant character in the play. He is represented as a divine artist, and stands for imagination as that of a poet, painter or sculptor. He himself declares that :

"I am Saṁskāra, the son of Anubhava (experience) and am an artist in the service of Viveka. I have learnt all the arts, and after having defeated Viśvakarmā, the artist of the gods, and *Māyā*, the artist of the *Asuras*. I left fatigued and slept for a long time. Finding it a suitable opportunity, the middle and the last *guṇas* of *Prakṛti* (*rajas* and *tamas*) who were sent by Mahāmoha, and are as powerful as the demons, Madhu and Kaiṭabha, wanted to kill me because I was the friend of *Sattva*. In the lives of men, negligence, indeed, lends a helping hand to their enemies. I was soon awakened from sleep by *Sahajadṛṣṭi* and *Sādṛśadṛṣṭi*, two handmaids of queen Sumati, who had been directed to do so by the mercy of the Supreme Deity. The enemies having fled in different directions for want of a resting place, His Majesty, King Viveka, is desirous, for some reason or other, to see the picture of the universe, and has communicated his orders to me through his commander-in-chief, Vyavasāya. Thus commanded, I have done his bidding. Only if officers act according to the needs of the occasion, can they hold their office permanently." Therefore –

"I have, by my skill, turned the mind of the man who pursues Brahma Vidyā into a wall, and painted theron the whole Universe which can be divided into two kinds, the pure and the impure".

Saṁskāra appears on the stage in the seventh Act. The forms of Brahmā, Śiva and others who are subject to *karma*, are not fit to be meditated upon and only the divinely pure forms of Lord Viṣṇu in his various *Avatāras* are viewed as most appropriate. As such, Viveka and Sumati together with Vyavasāya visit a picture-gallery to see diferent forms of Lord Viṣṇu painted by Saṁskāra with his imaginative skill.

Saṁskāra has full confidence in Viveka, that he would certainly appreciate the pictures drawn by him. Saṁskāra says that, his paintings are superior to that of Viśvakarmā, and that the picture-gallery would be an ornament even to the Lord who dwells within the heart.

At the close of the sixth Act, Tarka informs viveka that they should create in Puruṣa a clear realisation of the steps to the fulfilment of meditation, such as Dhāraṇa by arriving at a decision about the holy object of meditation. Concurrently, when King Viveka looks at the paintings drawn on the walls of imagination. The first picture that is seen too Viveka is of the supreme Viṣṇu called *Daharākāśa*. Therefore, king Viveka expresses his joy and says that "This picture-gallery, through limited in space, represents the boundless universe (in the form of artistic work) and affords a good illustration of the Divine Person called *Daharākāśa* who the Upaniṣad says, lives in the lotus of the heart. Or it reminds us of the child (the Lord) at the end of the *Kalpa*, having all the objects of the Universe in His stomach." Further he says,

"This painter has not painted the Universe here with external materials like the brush and paints; surely under the pretext of painting, he has brought out of his own varied imaginations painted with the brush of joy".

The other pictures which are painted by *Saṁskāra* are Lord Viṣṇu's forms of Matsyāvatāra, Kūrmāvatāra, Varāhāvatāra, Narasiṁhāvatāra, Vāmanāvatāra, Paraśurāmāvatāra, Rāmāvatāra, Kṛṣṇāvatāra and of Kalki Avatāra.

Though Saṁskāra is a character of a very high culture he shows humility and declares that he is to serve his master Viveka with all dedication.

To conclude, Saṁskāra represents truth of experience.

Tarka

Tarka's role in the drama is characterised as Viveka's charioteer. As the very name indicates, Tarka is indispensible to the activities of Viveka. He represents a power of reasoning or logic. He plays his role along with viveka in selecting a suitable place for Puruṣa's meditation. He is seen on the stage in the Sixth Act. Viveka moves in his chariot, run by Tarka. The extent of his travel is from the northern parts of *Bhāratavarṣa* to the extreme south. The holy places, Tarka shows are-the mountain Meru, Kailāsa, Gandhamādana, Himālaya, the Gaṅgā, Region of Vindhyā mountains, Ayodhyā, Mathurā, Sālagrāma, Vāraṇāsī, region of Sahyādrī mountains, Yādavācala, Paraśurāmakṣetra, Malaya mountain, Pāṇḍya country, Vṛṣācala, Coḷa country, Śrīraṅgam, Tuṇḍīramaṇḍala and Veṅkaṭācala.

Tarka points to important places and suggests their holy features too. But Viveka finds them not suitable to the purpose for one or the other reason. Finally, he decides that no other place is better suited for meditation than Hṛdaya-puṇḍarīka as it is free from any blemish.

Nārada and Tumburu

Nārada and Tumburu are two divine sages. They

enter the sage in the eight Act. they witness the battle between the forces of Viveka and Mahāmoha. In this battle, Kāma is killed by Vairāgya, Krodha by Kāma, Lobha by Santoṣa and Darpa by Atidṛṣṭi. In the terrible fight Viveka destroys Mahāmoha and sets Puruṣa free.

It is a rule of Sanskrit drama that secnes of battle should not be actually shown on the stage. They are described in the form of a narrative by eye-witness. Nārada and Tumburu are introduced here for this purpose.

Nārada is seen coming along with King Mahāmoha and Durmati. Mahāmoha shows high regard to Nārada for having visited his capital city *Māyā*. Both Mahāmoha and Durmati offer *Pādya* and worship the divine sage. However, Nārada refuses to accept any food because it was the day of *Ekādaśī*. In the words of Mahāmoha, the qualities of Nārada may be noted as seen in the following verse :

"Your gait has the charm of movements in dancing. Your *Vīṇā* with its many strings is extremely sweet to hear. Your body lights up the light of the moon. You have therefore come here to heighten our enjoyment."[90]

In fact, Nārada speaks to himself that Mahāmoha is a fool, but outwardly shows delight. It is a characteristic with divine sage, Nārada that he outwardly admires Mahāmoha and his achievements. The *Pratihārī* approaching Mahāmoha and telling that the messenger of Viveka has arrived. Mahāmoha welcomes the messenger. Finding Nārada already there, the *dūta* (Dṛṣṭapratyaya) is annoyed. Later Nārada admires Mahāmoha (sarcastically) and is confident of Viveka's success in the battle. Listening to the commanding message of Viveka, Mahāmoha gets angry at messenger. So, Mahāmoha orders that messenger should be sent out, after causing injuries to his body, Nārada obstructs it and advises Mahāmoha not to do like that. Thus, Nārada reminds Mahāmoha of the rules of polity.

Similarly, when Mahāmoha expresses anxiety and doubts about safety of Puruṣa in the ensuing battle, Nārada does not remain hesitant to say that no one can harm Puruṣa because he is firm in his action and does not fall a prey to his enemies.

Again Nārada is seen with Tumburu on the stage after the exit of Mahāmoha and Durmati. Tumburu and Nārada engage themselves in a conversation. As Nārada and Tumburu playing on their *Vīṇā*, moving in an aerial car, enter the stage, they see the indications of Viveka's victory over Mahāmoha. Comparing Viveka to the Sun, Nārada describes that the Sun is like the light of the Veda which causes the dawn of wisdom in Puruṣa. Similarly, comparing Mahāmoha to the darkness of night which is as black as groves of Tamāla trees in the forest of the sky, will be uprooted by the Sun. Further, Nārada forecasts that "the delight with which we witnessed the great battle between Rāma and Rāvaṇa is now a thing of the distant past. Now, fate is favouring us again with a similar experience, for, Mahāmoha, Dambha, Darpa and others are going to offer battle to Viveka, Vyavasāya and others. This tree of battle is deep rooted in hatred and its fruit will soon be within the reach of Viveka's hand."[91]

"In this great festival of battle which is to take place between the two kings, Viveka and Mahāmoha, who will stand in the very fore-front of the two armies of the gods and the asuras arrayed against each other, Viveka, whose weapon consists in explaining the difference between things (*i.e.* among *Īśvara, Cit* and *Acit*) and who wears the armour of true knowledge will (certainly) win over Moha who hides the whole world in darkness."[92]

"From the Kalpaka trees of the Vedas nourished in their growth by the different *Vidyās* (forms of meditation enjoyed in the Upaniṣads (like *Sadvidyā* and *Dahara-vidyā*;

on whose many branches (*śākhās*) wise Brahmins are engaged in study like birds seated on the branhces of trees — from these *kalpaka* trees of the Vedas thick showers of flowers will fall again and again, all at once, on the head of king Viveka, the conqueror of the formidable foe of the path to *Mokṣa*."[93]

Again, Nārada alone is seen on the stage, in the concluding scene of the ninth Act. He informs that Viveka has rescued Puruṣa from being sunk in the beginningless portion of *Saṁsāra* and has brought him near the shore of *Samādhi*. Though Viveka has levelled Mahāmoha, Nārada informs to be very cautious of any consequences. He expects Viveka to liberate Puruṣa from the wheel of *Saṁsāra* alertly. Further, Nārada guides him to reach the goal. He says "My friend, when at your bidding, I proclaim what is beyond the scope of the Śāstras and what has been revealed to me from his own experience as the reward of devotion to my *guru*, the aspirant to *Mokṣa* will soon attain *Samādhi* or intimate communion with the Supreme Being that dwells in the heart."[94]

And at last, Nārada gives assurance to both Vyavasāya and Viveka that he would proceed further to see the fulfilment of Viveka's accomplishment.

Dṛṣṭapratyaya

Dṛṣṭapratyaya is Viveka's messager. In the eighth Act, he makes his appearance in the presence of Māhamoha, Durmati and Nārada. He is supremely delighted to meet Nārada the divine sage in this context. He feels assured of Nārada's help in his errand. He brings a *Bhūrjapatra* from Viveka to be handed over to Mahāmoha. He gives it to Mahāmoha but he is asked to read the letter. To quote an interesting sentence from the letter. 'नीचाः कलहमिच्छन्ति सन्धिमिच्छन्ति

साध्वः.' He makes an appeal to Mahāmoha to give up wickedness and to make treaty with Viveka, but in vain. Finally, Mahāmoha orders that he should be sent out. However, he is wise enough to retreat at his own will.

Tārkṣya

Tārkṣya or Garuḍa is another character entering the stage in the concluding portion of the tenth Act. Having observed, Garuḍa's arrival before the palace of king Viveka. Viṣṇubhakti says that she is blessed by him. Also she says that "He is, as it were the chariot of the Lord of Lakṣmī and is ever eager to bring Him speedily to the houses of those who have surrendered themselves to Him and to whom He is bent on giving salvation. It is also most likely that He will bring *Saṅkalpa*, whose existence and might are inreparable from Him."[95] Viṣṇubhakti describes at length the glory of Garuḍa with utmost devotion.

Besides these minor characters, the play has a few characters who play an assisting role but not seen on the stage. Among them, mention may be made of Buddhi, Tuṣṭi, Virakti, Titikṣā, Jugupsā, Śama, Dama, Svādhyāya, Anubhava, Toṣa, Maitrī, Karuṇa and Mudita, Sahajadṛṣṭi and Sādṛśadṛṣṭi.

Buddhi

Buddhi is the wife of Puruṣa. She represents Puruṣa's knowledge of descrimination and intellect. Which are supposed to be rightly used. If rightly used she symbolises king Viveka and his followers; otherwise she symbolises king Mahāmoha and his group. In this play, Buddhi plays a concealed role in the first Act. She is referred to in the first Act as follows :

"In the course of the varied transformations wrought

in her by the dominance of one or otehr of the three qualities, *Sattva, Rajas* and *Tamas,* Buddhi, the wife of the progenitor of our two races, will become subservient to some one else and will, at a certain time, give birth to that terrible demon (*Parābhakti*) who will cherish the cruel and wicked thought of destroying our whole race."[96]

Tuṣṭi, Virakti, Titikṣā and Kṣānti are all maid-servants to Sumati. Among these unseen characters, Jigupsā representing disgust at sensible pleasures. Titikṣā symbolising endurance and *Ātmavidyā* representing knowledge of Ātman have been referred to in the eighth Act, spoken of by Abhiniveśa as getting ready for winning *Kāma, Krodha* and *Ahaṅkāra* respectively.

"My love ! Kāma by Aversion, Krodha by Patience, Lobha by Contentment, Conceit by Spiritual Study and so on"[97]

Tuṣṭi representing contentment is referred to by Nārada as swallowing Lobha in the eighth Act.

"Contentment with five heads came unexpectedly like another Ādiśeṣa newly created and has swallowed up Lobha as if he were a rat."[98]

Virakti is spoken of by both Nārada as well as Tumburu, and receives respects from them. Further Tumburu declares that Virakti destroys.

"What can we do to the goddess of Fate who is the embodiment of boundless cruelty, for she has persuaded men in *Saṁsāra* to give up wives, daughters, parents, sons and others whom it is their duty to support and to take up the role of *Saṁnyāsins*? we can only bow to her."[99]

"Having learnt, with great concern, that his friend, Lobha, whose loyalty had been proved to be sound by provocative tests in the form of bribes of three kinds (*dharma*, *artha* and *kāma*) having heard that this true friend, Lobha had been consumed in the great digestive fire of contentment, Manmatha entered into the fire of the broad vision of Virakti who was like the deity presiding over the battlefield and he became deprived of his body once again."[100]

Moreover, Kṣānti is praised by Nārada as silencing the pride of Krodha. Again Tumburu refers to Kṣānti as having levelled Krodha within a movement.

"Krodha's wrathful laughter was so loud as to deaden the roar of the waves of the ocean; it rocked the great mountains and made them echo; it scattered the array of the great winds which act as charioteers to *Agni* in the sky; it shook the walls of Brahmā's mansion and became many times louder still owing to the sound caused thereby. But with a bright and gentle smile from the lips of Kṣānti, Krodha was laid low."[101]

"The horrible might of this fire called Krodha is displayed in such cruel entertainment as parricide and its destruction of men reputed noble and great. It was notoriously seen an occasions like *Dakṣa's Yajña;* Krodha is (indeed) the enemy of all happiness (on earth) and bars the way to *Svarga* and *Mokṣa*. He is now reduced to the position of the short - lived lightning by Kṣānti."[102]

Then in the last Act, Viveka refers to Śama, Dama, Svādhyāya, Toṣa etc. as to create proper atmosphere for Puruṣa's attainment of *Mokṣa*.

"May the different branches of learning abide in those who are capable of refuting the doctrines of rival thinkers ! May Śama, Dama, Vedic study, contentment and others who have gained their purposes give leave to Puruṣa to depart; for now with me as his charioteer and seated in the chariot of mind, he is starting for his goal, the Supreme Being, by the path of *Arcirādi* without any more talk of his returning there from."[103]

Maitrī, Dayā, Mudita and Upekṣā

Glancing at Puruṣa Viṣṇubhakti says that Puruṣa is free from Kāma etc. and Maitrī, Dayā etc. are adorning Puruṣa as such it is easy for Puruṣa to engage himself in deep meditation.

Now, that Kāma and others have disappeared leaving only their names (in the memory), Puruṣa is endowed with the virtues of Śama, Dama and the like with his mind adorned with such graces as love to all beings, compassion and the like, and possessed of the wealth of faith, he attains *Samādhi.*[104]

Karuṇā

Karuṇā being one of the invisible roles is referred to by *Saṅkalpa* in the tenth Act. As *Saṅkalpa* describes :

"By the mother of all the worlds, by compassion the beloved spouse of Viṣṇu, I have been appointed to be your servant ever ready to do your bidding at the slightest movement of your brow."[105]

Viṣṇubhakti also praises Karuṇa by giving her privacy in connection with Nārāyaṇa. She says being resorted to Karuṇa, Lord Nārāyaṇa destroys all sins of Puruṣa. Thus, Karuṇa plays important role in protecting Puruṣa.

"The embodied being is deluded with the dance of *Māyā* or *Prakṛti*; and the Brahman who is the Lord of everything and whose greatness is unequalled, is besides Himself with compassion, which is bent on saving him and with the snow of the worship of His feet (*Śaraṇāgati*) quenches the fires of his suffering, and cancels his sins."[106]

Anubhava represents experience, the father of Saṁskāra, in the beginning of the seventh Act of the play.

Sahajadṛṣṭi and Sādṛśadṛṣṭi are represented as the servants of Saṁskāra, in the beginning of the seventh Act.

Sahajadṛṣṭi — When we happen to see one out of the two things or persons that are frequently seen together, the other comes to our memory.

Sādṛśadṛṣṭi — When we see one of two objects or persons that resemble each other, the other comes to the mind. It is in these two ways that remembrance or Saṁskāra is produced.

Needless to mention that all these characters belonging to the team of Viveka, have their relevance, when Viveka's victory and its auspicious consequences are taken to evaluation.

Mahāmoha

Among the characters who form the counterpart, king Mahāmoha is the chief of all evil ones. The characters following: Mahāmoha are Kāma, Krodha, Vasanta, Rāga, Dveṣa, Lobha, Dambha, Dapara, Stambha, Saṁvṛtti, Satya, Abhiniveśa, Tṛṣṇā, Kuhaṇa, Asūyā, Durvāsanā, Kali, Māna, Matsara, Śṛṅgāra and Bhrama. But the characters playing substantially an important role, are here taken up for a critical presentation.

King Mahāmoha or *Pratināyaka* is the counter hero. Mahāmoha literally means the great Delusion. It implies propensity of mind which brings about erroneous notions and which binds the person from a right understanding of the real values in conduct, action and achievement. Further, it is not mere ignorance and stupidity or even wickedness but delusion. Observing the movements of counter-hero, it can be said that he possesses the qualities of *Dhīroddhāta*[107] type of hero. He is proud of his valour, sufficiently envious, adept in deceipt, self-conceited, unsteady, wrathful and self-boasting.

Earlier, Mahāmoha is introduced in the first Act by Sūtradhāra, indicating the final sequel of the duel between himself and Viveka. Next in the same Act, the purpose of king Mahāmoha is declared by Vasanta. Such references to Mahāmoha have been made by Rati, Vasanta and Kāma, and others.

Then Mahāmoha is brought on the stage in the fifth Act. The very nature of king Mahāmoha is aptly pointed out by Viveka : "Mahāmoha by his very nature, holds fast to his view like the deadbody holding its fight tight."[108] In effect this nature of Mahāmoha is found amplified in his own words, in the following lines :

"My love, I have vowed to destroy that daring enemy of his own race, Viveka, and I sent Kāma, Krodha and others together for mutual protection as in the case of the lion and the forest, to bring about confusion in the mind of Puruṣa, who is now eager to meditate on Brahmān. Being overwhelmed with fear at that time, their battle array was broken and they began a retreat. Now being ashamed to look at my face, they have taken a vow to fast unto death. Therefore you should now go to their wives, Rati, Jigāsā and Tṛṣṇā and send them to their husbands to comfort them.[109]

He has his spouse Durmati, his right hand who closely follows Mahāmoha's words. As per the will of Mahāmoha she sends Rati, Jigāsa and Tṛṣṇā to misguide the persons and take them all to their side.

Mahāmoha is a symbolic of the utmost pride. He finds Viveka unequal to his status. He ofcourse expresses sorrow because he is forced to argue with him and also fight against him. With Durmati, Mahāmoha proclaims his superiority and underestimate Viveka and his followers.

The following verses illustrate Mahāmoha as self-boasting :

"All the multitudes of gods and *asuras* bear, on their heads, the scroll containing my orders. The letters in these orders are reflected in the gems shining in their crowns and the rays from their jewelled crowns seem to colour the letters with line."[110]

"The hosts of those that dwell in *svarga* are subject to my control. Is there any need to speak of the kings of the earth? The Trinity (Brahmā, Viṣṇu and Śiva) have been confined, respectively, within the lotus, the ocean, and the mountain. My brows never fail to accomplish my desires whether it is to create the world or to destroy it. Who is there, indeed to whom I am subject ? and who is there that is not subject to my authority ? Is there any need to describe my glory to any one ?"[111]

Mahāmoha is jealous of Viveka's glory. Therefore, he wants to pull Viveka down by deceitful deeds. Hence, he says :

"For some reason or other, Viveka is now in the ascendant. What are the tactics I should now adopt to bring him down ? Let it be. Am I not Mahāmoha ?"[112] These words show that Mahāmoha is adept in deceit.

King Mahāmoha represents the great delusion is well broughout in the following lines. He tells to Durmati that he has spread confusion in different systems of philosophy and proclaimed superiority to materialistic doctrine. According to him, body cannot find happiness after death; the body is the very soul and vice versa; what is perceived is real and regard it as important; acquisition of wealth and happiness through it as the soul end of life. This true doctrine gives rise to pride and is pleasing to the heart of everyone. These are enough to stultify Viveka's doctrine and his followers including Vaidika adherents. Further, Mahāmoha proclaims :

"The Upaniṣad, too, considers that the system of strong must (necessarily) be strong and calls this the Upaniṣad of the *Asuras*. So even, the Vedāntins support of the authority of the Upaniṣads is like a document of confession of our victory written by the hands of our very enemies."[113] He is confident of the doctrine of Bṛhaspati in his reply to Durmati's question. He compares Bṛhaspati's system to the real who can put to shame thousands of his imitation.

"These *Āgamas*, winning a number of wiseacresto their side prate of something or other as if it were true. If this system of the *guru* of the gods is properly promulgated, they will lose all their flavour and be reduced to (complete) silence."

Not even a thousand images of the Sun can never put the Sun to shame.[114]

To Mahāmoha, Mokṣa is attainment of heaven which is the abode of happiness. So, he is also sure of winning a victory over Viveka.

"The death of the body is *Mokṣa* what is called heavenly bliss is simply the enjoyment of sexual pleasure (here on earth) and the deities are women endowed with youth who give that pleasure."[115]

He is very egoistic as to make fun of "*Ṛṣis* who follow *Āgamas*, and who have disciplined themselves every day by the control of the senses and the proper observance of all religious rites, the picture of a beautiful woman not painted by the artist's hand but appearing on the wall of the mind (in the form of past impressions) can weaken the mind's concentration on God."[116]

"Even the students of the Upaniṣads declare that one who has attained the Supreme Being by giving up all the pleasure of sense-objects has (in *Paramapada*) (the pleasures of) eating and the enjoyment of the company of women who have unending delight in sex pleasures. This is indeed intriguing. Those who run away from fear of scorpions, should not fall into the mouth of (venomous) serpents."[117]

In his estimation even highly learned Puruṣa cannot remain unmoved before alluring pleasures. In this regard his opinion may be quoted as follows :

"Ha, Ha ! we find it stated in the *Śrutis* that even those who are esteemed as eternally pure, Garuḍa and others who fly in aerial cars in *Vaikuṇṭha* have quite a number of beautiful women existing solely and naturally for their enjoyment. It is also said in the *Śrutis* that the supreme Lord who grants deliverance from *Saṁsāra* to others is the consort of *Lakṣmī, Bhūmi* and *Nīlā,* so those persons who condemn love which is one of the ends of life, are like setting fire to their own cities."[118] He is so much swollen with pride that he does hesitate to say that even celestial beings and Lords of the Universe and Puruṣa's in worldly happiness with their spouses.

He considers such virtuous men as lacking in *vyavahārajñāna,* and illustrates his view with an example of a foolish Paṇḍit who receive twenty-five gold pieces when he is offered a hundred.

To Mahāmoha, Puruṣa's who observe *Brahmacarya* here aspire for pleasures in heaven.

He interprets creation in his own way which is broughout in the following verse :

"The relationship of husband and wife that exists between the parents of the whole world, namely Nārāyaṇa and Lakṣmī is natural and is the result of their will to be so. The division in creation as male and female is also to promote in Jīvās an eager desire to serve Nārāyaṇa and Lakṣmī. The other things that are done (in temples and the like) are also for the same purpose of promoting a thirst for service. The doctrine of Virocana (Cārvākism) which you now consider very interesting, alas, causes only aversion in the minds of the learned."[119]

He scorns other diverse schools of thought like Sāṅkhya, Yoga, Vaiśeṣika, Bauddha and Jaina, and upholds the system of Bṛhaspati which, alas ! does not appeal to Puruṣa. He finds no logic in other philosophical systems. Therefore, Mahāmoha proclaims that the followers of these schools engage themselves in futile disputations. Such views, in his opinion, make the world topsyturvy.

Mahāmoha is a firm believer of Virocana's teachings, because he propounded "The secret of the Upaniṣad of the *Asuras*." Upholding '*Asuropaniṣat*' he proclaims that "the older school of Cārvākas held that *Mukti* consisted in the disintegration of the body and the senses, he has added a corrective to it in my *Vārttika,* because he thinks their view is wrong."[120]

"*Mukti* or *Mokṣa* consists in the similarity of enjoyment to that of Brahmān (*Brahmaṇā bhoga sāmyam*), the Brahman being woman whose many attributes and glories entitle her to be called Brahman as seen from the big size of her two breasts. (They have *bṛhatvam* and therefore justify woman being called "Brahman.")[121]

Durmati enquires him as to why adherents of rival systems fail to understand him reightly. He replies that thieves cannot be made to change their nature. He sees adherent disputants as arrogant persons. He wishes to go in search of fresh men (Dambha and others) who would co-operate with him.

True to the proverb that 'Pride goeth before fall,' king Mahāmoha comes to notice the beginning of his end. He finds his supporters like Kāma and others fleeing away from their field and hide themselves somewhere. In his eagerness to know their where-abouts, he sends Dambha. Dambha also comes to know that by the effort of Viveka, Puruṣa has attained a state of mind in which he has an aversion to the body. He has to begun to hate Viveka for his evil design to destroy his race.

Like a swimmer loosing life in water but trying to catchhold of a straw, Mahāmoha begins to spread *Adharma* all over the world very carefully without being noticed by Viveka. He now wants to take away all strength of Viveka and implant his sovereignity. In this task, he expects much assistance from Durmati. He wants to know whether his supporters like Kāma, Krodha and Lobha are despondent at the efforts made by Viveka, or continue to give support to him. Riding in a chariot with Durmati as a charioteer, Mahāmoha observes Dambha blowing the trumpet and Darpa as his armour.

"Whether Kāma and his friends, Krodha and Lobha are despondent, or whether they come to my aid at the proper time, I will display the stand taken by Rāma in his battle with the *Rākṣasas* (*i.e.* fight single-handed with Viveka). Let this Kaliyuga be my chariot now, and you, my Durmati, will be my charioteer. Dambha will blow the trumpet at my victory and likewise Darpa will be my armour."[122]

As is common with all prototypes of Mahāmoha, he is praised by psychotant Dambha. Dambha says that Mahāmoha need not depend on support of others because he himself is capable of becoming victorious.

"Who is there that can stand before you when you play the game on the field of battle ? Who will long to become the enemy of Kāma, since he is always engaged in the persuit of the activities of love ? If only you cast an encouraging glance on Kroḍha, he will pound the earth to dust, throw off the great mountain-ranges (from their moorings) and drink off the waters of the ocean."[123]

Induced by his supporters and depending on his own strength, Mahāmoha strikes a plan to defeat Viveka. But suddenly he thinks of pleasures :

"Whenever the fire in the stomach burns (making me hungry) I will duly throw into it the four kinds of food and thus, with the help of Durmati will observe only the rite of *Prāṇāgnihotra*".[124]

With the assistance of Durmati and Durvāsanā king Mahāmoha gets draft orders to be prepared by skilled accountants and then circulated. It is the effect :

"The emperor Mahāmoha, the over-lord of all, issues these orders along with his queen. To my seven ministers, Kāma, Krodha, Lobha, Mada and Mātsarya. Dambha and Sthambha (Darpa) have been granted the seven holy capitals suitable for *Mokṣa* and the seven islands with their surrounding oceans."[125]

"Let the gods whose dread becomes intense at the mere sound of our name be now driven away from their offices and let the whole world employ (hereafter) the words *namaḥ, svasti, svāhā* and *svadhā* only in connection with Mahāmoha in the performance of the rites and even in ordinary conversation."[126]

At this act of Mahāmoha, a voice is heard proclaiming victory (from the group of Mahāmoha). He feels gratified and orders the cook to bring delicious food.

It is to be noticed that king Mahāmoha comes again on the stage in the eighth Act. The impact of Mahāmoha on persons is very much of an evil amounting to addiction to one habit or other. In the words of Abhiniveśa, the Finance Minister, persons who come under the evil influence of Mahāmoha cannot easily give up their habit; on the other hand they continue their habits and indulge in seven evils. Even Lobha supports Abhiniveśa and Mahāmoha. Truely he is a symbolic of *vyasanās.*

In spite of these powerful evil influences, Abhiniveśa gradually realises that Puruṣa cannot be finally conquered by his men because he is passing under the virtuous influence of Viveka and his followers.

Durvāsanā, the wife of Abhiniveśa even anticipates the destruction of Mahāmoha. "If so, our leaders, not excluding Mahāmoha may perish."[127] As a consequence, Abhiniveśa thinks of going out of the treasure — house of Mahāmoha and approaching Viveka. He even suggest Durvāsanā to reform herself.

Mahāmoha is adament. He decides to begin the battle with Viveka. Needless to pointout that he is the very representation of *chala* or stubborness. He decides to carryout his treachery to its highest degree almost to the end. Thus, he makes preparation for war and is ready to begin the battle.

Later, Nārada pays a visit to Mahāmoha's capital city called Māyā. He offers due respect to the divine sage. As they were conversing each other, a servant enters and informs that Viveka has sent a messenger to make a treaty. Because of Mahāmoha's pride and status, he calls this guesture of Viveka as an act of cowerdice. Following verses are an evidence to his status :

"What you have said is silly. Do not speak such timid

words even while dreaming. Am I not Mahāmoha ? Why do you think I am like others ? But the ways of statemanship are never properly understood by women. My love, please listen to this vow of Mahāmoha, the valiant, here."[128]

"Though my body is cut with saws, though I am thrown into the fire, I will never give up a pin's point of my territory, nor will I conclude peace with anyone.[129]

"Alas, I have ceased to be Mahāmoha and the Universe was not conquered by me at all (as it is thought to have been) if (as now) my boundless possessions should be looked upon as something to be partitioned."[130]

Mahāmoha is foolhardy and lacks practical vision. He expresses a concern over a false idea; *i.e.* his revered ancestor Puruṣa is being taken on the wrong path by Viveka. So, he thinks that the Puruṣa cannot occupy the place of *Kulapati*. He is anxious to make Puruṣa free from Viveka. He is assured by Nārada that Puruṣa would not be misguided by anyone. Still Mahāmoha flares with anger. He scoldes Viveka by several names — आः पाप। दुराचार, विश्वविद्वेष दूषित ! मूढ। But Nārada consols him — महाराज ! न श्रृतं न दृष्टं वा केन भवदपादानम्? आसंसारं प्रसिद्धवैभवः खल्वासि ।

The much thought off war then begins. Mahāmoha accompanied by Durāśā, Durmana, Mosa, Mada, Mātsarya, Paranindā and Droha — enters the battlefield. The manner in which he makes his entry into the battlefield is described in the following verse :

"The great battle against Viveka, in which Mahāmoha displays his terrific strength has begun. As a result of it, the oceans have been cast into the nether regions (*pātāla*); the great mountains have been broken to pieces and the earth shows extensive cavities where they stood; the Sun, the Moon, and the stars have disappeared leaving all the quarters in dense darkness; the mansion of Brahmā been subjected to cracks and the stars have fallen on account of the destruction caused by the wind."[131]

Mahāmoha is uncompromising one. He gives an expression to his false notion of *Svarga* and ancestors. Ultimately the battle turns a defeat for Mahāmoha. He fails to shatter the solid bedrock of what is Real, taught by Viveka. In fact, Mahāmoha gives up his mortal body.

"Mahāmoha of boundless strength who had stepped over the extremest bounds of praise due to all great warriors was, as it were, playing on the battle field which was difficult to leapover. For the first time in his life he has now met with death at the hands of the valiant king Viveka, who determines the true content of all the Upaniṣads."[132]

Durmati bemoans his death : "You are now going on a distant journey in the company of strangers. Why have you left behind, my lord, your dear wife, who is now in deep sorrow."[133]

Mahāmoha, in fullest sense of the term has been characterised in a significant manner. In each and every action of Mahāmoha, his sense of envy, deceit, self-conceit, unsteadiness etc., has been reflected. He is represented as a symbolic of utmost pride. He tries to establish his superiority over Viveka. He expresses the sense of jealousy on Viveka's glory. He is pictured as very egoistic as to make fun of the sages following the path of scriptures. He considers virtuous people as devoid of knowledge of descrimation. He shows himself as firmly believing in virocana's teachings. He carries out his treachery to its highest degree, but fails in his endeavour. In this manner, Mahāmoha's role is portrayed in a befitting manner to call him a counter-hero.

Durmati

Durmati, the spouse of Mahāmoha is the counterpart of Sumati.

Literally, the word Durmati means perversity of understanding. She symbolises the evil mind. The implication here is that those who are dispended to evil mindedness are so because of their folly and foolishness. They do not know that wickedness is not a paying position.

Vedānta Deśika brings the character of Durmati in the fifth Act. She is seen along with Mahāmoha. She is his right hand supporting him through and through. Mahāmoha aims at destroying the plans of Viveka. He sends Kāma, Krodha and Lobha to assist him in his ultimate object. But he learns that these assistants are not being able to get success. They fled somewhere. So he asks Durmati to send Rati, Jijñāsā and Tṛṣṇā to find their whereabouts. It is in this context, that Durmati shows her efficiency in evilminded work. She replies to Mahāmoha that she has already taken care in sending Rati and others to assist in Mahāmoha's task. Truly she stands for wicked acts and thought. By this she wins the praise of Mahāmoha.

Like Mahāmoha, she is also too egoistic. She agrees with Mahāmoha when he says that there is no one superior or equal to them. यथा त्वं नारीषु निःसमाभ्यधिकम्।(p.500) In another context, Durmati comes to know the system of philosophy held by Mahāmoha. It is *Asuropaniṣat* or Bṛhaspati's doctrine or Cārvākism (Materialism).

Having learnt Mahāmoha's faith, Durmati wants to know how Viveka can be conquered by the doctrine of Materialism ? Mahāmoha informs her in an elaborate manner that even the virtuous and *tapasvins* do have some laps or other owing to *Pūrvāvasana.* Such men can be brought on to their side. Still she has her own doubts as to how virtuous men can be cheated by charming women ? She is eager to know why persons take to other systems if what Mahāmoha holds is true and final. She also wants to know from Mahāmoha as to why he is censured without reason by believers in other systems if what is folds is the ultimate truth !

No doubt, Durmati entertains doubts about Mahāmoha's philosophy, but throughout the play she follows her spouse like a shadow. She gives all able assistance to him.

Accordingly, she suggests Mahāmoha to employ his ministers not only in preaching his doctrine but also to win a victory over Viveka. She is therefore complimented by Mahāmoha — *Kṛtyākṛtyavedinī khalvasi*. Acting on his direction Durmati invites Durvāsanā to help Mahāmoha.

Again, the dramatist brings Durmati in the eighth Act. Here she is seen along with Nārada and Mahāmoha. She offers respect to the divine sage. Later, in the same Act, she suggests to Mahāmoha (*Kāntāsammita*) to welcome Viveka in the pretext of making a treaty into their midst. After he joins their company, it will be easy for them to sack him. But Mahāmoha's concealed ego shows itself off. He says to Durmati that he is not a coward to do according to her suggestion. Because he is conscious of his prowess. Women like Durmati do not have a good knowledge of political craft. In this regard, Durmati's fore-thought suffers from practical knowledge.

Durmati is a silent spectator of the final battle. Though Mahāmoha gives her all hopes and strength, the poor lady has to witness defeat and demise of Mahāmoha on the battlefield. She weeps over the deadbody of Mahāmoha and mourns his death. All her hopes are foiled with *Sūryodaya* which are observed as festivals without knowing their significance. He is happy at the influence of *Kali* in every field of life. He also bemoans the performance of *Agnihotra* but takes delight because his master has succeeded in increasing evil mockery of doing *Sandhyā* and *Gāyatrī* and imparting Vedic knowledge among men.

The play has lengthy passages giving the observations of Darpa on this section of society. Namely, the wicked and the hypocrite. He sees the free play of Dambha everywhere among men. A graphic picture of his comments on Dambha's may be seen in certain pages.

However, all these observations made by Darpa provide him delight because he thinks that all such perverted attitudes of men are due to the impact of king Mahāmoha. At the sametime he shows regard for a few hermitages and *yogis* because they are generous and dedicated in their pursuits. He is also seen in the hermitage where he meets his wife as a *saṁnyāsinī*. He proclaims a superiority over his wife. He joins Dambha in achieving the common goal proclaimed by king Mahāmoha. Eventually Dambha, Darpa, Asūya, Kuhanā all join together because of supreme delight and satisfaction after listening to the aerial voice. At the end Dambha recognises the superiority of Darpa. Darpa equally compliments Dambha and Kuhanā.

At a later stage in the fifth Act, we notice Darpa in the company of Mahāmoha. He seeks direction from his master regarding the common plan of action. He is ultimately over-powered by king Mahāmoha and acts according to his instruction and desire.

Kāma, Rati and Vasanta

The roles of Kāma, Rati and Vasanta can be considered as the major ones. It is Kāma, who first enters the stage soon after the *Prastāvanā* of the first Act is over.

Kāma indeed has excelled all gods including Maheśvara.

"My bow is the tender sugarcane in my hand. My arrows are flowers, and the row of bees sitting on them forms the string of my bow. (with all that) can even Śiva when he went to conquer the demon of the three cities (Tripura) who had the mountain Meru as his bow and the wind and the fire as his arrows dare, even for an instant, to transgress my command ?"[134]

"Brahmā, the Primeval Deity, wears his wife in his mouths resonant with the chanting of the three Vedas; the left half of Śiva become transformed into that of a woman, and even that Supreme Being (Viṣṇu) is controlled by (subservient to), the Gopis. How, then, can lesser beings remain untroubled by the pangs caused by Manmatha ?"[135]

Rati is another role here brought in assisting her husband Kāma. She has full confidence in the valour of his husband. Yet she expresses a doubt, whether Kāma gets success. Because his enemy has resorted to a strong fortress of *Vairāgya* and is well guarded by his ministers like Śama and Dama. Having realised the doubt and entertained by Rati, Kāma says that the prowess and glory of Kāma never goes futile. His triumphant instruments are very strong to employ in the conquest the world. He says :

"My first bow is the incomparable body of beautiful women; this bow is slightly bent; its string (*guṇa*) is strong and consists of the quality of women's loveliness; its arrows are their eyes extending to the ears; the middle of this bow is their waist which is so slender as to be held within one's hand."[136]

"Even the very name of sweet - tongued women which is delicious to the ear like nectar, destroys one's self - possession; it puts down mental peace; it banishes shame and makes the spirit of detachment impossible. Is there any change that it does not produce ?"[137]

Kāma is confident of his strength. He is well-versed in discharging the arrows at his enemies, at proper time. Thus his arrows are unassilable even to Lord Nārāyaṇa.

"Leave the gods alone. The Supreme Nārāyaṇa whose words have the authority of the Vedas, who, in the assembly of sages, sings of the ways of winning *Mokṣa* and who performs austerities – even He displays His serenity of mind when He creates from His thigh that gem among young women (Urvaśī)".[138]

Like a true foe man, Kāma also does not bear the flattering of Viveka. He gets angry in such occasions. Therefore, when Rati starts describing the power of Viveka, Kāma says that she is mislead by the words of some fools. He tries to avoid entertaining, fear from Viveka.

Another quality of Kāma is not disclosing the secrecy of polity. When Rati enquires about the strategies employed by Viveka against Mahāmoha, Kāma does not disclose it though he knows it well. He does not hesitate to emphasize the point that the secrets of polity should not be revealed much less to a woman.

The entire source of Kāma's strength is his bow. As he says :

"Even the Moon and Indra, while condemning the forcible molestation of women as conduct resembling that of the cock, strayed from the path of virtue themselves. When my bow with the murmur of the rows of bees is bent, who is there that will desire even to look at the threshold of the house of *vairāgya* ?"[139]

"Friend Vasanta ! my bow is this sugarcane, so tender; these flowers are my arrows; this fine row of bees with their sweet humming sound is the string of my bow; women, timid and weak, are (the source of) my strength; this is the great truth; (with these) I have conquered Śiva and others and I grow in strength by mere thought."[140]

In the second phase, Kāma enters the stage again in the fourth Act being accompanied by Vasanta. As Vasanta tells, every person submits his deeds unto Kāma only. He exclaims that :

"What do you say ? You are, indeed, Kāma. Desiring this or that *siddhi,* and doing with their body and the senses this or that *karma* prescribed or forbidden, people then become wiser and throw the blame on you saying, "Kāma did so; Krodha did so."[141]

Further, it is described that Kāma's prowes delights in playing with persons like Śiva, the mansions of gods are free resource of Kāma. And Kāma's garden is the entire earth surrounded by the ocean. Thus, the splendour of Kāma's role is extraordinary.

On par with Kāma, Vasanta is also powerful. Kāma himself praises Vasanta as below :

"It is well-known that you are the cause of flowers; the whole world is filled by you with delight; of the six different kinds of seasons, you are the best *yajña* Jyotiṣṭhoma depends upon you (for it has to be performed only in spring); from you the goddess Lakṣmī gets the lotus which she holds in her hand (from you arises beauty); the Supreme Mādhava meaning Lord Nārāyaṇa and (also the month of Vaiśākha) depend upon you; Kāma is your friend and assistant. Who else among the seasons can compare with you ?"[142]

"You are a (great) fire; the breeze from the Malaya mountain is your charioteer; the Aśoka flowers are your flames (being red in colour); the rows of bees are your smoke; the moon (who sheds nectar) is the oil or ghee (which keeps that fire always burning; of you who never become extinct (who has conqured all talk of *Mokṣa*), the *Vairāgya* of even such (great persons) as Brahmā and Śiva is the fuel (which is these only to be consumed by you)".[143]

Though for some time Kāma and Vasanta forget themselves in praising each other, they are dutiful servants of Mahāmoha. Therefore, they recollect their duties. As Vasanta says :

"The common mission assigned to both of us is to confound the mind of Puruṣa now inclined to *Samādhi* or contemplation of God. The duty that rests with me is to create the proper atmosphere (like moon light, flowers and the like) for inciting love. Yours is to provide the proper support (in the form of beautiful women) and excite the required emotions."[144]

Kāma is clever in locating the weakness of Puruṣa. Therefore, he says that Puruṣa is unaccustomed to the contemplation on Brahman, therefore he can be easily diverted towards the contemplation of a lovely form of a woman, to which he has long been accustomed.

Having observed the condition of Puruṣa Vasanta informs to Kāma says :

"Puruṣa now dreads the great fears of *Saṁsāra*; at the same time, he longs also for the home (and other pleasures); he is eager to attain Brahman and, at the same time has an eye for the prosperity (of *Saṁsāra*). He has a passion for the pleasures of the senses and, at the same time, is ashamed of them. So his contemplation of the Supreme Brahman is both manifest and unmanifest, and is therefore in sure peril."[145]

Therefore, Kāma thinks that it is the proper time to discharge all his missiles at Puruṣa as his *yoga* is not complete. Therefore, he impels celestial women to enter Puruṣa's mind. Kāma further laughing in anger says :

"If Viveka grown arrogant by his association with Vyavasāya continues his efforts (to lead Puruṣa towards *Samādhi*), in disregard of me, he will then be himself the cause of creating in Puruṣa the condition of Soubhari (who was lured by a hundred women)."[146]

In the fourth Act, Kāma meets Krodha. So, the power of Kāma gets increased to vanquish Viveka. Therefore, Vasanta says that the meeting of Kāma and Krodha is just like a meeting of fire and wind in one place. Thus, Vasanta thinks that it is certain to get victory over Viveka with such abundant powers of Kāma and Krodha.

Addressing to Krodha, Kāma expresses his joy for getting abundant help from others to win over Viveka. He says :

"This moon is my dear friend and this moon light is my woman friend; Vasanta who shapes my arrows for me is my relative, worthy of the greatest regard; and you, Krodha, with your irresistible impetuosity come to my rescue in times of adversity. Who is there with a longing for life that can stand before me whose bow is made of flowers?"[147]

Vasanta too, is a close observer of Puruṣa's condition. Finding right time, Vasanta promotes Krodha to enter into Puruṣa to help Kāma in his deeds.

As Krodha has pointed out, Kāma's greatness is really remarkable :

Again, what is there to wonder at in my ability to break the beginning of meditation in Puruṣa, when I have succeeded in causing mental excitement even to such great persons as Maheśvara ?[148]

"If the elephant, Airāvata, bears the King of the gods, overthrows the army of the *Dānavas,* breaks down great mountain-ranges and destroys hundreds of forests, and if, without the least effort, he bears the sphere of the earth on his head as if it were only a bunch of flowers, is there anything to wonder at ?"[149]

Kāma and Vasanta further get an assistance of Lobha, as delineated in the last scene of the fourth Act. Yet, their power gets ceased before Puruṣa under the protection of Viveka. Therefore, both Kāma and Vasanta lose their courage and decide to quit the place for their own protection.

Again in the eight Act, Kāma makes his appearance in the battle scene. Suggesting Kāma's entrance in the battlefield Nārada describes as below :

"My friend, it is Manmatha who is now advancing bow in hand with an army consisting of women. He has arrows of different colours (flowers) tipped with honey given to him by his esteemed friend, Vasanta; *Kokilas* are the healds who sing his praise and swarms of bees from his twanging bow - string. He is allied with the breeze blowing from the mountain Malaya and has the shark as his banner."[150]

"Here is a woman of the *Padminī* type playing in front; on another side is a *Citriṇī;* elsewhere is a *Śaṅkhinī* and on another still, is a *Hastinī.* These four charming counsellors of Manmatha, the archer who assaults (every one in) the three worlds, promote his glory by their expressive glances and are indeed powerful."[151]

Similarly, observing Kāma's mearness to the chariot of Viveka, Tumburu anticipates thus :

"This insane Manmatha wants to fight with the great Viveka with the help of young women of the following description : the woman who has just had her bath after the period, the woman who is fatigued with dancing, the woman who is wearied on account of a long journey, the woman intoxicated with liquor, the woman who, after being angry with her lover, has relented, the woman who has become reconciled to her husband after a period of separation and the woman who has newly been wedded."[152]

On looking at Virakti, Kāma feels that his plans have failed. His attendants also appear to entertain doubts regarding his success. Yet Kāma tries to scatter the forces of Viveka. He plans to conquer Viveka and his allies banded together. Therefore he is marching ahead armed with his bow of flowers, along with the array of his lovely women in military formations resembling chariots, elephants, horses etc. in order to please Rati with his heroism. But atlast, Kāma entered into the fire of the broad vision of Virakti who is like the duty presiding over the battlefield. Thus, Kāma once again deprived of his body.

Thus "Kāma who proclaimed the doctrine that the only thing which had value was sexual union, who was keenly interested in dispelling the fear of hell, who was so great an artist as to shape the divine couple *Ardhanārīśvara* by uniting the two halves of two bodies cut into by his weapon — Kāma whose transgression of the code of virtue is notorious from the conduct of thousands of *Gopīs* enamoured of one who was not their husband (the Supreme Person, Śrī Kṛṣṇa) and whose valour was unsurpassed by that of any one else in the three worlds - Kāma has been slain."[153]

In this manner, in the drama the role of Kāma, Rati and of Vasanta has been described as holding in the highest esteem and whose power is fit to be borne on the heads of all people including gods. But as a matter of fact, the nature and movements of all these characters are backed up by

Mahāmoha. Hence their being ceased to exit, before Viveka's irrestistable power. These roles followed the wrong path and saw the dreadful end.

Krodha

The role of Krodha in the drama is drawn as the personification of anger. He is one of the assistants to Mahāmoha. He appears on the stage twice in the drama, *i.e.* first in the fourth Act, and second in the eight Act. He enters in a dreadful apparel. He rebukes the followers of Viveka : "who is the dependent of Viveka that indulges in the idle talk of subduing Kāma and Krodha ?"[154]

He is very proud of his power. He boasts of his valour, *i.e.*; "the dancing master who teaches the soldiers on the horrid field of battle to enact their defiant dance of war and how does this talk of Viveka arise ?" The *Asuras* are my followers and owing to the fever of fear arising from them, the wives of the gods find that the application of sandal paste to their breasts is all in vain. (for it fails to cool their body.)"[155]

Krodha has close friendship with Kāma. Therefore, listening to the Krodha's words of valour, Kāma first of all welcomes Krodha and happily calls him *Mahārathī,* then endorses Krodha's feelings he says that Krodha is able enough to obstruct Puruṣa's meditation.

So, too, Vasanta is another friend of Krodha. As all these are making their efforts to get victory for Mahāmoha, Vasanta informs Krodha to occupy the place in Puruṣa, so, that Krodha can easily vitiate Viveka's efforts.

Having the support of both Vasanta and Kāma Krodha's enthusiasm gets dubbled. Praising himself Krodha says that he has avoided the persons like sage Jamadagni who was once attacked by king of the Heyhayas and who bore it with patience and who did not invoke a curse of him.

He further says that he treats the path of the persons like Rāvaṇa and never bowdown to anyone. Further, he expresses that he has caused the fall of men of extraordinary power by his plans."[156]

Moreover, he proclaims that even though Puruṣa has given up his attachment to worldly things and sensual pleasures he causes in him on occasions such as the stealing and hiding of the articles like rags of cloth, grass seat and *Kamaṇḍala*, mental excitement; the uttering of lies, the desire to make false accusations (of others), tale-bearing and mental delusion and (thus) bring about the loss of *Samādhi* ."[157]

Sometimes Krodha praises the strength of others like Vasanta :

"Manmatha is ever bent on devouring the wealth of pure spiritual meditation; he is now fishing in the sea of sins which is thick with (six) heavy waves (hunger, thirst, delusion, grief, etc.) to catch silly creatures playing therein with the bait of pleasure and will use them as condiment for his meal."[158]

He expects Mahāmoha's help and guidance in attacking Viveka, though he himself is capable of doing it so. That is why, he does not like to take abrupt decision to march against Viveka.

Of course, as per the command of Mahāmoha Krodha enters the battlefield in the eighth Act. Seeing the entrance of Krodha in a dreadful manner. Nārada describes as below:

"Do you think it untrue that he made Himavān, the greatest of mountains, fuel for the fire of his hunger ? While thirsty, he sipped off five or six oceans in an instant. He broke down the rocks in mountain Meru and wears two of them as big ear-rings. This demon Krodha of such great renown, is now approaching the battlefield."[159]

His weapons are born with him. They are like hands, feet, legs, teeth etc. These weapons are his playthings."[160]

His actions are dreadful :

"This raging fire called Krodha is known to be very powerful and if roused, he will consume not only the entire army of his enemies but also all the mountains, the oceans and the earth itself."[161]

In spite of his irresistable might he could not fulfil the desire of Mahāmoha. He finally is reduced to death by Kṣānti. It is thus described :

"The horrible might of this fire called Krodha is displayed in such cruel entertainment as parricide and its destruction of men reputed noble and great. It was notoriously seen on occasions like Dakṣa's *Yajña,* Krodha is (indeed) the enemy of all happiness (on earth) and bars the way to *Svarga* and *Mokṣa.* He is now reduced to the position of the short-lived lightning by Kṣānti."[162]

Thus, Krodha's role has been portrayed just like a short-lived lightning. He shown as a dutiful servant of Mahāmoha. He make all efforts to the best of his capacity but everything is reduced to the destruction of himself.

Lobha and Tṛṣṇā

The role of Lobha is introduced in the play as he represents greed. Lobha's aim is to assist Mahāmoha and contribute to his success.

Similarly, Tṛṣṇā is brought in the play as she symbolises longing. She is the spouse of Lobha. Her purpose is also to aid Lobha and Mahāmoha in their task. Both Lobha and Tṛṣṇā enter the stage in the fourth Act. Their participation in the play has been described in the following verse which literally bringsout his nature :

"I have come here with my wife Tṛṣṇā bearing on my head the command of Mahāmoha as if it were a garland. Is there any one who can satisfy me with gifts of even spacious worlds all of gold and entire and undivided worlds long, broad and high."[163]

The conversation between Lobha and Tṛṣṇā as quoted below is a testimony to their literal characteristic nature :

"Though the mountain of gold, the mountain of silver and such others have been thrown into fill it up my dear Tṛṣṇā, the slenderness of your stomach shows no swelling at all."[164]

"It is surprising that the beauty of your beloved surpasses that of all other beautiful women ? However, you have to make, from all the gems to be found in the houses of all the gods and the *Asuras,* necklaces, armlets, girdles and anklets worthy of my loveliness."[165] True to the letter, the following verse graphically describes the nature of Lobha:

"What you have asked for is a very small matter. The gods, the *Asuras,* the *Kinnaras,* the *Kiṁpuruṣas,* the *Vidhyādharas,* sages, men and beasts — all these have been overcome by me. They themselves kill one another looking upon even a piece of chaff, as it were the mountain Meru. Listen to the condition to which, Kubera, the friend of Śiva, renowned as the bearer of the title *Dhanada,* has been reduced by me."

"Kubera, who is called the king of kings, never parts with what he has, nor does he enjoy his wealth, with a bewildered mind, he craves for more and more wealth; he never enjoys good sleep and is merely watching over his treasures like an evil spirit."[166]

His reply to Krodha as revealed in the following verses, shows what he really is :

"Kings get excited and confounded with the desire for a small particle of the earth's dust. The leaders of the gods tremble with fear at the thought that some one may be performing austerities somewhere for winning the position now occupied by them. When a few beggers are invited some where or other, they are insulted by the others. Thus, the world now stands on the side of Durmati's servants Envy and Jealousy."[167]

"Possessed by the boundless thirst for wealth, men wander about in all the ten directions; they dig into the earth (for gold and other forms of wealth) and make it uneven; they sing the praise of rich men and carry their paraphernalia; they cross the ocean in ships and declare vain wars."[168]

The associates of Mahāmoha resolve to construct a *Vyūha* with Tṛṣṇā in the centre and march against Viveka. But Vasanta has no confidence in this plan. At this context, Lobha tries to provide courage to his wife. He says, "mighty as our enemy is, there is no reason for you to be afraid; for, you are now surrounded by this array of our great warriors." Tṛṣṇā feels happy.

The *Vyūha* marches ahead. But all exhibit fear. Lobha in particular is not prepared to act in the absence of their king. Krodha comes out in great anger and wants to know what orders of the king they have carried out. To this Lobha's words of consolation :

"Time which flies with the great speed of the Sun's chariot cannot be stopped when there are no contrary winds. The wise man will not try to stop the flood that has run past but will start measures to present future dangers."[169]

Therefore, we should now save our lives. Do not the *Śrutis* say that one should protect oneself at all times and in all places and by all means."[170]

Dambha and Kuhanā

Dambha is another character assisting Mahāmoha. The literal meaning of Dambha is vanity or boastfulness. Hence, it may be said that Dambha in the drama is the personification of vanity. Dambha enters the stage in the fifth act, engaged in a conversation with Kuhanā, his wife. However, when Darpa and others are busy in mutual recrimination, Dambha is seriously considering his plan of action after Kāma, Krodha and Lobha have fled from the battle. At this juncture, Mahāmoha passes orders to Dambha to poision the mind of Puruṣa. Even for those who have conquered lust and anger, it is difficult to overcome certain enemies in their minds like pride, ego and hypocracy. In case of such persons Dambha finds scope for himself to influence them and to bring them under Mahāmoha.[171]

In the commencement of the fifth Act, Dambha calls his able and efficient mistress, and says that she is similar to Tārā (to Bṛhaspati) and Ahalyā to (Gautama). Appreciating very much her household in performing daily duties or rites, Dambha takes Kuhanā into confidence : She has shunned contact with any other man and is not able to endure his separation even for a moment. But Kuhanā does not entirely agree with Dambha, because she expects still higher approbation to the extent of comparing her to Arundhati (spouse of Vasiṣṭha). In this regard she excels her husband. She says to Dambha that she has been served by thieves, hunters, village-accountants, heretics and ministers of kings.[172]

Entering into a lengthy conversation both recollect to their minds, accomplishements and pat their bags. Further Dambha is seen rendering his excellent services to Durmati and Mahāmoha. Here he is at the height of his accomplishments. Dambha is asked to perform a sacrifice in order to bewitch the mind of Viveka who is foiling the plans of Mahāmoha.

Dambha's prowess in performing sacrifices is brought-out in the following verse :

"I am master of the four Vedas and of the fourteen branches of learning. The sixtyfour arts and crafts (*Kalās*) are also known to me. Thousands of *Yajñas* have also been performed by me at proper time and the banners to proclaim my having done all this have been planted in all the worlds."[173] Dambha thus is rightly praise as दम्भो धर्मध्वजाश्रयः ।

"Paraśurāma conquered the whole world and offered it to me again and again with great reverence, but by me to whom the whole Universe is not worth a straw, it was not accepted. (So also) I treated with contempt the offer made to me of *svarga* and of *Mokṣa* by the greatest of he gods in admiration of my greatness and glory."[174]

"Those rites that have been performed as *dharma* — even they will in general become witch-craft directed against Viveka owing to their association with me."[175]

Later, Dambha is seen awaiting Darpa, in his hermitage. He expects no help from Darpa for *Yajña* to be performed. Also Kuhanā wishes her husband all success. Dambha experiences a good omen that is a throb in the right eye. In this context, Dambha is seen sitting cross-legged to pretending to perform *Praṇāyāma.*[176] Meanwhile, he listens to the conversation between Darpa and Kuhanā. He tells that he does not want their advice as he is being helped by Kuhanā. Opening his eyes, Dambha scoldes his friends and asks them to get away. Darpa does not pay any attention to this, and proclaims his greatness, calling Dambha as a Ḍāmbhika. [177]

Dambha does not feel diffident at the self-praise of Darpa. He speaks out his brave qualities :

"I was once travelling in the outskirts of *Satyaloka*, when Brahmā come to welcome me at once with Śanaka and others, motionless and respectful and brought me *Arghya* in his own hand, having washed it seven times for the sake of purity."[178]

"How many, indeed, are the hermits of ancient times, born of the race of Brahmā, who have got over their deadly sins by having the holy water from my feet sprinkled on their heads !"[179]

Kuhanā strengthens this praise and tells that she is an eye-witness to Dambha's greatness.

Both Dambha and Kuhanā in the beginning were not rightly identified by Darpa and Asūyā, but afterwards the latter recognises the former and says :

"This must surely, be the revered Dambha and this Kuhanā, No one else could indulge in such exaggerated boast of their conduct and character. I will make these relatives of mine acknowledge it. (aloud) Revered Lady, you know all things. Still I will (now) inform you of some thing that I have arrived at by reasoning. This is the lady, Kuhanā, who with her deceitful mind, excels in the art of depriving others of their money and this is no other than Dambha, who performs *Yajñas* only in name, since in these Yajñas there is nothing more than the killing of animals."[180]

Responding to Darpa's feelings, Dambha too identifies him and says thus :

"I, too, guess who you are surely you are Darpa arrived here in person. You are always in the habit of vilifying those who are superior to others (in learning or in conduct) and you are good at raising a loud outcry. And this is certainly your wife, Asūyā, who has put on the disguise of *Saṁnyāsinī*."[181]

In short, the roles of Dambha and of his spouse Kuhanā, have been portrayed as subservient to Mahāmoha.

Darpa and Asūyā

Darpa is one of the associates of king Mahāmoha. Darpa is a symbolic of pride or arrogance. He plays his role after Kāma, Krodha and Lobha sustained a defeat.

Darpa is seen on the stage in the fifth Act. This Act is profuse in the self-proclamation of Darpa showing of his nature. He is walking on big sandals, waving and stout, hands and with a banner advertising his greatness hanging from his staff. He is to meet Dambha. He proclaims that he has come from *Brahmaloka,* and has made an extensive tour. He states his purpose. He is to vilify good and greatmen. He says that he received great honour from great persons like Indra and eight guardians on his tour. He calls himself the twelfth Āditya and the twelth among the Rudras and the nineth among the Vasus. His vanity is very aptly broughout by the dramatist in the following line:

"Ha ! how foolish this world is ! Even those who cannot be considered to occupy the position of my Śiṣya without evoking redicule — even they long in vain to be looked upon as equal to me or even as superior to me."[182]

Further his proud achievements are mentioned in the following verse :

"By me have been put to shame all learned men — those who are well-versed in the science of prosody (*Chandas*), those who have mastered grammar (*Vyākaraṇa*), those whose knowledge of the *Kalpa Sūtras* is free from doubts of any kind, those who have mastered the science of Śikṣā (Phonetics), those who can calculate the movements of the heavenly bodies (*Jyotiṣa Śāstra*), those who have made a critical study of Nirukta (Glossaries) those who have grown strong in the three branches of Mīmāṁsā and those who dance, as it were, in the wide expanses of *Nyāya Śāstra*."[183]

In spite of his proud and arrogant statements about his achievements he is evidently a malicious character. As such what is real or true makes him a laughing stock. This is broughout in the aireal voice, clapping his hands, the voice interrogates him as to from who he learnt his abilities. The voice directs him to realise the ultimate truth that what all we are and act, is on account of the grace of the Lord. Evidently, Darpa has forgotten this aspect. This has been broughtout in the form of an irony by the great scholar.

"From who did the swan learn the art of distinguishing between milk and water, unless it be by inexplicable causes? How many days did Agastya train himself to be able to drink the ocean ? (please) tell me."[184]

His foolishness is further highlighted in his lenghthy speech.

Darpa boasts of himself as having a large number of disciples who are heretics. He has no faith in *Pramāṇas*. He calls them as useless. He desires to bring the whole world under his control by his magical powers. He gives his own argument to disprove the *Pramāṇas*. He has no belief in the *Darśanas*.

Darpa manifests in several degrees among the followers of different religious and particularly in contending Supremacy of one's own religion like *Advaita, Dvaita*. He gives examples of Maṇḍanamiśra and Śaṅkara. Perhaps the only merit of this character is to expose hypocracy and ignorance among scholars. He has uttered disregard for men who pose themselves as learned with their beard and books hanging from their girdles. The reason for his disrespect at such scholars is broughtout in the following verse :

"They talk much but without any cogency; they have become arrogant on account of the meagreness of their knowledge; they have no respect for such men as *gurus*: they are unfit to pursue any of the four ends of life; they shake their limbs about in imitation of learned men. The only noticeable thing about them is the theatrical movements of their fingers. We have had enough of these ministers of foolish kings."[185]

Of course, Darpa is a loyal servant to Mahāmoha. Therefore, he sometimes wishes to know whether Īrṣyā (Jealousy) and Asūyā, (Envy) his wives, are carrying out their duties assigned by Mahāmoha.

Darpa is amazed at men of the same family following different religions. This is expressed in the following verse:

"His mother-in-law follows the doctrine of the Jains; his *sambandhis* (Parents of his daughter-in-law and son-in-law) are Buddhists; his mother and father belong to the set of Paśupatas; his *guru* is a logician of the Vaiśeṣika school (of Kaṇāda); his wife is an adherent of the schools of Sāṅkhya and Yoga and his friend is a *Śiṣya* of Cārvāka (materialist). His name is *Mithyācāra* (Hypocrite) and he professes to be a follower of the Vedās, while despising what is enjoined in them."[186] He calls such men as hypocrites. He is also puzzled at seeing men on the banks of sacred rivers like Gaṅgā and Yamunā. They are not able to understand his discourse. He pities men of these regions because they are pretending in the path of renunciation and have not given up their ego. They are bigger hypocrites and have not experienced *Śāntarasa*.

He concludes that the existance of these hypocrites is due to the impact of king Mahāmoha. He has nothing but abuse towards hypocrites. They earn money in day time being a guise of goodmen. But they indulge in drinking and pleasure during nights. He has no regard for Brahmins put up in the *Agrahāras* because of their hypocracy. He redicules rites like *Upanayana*.

Rāga and Dveṣa

Rāga and Dveṣa are the personification of desire and hatred respectively. They play their roles as the ministers to king Mahāmoha. They enter the stage right at the beginning of the third Act. The circumstance in which they make their appearance is naturally the time when Viveka and his friends are contemplating on the adoption of the Means for *Mokṣa.*

Both Rāga and Dveṣa have a common purpose and get busy to ruin the virtuous. When Rāga informs Dveṣa that external enemies have been overthrown by Viveka's deceitful plans, the former suggests :

"It is possible to make them helpless by pointing out, at great length, the good things of *Svarga* and the evils of *Mokṣa,* I know a thousand cunning devices with which to allure the poor Virakti away like Mārīca in luring Sītā. You have the precedent of Rāvaṇa to carry away Viṣṇubhakti by force."[187]

Both enter into a lengthy conversation on the followers of different doctrines such as Pūrvamīmāṁsā, Nirīśvaramīmāṁsā. But they have been defeated by Vāda, the Śiṣya, they try to accomplish their master's purpose.

Rāga is very enthusiastic of making Viṣṇubhakti defunct. He says :

"Well said, my friend; by such words as these, I feel sure that Viṣṇubhakti can be made to run away like a flight of birds from their nests on the tops of trees, when the forest-fire begin to consume them. How can Viveka, who is wanting in the power of reasoning. Succeed in creating in the self to get rid of *Saṁsāra* ? On the otherhand, the man who is desirous of defying the beauty and other charming qualities of earthly and celestial women will become more closely bound by those very qualities (*guṇas*), as if by ropes (*guṇas*). Look at these celestial women (the Apsarās), with lotus-like eyes who were born of ambrosia and who are like ornaments to *Svarga*. Of these celestial women –

"The bud of the breast opening, as it were, into flower desires to cover and conceal the space between the two arms; the eye, which has, as it were, stolen the beauty of the blue lotus, desires to leap over the ear; dalliances taught by Manmatha, the Ācārya, desire to adorn and beautify all the limbs; and the happy youth of beautiful women desires to conquer the whole - world."[188]

But, Dveṣa is all but ignorant of wise thinking. He replies to Rāga, "How can be Supreme Being who is considered to be supporting as His holy body the whole world of *Cit* and *Acit* be free from all sufferings and blemishes ? The Supreme Being is said to desire all desirable objects; how then can be said to be free from desires and to be Lord of Himself ?"[189]

Dveṣa thinks of conquerring Viveka by cutting the supporting tree, *i.e.* conquerring the class of learned men who are with Viveka. Rāga praises him. Dveṣa laughing aloud proclaims :

"As long as I am present, how will Viveka, whose understanding is (all) covered with the dust raised by ploughing in the salt marshes of the Upaniṣads, be able to establish the existence of God, who (said to be) the abode of hosts of auspicious qualities, who, it is said, has no equal nor superior, who (alone) can (according to them) cause the fulfilment of all the end of life and who is fit to be adored?"[190]

In the same Act, both listen to the voice behind the curtain and are in dreadful agitation. They anticipate the kings cause getting lost.

Abhiniveśa and Durvāsanā

Abhiniveśa plays the role of a Treasurer in the drama. He is represented as a obstinate addiction to some evil habits. He enters the stage in the eight Act. He introduces himself and reveals his nature in the Miśra-Viṣkambhaka:

"Under my influence, men delight in the seven evil habits in which they have begun to indulge to no purpose. Though beaten by a storm of obstacles they never give up what they have once begun. Though it is subject to various kinds of suffering and fear they never give up the eager pursuit of wealth as the (only) goal of life. I am Abhiniveśa the finance minister of Mahāmoha in charge of his treasury and am always addicted to some one thing or other (being blind to other interests) ?[191]

Further he continues that "I am the brother of the worthy Lobha born after him, and I grow in strength on my own account as a reaction to the feeling of dependency."[192]

He gives expression to distress and agony to which his entire family has fallen :

"Alas ! great danger confronts our race. For Puruṣa was first given instruction in Vedānta. His wavering faith in the scripture revealing the Supreme Brahman was made staunch and unshakable by an exhibition of the weakness of other systems of religious thought. He was then advised to adopt an *Upāya* with its *aṅgas* for the attainment of *Mokṣa*. Kāma, Krodha and others have been rejected. The place fit for meditation has also been investigated. A decision has been arrived at regarding a pure object for mental concentration. A strong desire has been created (in him) for the performance of the great *yoga* with a suitable object for meditation and accompanied by mental serenity, control of the senses, freedom from the desire for pleasures and the rest."[193]

The role of Durvāsanā, here can be brought together with Abhiniveśa, as she co-operates in Abhiniveśa's dealings. She is the spouse of Abhiniveśa. Durvāsanā is in close confidence of Durmati and hence the latter always takes the help of the former. She closely treads the path of Abhiniveśa. Therefore, Durvāsanā asks for details of the happenings to her husband — Abhiniveśa, the latter replies–

"My love ! Kāma is won by Aversion and Krodha by patience, Lobha by contentment, conceit by spiritual study and so on."[194]

After entertaining doubts of his efforts, Abhiniveśa decides to give up the camp of Mahāmoha. Disguised as *samādhyābhiniveśa*, he desires to approach Viveka; and he asks Durvāsanā to become *Suvāsanā*. They anticipate a calamity to Mahāmoha and the resultant *Pralaya* :

"Eagles are seen hovering round the top of the pillar supporting the triumphal arch at the portico; cyclones have torn to pieces the banner - clothes in our armies which are now without banners. The different quarters are seen occupied by Yama's servants armed with spears, daggers, swords, clubs, bows and other weapons as if by the agents who bring about *Pralaya*."[195]

But, both Abhiniveśa and Durvāsanā see king Mahāmoha getting ready for the battle, and become anxious to know about Mahāmoha's victory.[196]

Saṁvṛtisatya or Vyāvahārikasatya

In a similar way, the dramatist brings another envoy

of king Mahāmoha namely, Saṁvṛtisatya. He brings the message of Mahāmoha to king Viveka. Disclosing the letter, the messenger says thus :

"Your majesty, this letter contains the order of the emperor Mahāmoha, the ruler over the fourteen worlds, acting on the advice of his minister *Saṁśaya* (doubt) and who abides always by the wishes of his queen, Durmati. The orders were drafted by his acountant, Lobha, and are (now) communicated to you by me, his confidential envoy. They are on no account to be disobeyed."[197]

Further he continues to read that, "You have shown considerable earnestness in promoting the adoration of the Supreme Being and in doing so, have acted against our will. If, (now) you should transfer this earnestness towards the acquisition of wealth and lordship, we will hold you in high esteem."[198]

"My dear, have you heard this (message) which resembles the story of the beggar stretching his foot ? But it is only natural for Mahāmoha to hold fast to his view like the dead body holding its fist tight."[199]

Then he proclaims the glory of Kāma and the Krodha.

"By whose valour, indeed, will Kāma, who is superior to all others and whose greatness is well-known (even) among the gods of *Svarga*, be conquered ? By his prowess, the third eye of Śiva which had its origin in anger soon became cool with love."[200]

"The good Śruti says Kāma (desire) existed at the beginning." The first person (the Supreme Being) plays (the game of) creating the world maintaining it and destroying it, being impelled by desire; even the man who has attained freedom from desires wins *Mokṣa* which is hard to attain by a desire (Kāma) for it. On whom is Kāma dependent and is there any one in the world who is not subject to Kāma ?"[201]

No doubt, Mahāmoha's messenger though be under the command of Mahāmoha, is not influenced by his evil effects. Therefore, he has realised virtuous strength of both Viveka and Sumati. He has high regard for Viveka. Yet reluctantly he carries the orders of Mahāmoha. This idea is evident from the following verse :

"The world will (soon) show the greatest regard to Viveka who will kill Mahāmoha, defy Manmatha, and shake off Krodha with contempt."[202]

At last, when he exists, the statement he declares, is indeed remarkable, and shows his sense of morality as well as his knowledge of descrimination.

"Who is there to conquer Viveka, who, with is wife Sumati ever eager to awaken those who are asleep, promotes the welfare of the world ? And yet our master, Moha, orders us to do this."[203]

Besides these major and minor characters, playing their roles on the stage as assistance to Mahāmoha, two other characters *viz.*, Śṛṅgāra and Jighaṁsā have been just referred to, in the eight Act; but they are not physically seen on the stage.

All these characters as have been portrayed in detail, are brought in a significant manner. Vedānta Deśika has successfully portrayed these characters in his own inimitable style. Thus, Vedānta Deśika's skill of characterisation can be said as a superb one and meaningful.

2. RASA DELINEATION IN THE SAṄKALPASŪRYODAYA

Role of Rasa in General

Rasa or sentiment which has been considered as the soul of poetry,[204] is also called as it makes others relished. It is an integral aesthetic experience. Bharata, the foremost propounder of *rasa* theory, remarks that no Kāvya can be fully enjoyed without *rasa*.[205] Other rhetoricians like Bhāmaha etc. agree to Bharata's view, Providing predominance for *rasa* in the poetry, all poets and dramatists have incorporated *Guṇas, Rītis* and *Alaṅkāras* in their works as subscribing to the delineation of *rasa*.

The term *rasa* signifies '*aesthetic content*' of literary art and '*aesthetic relish*' which the reader or the spectator enjoys,[206] It arises from a proper combination of *Vibhāva* — stimulants, *Anubhāva* — physical consequents and *Vyabhicārī* — *Saṁyoga* — the transcient emotional states. As from a seed a tree grows, and from the tree flower and fruit, so also all sentiments stand as the root; the emotional states have their settled position for the purpose of manifesting the sentiments.[207]

As Bharata recognises, there are only eight *rasas*, such as: (i) *Śṛṅgāra* or Erotic, (ii) *Hāsya* or Humour, (iii) *Karuṇā* or pathetic, (iv) *Raudra* or Furious, (v) *Vīra* or Heroic, (vi) *Bhayānaka* or Terrible, (vii) *Bībhatsa* or Odious, and (viii) *Adbhuta* or Marvellous.[208]

Moreover, following Bharata some old poets like Kālidāsa[209] refer to these only eight *rasas*.

At this juncture, it is necessary to find out whether all these *rasas* are developed in the *Saṅkalpasūryodaya*. A close perusal of the drama makes it clear that the *rasas* like *Vīra, Śṛṅgāra* etc. have been delineated therein. But, none of these sentiments is prominent. As in other allegorical dramas, in *Saṅkalpasūryodaya* too, the prominent sentiment that is developed, is *Śānta*.

On the other hand, Edgerton denies the scope for the *Śānta rasa* in the drama. He says "it is forbidden to use it in the drama; it its inherently opposed to the very nature of the drama."[210] But, surely this is incorrect and baseless remark. There are sufficient and strong evidences to show *Śānta rasa* being accepted as one of the sentiments and essentially developed in this drama.

Udbhaṭa, the first commentator on the *Nāṭyaśāstra* of Bharata, recognises the inclusion of *Śāntarasa* in the drama. And it is held that he might have made necessary alteration in the texts of the *Nāṭyaśāstra* as shown below :

शृंगारहासकरुणाः रौद्रवीरभयानकाः ।
बीभत्साद्भुतशान्ताश्च नव नाट्ये रसाः स्मृताः ।।[211]

(*Nāṭyaśāstra,* VI.16)

Similarly, Śāradātanaya in his *Bhāvaprakāśa* on the *Nāṭyaśāstra*, accepts *Śāntarasa* as being one of the *rasas*.[212]

So too, the *Viṣṇudharmottara Purāṇa* states that the *Śāntarasa* is considered to be an independent and standing separate. And this *Śāntarasa* arises from *Vairāgya*. It can be enacted by means of taking on religious paraphernalia, and through such means as compassion for all beings, meditation, encouraging others towards the path of *Mokṣa* etc.[213]

Further, the Jain *Anuvogaddara sutta* (*Anuyoga-dvāra-Sūtra*) belonging to 5th century A.D., records a reference to *Śāntarasa*. Where it mentions all nine *rasa*s including *Śānta* and remarks that it can be characterised in the absence of perturbation and through tranquility.[214]

Abhinavagupta, one of the famous writers in the field of poetics, belonging to 10th century A.D. has advanced this idea of *Śāntarasa* in his *Abhinavabhāratī*, a scholarly commentary on the *Nāṭyaśāstra*. Therein, he says thus : In order to indicate that Śama is at the root of all *rasas*, it was named at the beginning. In ordinary wordly dealings, one does not mention separately a thing common to all, and so its *sthāyin* was not separately given. But even a thing which is common to a number other things, deserves to be separately reckoned by the descriminating man, and so *Śāntarasa* has become separate as the object of cognition in the form of the aesthetic enjoyment of the spectator who is admitted to be a descrimnating reader. In the *Itihāsas, Purāṇas*, Dictionaries etc, we hear of nine *rasas* as well as in the revered *Siddhāntaśāstra*. Thus, it is said : He should display the eight *rasas* in the places alloted to the eight gods. And in the centre he should display *Śāntarasa* in the place of the Supreme God.[215]

In the *Uttararāmacarita*,[216] Bhavabhūti speaks of *Karuṇā* sentiment as the dominant *rasa*, and all others are modifications thereof, just as the bubbles and waves of ocean are all forms of water. Abhinavagupta too applies a similar notion to *Śāntarasa* as synthesis of all *rasas*. It is evident from the previous paragraph that Abhinavagupta has sponsored the *Śānta*-syntesis by considering the *Śānta* as the one fundamental *rasa*, of which all other *rasa*s are modifications. He called Śānta the greatest *rasa*.[217]

In fine, *Śānta* is found to be an independent and the ninth *rasa* in addition to the group of eight *rasas*, spoken of by Bharata.

With regard to different *bhāvas* of *Śāntarasa*, Viśvanātha[218] remarks as below :

"*Śāntarasa* has *Śama* or calmness as its basic mood. It belongs to the very best of men. It has the white complexion of Kunda flower and of the moon, and Lord Nārāyaṇa is its presiding deity. Its *Ālambana-vibhāva* is the emptiness of all things because of their transient nature, or it is of the nature Supreme Self. Its *Uddīpana-vibhāvas* are holy hermitages, sacred places of pilgrimage, pleasant groves etc., and the company of great persons etc. Its

Anubhāvas are horripilation etc. Its *Vyabhicārībhāvas* are self-disparagement, joy, recollection, resolve, kindness towards all beings etc.

As has been said before; all nine sentiments have been developed in the *Saṅkalpasūryodaya*. But the instinct point to be understood is that, the Sentiment of *Śānta* is fundamental and predominant in this drāma, and the rest of the sentiments like *Śṛṅgāra, Hāsya* etc. are subordinate here. Of course, there are two reasons for holding *Śānta* as predominent here. One is its relation to ultimate goal of human life, *i.e. Mokṣa*; and the second one is the poetic delight which is always *Alaukika*, is above all mundane associations. Besides, Veṅkaṭanātha emphatically says that,

असभ्यपरिपाटिकामधिकरोति शृङ्गारिता
परस्परतिरस्कृतिं परिचिनोति वीरायितम् ।
विरुद्धगतिरद्भुतस्तदलमल्पसारैः परैः
शमस्तु परिशिष्यते शमितचित्तखेदो रसः ।। *S.S.*, I-19, p.47.

"*Śṛṅgāra* or the sentiment of love can give pleasure only to those who are unfit to be members of a decent assembly; the sentiment of heroism in war treats of attempts to disgrace one onother; the sentiment of wonder has to deal with incidents and situations that are difficult to imagine as true. Of what use are the oher *rasas* which are of little interest ? There is only one *rasa* that remains, and that alone can bring tranquility to the troubled heart."

In this context, it is felt necessary to quote the following verse from the drama :

विवेकप्रागल्भ्यस्फुरितरणवीरव्यतिकरः
परब्रह्मोदन्तप्रकटितदयावीरविभवः ।
प्रबुद्धक्षेत्रज्ञस्थितिघटितशान्ताकृतिरभूत
प्रयोगश्चित्रोऽयं भवरसभुजामप्यभिमतः ।। *S.S.*, I-9, p.32.

"This play rich with a variety of interests representing as it does, the spirit of war-like heroism in the person of the accomplished Viveka, revealing the heroism of grace and mercy while treating of the dealings of the Supreme Being with His creation, and embodying the spirit of tranquil resignation associated with the Self of *Jīvātmā* who has attained illumination, is sure to be welcomed even by those who experience the pleasure of *Saṁsāra*.

This verse indicates the presence of all nine *rasas* and *Śāntarasa* is superior to all. As indicated in this verve, Viveka fights against Mahāmoha with all his bravery. This seen begets *Vīrarasa*. After the destruction of Mahāmoha, the atmosphere become calm and quiet. Puruṣa with this tranquility follows the path of *Mokṣa* without any obstructions. This is the context in which *Śāntarasa* is developed. And in other cognated scenes other *rasas* like *Śṛṅgāra* have also been delineated. This idea is collectively brought by the dreamatist Veṅkaṭanātha in the following verse :

लक्षणसमृद्धिरनघा रसपरिपोषश्च सहृदयग्राह्यः ।
संपतति नाटकेऽस्मिन् स एष शैलूषसुकृतपरिपाकः ।।

S.S., I-21, p.52.

"Faultless and rich are seen the characteristics of a drama in this play. The development of the sentiments (*rasas*) is such as will appeal to men of taste. This is indicative of the good luck of actors."

Śāntarasa

As *Śāntarasa* is delineated predominently in the drama; it is evident that there are many references to the development of this *rasa*. For example :

दर्पोदग्रदशेन्द्रियाननमनोनक्तञ्चराधिष्ठिते
देहेऽस्मिन् भवसिन्धुना परिगते दीनां दशामास्थित ।

अद्यत्वे हनुमत्समानगुरुणा प्रख्यापितार्थः पुमान्
लङ्कारुद्धविदेहराजतनयान्यायेन लाल्यते॥ *S.S.*, I-71, pp.144-45.

"Like Sītādevī crying in Laṅkā in her imprisonment, having been informed at that time of the whereabouts of Śrī Rāma by Hanumān, Puruṣa is confined in the body surrounded on all sides by the seas of *Saṁsāra*, with the mind swayed by the ten senses like the proud *Rākṣasa* with ten heads. tormenting him and has reached a pitiable state being taught the great truths of spiritual life by a *guru* of the calibre of Hanumān, and cries his heart out."

Here, *Śāntarasa* is delineated. The state of calmness is obtained by the individual soul by the advise of a competent preceptor. So, individual soul finds all wordly things empty. Therefore, *Ālambanavibhāva* of *Śāntarasa* is brought here.

Another example from the seventh Act runs as follows :

क्वचिद्वाहाधीशः क्वचिदमरदन्तावलपतिः
क्वचित्प्रालेयांशुः क्वचिदमृतविच्छर्दितमिति ।
अतिक्षोभे सिन्धोरयमनघनिद्रो धृतगिरिः
विषादं देवानां विघटयति वैकुण्ठकमठः ॥ *S.S.*, VII-20, p.628.

"On one side, the horse *Ucchaiśravas*; on another, the celestial elephant *Airāvata*; here the moon and there the rising (out of the waters) of ambrosia — when, in these ways, the ocean was being turned inside out, the Great Tortoise, dispelled the grief of the gods by bearing the mountain on His back, while lying asleep without feeling any discomfort."

This stanza speaks of *Kūrma's* discarding Celestial elements like *Ucchaiśravās, Amṛta* etc. *Kūrma* stands unshaking in the ocean bearing a mountain on his back and dispels the grief of all gods. So, before Lord Nārāyaṇa in the form of *Kūrma* all elememts including *Amṛta* are Heya *i.e.* discardable. Due to the transient quality of even celestial things, they are said discardable, but it is not due to *jugupsā*.[219] Thus *Śāntarasa* is delineated here.

कामादिकेष्वपगतेषु कथावशेषं
संप्रत्यसौ शमदमादिगुणोपपन्नः ।
मैत्रीदयादिपरिकर्मविभूषितेन
श्रद्धाधनेन मनसा लभते समाधिम् ॥ *S.S.*, X-7, p.800.

"Now that Kāma and others have disappered leaving only their names (in the memory), Puruṣa is endowed with the virtues of Śama, Dama and the like and with his mind adorned with such graces as love to all beings compassion and the like, and possessed of the wealth of faith he attains *Samādhi*."

Here *Vibhāvas* of *Śāntarasa* are indicated, *i.e.* Puruṣa has completely turned away his face from *Saṁsāra* as he has given up all desires of mundane world. He is in close position of Śama, Dama etc. Hence, his mind is very much devoted to Lord Viṣṇu and hence he is engrossed in meditaion.[220]

Another example may be given *Anubhāvas* of *Śāntarasa* are present :

नियतपुलकिताङ्गी निर्भरानन्दबाष्पा
गलितनिखिलसङ्गा गद्गदस्तोत्रगीतिः ।
अमृतलहरिवर्णा हर्षनृत्तोपपन्ना
विगतनरकभीतिर्विष्णुभक्तिर्विभाति ॥ *S.S.*, X-24, p.816.

"Where is the noble Viṣṇubhakti, now, who is expecting the fulfillment of my endeavour and who removes all the sins (of mankind). It is to please her that we proceed to do all this — looking in front she, Viṣṇubhakti, shines as white in complexion as the wave of nector. Her hair always stands on end (owing to her deep devotion) and she sheds copious tears of joy. She has given up all attachment (to worldly things) and is ever singing hymns with flattering accents.

In the excessive joy (of her devotion) she dances and is absolutely free from the fear of hell."

This verse gives the description of Viṣṇubhakti. Viṣṇubhakti is overwhelmed with joy for Puruṣa is ascending the ladder of meditaion. She expresses her feelings of ecstacy in various ways like horripulation, shedding tears of joy, singing hymns and dancing. These are called Anubhāvas of *Śāntarasa*.[221]

In this manner, we find many examples delineating *Śāntarasa*. I-32, II-65, IV- 57, VI-61, VIII-42, VIII-48, X-7, and X-38. Most of the examples are found in the tenth Act as it describes the culminating stages of Puruṣa.

Śṛṅgārarasa or Erotic Sentiment

This sentiment is so called because its Capacity of atracting the minds of readers is unparalled. In this context, it is said that the nature of *Śṛṅgāra* is Supreme. It is caused due to the advent of Manmatha.[222]

Now, some exámples delineating *Śṛṅgāra* sentiment may be illustrated as below :

चूडावेल्लितचारूहल्लकभरव्यालम्बिलोलम्बकाः
क्रीडन्त्यत्र हिरण्मयानि दधतः शृङ्गाणि शृङ्गारिणः ।
तन्वङ्गीकरयन्त्रयन्त्रणकलातन्त्रक्षरद्धस्त्रिका-
कस्तूरीपरिवाहमेदुरमिलज्झम्बाललम्बालकाः ॥ *S.S.*, I-33, pp.74-75.

"Here are young pleasure seekers wearing lovely flowers of red lotus in their plaited hair from which bees hang down and they are playing with golden syringes in their hands. Their locks of hair are thick with the liquid sprayed on them by the hands of slim young women, from bellows containing the paste of musk dissolved in water".

This verse gives a beautiful description of young women. The red lotuses, golden bangles and the locks of hair — these are the elements highlighting the beauty of women. Therefore these are called *Uddīpanavibhāvas* of *Sṛṅgārasa.*[223] Some other examples of *Śṛṅgārarasa* are I-3, II-26, III-31, IV-60, IV-18, and VIII-61.

The following is another example illustrating the delineation of *Sombhogaśṛṅgāra*. It arises when both hero and heroin fallen in deep love, see each other with amorous look and experience the lovely touch of other ones.[224]

जनितवलयभङ्गे दत्तहारावमर्दे
मुषितनिखिलखेदे मोहसंतोषहेतौ ।
सचकितपरिरम्भे सांप्रतं कातराक्ष्या-
स्त्यजति युगलचिन्तामङ्गयोरन्तरात्मा ॥ *S.S.*, I-54, p.112.

"In this close and frightened embrace of my beloved with looks expressive of timidity, her bangles have broken, neckless has been split into two, all thought of pain or fatigue is lost; it is such as will give delight to Moha; and my inner self has lost all sense of our bodies being two."

As described in this verse, both Kāma and Rati immersed in deep love, experience the joy of close touch, *i.e.* embrace. Hence, it is an example of *Sambhogaśṛṅgāra*.

There are many other examples where *Sambhoga-śṛṅgāra* is developed. They are : III-35, III-47, IV-46, and V-19 etc.

Here is an example of *Vipralambhaśṛṅgāra*. *Vipralambhaśṛṅgāra* arises when hero and heroin are seperated from each other though they are in deep love. And they are not in a position to meet each other.[225]

दिनाधिपविनाकृतिव्यसनखिन्नसंध्यावधू-
विधूतकबरीभ्रमरप्रसरकौतुकापादकम् ।
विशृङ्खलकलिन्दजाजलतरङ्गभङ्गावली-
मलीमसमिदं तमो जगदशेषमाचूषति ॥ *S.S.*, III-46, p.392.

"The Sun having set, light shrinks everywhere, my lovely dear and the spread of dense darkness covers the face of the eastern quarter. And now the irrepressible Manmatha advances to afflict the world in the company of his friend, the Spring, doing various acts of an evil nature."

This verse describes an advent of night. Before night appears, the dramatist describes that damsel of twilight, *i.e. Sandhyā* suffers from the pangs of seperation from her lord the Sun. Here both *Sandhyā* and the Sun are in deep love. But they are seperated. Thus, here in the sense of seperation (*Pravāsa*), *Vipralambhaśṛṅgāra* is developed.

Similarly, there are some other examples of the same coin. They are I-74, and IV-6 etc.

Hāsyarasa or Humour

Hāsya or humour is one of the sentiments keeping the things lively. It arises through *Ceṣṭā* or the movements, *Veṣa* or dress and through *Vāṇi* or speech of a person whose mind is *vikṛta*. The person causing humour through his speech etc. is *Ālambana* ; and his movements are *Uddīpana's* of this sentiment. This sentiment of Humour is of six types. (1) Laughing or smiling of high-souled person. (2) *Vihasana* or a gentle laugh laugh and *Avahasana* or mocking laugh of middle class person. (3) *Apahasana* or causeless laugh and *Atihasana* or a violent laugh of low class person.[226] Thus, here we can see six types of humour in three sets corresponding to different classes of person.

There is a very good example in the fifth Act of *Hāsyarasa*.

जातिमात्रशरणा बहिष्कृताः केचिदादृतजघन्यवृत्तयः ।
रोषणा विपरिधाविनो मुधा ह्रेपयन्ति जनमुज्झितह्रियः ॥

S.S., V-39, p.494.

"There are some men who have nothing else in their favour but their birth in a good caste, who are outcasts in their community, who adopt mean ways to getting a livelihood and who are ever wrathful (by treatment) and are constantly wandering about (from place to place) aimlessly. They have no sense of shame in themselves and make others feel ashamed at their conduct, just like certain animals which are found living on heaps of rubbish (*jāti*) which are driven out of the houses of men, which live on fifth and which are ever angry and roam about the streets (aimlessly). These animals, too, have no shame and make men feel ashamed at their sight."

First of all it should be noted here that here Humour arises through the rough speech of Dambha. Hence, Dambha is *Ālambana* of the Humour; and his speech contains *Uddīpanabhāva*. His face in anger is *Anubhāva*; and Dambha's mocking contains *Vyabhicārībhāva*. In the example given above the sense of Humour lies in the element of *Apahāsa* by Dambha, who may be considered here as belonging to a low class.

Therefore, this is an example of showing the delineation of fifth type of *Hāsya* or Humour.

Karuṇarasa or Sentiment of Pathos

Karuṇarasa is produced through *Iṣṭanāśa* or destruction of desired fruit and through *Aniṣṭanāśa* or obtaining undesred fruit. Here *Śoka* is *Sthāyībhāva*. And *Śocanīyavastu* or the thing subjected to grievance is *Ālambana*; and the state of taking to the deadbody to the funeral field etc. is *Uddīpanavibhāva*. Moreover, *Daivāṇinda* or denouncing fate, Bhūpata or falling down to the earth, *Rodanam* or lamentation etc. are *Anubhāvas*; and *Nirveda* or detachment Moha, swooning, *Apasmāra* or uncurable disease, *Vyādhi* or curable disease, *Glāni* or decline, *Smṛti* or rememberance, *Unmāda* or intense passion, *Viṣāda* or grief, *Jāḍya* or steadyness etc. are *Vyabhicārībhāva*'s of sentiment of Pathos.[227]

In this connection, two verses selected from the Pathetic scene at the end of the eight Act may be quoted to show the delineation of *Karuṇarasa*.

बाह्यजनैः सार्धं दीर्घमार्गं त्वया प्रकान्तेन ।
दीनदशासंतप्तो दयितजनो नाथ किमिति संत्यक्तः ।।

S.S., VIII-104, p.744.

"You are now going on a distant journey in the company of strangers. Why have you left behind, my lord, your dear wife, who is now in deep sorrow."

हतजीवजीवितेशां विषादमूर्च्छादिलुप्तनिश्वासाम् ।
तृष्णादयः सकुल्या दुर्मतिमभितो निपत्य विलपन्ति ।।

S.S., VIII-105, p.745.

"By the side of Durmati who has lost her beloved husband and who, on account of the swoon caused by sorrow, does not even breathe, other ladies like Tṛṣṇā, who belong to the same family, fall on the ground and raise their lament."

Here the sentiment of Pathos is developed through *Iṣṭanāśa, i.e.* the destruction of Mahāmoha who is the beloved husband of Durmati, and through *Aniṣṭaprāpti, i.e.* obtaining widowhood, (this elememt is not evident). Here lamentation of Durmati is *Sthāyibhāva*; Mahāmoha who is already dead is *Ālambana*; *Uddīpanabhāva* is silent. Tumburu's denouncing the fate, lamentation of Tṛṣṇā etc. are *Anubhāvas*; Durmatis falling in swoon, decline of her status and sorrowful condition are *Vyabhicārībhāvas*.

Thus, these two are apt examples delineating *Karuṇarasa*.

Raudrarasa or Furious Sentiment

Raudrarasa is usually developed in the battle scene. Krodha or Anger is its *Sthāyībhāva*; Redness is its colour and *Raudra* is the deity of this sentiment. Enemy is the *Ālambana-Vibhāva* and the actions of the person like first fighting become *Uddīpanabhāvas*. Moreover, fist fighting making enemy to fall ground, deceitful actions, rushing to the battlefield etc. Then biting one's lips, clapping, sensuring, declaring one's own valour, holding a weapon etc. are *Anubhāvas*. And *Ugratā* or *Āvega*, *Romāñcana, Sveda, Vepata, Mada* etc. are *Vyabhicārībhāvas* of *Raudra* sentiment.[228]

There are copious examples delineating this sentiment. For example ;

अतिघोरचेष्टितः खल्वसावशेषविध्वंसनतर्षवानमर्षः ।

S.S., VIII, p.726.

"Krodha's movements are dreadful and he seems to be thirsting for the destruction of everything without exception."

अपि वैरवरूथिनीमशेषामपि शैलानपि सागरानपि क्षमाम् ।
ग्रसितुं प्रभवत्यतं प्रदीप्तः प्रथितः कोपतनूनपादनूनः ॥

S.S., VIII-68, p.726.

"This raging fire called Krodha is known to be very powerful and if roused, he will consume not only the entire army of his enemies but also all the mountains, the oceans and the earth itself."

जिघांसाजानिनानेन स्थिरत्रसमिदं जगत् ।
वध्यघातकभावेन विभज्य विनियुज्यते ॥ *S.S.*, VIII-69, p.726.

"The world consisting of the moving and the unmoving, has, for his own purpose, been divided by Krodha, the husband of Jighāṁsā, into two classes, those that kill and those that are killed."

करचरणनखरदन्तप्रभृतिकमपि जगति सहजमितरदपि ।
प्रतिघसुभटस्य विश्वं प्रहरणमथवा विहर्तुमुपकरणम् ।।

S.S., VIII-70, p.726.

"To this warrior striking against his enemies, all things in the world — those that were born with him like hands, feet, nails, teeth and the like, as well as others like stones, swords and the like serve as weapons or, shall I say, as playthings."

Here, anger Krodha is *Sthāyibhāva*; his enemy foe, *i.e.* Kṣānti is *Ālambana*; and his action of burning enemies in the fire of his anger is *Uddīpanabhāva*; Krodha's holding the inborn weapons like his nails, teeth etc. is *Anubhāva*; and Krodha's drastic actions against enemies is *Vyabhicārībhāva* of *Raudra* sentiment.

Thus, these are apt examples illustrating the existence of *Raudrarasa*.

Virarasa or Heroic Sentiment

Vīrarasa is developed where hero is extraordinary one. Its *Sthāyibhāva* is *Utsāha*; and the enemy to be win over, *i.e.* *Ālambanavibhāva*; and the movements of hero for achieving his goal are the *Uddīpanavibhāvas*; and the support etc. for his activities are *Anubhāva's* of *Vīrarasa*.[229]

अनिद्राणप्रज्ञासहजबलधीराद्भुतगति-
स्तितिक्षासंतोषस्थिरतरतनुत्राणघटितः ।
प्रयुक्तं केनापि प्रणवरथमास्थाय पुरतो
विवेकः प्रत्युद्यन् विघटयति मे व्यूहघटनाम् ।। *S.S.*, IV-58, p.444.

"Viveka with unfailing good sense as his source of strength and with a courageous and wonderful movement is now wearing the thick armour of Patience and contentment, and seated in the chariot of *Praṇava* driven by some one, (*Praṇava* composed by Brahmā), comes in front of us and breaks our battle-formation."

As described the above example, Viveka is the irresistable extraordinary hero; his courageous wonderful movements are due to *Utsāha*, which is *Sthāyībhāva*; his chariot of *Praṇava* possesses golden splendour, Mahāmoha enemy king to be won over Viveka. By Viveka is its *Ālambanavībhāva*; and his efforts of breaking enemies *Vyūha* is *Uddīpanavībhāva*; and the armour of patience and contentment to which Viveka is resorted is *Anubhāva*.[230]

Thus, the above example is an illustration of *Vīrarasa*. Some other examples are IV-7, IV-18, V-64, VII-36, VIII-57, and VIII-33 etc.

Bhayānakarasa or Terrible

Bhaya or fear is *Sthāyībhāva* of *Bhayānakarasa*; its deity is god Yama. The thing from which fear arises is *Ālambana*; actions of dreadful person are *Uddīpana-vibhāvas*; paleness, stumbling speech, swooning, swetting, horripilation, trembling, looking towards different directions are *Anubhāvas*.

Following is the verse showing that delineation of *Bhayānakarasa*:

पातालक्षिप्तसिन्धुः प्रशकलितकुलक्ष्माभृदुत्कीलभूमि-
निर्धूतादित्यचन्द्रद्युतिगणनिबिडध्वान्तनीरन्ध्रदिक्कः ।
वेधःसौधप्रभेदी विघटितपवनस्कन्धपर्यस्ततारः
प्रारब्धोऽसौ विवेकप्रतिरथिनि महानाहवे मोहवेगः ॥

S.S., VIII-96, p.740.

"The great battle against Viveka, in which Mahāmoha displays his terrific strength has begun. As a result of it, the oceans have been cast into the nether regions (*Pātāla*); the great mountains have been broken to pieces and the earth shows extensive cavities where they stood; the Sun, the Moon and the Stars have disappeared leaving all the quarters in dense darkness; the mansion of Brahmā being subjected to cracks and the Stars have fallen on account of the destruction caused by the wind."

Here fear on account of Mahāmoha is *Sthāyībhāva*; Mahāmoha who is the source of fear is *Ālambana*; plightful conditions of ocean, mountains, the earth, the sun, the moon, the stars, different horizons and of the mansion of Brahmā are *Vyabhacārībhāvas*. Here *Anubhāva* is silent.

Therefore, this is an apt example where *Bhayānakarasa* is developed.

Bībhatsarasa or Odious Sentiment

Jugupsā is the *Sthāyībhāva* of *Bībhatsarasa*. Its colour is bluish and *Mahākāla* is the deity. Meat, blood etc. are *Ālambanavibhāvas*. And falling of insects on such things is *Uddīpanavibhāva*. Spewing, turning away the face closing the eyes are *Anubhāvas*; and swooning, falling sick or dieing are *Vyabhicārībhāvas*.[231]

Following are the examples showing the delineation of *Bībhatsarasa*.

क्षतजमधु रणस्थैर्दत्तमुत्तम्भिताग्र ध्वजपटपुनरुस्वर्धनीकैरनेकैः ।
पलभुज इह जाग्रन्नन्दथूनां वधूनां पृथुकरटिकरोटीकर्षैरैरर्पयन्ति ॥

S.S., VIII-33, p.700.

"The white clothes in the uplifted banners of the armies create the impression of a second *Gaṅgā* in the sky. Evil spirits are here offering, to their delighted wives, the liquor of blood shed by the armies, in the capacious skulls of elephants (which serve as drinking cups)."

पत्तीनुद्यद्विपत्तींस्त्रुटितपृथुशिरःकन्धरान्सिन्धुरेन्द्रान्
वाहनाकीर्णदेहान् व्यतिहननमिथःखण्डिताङ्गांशताङ्गान् ।
शस्त्राशस्त्रिप्रसङ्गप्रभवचटचटारावघोरप्रचाराः
कुर्वन्त्युद्दामगर्वाः कृतिन इह रणे विक्रमैरक्रमेण ॥

S.S., VIII-34, p.701.

"Fierce warriors who are experts in fighting exhibit their valour by driving foot-soldiers pell-mell into dangers. They cut off the heads and necks of proud elephants, lop off the limbs of horses and by dashing their chariots against those of their enemies cause them to be shattered to pieces and they rush to and fro striking their weapons against those of their foes and cause a loud clatter thereby."

Here *Jugupsā* arising from the cite of flowing of the blood in the battlefield is *Sthāyībhāva*; flow of blood, scattering of meat here and there are *Ālambanavibhāvas*. *Uddīpana* and *Anubhāva* are however silent here. Death of soldiers, wounded horses and elephants are *Vyabhicārībhāvas* of *Bībhatsarasa* here.

Adbhutarasa or Marvellous Sentiment

Vismaya is *Sthāyībhāva* of *Adbhutarasa*; its colour is Yellow. Extraordinary object is *Ālambanavibhāva*; and the glory of the qualities of that object is *Uddīpanavibhāva*; horripilation, swetting, standing, staying, unclear speech, anxiety, opening the eyes etc. are the *Anubhāvas*; reasoning or imagination, hasty, happiness etc. are *Vyabhicārībhāvas*.[232]

Here is an example where *Adbhutarasa* is developed.

अमी पुनः सात्त्वतं शास्त्रमधीयानास्त्रय्यन्तवादिभिरैक्यमिवापन्ना बल्बजप्राय-बहुविधविद्याजल्पविमुखीकृतमानसा बहिरन्तश्च शुद्धाः श्वेतद्वीपवासिन इव शुभंयवः पुरुषास्तामिमामौपनिषदीं परिषदमुपजिगमिषन्ति ।

S.S., II-82, p.303.

"And now, here are pure souls (pure in body and pure in mind) who have studied the scripture of the *Sāttvatas* (*Pāñcarātra*), and seem to be in no way different from the followers of Vedānta. They turn away their mind from the varied prate of the *Vidyās* which are as gross and coarse as grass. They long for the good (of all) like the resindents of

Śvetadvīpa and are now approaching this assembly of the followers of the Upaniṣads."

This example is from the context of discouse between the preceptor and desciple on different systems of philosophy. Improvement in the mental status of the individual souls causes *Vismaya*; and this *Vismaya* is *Sthāyibhāva* here. The desciple and preceptor may be considered here as extraordinary objects through the discourse of whom individual souls are taking much interest in Vedānta; the glory of these two unique personalities is *Uddīpanavibhāva*; internal and external purity of the individual souls, the desire for participating in Vedānta discussions etc. are *Anubhāvas*; brightness of individual souls resembling that of beings in the *Śvetadvīpa* is *Vyabhicārībhāva*.

Thus, this is an apt example delineating *Adbhutarasa*.

3. ALAṄKĀRAS IN THE SAṄKALPASŪRYODAYA

The excellence of a literary work, be it a drama or a poem, lies in its richness of the use of figures of speech and of the sentiments. Rhetoricians have considered the figures of speech as one of constituents of poetry. Therefore, the dramatists or poets have made good use of different figures in proper contexts.

The figures of speech indeed, adorn the substance of poetry. Bhāmaha and Daṇḍin, famous rhetorians of the old school, have regarded them as invariable elements of the poetry. Bhāmaha says that an unornamented poem, though full of poetic sentiments, does not attract a *Sahṛdaya* (lover of poetry) like a beautiful but unornamented face of a lady.[233] Ānandavardhana, the foremost propounder of the *Dhvani* Theory, regards that figures of speech should be used with great discretion in such a way as to subserve the delineation of *Rasa*. Figures should be evolved without special effort on the part of the poet.[234]

Daṇḍin also has highlighted the importance of figures of speech as a means of adding charm to poetry.[235] Though Vāmana has laid much emphasis on *Rīti*, he has readily accepted the importance of the figures. He says that beauty is *Alaṅkāra*, and a poem appeals to the mind of a reader if it has *Alaṅkāras*.[236] Thus, it is evident that figures add to the poetic charm. Rhetoricians have mentioned two types of figures of speech. (1) *Śabdālaṅkāra* (decorating the words), and (2) *Arthālaṅkāra* (decorating the sense). Vedānta Deśika may be said to be equally well-versed in the science of rhetorics as can be seen further from copious examples of various figures of speech. A close reading of the *Saṅkalpasūryodaya* makes it evident that Vedānta Deśika has made use of various figures of speech in suitable contexts. No doubt, Vedānta Deśika's use of *Śabdālaṅkāras* is considerably scanty as comparing to the use of *Arthālaṅkāras*. Yet, a few examples of *Śabdālaṅkāra* may be seen as below.

(a) Anuprāsa or Alliteration

Anuprāsa is that, where same sound is repeated for number of times in the same order even if their vowels differ in such repetition.[237]

A verse from the first Act of the *Saṅkalpasūryodaya* exemplifies *Anuprāsa*.

महत्यारम्भेऽस्मिन्मधुरिपुदयासंभृतधृतिः
बहिष्कृत्यारातीन्सुमुखि बहिरन्तश्च भवतः ।
समाधावाधाय क्षपितवृजिनं क्षेत्रिणमहं
परप्राप्त्या धन्यं परिणमचितुं प्राप्तनियमः ॥

Here the first line of the verse repeats '*Ma*' sound twice. similarly, in the second line bahi sound, in the third line sound '*dha*' and '*kṣa*'. The sound *para* and *prāpta* are repeated twice in the last line. Therefore, it can be said as an example of *Anuprāsa*.

(b) Cchekānuprāsa or Single Alliteration

It is called *Cchekānuprāsa* where there is single repetition of similar consonants. And this similarity of consonants should be without change of order.[238] There is an example of this kind of Alliteration :

क्षमृदुहृदये दये मृदितकामहितें महिते
धृतविबुधे बुधेषु निहितात्मधुरे मधुरे
वृषगिरिसार्वभौमदयिते मयि ते महतीं
भवुकनिधे निधेहि भवमूलहरां लहरीतम् ।। (VI-76)

In this verse, the first line consists of single repetition of consonants *daye daye* and *hite hite*. And, in the second line budhe budhe and *madhure madhure*, in the third line *yite yite*; and in the last line of the verse *nidhe nidhe* and laharī laharī are repeated. Therefore, it is an example of *Cchekānuprāsa*.

(c) Upamā or Simile

There are a few examples illustrating *Upamā*[239] figure of speech. For example :

दृश्यमानो दिवसेश्वर इव बहलमन्धकारप्राग्भारकं ।
दीप्यमानश्च दवानल इव विपुलं विन्ध्याटवीमण्डलम् ।।
त्वरमाणश्च प्रभञ्जन इव तुलितं शैलेन तूलोत्करं ।
प्रेक्षमाणो निखिलमपि दुर्मतिमतं भेत्तुं विवेकः प्रभुः ।। (II-4)

"Like the Sun whom we see dispelling wide and dense darkness, like the blazing forest — fire (burning away) the broad expanses of Vindhya forests, like a swift gale dispersing mountain — like heaps of cotton, our king Viveka will refute all the rival systems of perverse minds in the sight of every one."

According to Mammaṭa, the definition of *Upamā* runs thus : *Upamā* exists where there is similarity of attributes between two things, when there is distinction between them.

Here Viveka's refuting all the rival systems of perverse minds by mere sight is compared with Sun's dispelling the darkness, forest — fires (*dāvānala*) burning the wide Vindhya forest and to swift winds dispersing mountain like heaps of cotton. Thus, here the *Upameya* statement of Viveka's dispelling the darkness is adorned and strengthened by three *Upamāna*s given above. As three *Upamāna*s are enlanced here, this verse may be said as an example of *Mālopamā*.

In this verse above *iva* is the term expressing the idea of comparison. Since *iva* is used as *Upamā Pratipādaka* term in the said example, this is of the type of Śrautī Upamā as Mammaṭa calls.

In the same manner, other examples of *Upamā* figure of speech like I-59, I-87 etc. should be understood.

(d) Rūpaka or Metaphor

The benedictory verse of the *Saṅkalpasūryodaya* is an example of *Rūpaka* figure of speech :

यद्भक्तिप्रचयात्मके दिनमुखे दृष्टिक्षमः क्षेत्रिणः
क्षिप्रं संसृतिशर्वरीं क्षिपति यत्संकल्पसूर्योदयः ।
तत्त्वैरस्त्रविभूषणैरधिगतः स्वाधीननित्योन्नतिः
श्रीमानस्तु स मे समस्तविपदुत्ताराय नारायणः ॥ (I-i)

"May Śrīman Nārāyaṇa (Nārāyaṇa with His consort Śrī) be pleased to convey me over all the ills (of life) — Nārāyaṇa whose *will* like Sunrise dispels at once the night of *Saṁsāra* (or the recurring cycle of births and deaths), who is capable of being seen by the *Jīva* (or embodied soul) when its deep devotion has attained to the state of the dawn of day Nārāyaṇa whose supremacy is self-dependent and eternal, arising, as it does, from His missiles and ornaments which are symbolic of the various *tattvas* or 'reals' of the Universe."

As Mammaṭa defines, *Rūpaka* consists in the identification of the standard of comparison and the object of comparison.[240]

Here the dramatist invokes Lord Nārāyaṇa for the removal of the phenomenal obstacles and for gaining transcendental fruit. Here in the three *Rūpakas* are seen :

(1) यद्भक्तिप्रचयात्मके दिनमुखे

(2) संसृति शर्वरी

(3) संकल्पसूर्योदयः

Therefore, it is evident that in the above verse, there are three *Upamānas* such as *dinamukha* (early morning) *śarvarī* (night) and *sūryodaya* (sunrise). And the *Upameyas* are also three respectively , such as *bhaktipracaya* (deep devotion), *saṁsṛti* (recurring cycle of births and deaths) and *saṅkalpa* (will). The identification here has sprung from extreme resemblance between these *Upamāna* and *Upameyas*. Each *Upamāna* endows the *Upameya* with its own form by superimposing it thereon. Hence this verse is an apt example of *Rūpaka*.

In a similar manner, many good examples illustrating *Rūpaka* are found in the drama. They are : I-2, I-38, and II-80 etc. These examples should be understood in the manner described above.

(e) Śleṣa or Paronomasia

In the drama, there are some examples of Śleṣa figure of speech. One of such examples may be seen as below:

वित्रासिनी विबुधवैरिवरूथिनीनां पद्मासनेन परिचारविधौ प्रयुक्ता।
उत्प्रेक्ष्यते बुधजनैरुपपत्तिभूम्ना घण्टा हरेः समजनिष्ट यदात्मनेति।। (I-14)

"It is considered by wise men, on the strength of abundant

and appropriate reason, that the bell of Hari (Hari's temple) which frightens away the hosts of the enemies of the gods, and which was used by Brahmā in the service of the Lord, was born as an incarnation in the form of this poet."

As defined in the *Kāvyaprakāśa Śleṣa* arises when words which ordinarily have one sense, convey two meanings owing to peculiar circumstances.[241]

In the given example above, Vedānta Deśika's divine incarnation is described. The stanza conveys that Vedānta Deśika is the divine incarnation of the bell of Lord Hari (the bell in the temple of Tirupati), which dispels the enemies of the Gods.

In this stanza there is a Pun on the following terms :

तामभिप्रेत्याह - वित्रासिनीति। विबुधवैरिणो राक्षसाः तेषां वरुथिन्यः सेनाः। अन्यत्र कुदृष्टिवर्गाः तासां वित्रासिनी। पद्मासनेन प्रयुक्ताः चतुर्मुखेन समर्पिता। अन्यत्र श्रियः पत्या दत्ता। उपपत्तयः विबुधवैरिवित्रासकत्वकैंकर्योपयुक्तत्वादयः तेषां भूम्ना बाहुल्येन। यद्वा उक्तोपपत्तिद्वय सामर्थ्येनेत्यर्थः यदात्मना यस्य वैदान्ताचार्य स्यात्मना स्वरूपेण घण्टानादो रक्षोघ्न इति प्रसिद्धिः। (pp.40-41)

विबुधवैरि वरुथिनीनाम्, पद्मासनेन प्रयुक्ताः and उपपत्तिभूम्नाः ।

(1) विबुधवैरि वरुथिनीनाम् — Army of the demons. The hosts of wicked people.

(2) पद्मासनेन प्रयुक्ताः — Given by four-faced Brahmā given by Goddess Lakṣmī consort of Lord Hari.

(3) बुधजनैः उपपत्तिभूम्ना — (a) Strongly upheld by the competant scholars.

(b) Fully realised by means of *Kaiṅkarya.*

Thus, the terms in the stanza above convey two senses and hence, it is an example of *Śleṣa.*

(f) Atiśayokti or Exaggeration

Following is an example of *Atiśayokti* figure of speech.

मयि चरति कदाचित्सत्यलोकोपकण्ठे
सपदि सनकमुख्यैः साकमभ्युज्जिहानः
सविनयनिभृताङ्गः सप्तशः क्षालितेन
स्वयमुदवहदर्घ्यं पणिना पद्मयोनिः ॥ (V-40)

"I was once travelling in the outskirts of *Satyaloka*, when, Brahmā came to welcome me at once with Sanaka and others, motionless and respectful and brought me *Arghya* in his own hand, having washed it seven times for the sake of purity."

Atiśayokti means the statement of excellance of *Upameya*. This element is broughtout on account of its complete identification with the *Upamāna*.

As Mammaṭa defines *Atiśayokti* figure of speech is explained as having four types.[242]

Of these four, the third type of *Atiśayokti* is here illustrated. The third type occurs when there is a supposition or assumption of an impossible thing as a result of expressing the sense of *yadi*. Here, in the said example Dambha boasts of himself as inheriting great honour even by Brahmā, Sanaka and others in the out-skirts of *Satyaloka*. Dambha's having such exhaulted honour, is just impossible. This is a clear assumption. Hence it is an apt example of *Atiśayokti*. Other examples of the *Atiśayokti* are V-41, 59, and VI-63 etc.

(g) Nidarśana or Illustration

There is an example of illustrating the *Nidarśana* figure of speech. It is as below :

सौहार्दमित्थमनवाप्य सहोदराणा-
मासीत्स्वमूलगुणभेदवशाद्विरोधः ।

एकप्रजापतिभुवामपि वैरबन्धः
स्वात्मावधिः स्वयमुदेति सुरासुराणाम् ॥ (I-48)

"Thus between us, all fraternal feelings have dis-appeared and enmity has arisen (in their place) owing to the basic difference between our natures. Though born of one and the same father — the sage Kāśyapa Prajāpati — has not hatred arisen between the *Suras* and the *Asuras* lasting till death ?"

Nidarśana is defined as an impossible connection between two things which leads to comparison.[243]

In the verse mentioned above describes how enemity has arisen between Viveka and Mahāmoha the brothers born of Puruṣa (Individual soul).

These two brothers Viveka and Mahāmoha are described as related to Gods and demons.

In fact, it is just impossible to say that Viveka and Mahāmoha are related to Gods and demons respectively. Thus the impossible connection between these two senses links to comparison between them. *Vairabandha* or *Virodha* is the term here shown the sense of similarity between them. Thus, in *Nidarśana* the comprehension of the similarity makes the sentences understandable. Hence, it is an example of *Nidarśana*.

(h) Samāsokti or the Speech of Brevity

There is a beautiful stanza standing as an example of *Samāsokti*, *i.e.*

मुकुलयति विवित्सां मोहविध्वंसमिच्छन्
विमृशति निगमान्तान् वीक्षते मोक्षधर्मान् ।
निशमयति च गीतां नित्यमेकान्तभक्त्या
गुणपरिषदवेक्षी गुप्यमन्त्रो विवेकः ॥ *S.S.*, I-61

"He gets all his doubts cleared; desirous of destroying Moha, he studies Vedānta thoughtfully and reads about those observances or duties which lead to *Mokṣa*. He cultivate virtues like self-control and guards his policies from being known to others (Practising in secret the repetition of *Aṣṭākṣara*) and is always trying to understand the Gītā with undivided devotion."

As Mammaṭa has explained *Samāsokti*[244] is the statement of another by means of Paronomastic adjectives, *i.e.* (1) from the description of a relevant matter, an irrelevant matter is understood, (2) such irrelevant is understood by means of Paronomastic adjectives, and (3) the substantive in the sentence which describes a relevant matter is not Paronomistic.

In the example mentioned above Vedānta Deśika describes the nature of Viveka through Kāma, one of the ministers of Mahāmoha. From the description of Viveka who is *prakṛta*, we understand the description of a king who is *aprakṛta*. This is done by means of Paranomistic adjectives. They are :

विवित्सां मुकुलयति – (i) removing the doubts,

(ii) removing desire for physical wealth.

निगमान्तान् विमृशति – (i) one who studies Vedānta philosophy thoughtfully,

(ii) one who counsels indeep with the ministers well versed in polity (*nigama*).

गुणपरिषदवेक्षी – (i) possessing virtues,

(ii) cultivating good qualities like self-control etc.

गुप्तमन्त्र – (i) one who preserves the secracy of Vedic *Mantra*s and instructs them to a qualified student,

(ii) one who guards his strategyes from being known to others.

Thus, the adjectives shown above are Paronomistic and significant. But the substantive Viveka is not Paronomistic and does not in anyway help us to understand the irrelevant matter (*aprakṛta*).

Thus, the stanza given above is an example of *Samāsokti*.

(i) Arthāntaranyāsa or Corroboration

The following verse is an example of *Arthāntaranyāsa* figure of speech:

> इमामधर्मेण विभाव्य संप्लुतामुदन्वता द्वारवतीमिवाधुना ।
> न भावये संयमसंपदास्पदं न कालतः कस्य गुणव्यतिक्रमः ॥ (VI-33)

"Well, driver! This city of Mathurā now bears witness to the story of the gopis in whose company Bhagavān enjoyed Himself. In the same way as the city of Dvārakā was enveloped by *adharma*. I do not therefore consider it suitable for acquiring the wealth of Yoga. What is there that does not undergo a change in its nature in the process of time ?"

Before seeing the illustration of *Arthāntaranyāsa* it is better to know the definition there of. As Mammaṭa defines that is *Arthāntaranyāsa* when a general proposition is supported or corroborated by a particular — or a particular by a general either through similarity or through dissimilarity.[245]

This stanza explains the decline of *dharma* in Mathura city. Hence, it was considered as an improper place for meditation by Viveka. The stanza above is an example of *Sāmānyena viśeṣasya samarthanaṃ* — सामान्येन विशेषस्य समर्थनम्।

The latter part of the second line of the staza enunciates a general proposition, which supports the particular illustration explained in the remaining portion of the verse. The particular case describes that the city of Mathurā is enveloped by *adharma*. Therefore, it cannot be considered as suitable place for acquiring the wealth of Yoga. This is supported by a general proposition "what is that that does not undergo a change in its nature in the process of time ?"

This is an example of figure of *Arthāntaranyāsa*.

(j) Viśeṣokti or Speech of Speciality or Peculiar Allegation

An example of *Viśeṣokti* figure is employed by the author in the fifth Act of the drama :

अनन्तविषयस्पृहाजलधिसंप्लुते मानसे
वसन्तसमये स्थिते मलयमारुते जीवति ।
सकृद्विहितसौप्तिकंप्रतिनिवृत्तिवैलक्ष्यतः
प्रसुप्त इव हन्त न स्पृशति पञ्चबाणः शरान् ॥ (V-61)

"While the mind is still sunk in the sea of endless desires for objects of sense, while the spring is in full swing, and while the breeze from the mountain Malaya is blowing gently. Kāma, having been obliged to retreat from a night - attack, is now ashmed, and being dazed like one asleep, does not (even) touch his arrows."

As has been defined by Mammaṭa, *Viśeṣokti* consists in the statement representing an effect as not following inspite of the causes working properly.[246]

The verse quoted above describes how unattackable and invincible is Viveka.

Here, (1) अनन्तविषयस्पृहा — endless desires for objects of sense,

(2) वसन्तस्थितिः — presence of spring in full swing,

(3) मलयमारुत जीवनम् — gentle blowing of breeze from Malaya mountain and

(4) सौप्तिकविधान — a retreat from night attack.

are the causes which should produced the result, *i.e. Viveka parājayaḥ* or Viveka's defeat. But this result has not followed अत्र वसन्तादिसमवधानेऽपि कामस्याकार्याकरत्वोक्तेविशेषोक्तिर्व्यज्यते ॥

Though Vasanta is providing full co-operation, it is not possible for Kāma to achieve his goal of defeating Viveka. The cause which prevented this result from happening is the Viveka's firmness. This cause has not been mentioned. Therefore, the staza is an example of *anuktanimittā viśeṣoktiḥ*.

(k) Anumāna or Inference

There is one of the rare examples of *Anumāna* figure of speech.

उपवनशुकबृन्दैरुद्गृणद्भिस्त्रिवेदीं
प्रतिकलमनुमेयप्राच्यधर्मानुबन्धम् ।
चिरगतजनघोषं तीरमेतन्सरय्वा
रघुकुलनृपतीनां शोभते रत्नयूपैः ॥ (VI-27)

"In the Parks here, large number of parrots repeat the three Vedas ; it may be inferred from this at every instant that in fromer times, Vedic *dharma* was observed here (in its fulness). The bank of the Sarayū, though for a long time without the sound of men, looks beautiful on account of the large number of sacrificial posts adorned with gems which were planted there by the king of the race of the Raghus."[247]

As Mammaṭa defines *anumāna* consists in the statement of the reason (*sādhanaṁ*) and the conclusion (*sādhyaṃ*). The verse cited above is addressed by Viveka. It descirbes the beauty of the Penance groves on the bank of river Sarayū. The first line of the verse referring to the chanting of the Vedic *Mantras* by the Parrots, is the statement of the reason (*sādhana*) and the second line infering the observance of religious activities, is the statement of conclusion (*sādhyaṃ*). Hence, this is an example of (*anumāna*) figures of speech.

(l) Paryokti or Round about Speech or Circumlocation

Here is an example of *Paryokti* figure of speech.

एष मैनाकजनको धरणीधेनुतर्णकः ।
त्रिदशाचलजामाता त्र्यम्बकश्वशुरो गिरिः ॥ (VI-21)

"This Himālaya is the father of the mountain Maināka : he is, as it were, the calf of the cow named Earth; he is the Son-in-law of Meru and the father-in-law of Śiva."

In *Paryokti* there is a certain thing whcih is intended to be expressed in order to explain the expressed meaning usual procedure of using the words is not adopted here. But the intended sense is here conveyed by a different mode.[248] Thus, *paryokta* is the statement of a certain thing without the relation of *vācya* and *vācaka* existing between it and the words which convey it.

The stanza quoted above refers to the glory of Himālayan mountain. But instead of expressing this idea directly poet resorts to a different mode and wherein other Phrases such as *janaka*, *tarṇaka* (calf) *jāmāta śvaśura* are used indicating the glory of Himālaya.

जनक - मैनाक जनक — (Father of Maināka)

तर्णक - धरणीधेनु तर्णकं — (Calf of the cow named earth)

त्रिदशाचलजामाता — (Son-in-law of Meru mountain)

त्र्यम्बक श्वशुरः — (Father-in-law of Lord Īśvara)

Therefore, as the intended sense is here conveyed by means of a different mode without *vācya*, *vācaka*, *bhāva* this stanza is an example of *paryoktaṃ*.

(m) Samuccayālaṅkāra or Conjunction

There is a verse in the first Act dealing with the accomplishments of scholars, devotees and the Viveka. It runs as below:

दुर्जनं प्रतिपक्षं च दूरदृष्टिरयं जनः ।
विवेकश्च महामोहं विजेतुं प्रभविष्यतः ॥ (I-29)

"With fore-sight, I shall be able to defeat the plans of my wicked rivals in the profession in the same way as king Viveka will defeat by his forethought the wicked Mahāmoha."

Samuccaya figure of speech occurs where many causes conjoin to produce a certain result. To explain, there is a certain result which is intended to be produced. For, one cause capable of producing that result exist. Simultaneously with it, other causes which are capable of producing the same result are mentioned. Thus, *samuccaya* consists in the simultaneous operation of many causes each of which is severally capable of producing the intended result. [249]

In the example quoted above the proper efforts of scholarly persons hamper the activities of wicked ones prompted by *tamas*. The efforts of a devotee being a righteous path, destroy the envious activities. Similarly, Viveka by means of well-timed strategyes like *Vairāgya* etc. defeat Mahāmoha.

Thus, the efforts of learned scholars, devotee and of Viveka yield the fruit of defeating Mahāmoha. In this way, here three causes simultaneously begin to operate in order to produce the same result. Thus, it is an illustration of *samuccaya* figure.

(n) Kāvyaliṅga or Poetical cause

Following verse from the third Act is an example of *Kāvyaliṅga* figure of speech:

स्वस्यावाप्तिः सुखमिति मृषा स्वेतरस्यानुभूतौ ।
कामादन्यः क इव घटते मोक्षनामा पुमर्थः ॥
तस्मादस्मद्बहुमतनिरध्यक्षमीमांसकोक्त्या ।
स्वोच्छानृत्यद्बहुगुणनिधिः स्वर्ग एवापवर्गः ॥ (III-3)

"If bliss means the attainment of one's self, it is false (because we are already in the attainment of our self); if on the other hand, bliss means the attainment of something other (than one's own self), then since it is the desire for something else, there cannot be a *Puruṣārtha* called *Mokṣa* other than Kāma which is desire. Therefore, *Svarga* which results form our own desire and which dances (before our eyes) as a treasure of good experiences should itself be called *Mokṣa* as stated by the atheistic Mīmāṁsakas whom we hold in high esteem."

The figure of *Kāvyaliṅga* arises when the reason for a certain thing is contained in *vākyārtha* or the meaning of a sentence.[250] The reason to be dealt with in this figure, is poetical one and not the logical one of Naiyāyikās. Hence, it is called *Kāvyaliṅga.* The stanza adduced here describes the influence of Rāga over an ordinary person desiring for perishing pleasures of this life. And it explains, there is no other *Mokṣa* than fulfiling one's desire.

Here the first two lines contain the statement providing the reason for identifying the fulfilment of one's desire with

Mokṣa. And the substantiation of this view is presented in the last two lines. Thus, it is an example of *Kāvyaliṅga*.

(o) Parikara or Significant

Another stanza is seen in the second Act illustrating *Parikara* figure of speech.

सत्त्वस्थान्निभृतः प्रसादय सतां वृत्तिं व्यवस्थापय
त्रस्य ब्रह्मविदागसस्तृणमिव त्रैवर्गिकान्भावय ।
नित्ये शेषिणि निक्षिपन्निजभरं सर्वंसहे श्रीसखे
धर्मं धारय चातकस्य कुशलिन् धाराधरैकान्तिनः ।। (II-38)

"Behave with proper care (and attention) towards righteous men and win their favour. Establish firmly the code of conduct upheld by the good; be in dread of giving offence to those who have realised Brahman, treat as straw those who pursue the three worldly ends (*dharma*, *artha* and *kāma*); having surrendered the responsibility for your protection to the eternal Lord of Lakṣmī who forgives everything and for whose purpose (alone) we exist, observe, my good sir, the code of the bird Cātaka, which depends solely and exclusively on the cloud (for its welfare and for its life)."

As Mammaṭa defines[251] *Parikara* arises when a certain thing is described by means of significant adjectives. To be explicit, this figure arises when a certain substantive is qualified by many adjectives that express one sense and suggests another.

In the stanza cited above, the king Viveka asks his disciple (Vāda) to remain engaged in the efforts leading to grace of God. All the words expressing the command of the king are very significant. And these commanding words relate to the king himself which is here a substantive. The expression of these adjectives suggests another meaning in a prohibitive order, *i.e.*

सत्त्वस्थान्निभृतः प्रसादय — (i) Win the favour of *Sāttvika* people.

(ii) keeping oneself far from wicked ones which means they should not be pleased.

सतां वृत्तिं व्यवस्थापय — (i) Establising firmly the code of conduct upheld by the good.

(ii) one should not follow the path of wicked men.

त्रैवर्गिकान् तृणमिव भावय — (i) one should treat the three phenomenal ends (*dharma, artha, and kāma*) as straw.

(ii) one should not consider these *Puruṣārthas* as highest ones.

(p) Viṣama or Unequal

A stanza illustrating *Viṣama* figure of speech is found in the third Act.

प्रपञ्चकृतकञ्चुकं यदि परं महः प्राप्यते
न दुःखमपहस्तितं भवति नैकधोपप्लवात् ।
अथैकमखिलोज्झितं न खलु भोग्यतामेति तत्
ततो निगममस्तकैर्निगदमात्रशेषैः स्थितम् ॥ (III-4)

"If it is held in accordance with Viśiṣṭādvaita that *Mokṣa* is the attainment of Supreme splendour (called Brahman), whcih has for its covering or body this world of *Cit* and *Acit*, (which would cling to Brahman owing to that covering (or body) will be ours. If, on the other hand, the Advaitin's view is accepted that *Mokṣa* is being Brahman without any attribute or distinguishing feature, then it cannot be enjoyable. So, the Upaniṣads (the head of the Veda) can remain only as a subject of study without any practical use."

Viṣama arises due to the contradiction between two things. As Mammaṭa defines[252] the figure *Viṣama* has four varieties :

(1) Where the Union between two things could not take place due to their extreme dissimilarity.

(2) Where not only is there no accomplishment of the fruit of an action by an agent but a calamity occurs in addition.

(3) Where the quality of the cause is mutually opposed to the quality of the effect.

(4) Where the action of a cause is mutually opposed to the action of the effect.

The present stanza exemplifies the third variety of *Viṣama* figure of speech, *i.e.* the role of Dveṣa asserts that the Philosophy of Viśiṣṭādvaita is ambiguous and hence, he calls it atheistic school in explaining this line of defective thought he shows the contradiction in this philosophy, *i.e.* the first line of the verse above says that *Mokṣa* is the attainment of Supreme Brahman who has for his body this world of *Cit* and *Acit*. The second line there of shows that the world of *Cit* and *Acit* is full of suffering. These two lines bring out the contradictory elements, *i.e.* the quality of the cause, *i.e.* Brahman is bliss. While the quality of the effect, *i.e.* the world of *Cit* and *Acit* is sorrow. These two qualities bliss and sorrow of cause and effect respectively are quite contradictory to each other.

Moreover, the third line illustrates another sort of contradiction between the qualities of cause and effect, *i.e.* attributeless Brahman is attainable according to Advaitins but there is absolute absence of such thing which is attributeless in the Universe. It is just like horn of the hare. The quality of *nirviśesa brahma* that is cause is *prāpyatva*.

This quality is totally absent in the Universe, *i.e.* effect. Thus, the quality of cause and effect here too are contradictory. This is how *Viṣama* figure of speech can be shown here.

(q) Vyatireka or Distinction

The stanza mentioned below illustrated the figure of *Vyatireka*.

पदे विष्णोरेषा प्रभवमधिगम्य प्रसृमरा
स्फुरत्ताराफेनस्तबक परिपाटी परिगता ।
क्षरन्ती पूर्वाद्रेरमरतटिनीसंप्लवसखी
तमिस्राकालिन्दीं शबलयति चन्द्रांशुपटली ॥ *S.S.*, IV-31

"Like the flood of the celestial Gaṅgā covered with bunches of foam looking like shining stars and taking its source from the feet of Viṣṇu and flowing down to mingle its waters with the dark waters of the Yamunā and giving them a variegated colour, these multitudinous rays of moon light taking their orgin from the sky and surrounded by the shining stars looking like the foam on the surface of the Gaṅgā and coming down the eastern mountain mingle with the darkness and give it a variegated appearance."

As Mammaṭa defines[253] the *Vyatireka* figure consists in the excellence of the *Upameya* over the *Upamāna*. The stanza given above contains the description of moon light. That is here *Upameya*. This is compared to Gaṅgā. Hence, Gaṅgā is *Upamāna*. The beauty of multitudinous rays of moon light is very striking and therefore which is superior to Gaṅgā's work of giving a variegated colour to the dark waters of the Yamunā which is the usual *Upamāna* here. Thus this stanza illustrates the *Vyatireka* in the proper manner.[254]

There are some other examples of this figure like V-59, and VI-32 etc.

(r) Bhrāntimān or Error

The following stanza illustrating *Bhrāntimān* figure, occurs in the Śuddha-viṣkambhaka of the seventh Act. The context is that Viveka and Sumati visit a picture gallery where Saṁskāra has depicted the forms of ten incarnations of Lord Hari. Saṁskāra looks round the picture-gallery, and describes the excellence of the paintings. In his own words:

विश्वप्रीणनविश्वकर्मरचनाचातुर्यकातर्यदैः
शिल्पैः कल्पयतीव मण्डनमसौ चेतः स्थितेर्मण्डपः ।
रत्नस्तम्भभुवोऽपि रश्मय इमे सोपानगोपानसी -
मध्यं यत्र गवाक्षयन्ति विहितप्रत्यग्रचित्रक्रमाः ॥ (VII-3)

"The Picture-gallery containing paintings which will put tp shame the skill of even Viśvakarmā who can please all beings with his artistic work, — this picture gallery will be an ornament even to the Lord who dwells within the heart. The brilliant rays which issue from the pillars set with gems will look like windows in the middle of staircase and in the ridge of the roof, as it were, a new painting executed there."

As stated in the *Kāvyaprakāśa* the figure *bhrāntimān* consists in the comprehension of *Upameya* as identical with *Upamāna*. In other words, the *Upameya* is mistaken for *Upamāna* and this mistake is due to close similarity between *Upameya* and *Upamāna*. Further this error is not intentional but real.[255]

In the stanza adduced above, author describes that the brilliant rays issuing from the pillars set with gems appear like the windows in the middle of stair-case. The brilliant rays of the pillars in the picture scroll, are mistaken for the windows, due to utter similarity of the brightness. Therefore, the stanza is an example of *bhrāntimān*.

(s) Ākṣepa or Paralipsis

In the fourth Act of the *Saṅkalpasūryodaya* there is a verse exempligying *Ākṣepa* figure of speech.

मा भूदमोघविशिखं नमितं धनुस्ते
मौर्वी च मा भवतु पुङ्खितचित्रपुङ्खा।
मद्दर्शितैरपि सखे विभयाद्विवेकः
शाखानिषङ्ग निहितैः शतशस्त्वदस्त्रैः ॥ (IV-14)

"My friend, let not your bow with its unfailing arrows be bent; let not your arrows of varied colours be placed in the bow-string. The very sight of your multitudinous arrows brought to his notice by me in the quiver — like branches of trees will frighten Viveka."

The figure *Ākṣepa* arises when there is a denial of something which is intended to be said, with a view to express some special meaning.[256]

This stanza given above is an address to Kāma by Vasanta. He therein, describes that victory over Viveka is not a difficult task. The speaker, Vasanta first avoids Kāma from discharging an arrow at Viveka. Then he says that Viveka gets frightened by mere seeing different types of missiles like flowers in the quiver - like branches.

Thus, the denial of discharging an arrow conveys the special menaing that gaining victory over Viveka is very easy. As this description involves apparent throwing off of the *iṣṭārtha, i.e.* victory over Viveka. Hence, the stanza above is an apt example of *Ākṣepa* figure of speech.

(t) Mudrālaṅkara

Here is an exmple illustrating *Mudrā* figure of speech.

संसारवर्तवेगप्रशमनशुभदृग्देशिकप्रेक्षितोऽहं
संत्यक्तोऽन्यैरुपायैरनुचितचरितेष्वद्य शान्ताभिसंधिः ।

निःशङ्कस्तत्वदृष्टया निरवधिकदयं प्रार्थ्य संरक्षकं त्वां
न्यस्य त्वत्पादपद्मे वरद निजभरं निर्भरो निर्भयोऽस्मि ॥ (VI-74)

"I have obtained the gracious glance of my ācārya which can arrest the speed of the whirlpool of *Saṁsāra* I have no other *Upāyas* (for my salvation) like *bhakti* or *Upāsanā*, and have given up all interest in activities which are improper. Having a mind free from doubts and with full knowledge, I have sought Thee as my saviour and have laid the responsibility for my salvation, O Varada ! at your lotus - feet. Here after I have no responsibility of my own for my protection and am free from all fears."

As Appayya Dīkṣita defines that an intended meaning is suggested by the words explaining the glory of the character related to the particular context.[257]

The present verse describes the glory of the deity of Śrīraṅgam, Lord Nārāyaṇa. As Viveka being in search of proper place for his meditation, he moves together with Tarka towards the holy place of Śrīraṅgam. In this context, Viveka glorifies the greatness of Lord Nārāyaṇa.

In this verse, the author uses an invoking word *varada* which means protector, fulfiller of devotees desires. This meaning tends to show Supremacy of Nārāyaṇa. His being Supremacy should have been expressed by using the word *nṛvara*; whereas this intended sense is suggested here by the term *varada*.[258] Hence, this is an example of *Mudrālaṅkāra*.

It is one of the glaring literary merits of Vedānta Deśika that he has made rare use of various types of *Nāṭyālaṅkāra*. They are as below :

(i) (a) प्राप्तिर्नाम नाट्यालंकारः[259]

प्रमाणपथ विभ्रष्टप्रधानार्थविमर्दनैः ।
स्थालीपुलाकनीत्यैव निवर्त्याः प्रतिवादिनः ॥ (II-40)

"Try to correct your oppenents by pointing out one or two important passages of scriptural tracts where they give wrong interpretations that are contrary to the *Pramāṇas*. While trying to see whether the rice in the pot has been well cooked or not, it is enough if one or two grains are taken out and tested with the hand. To determine the quality of the gold, no one ever thinks of rubbing the whole piece away on the touchstone."

(b) अनुनयोनाम नाट्यालंकारः[260]

असदद्रव्यसृष्टिप्रभृत्यर्थक्लृजया श्रुतिप्रक्रियाणामधिक्षेपतश्च ।
उलूकोपदेशापदेशप्रवृत्तः कथाशेषितोऽसौ कणादप्रणादः ॥ (II-70)

"Here, This system assumes the creation of new objects which did not exist before (as pots from mud). In other respects, too, it rejects the doctrines of the *Śrutis*. This tall talk indulged in by Kaṇāda is said to have begun from the teaching of Ulūka and, at present, it survives only in name."

(c) उद्दिष्टं नाम नाट्यालंकारः[261]

गाथा तथागतानां गलति गमनिका कापिली क्वापि लीना
क्षीणा कणादवाणी द्रुहिणहरगिरः सौरभं नारभन्ते ।
क्षामा कौमारिलोम्निर्जगति गुरुमतं गैरवाद् दूरवान्तं
का शङ्का शंकरादेर्भजति यतिपतौ भद्रवेदीं त्रिवेदीम् ॥ (II-89)

"When the prince of *Saṁnyāsins*, Śrī Rāmānuja, occupies the throne of the Vedas, the composition of the followers of Tathāgata (Buddha) which are mostly in dialect, glides away (unseen); the path of Kapila and his followers (the Sāṅkhyas) hides itself somewhere; the speech of Kaṇāda's disciples (Tārkikas of the Vaiśeṣika school) is growing thinner and thinner; the words of Druhiṇa (*i.e.* Hiraṇyagarbha or Brahmā) expounding Yoga, and of Hara (Paśupati's system) have lost their flavour; the doctrine of Kumārilabhaṭṭa (*Mīmāṁsā*) has become lean and that of

Guru (Prabhākara) has been thrown out to a distance owing to (indigestible) heaviness, such being the case, what doubt is there about (the fate of Śaṅkara) and others (Bhāskara and Yādavaprakāśa)?"

(d) प्रतीतेर्दाक्षिण्यं नाम नाट्यालंकार:[262]

तत्त्ववृत्तोभयभ्रष्टपाषण्डि गुणसंकुलः ।
कृती भवति कालोऽयं कृतिना संप्रति त्वया ।। (II-95)

"This age crowded with the multitudes of heretics who have strayed both from truth and from righteous conduct is now fortunate in having such an intelligent person as yourself."

(e) गर्हणं नाम नाट्यालंकार:[263]

जटालवृजिनाविले जवनयौवनास्वादने ।
जरामरणभीषणे जगति जन्तुरावत्यते ।। (III-16)

"By the floods of the wild stream of fate ordained, by the force of the gale of Lord's *Līlā* which blows with a wonderful speed, the embodied being is tossed to and fro in this world full of sins interlocked and entagled, with the enjoyment of a youth which flies fast and with the terrors of old age and death."

(f) पश्चात्तापो नाम नाट्यालंकार:[264]

प्रथितं पातकिवर्गं कृतघ्न एको हि कृत्स्नमतिशेते ।
तमिमं क्रियामाणघ्नंस्तमपि दुरात्मा करिष्यमाणघ्नः ।। (III-33)

"It is well known that man who is ungrateful for a past act of kindness is worse than all other groups of sinners. The man who is ungrateful for a present act of kindness is worse than the ungrateful man spoken of before. The wicked man who is ungrateful for a future act of kindness is the worst of all."

(g) क्षोभो नाम नाट्यालंकार:[265]

अवहितैरस्माभिर्भवितव्यम् अत्र हि —
वितमसि पदे विधास्यन् मायाजलधेः समुद्धृतं पुरुषम् ।
विमृशति किमपि रहस्यं सुमतिसहायो विवेक एकान्ते ॥ (IV-55)

"Viveka has lifted up Puruṣa from the sea of *Prakṛti* and in eagerness to place him in the region (Vaikuṇṭha) which is far removed from *tamas* (and *rajas*) is planning a secret strategy in the company of Sumati."

(h) परिहारो नाम नाट्यालंकार:[266]

ध्रुवमत्र गुणोत्तरापवादी ध्वनिसारः स्वयमागतोऽसि दर्पः ।
परिकल्पितवीतरागवेषा तव भार्यैव भवेदसावसूया ॥ (V-43)

"I, too, guess who you are ; surely you are Darpa arrived here in person. You are always in the habit of vilifying those who are superior to others (in learning or in conduct) and you are good at raising a loud outcry. And this is certainly your wife, Asūyā, who has put on the disguise of a *Saṁnyāsinī*."

(i) नीतिर्नाम नाट्यालंकार:[267]

परमनुगणयन्तः पण्डितंमन्यवर्गा-
नवितथमिव जल्पन्त्यागमाः किंचिदेते ।
विबुधगुरुमतेऽस्मिन् व्यक्तमुत्तभ्यमाने
मुषितनिखिलसारा मौनमुद्रां भजन्ते ॥ (V-48)

"These Āgamas, winning a number of wiseacresto their side prate of something or other as if it were true. If this system of the *Guru* of the gods is properly promulgated, they will lose all their flavour and be reduced to (complete) silence."

(u) Virodhābhāsa[268]

ललितमनसां प्रीत्यै बिभ्रद्रसान्तरभूमिका-
मनवमगुणो यस्मिन्नाट्ये रसो नवमः स्थितः ।

जनपदवीजङ्घालार्तिच्छिदानुगुणीभव-
न्नटपरिषदा तेनास्वादं सतामुपाचिन्वति ॥ (I-3)

"Provide for the enjoyment of good men with the help of actors personating the varied qualities of men, and capable of relieving the fatigue of all those who tread the path of *Saṁsāra*, by staging a play in which the ninth *rasa*, *Śāntarasa* (or sentiment of tranquil resignation), full of noble features, takes the place of other *rasas* or sentiments (like love and valour) for the delight of those gentle natures who cannot stand mental strain."

(v) Ūhālaṅkāra

कुलपतिमोक्षणोत्सवमृदङ्गकथा कदा
नवसमरोत्सुकापि न च भवति गजेन्द्रघटा ।
तथापि युगान्तभवत्स्तनयित्नुनिभक्कणितः
कथं कथं कोऽपि हन्त निखिलं मुखरयति नभः ॥ (I-98)

"The drum is not beaten yet for the festival of our progenitor's deliverance ; nor do we find the elephants set in array for the battle that is to begin. And yet, there is great blast of sound similar to the thunder of clouds, which will happen at the end of the *Yuga*, now filling the whole sky from somewhere or other."

This *Alaṅkāra* is defined as ऊहो वितर्कः स द्वेधा निर्णयानिर्णयात्मकः ।(*Prabhāvilāsa*, p.193) Here *Ūhā* determines that the sound of the drum suggesting victory of Viveka over Mahāmoha, is not proper as it is not achived yet. However, *Ūhā* determines Viveka's victory which is here as a suggestive element.

(w) Vinokti

सौवाकृतिस्तव त एव गुणानुभावाः
स्यादेव सागरसुता लिखिता त्वमेव ।

शिञ्जानमञ्जुमणिनूपुरमेखलस्ते
संचार एष चतुरो यदि नान्तरायः ॥ (VII-26)

"You have the same form, the same complextion and the same virtues and the daughter of the ocean might be thought of as yourself painted here, if only this graceful movement of yours with the jingling of your anklets and your girdle did not make a difference."

This *Alaṅkāra* is defined in the *Prabhāvilāsa*.

विना संबन्धि यत्किञ्चिद्यत्रान्यस्य परा भवेत् ।
रम्यतारम्यता वा स्यात्सा विनोक्तिरिति स्मृता ॥ (p.632)

This is further illustrated there itself :

अत्र नूपुरसंचारं विना शोभनत्वप्रतीते ।
रम्यतारूपविनोक्तिरलंकारः ॥ (p.632)

(x) Kārakaheturnāmālaṅkāra[269]

प्रह्लादह्लादनानि प्रणतसुरगणप्राणनप्रीणनानि
प्रत्यूढस्थेमभीमप्रलयघनघटाघोषणाडम्बराणि ।
क्षुभ्यत्सप्ताम्बुधीनि क्षुरपरुषनखक्रीडितक्षुण्णशात्रो-
रस्मद्भीतव्यपोहं विदधतु नृहरेरट्टहासाद्भुतानि ॥ (VII-40)

"May the wonderous roars of Narasiṁhā, who killed His foe by the play of His claws sharp as a sword, bring about the disappearance of all our fears - roars which made Prahlāda rejoice, which brought delight into the lives of the gods who worshipped Him with devotion, which belittled the loudness of the thundering sounds of the terrible multitudes of clouds at the time of *Pralaya* and which convulsed the seven seas."

(y) Preyo'laṅkāra[270]

शाक्यौलूक्याक्षपादक्षपणककपिलामर्त्यवन्द्यप्रधानै-
रन्यैराम्नायचर्चाकवचधृतिकनद्रोमुखद्वीपिभिश्च ।

बंहीयः क्षोभितापि श्रुतिरिह बहुधा जायमानेन गोज्रा
काले कालेऽभिगुप्ता कलहमतितरन्त्यक्षता रक्षतात्त्वाम् ।। (II-36)

"The *Śruti* which has been many times subjected to affliction by Buddhists, by Vaiśeṣikas who follow Kaṇāda, by Naiyāyikas under the leadership of Gautama, by the Jains, by Kapila (the Sāṅkhyas), by Bṛhaspati (the materialistic thinker) and so also by others who ostentatiously wear the cloak of students of the Vedas, like tigers with the faces of cows (Advaitins) the *Śruti* has been protected every now and then without any scathe by the great Saviour who is born as incarnation at the proper time and who is also your protector and in this way the *Śruti* has been getting rid of her afflictions."

In his *Kuvalayānanda*, Appayya Dīkṣita has identified *Preyolaṅkāra* with *Bhavalaṅkāra*, where he says—

प्रेयोऽलंकार एव भावालंकार उच्यते। (p. 270)

Besides *Prabhāvilāsa* defines this *Alaṅkāra* as प्रेयः प्रियतरारव्यानम्। (p.249) which means narration of a thing causing happiness. In the verse above the protection of *Śruti* is described and this itself is subject of creating joy in the present context.

(z) Pariṇāmālaṅkāra[271]

आरोहन्त्वनद्यतर्कपदवीसीमादृशां मादृशां
पक्षे कार्तयुगे निवेशितपदाः पक्षे पदद्भ्रयः परान् ।
सर्वानुश्रवसारदर्शिसशिरः कम्पद्वीजिह्वाशन-
क्रीडाकुण्डलमैलिरत्नघृणिभिः सारात्रिकाः सूक्तयः ।। (II-85)

"The wise saying of the *Pāñcarātrȧśāstra* which are lit up, as it were, with cremonial flames by the gems in the heads of the serpents worn on the ears as ornaments by Garuḍa, who knows the essence of all the *Śrutis* and who nods his head in high appreciation of them — let these sayings which are in consonance with the (Vedantic) system of the

Kṛtayuga maintained by us who have seen the outermost bounds of the region of the irreproachable."[272]

REFERENCES

1. A.B. Gajendragadkar, *Abhijñāna-Śākuntala of Kālidāsa,* Bombay, 1934, p.50 (*Introduction*).

2. अवधारितनाट्यदेशिमार्गैरसमीचीनपराङ्मुखैरमीभिः ।
भरतागमदैवतैरिवैषा परिषत् संप्रतिभासते महद्भिः ॥ *S.S.,* I-4, p.19.
धीरोदात्तानुकूलोत्तमगुणमहिमा नायकेष्वग्रणीस्त्वं
स्वाधीनत्वत्सनाथा सुमतिरभिमता धर्मपत्नी तवासौ ।
स्वायत्ता चाद्य सिद्धिः समजनि भवतः स्वामिनिःश्रेयसार्था
रामस्त्वं च त्रिलोक्यां रण विह्वतिमुखैरप्रदृश्यानुभावौ ॥ *S.S.,* X-71, p.859.

3. महासत्त्वोऽतिगम्भीरः क्षमावानविकत्थनः ।
स्थिरो निगूढाहङ्कारो धीरदात्तो दृढव्रतः ॥
Dhanañjaya, *Daśarūpakam,* Motilal Banarasidass, Delhi 1979, II-4, p.137.

4. त्रिगुणघाटिताद्भोक्तुर्बुद्धिः सती तदनुव्रता समयनियतोच्छ्रायं त्रेधा कुलं समजीजनत् ।
प्रथममिह तद्भोगद्वेष्यं विवेकपुरः सरं द्वितीयमितरज्जुष्टं रागप्रमोहमुखं मिथः ॥
S.S., I-46, p.96.

5. आर्यपुत्र, एवमेतत्। तथापि विषमास्थिरसंस्थानवैराग्यदुर्गप्रतिष्ठितोऽप्रमत्तैः शमदम-प्रमुखैरमात्यैरभिरक्षितः स्वयम्-सहायशूरोऽनपायसाहसश्च विपक्षः किं नाम कदा करिष्यतीति कलुषित हृदयास्मि ॥ *S.S.,* I, p.85.

6. मुकुलयति विवित्सां मोहविध्वंसमिच्छन् विमृशति निगमान्तान् वीक्षते मोक्षधर्मान् ।
निशमयति च गीतां नित्यमेकान्थक्त्या गुणपरिषदवेक्षी गुप्तमन्त्रो विवेकः ॥
S.S., I-61, p.123.

प्रत्यङ्मुखीं सुमतिदीप्तिमिह प्रचिन्वन् प्राप्तोदयोऽप्यामितरागबलोपपन्नः ।
क्षाम्यन्नहंकृतिमयीमवशो हिमानीं भास्वानसौ भजति विष्णुपदं विवेकः ॥
S.S., I-62, pp.124-25.

7. मदनमत्सरमानमयः पुमान् बहुपिशाचगृहीतः इवार्भकः ।
निगमसिद्धनरेन्द्रनिरीक्षणान्निपुणपद्धतिमभ्यवपद्यते ॥ *S.S.,* I-76, p.153.

अनघदेशिकदृष्टिसुधाप्लवे विधिवशादुपसेदुषि देहिनः ।
विमलबोधमुखा विविधा गुणाः परिणमन्त्यपवर्गदशाङ्कुराः ॥ *S.S.,* 77, p.154.

स्वाधीनेतरपात भीतिपरुषस्वर्वासदुर्वासनापाशाकर्षणयन्त्रणाभिरभितः क्षिप्तात्मनः क्षेत्रिणः।
निष्प्रत्यूह विजृम्भमाणकरुणादुग्धार्णवे निर्भरा भक्तिः सेत्स्यति भागधेयवशतः प्राप्ये परे ब्रह्मणि॥

S.S., 78, p.155.

8. पुरावेधःस्तम्बावधिपुरुषसृष्टेः स्थितिमति स्थिरा भक्तिः सूते विपदुपरतिं पुंसि परमे।
तदन्यानभ्यर्चन्नभिलषितमुक्तिः सुरगणानुदन्यां प्रालेयैरुपशमयितुं वाञ्छति जडः ॥
S.S., I-86, p.174.

आबध्नति विगतशान्तिमनादि निद्रां चेतस्विनस्त्रिगुणशक्तिमयी त्रियामा ।
नाथस्य केवलमसौ नरकान्त कर्तुः संकल्पसूर्य विभवेन समापनीया ॥
S.S., I-87, p.175.

9. त्वया जुष्टः पत्न्या विधिवदिह यष्टा स्वयमहं विधत्ते चार्त्वियं शमदममुखोऽयं गुणगणः।
अकस्मादुद्देश्यो भवति भगवानात्महविषः पशुर्बद्धो मुक्तिं भजति विगलत्कर्मनिगलः॥
S.S., I-79, p.157.

स्वरक्षणभरार्पण क्षणिकसत्रिणः क्षेत्रिणः प्रवर्त्य कृपया स्थितिं प्रभुरभूतपूर्वोदयाम् ।
जगद्विपरिवर्तनप्राथित नित्यशक्तिः स्वयं क्षिपत्यपुनरङ्कुरं दुरितमस्य लक्ष्मीपतिः॥
S.S., I-80, p.159.

निरपायदेशिकनिदर्शितामिमां कमलासहायकरुणाधिरोहणीम् ।
क्रमशोऽधिरुह्य कृतिनः समिन्धते परिशुद्धसत्त्वपरिकर्मिते पदे ॥
S.S., I-81, pp.161-62.

स्वयमुपशमयन्ती स्वामिनः स्वैरलीलां स्वमतमिह दुहाना स्वादु पथ्यं प्रजानाम् ।
नियतमियमिदानीमन्यदा वा भवित्री निरवधिसुखसिद्धयौ निष्प्रकम्पानुकम्पा ॥
S.S., I-82, p.163.

10. पश्यति परेषु दोषानसतोऽपि जनः सतोऽपि नैव गुणान् ।
विपरीतमिदं स्वस्मिन् महिमा मोहाञ्जनस्यैषः ॥ *S.S.*, I-63, p.128.

11. अतिक्रान्तावस्मद्भ्रुकुटिनटनारम्भसमयप्रदीप्तः क्रोधादि प्रतिभटनिरुद्धो न भवसि ॥
S.S., III-38, p.385.

12. प्रिये, स्वधर्मनिरतानस्मान् प्रति सोऽयमाशीर्वादः ॥ *S.S.*, III, p.385.

13. प्रिये, स्थानक्रोधो न खलु दोषाय।
योऽसौ कामादिनिरसनार्थतया परमार्थवेदिभिः प्रशस्यते। *S.S.*, III, p.388.

14. देवि विवेकवल्लभे, अनधिगतप्रमाणतर्कसरणिरिव कथमेवमाशङ्कसे। *S.S.* I, p.141.
कालस्वभावनियतियदृच्छादिषु वस्तुषु ।
कारणं किमिवात्रेति तापसैरपि तर्कितम् ॥ *S.S.*, I-69, p.142.

कर्माविद्यादिचक्रे प्रतिपुरुषमिहानादिचित्रप्रवाहे
तत्तत्काले विपक्तिर्भवति हि विविधा सर्वसिद्धान्तसिद्धा ।
तल्लब्ध स्वावकाशप्रथमगुरुकृपागृह्यमाणः कदाचिन्
मुक्तैश्वर्थान्तसंपन्निधिरपि भविता कश्चिदित्थं विपश्चित् ॥ *S.S.*, I-70, p.143.

अनुचितपदवीभिश्चिन्तयित्वा प्रयातान्यलमलमतिमात्रैरद्य बाले विषादैः ।
उपनिषदमुदारामुद्वमन् क्वापि लक्ष्ये शरणमुपगतान्नस्त्रायते शार्ङ्गधन्वा ॥
S.S., III-14, p.352.

15. स्वस्ति श्रीश्वेतद्वीपविहारमण्डपिकामातस्थुषा विबुधमहितवृत्तिना महाराजविवेकेन महामोहाय संदिश्यते । प्रसिद्धं खल्विदम् - नीचाः कलहमिच्छन्ति संधिमिच्छन्ति साधवः । *S.S.*, VIII, p.679.

दीयन्तामिह दक्षिणापथभुवो यावत्कलेरत्ययस्तत्र स्थावरतिर्यगंशमखिलं भुङ्क्ष्व त्वमप्यक्षतः । इत्थं नाम कुलक्षयोपशमनोपाये त्वया तस्थुषा संधिः सत्यगिरामतुच्छ-मनसामच्छात्मनामस्तु नः ॥ *S.S.*, VIII-11, p.680.

16. प्रभुणैव सर्वजगदुद्भवस्थितिप्रलयप्रवाहपरिरब्धकेलिना ।
अहमस्त्रमन्त्रपरिमृष्टदर्भवद्गमितः स्ववध्यनिधने निमित्तताम् ॥*S.S.*, IX-7, p.753.

17. For details see from page 718 to 746.

18. अथ नायिका त्रिभेदा स्थाऽन्या साधारणा स्त्रीति ।
नायकसामान्यगुणैर्भवति यथासंभवेर्युक्ता ॥
विनयार्जवादियुक्ता गृहकर्मपरा पतिव्रता स्वीया ॥
Viśvanātha, *Sāhitya Darpaṇa,* III-56-57, pp.131-32.

19. अस्ति खल्वनभिज्ञकुल सार्वभौमविवेकहतकमूलाकर्तृत्वाभिमानादिनानाविधविषमदृष्टि-सहकृतः कश्चिदस्मत्कुलाभिचारकाङ्क्षिभिरुपनिषदूषरनिष्ठैः कैश्चिन्निष्ठुरैरनुष्ठीयमानो निवृत्तिसंज्ञको धर्मः । यन्निष्ठस्य पुरुषस्य परदोषदर्शनादिष्वन्धवधिरमूकषण्डादिवदत्यन्त मवसन्नावस्थानमाकर्ण्यते ॥ *S.S.*, I, pp.106-107.

20. आर्यपुत्र, विरूपाः खलु जना निजमुखदोषं
निर्मलेष्वपि दर्पणेषु समर्पयन्ति । *S.S.*, I, p.129.

21. देवि, सत्यमेतत् । यथार्थदर्शिनी, यथार्थवादिनी च भवति । किंच ;
निर्धूतनिखिलदोषा निरवधिपुरुषार्थलम्भनप्रवणा ।
सत्कविभणितिरिव त्वं सगुणालंकारभावरसजुष्टा ॥ *S.S.*, I-64, p.129.

22. आर्यपुत्र, कथं स नित्यनिर्मलमहानन्दशान्तस्वयंप्रकाशसर्वजनदर्शनयोग्यस्वभावः पुरुषो महामोहेन मानमदमत्सरप्रमुखैरपिदुर्विनीतैर्दुर्वारगर्वसंकुलदुरितमहोर्मिसंघात-संघटनभीषणे दुःखसागरे निक्षिप्तः ? *S.S.*, I, p.135.

23. प्रिये सूक्ष्मदर्शिनि, किं दृष्टमपह्नोतव्यम् ?
आगमिकं वा किं न प्रत्येतव्यम् ? *S.S.*, I, p.135.

24. आर्यपुत्र, अनादौ गते काले अलब्धपूर्वो मीक्षः।
अनन्तेऽप्युपरितनकाले केन कथं लभ्यत इति शङ्काकलङ्ककर्बुरितं मे हृदयम् ।।
S.S., I, p.141.

25. देवि अनवरतशोभनशंसिनि, निदानमिह निपुणमुपपादयन् प्रतिपन्नामेव भवतीं प्रत्यभिज्ञापयामि । दुरासेघस्थेम्ना दुरितपरिपाकेन भविनः प्रमाथी संसारः प्रशमरहितोऽयं प्रभवति । निरोधे तस्यैका निरूपधिककारुण्यघटितस्वतन्त्रेच्छा-शक्तिः स्वयमुपधिमाधाय रमते ।। *S.S.*, I-75, p.151-152.

26. यथैष महावराहः प्रलयार्णव निमग्नं भूमिमुद्धरति, तथार्यपुत्रोऽपि संसारसागरनिमग्नं पुरुषमुद्धरेत् ।अन्यदपि भणामि। दृढतरदंष्ट्राग्रदारित हिरण्याक्षवक्षस्तटकठिनक-वाटसंपुटोत्थितघनशोणितनदीप्रवाहघणघणायमानघोणान्तरस्य यज्ञवराहस्ये वार्यपुत्रस्य जन्य नौपुणं द्रष्टुमुत्कण्ठितास्मि ।। *S.S.*, VII, p.638.

27. सुमतिबहुमतेन स्वात्मना सत्त्वधाम्ना बहिरबहिरुदीर्णे वारिते वैरिवर्गे ।
जनयति पुरुषस्य ज्यायसीं चित्तवृत्तिं समविषमविभेदी सार्वभौमो विवेकः ।।
S.S., IX-34, p.778.

28. मानुषस्य योगिनो मानुषसदृशे चित्तसङ्गः संपादनीयः । आर्यपुत्र, एतेनेव त्वया सागरनिमग्ना वेदा इव मोहान्धकारनिमग्नाजना उद्धृत्य रक्ष्यन्ते । किं नाम परमपुरुषस्यैतादृशानि रूपान्तराण्यपि भवन्ति ।। *S.S.*, VII, p.625.

29. सुमतिनिकेतनमेतत्स्वयंप्रभमासीदामि ।
बलदर्शनमण्डपं श्रुतिनां बहुभिर्भावितवैभवं प्रमाणैः ।
अवधूतरजस्तमस्कमेतत् सुमतेस्तत्त्वमयं विभाति सौधम् ।।*S.S.*, IX-51, p.792.

30. त्रिगुणघटिताद्भोक्तुर्बुद्धिः सती तदनुव्रता समयनियतोच्छ्रायं त्रेधा कुलं समजीजनत् ।
प्रथममिह तद्भोगद्वेष्यं विवेकपुरः सरं द्वितयमितरज्जुष्टं रागप्रमोहमुखं मिथः ।।
S.S., I-46, p.96.

31. जात्यन्धः परदोषदृष्टिषु परीवादेषु मूकाग्रणीर्बाधिर्यप्रथमावतारसरणिर्निन्दासमाकर्णने ।
स्त्रीप्रायः परदारसंग्रहविधौ तद्वत्परावर्जने संपद्येत समीक्षणेऽपि विकलः पापैर्विवेकादिभिः।।
S.S., I, p.100.

32. स्वाधीनसंसरणनाट्यनिरूढवृत्तेः संतोषितः प्रणति भूमिकयास्य पुंसः ।।
S.S., I, p.120.

33. महत्यारम्भेऽस्मिन् मधुरिपुदयासंभृतधृतिर्बहिष्कृत्यारातीन् सुमुखि बहिरन्तश्च भवतः।
समाधावाधाय क्षपितवृजिनं क्षेत्रिणमहं परप्राप्त्या धन्यं परिणमयितुं प्राप्तिनियमः।।
S.S., I-65, p.134.

34. स्वतः प्राप्तं रूपं यदिह किल भावेषु तदपि त्यजन्तस्ते दृष्टा नियतिघटितोपाधिवशतः ।
प्रकृत्या तिष्ठन्ति ह्युपधिविगमे ते च र्तसावनादिः संसारः पुरुषमुपरुन्ध्वे गलति च।।
S.S., I-66, p.136.

35. मदनमत्सरमानमयः पुमान् बहुपिशाचगृहीत इवार्भकः ।
निगमसिद्धनरेन्द्रनिरीक्षणा न्निपुणपद्धतिमभ्यवपद्यते ॥ *S.S.*, I-76, p.153.

36. निरपाय देशिकनिदर्शितामिमां कमलासहायकरुणाधिरोहणीम् ।
क्रमशोऽधिरूह्य कृतिनः समिन्धते परिशुद्धसत्त्व परिकर्मिते पदे ॥
S.S., I-81, p.262.

37. स्वयमुपशमयन्ती स्वामिनः स्वैरलीलां स्वमतमिह दुहाना स्वादु पथ्यं प्रजानाम् ।
नियतमियमिदानीमन्यदा वा भवित्री निरवधिसुखसिद्ध्यै निष्प्रकम्पानुकम्पा ॥
S.S., I-82, p.263.

38. निषिद्धं विद्यार्थादधिकमपि काम्यं च विजहत् परप्रीत्यै कर्म प्रतिनियतमादाय मुदितः ।
शुभश्रद्धादुग्धोदधिनवसुधोल्लासललिते समाधावाधातुं त्वरयति मुनिः संप्रति मनः ॥
S.S., III-23, p.363.

39. विलक्षोपक्षिप्तं विषयरसगन्धर्वनगरप्रशंसायाथार्थ्य प्रणिदधति चित्तेऽपि ननुभृत् ।
मया दत्ते हस्ते मतिकलुषमुल्लङ्घ्य तरसा परब्रह्मैकान्ती भवजलनिधिं गोष्पदयति ॥
S.S., III-24, p.363.

40. स्मरति महतामातङ्कानां मनस्कुरुते गृहान् प्रसजति परब्रह्मप्राप्तौ समृद्धिमपेक्षते ।
अभिनिविशते भोगोदन्वत्यपत्रपते पुनः प्रणिधिारधुना सिद्धापायः सितासितपद्धतिः ॥
S.S., IV-18, p.409.

41. प्रणिधानविशेषभावितात्मा करणग्रामनिरोधनिष्प्रकम्पः ।
निभृतश्वसनो निवृत्तिधर्मा पुरुषस्त्यक्तपरिग्रहोऽयमास्ते ॥ *S.S.*, IV-54, p.440.

42. भयस्थानग्रन्थान्परिपठति निद्राति च मुहुः स्वमात्मानं
पश्यत्युपचरति देहं च विधिना ।
निवृत्तिं दुःखाब्धेरभिलषति रज्यत्यपि सुखे द्विधा वृत्त्या
दुःख्यानपुरुष इह डोलायित इव ॥ *S.S.*, IV-34, p.421.

43. तितिक्षुर्दून्द्वानि द्रुतमतिरयत्नोपनतभुक्परित्याज्यत्यागी भ्रमर इव सारग्रहरुचिः ।
कृतज्ञः प्राप्तव्ये नियतधृतिरेकान्तरसिको मुमुक्षुः संधत्ते मुनिरनिभृतं ब्रह्मणि मनः ॥
S.S., IX-35, p.778.

44. विषयमदिरामुग्धैस्त्यक्तः स एष पृथग्जनैः क्वचन समये यत्रैकाग्रयं क्वचिच्च तथास्पदे ।
निभृतकरणग्रामस्तृप्यन्निरुद्धमरुद्गणः परमिह परे धाम्नि प्रत्यङ्मुखः प्रतितिष्ठिति ॥
S.S., IX-45, p.788.

45. पुलकमुकुलोत्तुङ्गैरङ्गैरुदश्रुभिरीक्षणैरयमनुभवत्यन्तर्दृष्टिः समाधिरसं पुमान् ।
ध्रुवमिह महानन्दब्रह्मोपलम्भनलक्षणे महति विभवे निष्प्रत्यूहा मनोरथपद्धतिः ॥
S.S., IX-46, p.789.

46. मुमुक्षुत्वे सिद्धे मुषितमतिमोहस्य मुरभित्समाधिः संरोहन्नुपहरति सर्वाधविरतिम् ।
परस्तादास्थेयं यदिह विदुषानिष्टजनुषा फलार्थं तत्किं वा फलमिति वितर्कः श्रमफलः ॥
S.S., X-4, p.798.

47. कलत्रसुतसोदरप्रभृतिकल्पनाबर्बरैरशक्यविनिवर्तनैरहितशृङ्खलैर्यन्त्रितः ।
निसर्गसुहृदि प्रभौ निहितगुप्तिभारः पुमानुपस्थितमुपस्थितं हितमशेषसुद्वीक्षते ॥
S.S., X-34, p.823.

48. न मुक्तो न च बद्धोऽहं यथा पश्चाद्यथा पुरा ।
कृपणः किं करिष्यामि न करिष्यामि वा स्वयम् ॥ *S.S.*, X-41, p.830.

49. अमतिविहितैरंहः स्तोमैर्झटित्यहमुज्झितः शमितविपथैः सत्त्वोदग्रैः शमादिभिराश्रितः ।
परमपुरुषध्यानस्तोत्रप्रणाममुखैर्मखैः परिहृतमुधाकालक्षेपः फलोदयमाद्रिये ॥
S.S., X-42, p.831.

50. नाथे नस्तृणमन्यदन्यदपि वा तन्नाभिनालीकिनीनालिकस्पृहणीयसौरभमुचा वाचा न याचामहे ।
शुद्धानां तु लभेमहि स्थिरधियां शुद्धान्तसिद्धान्तिनां मुक्तैश्वर्यदिनप्रभातसमयासत्तिं प्रसत्तिं मुहुः ॥ *S.S.*, X-50, p.839.

51. निरपायमुख्यरागं निजपक्षनिविष्टनित्यहरितत्त्वम् ।
गुणपञ्जरस्थितं त्वां शुकमिव मोक्ष्यामि दिव्यगतियोग्यम् ॥*S.S.*, X-58, p.847.

52. श्रीरङ्गं वृषभाचलं करिगिरिं श्रीमद्यदुक्ष्माधरं साकेतं मधुरामुपैष्यति हरिक्षेत्रं बदर्याश्रमम् ।
अन्तः संभृतसप्ततन्त्ववभृयाथा देहपातोदयाद्यद्वा संप्रति यत्र कुत्रचिदसौ यत्रैकतानं मनः ॥ *S.S.*, X-89, p.878.

53. स्वयं व्यक्तक्षेत्रे विपिनविषये वा विधिवशात् प्रशस्ते दुष्टे वा क्वचन समये त्यक्तवपुषः ।
मुकुन्दस्त्रय्यन्तप्रथितमहिमा सोऽयमनघान् प्रपन्नानुद्धृत्य स्वपदमनपायं शमयति॥
S.S., X-90, p.880.

54. निर्णिक्तत्रिगुणाञ्जनस्य परब्रह्मोपसंपत्तितः प्रादुर्भूतगुणाष्टकस्य च परं साधर्म्यमभ्येयुषः पारावर्यविभागलक्षणपरित्यागप्रसङ्गोज्झिता शेषादेरिव शेषवृत्तिरपि ते सत्तावधिः सेत्स्यति ॥ *S.S.*, X-59, p.848.

55. त्वया त्रय्यन्तविज्ञानं पुरुषस्य विभावितम् ।
श्रद्धावैकल्यमात्रं तु शमनीयमतः परम् ॥ *S.S.*, II-9, p.213.

56. विवेकस्य गुणश्रेयान् व्यवसायश्चमूपतिः ।
स्वपक्षे तिष्ठमानेभ्यः स्वयमागत्य तिष्ठते ॥ *S.S.*, II-35, p.247.

57. अलमिह मिथः श्लाघामाद्यन्मितंपचसंमतैरनघपरिषत्प्रत्यादिष्टैरलीकविकत्थनैः ।
अवितथकथाधौरेयाणामनुप्रसृतौ सतां ध्रुवमिह भवद्वृत्तेराविर्भविर्भविष्यति पङ्गुता॥
S.S., II-56, p.274.

58. अध्यासीनतुरङ्गवक्त्रविलसज्जिह्वाग्रसिंहासनादाचार्यादिह देवतां समधिकामन्यां न मन्यामहे ।
यस्यासौ भजते कदाचिदजहद्भूमा स्वयं भूमिकां मग्नानां भविनां भवार्णवसमुत्ताराय नारायणः ॥ *S.S.*, II-63, p.282.

59. एकयैव गुरोर्दृष्टया द्वाभ्यां वापि लभेत यत् ।
न तत्तिसृभिरष्टाभिः सहस्रेणपि कस्यचित् ॥ *S.S.*, II-62, p.281.

60. देव, अमी पुनरार्यवचनमसहमाना दिगम्बरादिवत् केनापि विप्रलम्भोपायेन स्वसिद्धान्त-श्रद्धासंवर्धनाय प्रयतन्ते । तत्र तावदिमां प्रत्यायनामारचयन्तिद्धूयदकाण्ड एव वर्षासमयमादर्शयन्ति ॥
S.S., II, p.299.

61. विविधविषयद्वीपारोहावरोहविसंस्थुलस्थितिभिरमुकैरन्योन्यस्मादुपस्थितसाध्वसैः ।
कमठमकरग्राहप्रायैरबुद्धिभिराश्रितस्त्रिगुणजलधिर्न द्रष्टव्यः समीहितसंयमैः ॥
S.S., VII-10, p.617.

62. मनसि वचसि काये पुण्यपीयूषपूर्णास्त्रिभुवनमुपकारश्रेणिभिः प्रीणयन्तः ।
परगुणपरमाणून् पर्वतीकृत्य नित्यं निजहृदि विकसन्तः सन्ति सन्तः कियन्तः ॥
Bhartṛhari, *Nitiśataka*, Ed. D.N. Shanbhag, Dharwad, verse 73, p.24.

63. मयस्त्वष्टान्यो वा विपुलमहिमा विश्वसृडपि स्वशक्त्येदं
चित्रं किमपि न विधातुं कृतमुखः ।
अखण्डब्रह्माण्ड प्रथमतमशिल्पी स भगवान् स्वयं
पद्माजानिर्व्यलिखदिह शिल्पं स्वविषयम् ॥ *S.S.*, VII-16, p.623.

64. देव, वयं हि भगवतो वाहनादिवदुपकरण मात्रम् ।
प्राधान्यं तु सर्वत्र भवत एव ॥ *S.S.*, IX, p.749.

65. यद्वाक्तिप्रचयात्मके दिनमुखे दृष्टिक्षमः क्षेत्रिणः
क्षिप्रं संसृतिशर्वरीं क्षिपति यत्संकल्पसूर्योदयः ।
तत्त्वैरस्त्रविभूषणैरधिगतः स्वाधीननित्योन्नतिः श्रीमानस्तु
स से समस्तविपदुत्ताराय नारायणः ॥ *S.S.*, I-1, p.1.

66. अहो नु खलु विष्वक्प्रकाशा दिशो विदिशश्च ।
तदासीदतीव देवस्य दयावल्लभस्य संकल्पः ॥ *S.S.*, X, p. 813.

67. व्यक्तौ संनाहसंकल्पौ विश्वगोपुरिमौ हरेः ।
प्रथितावागमग्रामे पक्षीश्वरसुदर्शनौ ॥ *S.S.*, X-19, p.813.

68. वैकुण्ठकृपया देव्या मदभीष्टे व्यवस्थितम् ।
प्राध्वं संकल्पमार्ताण्डं प्रवर्तयितुमुत्सहे ॥ *S.S.*, X-12, p.805.

69. यस्मिन्विस्मयनीयभूमनि मनागुन्मीलिते नैकधा सिध्यन्त्यस्य सितासितस्य जगतः स्वर्गापवर्गादयः। ऐशः सोऽहमवासरात्ययभवन्मायामहायामिनीसत्ताशेषसुषुप्त बोधन-पटुः संकल्पसूर्योदयः ॥ *S.S.*, X-20, p.813.

70. आदिष्टः सोऽहमिदानीमनघपरविद्याप्रसादितया प्रदित्सितपारितोषिकया सकलगुणसेव्यया देव्या भगवदनुकम्पया। यथा — मदधीनवृत्तिना मोहादिविजयिना विवेकेन जनितभूमा

विनिष्पन्नसमाधिः पुरुषस्त्वयैव मोचनीय इति । अहं च सर्वथा निखिलजगदम्बायास्तदनुकम्पायाः प्रियमाचरामि । न च मया तदनुरोधिपरित्राणे तद्विरोधिनिरसने च दुष्करं किंचित् ॥ *S.S.*, X, p.814.

71. अचरन्मधुकैटभान्पयोधीनहिरण्याक्षहिरण्यविप्लुतां द्याम् ।
अदशाननकुम्भकर्णघोषां पुनरूर्वीमपि विक्रमैरकार्षम् ॥ *S.S.*, X-21, p.815.

72. अनिदंप्रथमां निद्रामपावर्त्य क्षणादहम् ।
अनिदंपश्चिमां पुंसो जनयिष्यामि जागराम् ॥ *S.S.*, X-22, p.815.

73. मयि विनिहितभारं मध्यमे वृत्तिभेदे स्थिरमनसमुपायापायरथ्या निवृत्तम् ।
मुरमथनसमीक्षाशेखरेण स्वभूम्ना मुषितनिखिलदोषं मोचयिष्यामि जीवम् ॥
S.S., X-23, p.816.

74. महाभाग, अहं किल परमपुरुषसंकल्पः परमैकान्तिपरिषदग्रगण्यमनन्तसुकृतदुष्कृतनिगलयुगलविगलनपूर्विकया परमपदपर्यङ्क परिष्कारपरब्रह्म सेवापर्यन्तया भक्तिपरिपाकसंपदा संघटयितुं तदेकवल्लभया कृपणजनविषयकृतपक्षपातया कृपया नियुक्ताश्चिर प्रार्थितदर्शनं भवन्तमुपगच्छामि। तदिह निकटवर्तिन्यां निःश्रेयस संपदि निर्विशङ्केन भवता भवितव्यम् ॥ *S.S.*, X, pp.841-42.

75. भगवति निहितात्मा भागधेये श्रुतीनां पुरुष इह महात्मा वर्तते भूतधात्र्याम् ।
तदयमवधानैः सर्वमन्तेवसद्भिः पृथुमतिभिरभीष्टं पृच्छयतां विश्वदशीम् ॥
S.S., X-65, p.853.

76. इयमखिलपुमर्थप्रार्थनाकल्पवल्ली सितमतिभिरनन्यैः सेविता सिद्धवृन्दैः ।
द्युतिभिरविरलाभिर्द्योतयन्ती दिगन्तान् विशति सुमति सौघं विष्णुभक्तिर्विशुद्धम् ॥
S.S., IX-52, p.793.

77. अहं वैकुण्ठदास्यैकलास्यलीलाविनोदिनी ।
विश्वकिल्बिषसंहार विभ्रमारभटीनटी ॥ *S.S.*, X-1, p.795.

78. अम्बा मे पुरुषस्य बुद्धिरनघा नातः स धर्मोत्तरः
संतुष्टिः सहजा क्षमा प्रियसखी सद्‌वृत्तिराज्ञाकरी ।
विद्यैव स्वयमस्मि विश्ववृजिन प्रध्वंसनं क्रीडितं
साहं प्राणिमि विष्णुभक्तिरचला संतिष्ठते संसृतिः ॥ *S.S.*, X-2, p.796.

79. अघपरिणमितैरमित्रभेदैः करणकलेबरपुत्रदारिकाद्यैः ।
ग्रहिल इह मयैव मोचनीयो मुरभिदनुग्रहलीलया मुमुक्षुः ॥ *S.S.*, X-5, p.799.

80. शरणागतरक्षणैकदीक्षः समये तत्परिपन्थिनो निरुन्धन् ।
प्रभुरायतते परः कृपायां सचिवास्तस्य च सर्व एव देवाः ॥
S.S., X-13, p.805.

81. क्षुण्णक्षोणीधराणि क्षुभितचतुरकूपारतिम्यद्दरुन्ति त्रुट्यत्तारासराणि स्थपुटितविबुधस्थानकानि क्षिपेयुः ।

पातालब्रह्मसौधावधिविहितमुधावर्तनान्यस्मदार्ति ब्रह्माण्डस्यान्तराले बृहति खगपतेर्भक-क्रीडितानि ॥ *S.S.*, X-18, p.808.

82. नियतपुलकिताङ्गी निर्भरानन्दबाष्पा गलितनिखिलसङ्गा गद्गदस्तोत्रगीतिः ।
अमृतलहरिवर्णा हर्षनृत्तोपपन्ना विगतनरकभीति विष्णुभक्तिर्विभाति ॥
S.S., X-24, p.816.

83. नियताक्षहयं सैषा स्फुरत्प्रशमपत्तिकम् ।
मनोरथमधिष्ठाय विष्णुभक्तिरिह स्थिता ॥ *S.S.*, X-25, p.817.

84. शमधननिधिः संविद्वल्लीसमग्रफलोदयः श्रुतपरिणतिः शुद्धस्थेमा सुखप्रतिभूरसि ।
भवभयतमः प्रातः संध्या परावरदीपिका भगवति हरौ भक्तिर्दिव्या परिष्कृतिरात्मनः ॥
S.S., X-26, p.818.

85. अहं त्विदानीमभिनिर्वर्तिताभिगमननियतिरहिंसादिमयीमष्टपुष्पीमुपादाय त्वत्प्रभावनष्टाश्लिष्ट पूर्वोत्तरपुण्यपापराशिमनन्य याजिनमनन्यध्यायिनं च पुरुषमासन्नमुक्तिलाभव्यवसाय जनित निरवधिकप्रमोदमनुमोदितुं त्वदेकान्तिना विवेकेन सह त्वरितमागमिष्यामि ॥

S.S., X, p.827.

86. नासौ महाराजस्य निर्वेदावसरः। अद्य हि परसंकल्पकल्पान्तपावकेन प्रारब्धकर्मलेश-परिशेष उपशोषितः पुरुषस्य दुरितार्णवः प्रकृतिरपि निर्मोककल्पा शेषपरिशुद्ध-स्वभावं पुरुषमायुषः पारे तमसः पारे निर्मोक्ष्यति ॥ *S.S.*, X, p.865.

87. देवर्षिभूतपितृमत्यऋणातिलङ्घी दत्ताभयस्य कृपया दृढभक्तिशाली ।
पत्युः समस्तजगतां परमं पदं तत् प्राप्यत्यसौ गुरुजनैः प्रथमाधिरूढम् ॥
S.S., X-91, p.881.

88.(a) "The *Guru* here is Śrī Rāmānuja and the Śiṣya is Śrī Vedānta Deśika himself, separated though they were by several centuries in fact."
Rajagopala Iyengar, M.R., *Saṅkalpasūryodayam,* Vedānta Deśika Research Society, Madras, 1977, p.76.

(b) अनेन च गुरुशिष्यवृत्तान्तप्रसङ्गेन कविरयं भगवद्रामानुजं गुरुमात्मानं च शिष्यमनामोल्लेखं परिकल्प्य चिरात् स्वहृदये विपरिवर्तमानमात्मनो भगवद्रामानुजसाक्षाच्छिष्यत्वालाभजनितं खेदं लघयितुकाम् इव संदृश्यते ॥
Saṅkalpasūryodaya, Ed. Krishnamacharya V (in Sanskrit), Adyar Library, Madras, 1948, upodghata, p.15.

89. दयया देशिकेन्द्रस्य दृष्टया चास्य महीपतेः ।
परितोषेण चैवं ते प्राप्तोऽहं पारितोषिकम् ॥ *S.S.*, II, 99, p.329.
अहं खल्वनुभवामुष्यायणः संस्कारनामा देवस्य विवेकस्यशिक्षितसर्वविद्याकलापः शिल्पी देवशिल्पिनं विश्वकर्माणमसुरशिल्पिनं मयं च विजित्य विश्रमाभिलाषी

चिरमस्वाप्सम्। तावच्चेदमन्तरमासाद्य महामोहप्रयुक्ताभ्यां मधुकैटभाभ्यामिव महाबलाभ्यां मध्यमचरमगुणांभ्यां सत्त्वमित्रमसविति महाबलाभ्यां मध्यमचरमगुणांभ्यां सत्त्वमित्र-मसाविति जिघांसितः। नूनमप्रबुद्धतैव पुरुषेषु प्रतिपक्षजनस्य हस्तावलम्बः। ततश्चाहं प्रबोदितः सहसैव परमपुरुषदयाचोदितया देव्या सुमत्या सहदृष्टि सदृशदृष्टिसंज्ञाभ्यां दासीभ्यां, निरवकाशतया ततस्ततः पलायिते प्रतिपक्षे केनापि हेतुना विश्वचित्रं दिदृक्षमाणस्य देवस्य महाराज विवेकस्य सेनापतिना व्यवसायेन स्वामिसंमत-मादिष्टोऽस्मि। यथादिष्टं च तदाहितदृष्टिरन्वतिष्ठम्। अवसरानुकूलवृत्तीनां खल्वधि-कारिणामाधिपत्यं प्रतितिष्ठति। ततश्च, *S.S.*, VII, pp.608-9.

विदुषश्चिन्तानां शक्त्या चित्रभित्तिं वितन्वता।
शुद्धाशुद्धविभागार्हं विश्वं विलिखितं मया॥ *S.S.*, VII-1, p.609.
परिमितमपरिमितानामास्पदमेतत्प्रपञ्चचित्राणाम्।
दहरगगनाभिधानं दिव्यं पुरुषं निदर्शयति॥ *S.S.*, VII-6, p.615.
नैतद्बाह्यैस्तूलिकावर्णकाद्यैः क्लृप्तं चित्रं किंतु संतोषलिप्ताम्।
नानाकारां भावनामेव शिल्पी शिल्पव्याजान्नूनमत्रोज्जगार॥ *S.S.*, VII-7, p.615.

90. लास्यान्विता च ललिता च गतिस्त्वदिया मञ्जुस्वना बहुगुणा च विभाति वीणा।
देहश्च दर्शयति चान्द्रमसीमभिख्यां प्राप्तोऽसि नस्त्वमिह भोगसमृद्धिहेतुः॥
S.S., VIII-8, p.676.

91. तदिह रामरावणरणावलोकनरसश्चिरातिवृत्तोऽपि नियतिवृत्त्या पुनरिदानीमस्माकं प्रादुर्भविष्यति। यदिह महामोहदम्भदर्पादयो विवेकव्यवसायादिभिर्योत्स्यन्ते। अद्य चाति गाढवैरमूलस्याहवानोकहस्य फलं हस्तापचेयं भविष्यति विवेकस्य॥
S.S., VIII, p.696.

92. द्वेधा कल्पितदेवदानवचमूनासीरमासीदतोरारब्धे तु विवेकमोहनृपयोरायोधनैकोत्सवे।
वैलक्षण्यनिरूपणप्रहरणो बिभ्रत्प्रमाकङ्कटं जेतासौ जगदन्धकारमितरं देवो विवेकेश्वरः॥
S.S., VIII-27, p.696.

93. विद्याभेदैरूपचयवतां वेदकल्पद्रुमाणां व्यक्तोल्लासद्विजपरिवृढव्याप्तशाखाशतानाम्।
श्रेयोमार्गप्रतिभयजितः श्रीविवेकस्य मौलौ भूयो भूयः सपदि भविता भूयसी पुष्पवृष्टिः॥
S.S., VIII-28, p.697.

94. अधिकमिह मुमुक्षोरागमग्राह्यवर्गात् स्वयमिह गुरुभक्त्या दर्शितं स्वानुभूतौ।
प्रथयति मयि सौम्य त्वन्निदेशेन मन्ये सपदि भवति लग्ने गाढलग्नः समाधिः॥
S.S., IX-43, p.785.

95. आनेतुमात्मरभसेन समीहमाने रक्षोन्मुखं नतगृहेषु रमासहायम्।
प्रायः प्रभोस्तदपृथक्स्थिति वृत्तिशक्तिं संकल्पमप्युपहरिष्यति तद्रथोऽसौ॥
S.S., X-16, p.807.

96. गुणनेत्रोन्मेषक्रमपरिणतानन्तविकृतिः क्वचित्काले बुद्धिः कुलयुगलकूटस्थगृहिणी।
अतिक्रूरात्यन्तप्रलयविधिदुर्मन्त्रपरुषां पुरा भीमाकारां सृजति परभक्तिं परवती॥
S.S., I-52, p.109.

97. कामो जुगुप्सया, कोपस्तितिक्षया, लोभस्तुष्टया, अहंकार आत्मविद्या ।
S.S., VIII, p.669.

98. सैषा पञ्चमुखी तुष्टिः शेषसृष्टिरिवापरा ।
अतर्कितमुपस्थाय ग्रसते लोभमूषकम् ॥ *S.S.*, VIII-41, p.705.

99. स्वभर्तव्यं भार्यादुहितृपिनृपुत्रप्रभृतिकं विसृज्य प्रव्रज्यामुपनिहितवत्यै भवभृतः ।
अमुष्यै किं कुर्मोनिरवधिकनैर्धृण्यवपुषे नियत्यै भूयिष्टं भवतु भगवत्यै नम् इदम् ॥
S.S., VIII-53, p.714.

100. स्वमित्रमुपधात्रयप्रथित शुद्धिलोभात्मकं झटित्यलघुतुष्टिकुक्ष्यनलदग्धमित्याकुलः ।
विरक्तिरणदेवतानिपुणदृष्टिवैश्वानरं प्रविश्य मकरध्वजः पुनरनङ्गतामागतः ॥
S.S., VIII-60, p.721.

101. रुन्धानः सिन्धुघोष प्रथनमनिभृतं क्रन्दयन्क्ष्माधरेन्द्रान्
भिन्दानः स्कन्धभेदान्सुरपथरथिनां शुष्मणः सारथीनाम् ।
शुद्धालोकेन सद्यः क्षयमुपगमितः क्षान्तिमन्दस्मितेन
क्षुभ्यद्वैधात्रसौधध्वनिगुणितरवः कोऽपि कोपादृहासः ॥ *S.S.*, VIII-71, p.727.

102. गुरुवधमुखक्रूर क्रीडाकठोरपराक्रमः प्रथितमहितध्वंसो दक्षाध्वरप्रभृतिष्वसौ ।
स्वयमिह सुखारातिः स्वर्गापवर्गाविघातकः क्षणरुचिपदं क्षान्त्या गच्छत्यमर्षहुताशनः ॥
S.S., VIII-77, p.730.

103. विद्याभिः स्वविपक्षभङ्गपटुषु स्थानेष्ववस्थीयतां
सिद्धार्थैरनुमन्यतां शमदमस्वाध्याय-तोषादिभिः ।
मत्सूतस्य मनोरथस्य रथिना दृष्टाध्वना संप्रति
प्रत्यावृत्तिकथोज्झितेन परमं बह्म प्रतिष्ठास्यते ॥ *S.S.*, X-76, p.866.

104. कामादिकेष्वपगतेषु कथावशेषं संप्रत्यसौ शमदमादिगुणोपपन्नः ।
मैत्रीदयादिपरिकर्म विभूषितेन श्रद्धाधनेन मनसा लभते समाधिम् ॥
S.S., X-7, p.800.

105. जनन्या सर्वलोकानां विष्णुवल्लभया तया ।
कृपया कल्पितः सोऽहं त्वद्भ्रूविभ्रमकिंकरः ॥ *S.S.*, X-27, p.818.

106. स्वमायशैलूषीविहरणपरिभ्रान्ततनुभृत्परित्राणोद्योगप्रवणकरुणावेशविवशः ।
प्रतिक्षेप्तुं तापान् प्रभुरयमपर्यन्तमहिमा हिमानीमानीय स्वपदनतिमेनः प्रणुदति ॥
S.S., X-30, p.820.

107. दर्पमात्सर्यभूयिष्ठो मायाछद्मपरायणः ।
धीरोद्धातस्त्वहङ्कारी चलश्चण्डो विकत्थनः ॥
Dhanañjaya, *Daśarūpakaṃ*, Motilal Banarasidass, Delhi, 1979, II-5, p.142.

108. स्वभाव्यमेव शवमुष्टिवद् गृहीतग्रहिता महामोहस्य ॥ *S.S.*, III, p.385.

109. प्रिये ! महासाहसिकस्य कुलघ्नस्य विवेकस्य विध्वंसनाय कृत प्रतिज्ञेन मया समाधिसाकाङ्क्षपुरुष संक्षोभणाय प्रेषिताः । सिंहवनगुप्तिन्यायेन परस्पराभिरक्षिताश्च कामक्रोधादयः कालोपपन्नकार्तर्यकलुषिताः सैकत सेतवे इव भग्नव्यूहाः प्रतिनिवृत्य कथमप्यस्मन्मुखमवलोकयितुमक्षमाः प्रतिदिशं प्रस्थाय प्रायमास्थिता इत्युपश्रुत-मस्माभिः । तदिह भवत्या तत्प्रेयसी रतिजिघांसातृष्णास्तत्सकाशं गमयित्वा मामकास्ते मन्त्रिणः समाश्वासयितव्याः ॥ *S.S.*, V, p.499.

110. सुरदनुगणाः स्वमूर्ध्नि नित्यं निदधति शासनपत्रिकां मदीयाम् ।
प्रतिफलितलिपिप्रकारदीप्यन्मणिमकुटांशुमषीरसानुलिप्तम् ॥*S.S.*, V-44, p.500.

111. वर्गः स्वर्गसदां मया नियमितः क्षोणीभृतः किं पुनः
पद्माम्भोनिधिपर्वतेषु निहितास्तिस्रो मया मूर्तयः ।
विश्वं कर्तुमकर्तुमन्यथयितुं मदभ्रूरमोघक्रमा सोऽहं
कस्य वशे क एष न च मे किं कस्य वा कथ्यते ॥ *S.S.*, V-45, p.501.

112. किं तावदद्य केनापि हेतुना प्रदीप्यमाने विवेक ।
प्रतिविधातव्यम् ? अस्तु नान्वहं महामोहः ॥ *S.S.*, V, p.501.

113. परमनुगुणयन्तः पण्डितंमन्यवर्गान्वितथमिव जल्पन्त्यागमाः किंचिदेते ।
विबुधगुरुमतेऽस्मिन्व्यक्तमुत्तभ्यमाने ।
मुषितनिखिलसारा मौनमुद्रां भजन्ते ॥ *S.S.*, V-48, p.504.

114. न खलु सहस्रमपि प्रतिसूर्याः कदाचिदपि सूर्यमभिभवन्ति । *S.S.* V, p.505.

115. शरीरप्रलयो मुक्तिर्भोगस्तु रतिरुत्तमा ।
देवतास्तत्प्रदायिन्यः स्त्रियस्तारुण्यभूषणाः ॥ *S.S.*, V-49, p.505.

116. अपि तपसि रतानामप्यधीतागमानां अपि यमनियमाद्यैरन्वहं शिक्षितानाम् ।
शिथिलयति समाधिं शिल्पिहस्तानपेक्षं वरतनुमयचित्रं वासनाभित्तिलग्नम् ॥
S.S., V-50, p.506.

117. पठन्ति चौपनिषदाः परिहृतविषयानुरागतया परमपुरुषमुपसन्नस्यापि जक्षणादिक-मक्षीणविहृतिशालिनीभिरुपभोगं चेति महदिदं सारस्यम् । न खलु वृश्चिकभयात्पला-यमानैराशीविषमुखे निपतितव्यम् । *S.S.*, V, pp. 506-507.

118. अहह । अनादिशुद्धतया संमतानां वैकुण्ठवैमानिकानां वैनतेयादीनामाजानसिद्धाः कति कति विलसिन्यः श्रूयन्ते । श्रूयते किल सकल संसारनिवर्तकः सर्वेश्वरो लक्ष्मीभूमिनीलानायकः तदिह कामपुरुषार्थप्रतिक्षेपकैः कापेयवृत्तिभिः प्रतिभटन-भवनदिधक्षानिक्षिप्तेन पावकेन स्वनगमपि दंदह्यते ॥ *S.S.*, V, p.508.

119. दापत्यं सहजं समस्तजगतां पित्रोस्तदिच्छावशात्
कामिन्यादिविभागक्लृप्तिरपि तत्कैंकर्यसिद्धयै नृणाम् ।
इत्थं शेषमशेषमद्य तु भवत्सारस्यसंवर्धकं वैरस्यं
विदधाति हन्त विदुषां वैरोचनं दर्शनम् ॥ *S.S.*, V-54, p.510.

120. चिरसेवनतोषितेन धात्रा निपुणस्थानविदा निवेदितार्थः ।
असुरोपनिषद्रहस्यमग्रयं प्रथयामास विरोचनः प्रजानाम् ॥ *S.S.*, V-58, p.514.

121. करणविलयरूपा मुक्तिरित्युक्तमाद्यैः वितथमिति मयान्यद्वार्तिके विन्यवेशि ।
स्तनयुगलबृहत्त्व स्थापनीयस्वभूम्ना बहुगुणविभवेन ब्रह्मणा भोगसाम्यम् ॥
S.S., V-59, p.514.

122. कामास्ताम्यतु कोपलोभसहितः काले समभ्येतु वा रक्षः संयति राघवस्थितिमहं व्यङ्क्ता विवेकाहवे ।
कालस्त्वेषु रथो भवत्विह कलिस्त्वं सारथिदुर्मते दम्भः संप्रति जैत्र दुन्दुभिरसौ दर्पस्तथा कङ्कटः ॥ *S.S.*, V-64, p.519.

123. कस्तुभ्यं रणरङ्गखेलनकलामातिष्ठते तिष्ठते कश्च
प्रेप्सति कामतन्त्रनियतस्वैराय वैरायितम् ।
येन क्षोदयितुं क्षमां प्रभवति क्षेप्तुं कुलक्ष्माभृतः
पातुं सप्त सरस्वतोऽपि भवता साकूतमालोकितः ॥ *S.S.*, V-65, p.520.

124. प्रज्वलति जठराग्नौ क्षिपन्यथावच्चतुर्विधं हव्यम् ।
प्राणाग्निहोत्रमेकं परिपालयितास्मि दुर्मतिसहायः ॥ *S.S.*, V-67, p.521.

125. आदिशति भवतो महाराजाधिराजपरमेश्वरो दुर्मत्या सह महामोहः। कामक्रोधलोभ-मदमात्सर्यडम्भरस्तम्भेभ्यः सप्तभ्यः सचिवेभ्यः सप्त मुक्तिक्षेत्रतया प्रसिद्धाराजधान्यः ससागराश्च सप्त महाद्वीपा दत्त महामोहेनेति लिव्यताम् । अपि च,
S.S., V, p.524.

126. स्वकीयाख्यामात्रच्छुरणपरिणाह्यद्भयहरान् बहिष्कृत्येदानीं विजहदधिकारान्क्रतुभुजः ।
यदृच्छावाक्येऽपि व्यवहरतु लोकोऽयमखिलो नमः स्वस्तिस्वाहास्वधामिह महामोह विषयाः ॥ *S.S.*, V-69, p.525.

127. यद्देवं महामोहपर्यन्तानामस्मत्प्रभूणां विनाशो भवेत् ? *S.S.*, VIII-50, p.670.

128. मुग्धे ! स्वप्नेऽप्येवंविधं कातर्यवचनं मा वोचः । नन्वहं महामोहः ? किमिदानीमन्यमिव मामभिमन्यसे। अथ वा, न हि कदाचिदपि परिस्फुरन्ति प्रमदाजनानां राजकार्यगतयः। प्रिये, शृणु चैतन्महामोहस्य वीरव्रतम् । *S.S.*, VIII, p.682.

129. क्रकचैः कृत्तदेहोऽपि दीपितोऽपि दवाग्निना ।
न सूच्यग्रं प्रदास्यामि न सन्धास्यामि केनचित् ॥ *S.S.*, VIII-13, p.682.

130. नाहमस्मि महामोहः न च विश्वं जितं मया ।
विभूतिरमिता यस्य विभक्तव्यपदास्पदम् ॥ *S.S.*, VIII-14, p.683.

131. पातालक्षिप्तसिन्धुः प्रशकलितकुलक्ष्माभृदुत्कीलभूमिनिर्धूतादित्यचन्दद्युतिगणनिबिड-ध्वान्तनीरन्ध्रादिक्कः ।
वेधःसौधप्रभेदी विघाटितपवनस्कन्धपर्यस्ततारः प्रारब्धोऽसौ विवेकप्रतिरथिनि महानाहवे मोहवेगाः ॥ *S.S.*, VIII-96, p.740.

132. निखिलसुभटश्लाघारेखाविलनजाङ्घिकोः निरवधिबलो मोहः क्रीडन्ननुत्तरणे रणे ।
विविधनिगमग्रामस्थेयाद्विवेकमहीभृतो विपदमधुनावीरादस्मदिदंप्रथमां गतः ॥
S.S., VIII-101, p.742.

133. बाह्यजनैस्सार्धं दीर्घमार्गं त्वया प्रकान्तेन ।
दीनदशासंतप्तो दयितजनो नाथ किमिति संत्यक्तः ॥ *S.S.,* VIII-104, p.744.

134. करधृतललितेक्षुधन्वनो मे भ्रमरगुणार्पितपुष्पमार्गणस्य ।
मरुदनलशरोऽपि मेरुधन्वा क्षणमतिलङ्घितशासनः कथं स्यात् ॥
S.S., I-35, p.81.

135. वहति महिलामाद्यो वेधास्त्रयीमुखरैर्मुखैर्वरतनुतया वामो भागः शिवस्य विवर्तते ।
तदपि परमं तत्त्वं गोपीजनस्य वशंवदं मदनकदनैर्न क्लिश्यन्ते कथं न्वितरे जनाः ॥
S.S., I-36, pp.82-83.

136. वपुरप्रतिमं नितम्बिनीनां दृढसौन्दर्यगुणं दरावनम्रम् ।
श्रवणावधिनेत्रचित्रपुं धनुराद्यं मम मुष्टिमेयमध्यम् ॥ *S.S.,* I-38, p.85.

137. शैलीं विलोपयति शान्तिमधः करोति व्रीडां व्युदस्यति विरक्तिमपह्नुते च ।
कर्णामृतं किमपि तत्कलभाषिणीनां नामापि किं न विकरोति निशम्यमानम् ॥
S.S., I-39, p.86.

138. अलमिह विबुधाद्यैरागमग्राह्यवाचो मुनिपरिषदि धर्मान् गायतो मुक्तिहेतून् ।
तपसि नियतवृत्तेस्तस्य देवस्य शान्तिं जनितयुवतिरत्नं दर्शयत्यूरुकाण्डम् ॥
S.S., I-45, p.94.

139. कुवृत्तिमिति कौक्कुटं व्रतमधिक्षिपद्भिस्तथा सुधाकरशतऋतुप्रभृतिभिः स्वयं चस्खले।
नदद्भ्रमरपङ्क्तिके नमति कार्मुके मामके विरक्तिगृहदेहलीं क इह दोहली वीक्षते॥
S.S., I-55, p.114.

140. इक्षुः पेशलमीदृशं मम धनुः पुष्पाण्यमी सायकास्तन्त्रीमञ्जुलनिःस्वना मधुकरश्रेणी शुभा शिञ्जिनी ।
भीरुः सन्नबलाजनो मम बलं तथ्यं परं कथ्यते सोऽहं निर्जितशूलभृत्प्रभृतिकः संकल्पसिद्धोदयः॥ *S.S.,* IV-1, p.396.

141. कामं कामं कामपि सिद्धिं करणैः स्वैः कारं कारं कर्म निषिद्धं विहितं वा ।
न्यस्यन्ति त्वय्यद्भुतसीम्नि प्रतिबुद्धाः कामोऽकार्षीन्मन्युरकार्षीदिति नाम ॥
S.S., IV-3, p.397.

142. प्रख्यातस्त्वयि संभवः सुमनसां विश्वं त्वया नन्द्यते मुख्यस्त्वं किल षड्विधेषु ऋतुषु ज्योतिस्त्वदेकाश्रयम् ।
यत्र श्रीर्धृतपङ्कजा स च परस्त्वत्संश्रयो माधवः कामस्ते सचिवः क एव भविता कालोत्तमस्त्वत्समः॥ *S.S.,* IV-5, p.398.

143. वसन्तस्त्वं वह्निर्मलयपवनः सारथिरसावशोकादिर्ज्वाला मधुकरगणो धूमपटली ।

सुधासूतिः स्नेहस्तदिह जितनिर्वाणवचसो विरक्तिस्ते दाह्या द्रुहिणगिरिशादेरपि सतः ॥

S.S., IV-6, p.399.

144. तदिह समानभावयोः समाधिप्रवणपुरुष चेतः क्षोभणे ।
शृङ्गारोद्दीपनविभावकृत्यं मय्यायत्तम् ।
भवता पुनरालम्बन विभावसंपत्तिरुपपादनीया । *S.S.,* IV, p.400.

145. स्मरति महतामातङ्कानां मनस्कुरुते गृहान् प्रसजति परब्रह्मप्राप्तौ समृद्धिमपेक्षते ।
अभिनिविशते भोगोदन्वत्यपत्रपते पुनः प्रणिधिरधुना सिद्धापायः सितासितपद्धतिः॥

S.S., IV-18, p.409.

146. यदि मामवमत्य संयतेत व्यवसायान्वयदर्पितो विवेकः ।
वनिताशतवञ्चितस्य पुंसः स्वयमाधास्यति सौभरेरवस्थाम् ॥

S.S., IV-12, p.405.

147. ताराकान्तः प्रियसुहृदयं चन्द्रिकेयं वयस्या बाणारम्भाद्बहुमतिपदं बान्धवो मे वसन्तः ।
त्वं च त्राता विपदुपगमे क्रोध दुर्वारवेगः को वा मह्यं कुसुमधनुषे तिष्ठते जीवितार्थी॥

S.S., IV-32, p.420.

148. प्रख्यातमिदमित्थं भवतश्चातुर्यम् । तथाऽप्यत्यन्तवीतरागे क इव तवावकाशः ॥

S.S., IV, p.428.

149. पुंसस्त्यक्तपरिग्रहस्य विषयग्राहोज्झितस्याप्यहं
कन्थाविष्टरकुण्डिकादिहरणप्रच्छाद-नाद्याश्रयः ।
अन्तः क्षोभमलीकजल्पमसदारोपस्पृहां पैशुनं
संमोहादि च संमुखय्य सहसा दास्ये समाधिक्षयम् ॥ *S.S.,* IV-41, p.428.

150. महितमधुप्रदिष्टमधुदिग्धविचित्रशरः परभृतवन्दिमान् भ्रमरसंहतिगीतगुणः ।
मलयमरुत्सखो मकरलक्षणकेतुरसौ धृतधनुरभ्युपैति मदनः प्रमदापृतनः ॥

S.S., VIII-48, p.710.

151. काचित्क्रीडति पद्मिनीह पुरतः काप्यन्यतश्चित्रिणी
शन्यिप्यपरत्र काचिदितरा हस्तिन्यसावन्यतः ।
तस्यैतस्य समृद्धिमेति सरसप्रेक्षानिरूढोदयं चित्रं
मन्त्रिचतुष्टयं त्रिभुवनावस्कन्दिनो धन्विने ॥ *S.S.,* VIII-49, p.711.

152. ऋतुस्नाता नृत्तग्लपिततनुरध्वश्रमवती मदक्षीबा क्रुद्धप्रसदनवत भिन्नघटिता ।
इदंपूर्वेत्येवंविधयुवतियूथेन सहितो युयुत्सत्युन्मत्तः स्मर इह विवेकेन महता ॥

S.S., VIII-50, p.712.

153. संभोगैकान्त्यवादी निरयभयकथाभङ्गसङ्गी निकामं
शस्त्रच्छिन्नार्धदेहद्वयघटनभवद्दिव्य-दांपत्यशिल्पी ।
प्रख्याततिक्रमोऽसौ परपुरुषवशैर्गोपकन्यासहस्रै
रेकस्त्रैलोक्यवीरः स्मर इह मृदितः क्वावतिष्ठेत कोपः ॥ *S.S.,* VIII-66, p.724.

154. कः खल्वसौ विवेकवशवर्ती कामक्रोधप्रशमन कथावृथा जल्पमुपकल्पयति ॥
S.S., IV, p.413.

155. अयमहमुद्भटप्रथनचारभटारभटीनटपतिरुत्थितः कथमुदेतु विवेककथा ।
यदनुविधायिदैत्यभयसंज्वरितासु मुधा सुरसुभटीपयोधरतटीषु पटीररसः ॥
S.S., IV-24, p.414.

156. जमदग्निमुखान् परित्यजन् परिगृह्णन् दशकंधरादिकान् ।
विनिपातितवानुपायतः पुरुषानद्भुतपौरुषानहम् ॥ *S.S.*, IV-40, p.428.

157. पुंसस्त्यक्तपरिग्रहस्य विषयग्राहोज्झितस्याप्यहं
कन्थाविष्टरकुण्डिकादिहरणप्रच्छाद-नाद्याश्रयः ।
अन्तःक्षोभमलीकजल्पमसदारोपस्पृहां पैशुनं
संमोहादि च संमुखय्य सहसा दास्ये समाधिक्षयम् ॥ *S.S.*, IV-41, p.428.

158. अनघसमाधिसंपदुदरंभरिरात्मभवः प्रबलमहोर्मिजालभरिते दुरिताम्बुनिधौ ।
जडमति जन्तुजातमुपजातविहारमसौ सुखबडिशावकृष्टमुपदंशदशां नयति ॥
S.S., IV-56, p.441.

159. क्षुदिन्धनवसुंधराधरधुरंधरः किं मृषातृषारभसचूषणक्षपित पञ्चषाम्भोनिधिः ।
हठत्रुटितहाटकाचलतटीबृहत्कुण्डलः प्रसर्पति रणाङ्कणं प्रथित एष कोपासुरः ॥
S.S., VIII-67, p.725.

160. करचरणनखरदन्तप्रभृतिकमपि जगति सहजमितरदपि ।
प्रतिघसुभटस्य विश्वं प्रहरणमथवा विहर्तुमुपकरणम् ॥ *S.S.*, VIII-70, p.726.

161. अपि वैरिवरूथिनीमशेषामपि शैलानपि सागरानपि क्ष्माम् ।
ग्रसितुं प्रभवत्ययं प्रदीप्तः प्रथितः कोपतनूनपादनूनः ॥ *S.S.*, VIII-68, p.726.

162. गुरुवधमुखक्रूरक्रीडाकठोरपराक्रमः प्रथितमहितध्वंसो दक्षाध्वरप्रभृतिष्वसौ ।
स्वयमिह सुखारातिः स्वर्गापवर्गविघातकः क्षणरुचिपदं क्षान्त्या गच्छत्यमर्षहुताशनः ॥
S.S., VIII-77, p.730.

163. महामोहस्याज्ञां शिरसि निदधानः स्रजमितामहं तृष्णाजानिस्त्वरितमिह लोभः समुदितः।
प्रदिष्टैस्तत्तादृक्प्रथिमविकटैर्हाटकमयैरखण्डैर्ब्रह्माण्डैर्मम क इव तृप्तिं घटयिता ॥
S.S., IV-47, p.433.

164. कनककलधौतशैलप्रभृतिभिरपि हन्त पूरणैः क्षिप्तैः ।
तृष्णे भजति समृद्धिं भूयो भूयस्तवोदरे कार्श्यम् ॥ *S.S.*, IV-49, p.434.

165. आर्यपुत्र, तव वल्लभाया मम रमणीयत्वं सर्वरमणीसमभ्यधिकमिति किमाश्चर्यं तथापि देवासुरगृहगतसकलरत्नोपहारेण मम सौभाग्यसदृक्षाणि हारकेयूरमेखलानूपुराणि त्वया करणीयानि। *S.S.*, IV, p.435.

166. प्रिये, ईषत्करमिदमभ्यर्थयसे। निर्जिताः खलु मया देवासुरकिंनरकिंपुरुषविद्याधर-मुनिमनुष्यतिर्यञ्चः, यथा परस्परमेव व्यतिहन्यन्ते, यथा वा तुषकणमपि मेरुं मन्यन्ते।

तत्र तावद्धनदबिरुदविख्यातस्य त्र्यम्बकसखस्य मत्कृतामवस्थामाकर्णय लब्धं न मुञ्चति विलक्षमतिर्न भुङ्क्ते धत्ते पुनः पुनरसौ महतीं धनायाम् । निद्रारसं न लभते महतां निधीनां रक्षापिशाच इव संप्रति राजराजः ॥ *S.S.*, IV-50, p.435.

167. क्षुद्रक्षोणिरजःकणस्थिरतृषः क्षुभ्यन्ति पृथ्वीभृतस्तप्येत स्वपदाय कः क्वचिदिति त्रस्यन्त्यमर्त्येश्वराः । भिक्षाकेष्वपि केषुचित्क्वचिदुपक्षितेष्वधिक्षेपतः पक्षे दुर्मतिभृत्ययोरिह जगत्तिष्ठत्यसूयेर्ष्ययोः ॥ *S.S.*, IV-51, p.437.

168. अटन्ति हरितो दश स्थपुटयन्ति विश्वंभरां पठन्ति धनिनां चटून् परपरिच्छदं बिभ्रति ।
तरन्ति जलधिं प्लवैः समरमारभन्ते मुधा दुरन्तधनदोहलग्रहिलचेतसो देहिनः ॥
S.S., IV-52, p.438.

169. अतिक्रामन् कालस्तपनरथवेगेन महता न रोद्धुं शक्येत प्रतिवहनवातूलरहितः ।
गतस्त्रोतोरोधे न खलु यतितव्यं कुतधिया तदारम्भः श्रेयानुपरितनभीतिप्रतिभटः ॥
S.S., IV-60, p.445.

170. दत्रायुस्तावदस्माभिरभिरक्षणीयम् । "सर्वत एवात्मानं गोपायेत् इति हि श्रूयते।"
S.S., IV, p.446.

171. अहह अरे, त्वां धर्मपत्नि, कुहने संबोधयामि । त्वं हि मे तारेव बृहस्पतेः, अहल्येव गौतमस्य, अस्पृष्टपुरुषान्तरा क्षणविरहाक्षमा सहधर्मचारिणी ॥ *S.S.*, V, p.448.

172. यद्ब्राह्मणेश्वरो भणति । तथापि लज्जामि निर्दिष्टान्निदर्शनात् । अरुन्धतीव वसिष्ठस्येति वचनीयं गृहस्वामिना । यदाहं तस्करैः कितवैर्ग्रामणीभिः नरेन्द्रामात्यैः पाषण्डिभिरन्यैरपि तादृशैः प्रार्थितास्मि, तदापि तान् त्वामेव स्मृत्वा सेवे । *S.S.*, V, p.449.

173. विद्याश्चतुष्कसहिता विदिता द्विसप्त क्षिप्रं चतुर्गुणितचन्द्रकलाः कलाश्च ।
काले च साधुं विहिताः क्रतवः सहस्रं धर्मध्वजाश्च भुवनेषु मया निबद्धाः ॥
S.S., V-1, p.454.

174. निर्जित्य क्षितिमण्डलं भृगुपतिर्मह्यं प्रदातुं पुनः प्रह्वः प्रार्थयत न्यषेधि च मया विश्वं तृणीकुर्वता।
अस्मद्वैभवदृष्टिसंभृतचमत्कारैरमर्त्येश्वरैर्दत्तौ धिक्कृतवानहं शमधनः स्वर्गापवर्गावपि ॥
S.S., V-2, p.456.

175. ये तु धर्मतयाऽधीतास्ते सर्वे मत्परिग्रहात्।
अविशेषेण गच्छन्ति विवेकस्याभिचारताम् ॥ *S.S.*, V-3, p.457.

176. अकामोपनतमिदमसंभाष्यसंभाषणम्।(प्रकाशम्) रेरे व्रात्यब्राह्मण मूढजनमूर्धाभिषिक्त ! स्वमौढ्यप्रच्छादकं मां प्रख्यापयसि ? दिष्टया खलु मया तपःसंक्षयभीरुणा नैतावन्तं कालं शप्यसे। शप्ताः खलु मया कति कति भस्मसात्समपद्यन्त। अविदितपूर्व दुराचार ! दूरं गच्छ। मा ते भून्मम दृष्टितेजसा भस्मीभावः। *S.S.*, V, p.490.

177. अहो महादाम्भिक, अविदितमदीयाचारः किमिति दुराचार इत्युपक्रोशसि। अथवा

कः खल्वयं मया विना मत्प्रभावभिज्ञः यस्य से महायोगिनोऽपि अभिजनविद्यावृत्तेषु षोडशीमपि कलां नार्हन्ति। किमुत पृथग्जनाः अत एव हि श्रोत्रियानपि त्रिवर्षपूर्वान्न नमस्करोमि। किं न वेत्थ मामकं धर्मप्रवर्तनाभिसंधम् ॥ *S.S.*, V, p.492.

178. मयि चरति कदाचित्सत्यलोकोपकण्ठे सपदि सनकमुख्यैः साकमभ्युज्जिहानः ।
सविनयनिभृताङ्गः सप्तशः क्षालितेन स्वयमुदवहदर्घ्यं पाणिना पद्मयोनिः ॥
S.S., V-40, p.496.

179. कति कतीह पुरातनतापसाः कमलसंभववंशसमुद्भवाः ।
अतितरन्ति महान्त्यपि पातकान्यहह मामकपादजलाप्लुताः ॥ *S.S.*, V-41, p.496.

180. (स्वगतम्) नूनमयमार्यो दम्भः, इयमपि कुहना । न खल्वन्येषामीदृशं चारित्रमतिवादनं वा संभवति । तदेतावेवास्महबन्धुभूता — वभ्युपगमयामि । (प्रकाशम्) भगवति विश्ववेदिनि, युक्तिसिद्धमिह किमपि भगवत्यै निवेदयामि — *S.S.*, V, p.496.

परधनहरणप्रवीणभावा कुटिलमतिः कुहनैव सेयमार्या ।
पशुवधपरिशेषनामयज्ञः स्ववशजनः स्वयमेव दम्भ एषः ॥ *S.S.*, V-42, p.497.

181. ध्रुक्मत्र गुणोत्तरापवादी ध्वनिसारः स्वयमागतोऽसि दर्पः ।
परिकल्पितवीतरागवेषा तव भार्येव भवेदसावसूया ॥ *S.S.*, V-43, p.497.

182. त्रयोदशमिवादित्यं रुद्राणां द्वादशं तथा ।
मन्वीत नियतं लोको वसूनां नवमं च माम् । *S.S.*, V-4, p.460.

अहो नु खलु जगतो मौढ्यं येषामस्मदनुचरप्रतिनिधिपर्वण्यप्यवस्थानमपहास्यं, तेऽपि मत्साम्यं मदाधिक्यं वा प्रतिलब्धुं मोघवृत्तिं मनोरथमारोहन्ति ।
S.S., V, p.460.

183. छन्दश्छन्दितबुद्धयः पदविदः कल्पे विकल्पत्यजः शिक्षाशिक्षितमानसा विगणितज्योतिर्गणावृत्तयः।
निर्णीतार्थनिरुक्तयस्त्रिविधया मीमांसया मांसला नृत्यन्तो नयविस्तरे च सुधियः सर्वे मया खर्विताः ॥ *S.S.*, V-5, p.460.

184. विधिमन्तरेण विहगेन कुतः पयसोरशिक्ष्यत विवेकविधिः
कति वा दिनानि वद पर्यचिनोत्कलशीसुतः कबलयञ्जलधिम् ।
S.S.,V-6, p.461.

185. अनियतबहुजल्पैरल्पबोधावलिप्तैरवमतगुरुवर्गैरत्रिवर्गापवर्गैः।
अभिनयविधुताङ्गैरङ्गुलीनृत्तसारैरलमिह जडभूभृत्पीठमर्दैरमीभिः॥
S.S., V-14, p.468.

186. श्वश्रूरस्य दिगम्बरव्रतवती संबन्धिनः सौगता माता चास्य पिता च पाशुपतिनौ वैदेशिको देशिकः ।
जाया तिष्ठति सांख्ययोगसमये चार्वाकशिष्यः सखा मिथ्याचारसमाह्वयः स्वयमसौ विप्लावको वैदिकः ॥ *S.S.*, V-15, p.470.

187. संभवति च सर्वथा सर्वतः प्रसारिताभ्यां स्वर्गापवर्गगुणदोष जालाभ्यां तयोरूपरोधः । अहं पुनर्मायासहस्रवेदी मारीचमैथिलीन्यायेन विरक्तिं तावत्तपस्विनीं विप्रलभे । भवतस्तु विष्णुभक्तिविमथने पौलस्त्य एव प्रमाणम् ।

S.S., III, p.335.

188. सखे, साधु भाषितम् । नूनमीदृशेन वचसा दवदहनदन्दह्यमानतर्विशिखरकुलाय-कुहरनिष्कान्ता विहगपङ्क्तिरिव विष्णुभक्तिरपसर्पति । अद्य खल्वनादिभोग-वासनाजालजटिलबुद्धेरात्मनः कथं नाम निर्विवेको विवेकः संसारजिहासां साधयिष्यति प्रत्युत दिव्यभौमयुवतिगुणपल्लवकुतूहली तद्गुणैरेव निबिडं निबध्यते । पश्य तावदमृतोद्भवास्त्रैलोक्यललामभूताः पद्मलोचनाः ॥ *S.S.*, III, p.340.

स्मेरेण स्तनकुङ्मलेन भुजयोर्मध्यं तिरोधित्सितं नेत्रेण श्रवणं लिलङ्घयिषितं नीलोत्पलश्रीमुषा ।

अङ्गं सर्वमलंचिकीर्षितमहो भावैः स्मराचार्यकैस्तन्वीनां विजिगीषितं च वयसा धन्येन मन्ये जगत् ॥ *S.S.*, III, 5, p.341.

189. सर्वाधारः कथं भूयात्सर्वदोषविवर्जितः ।
तथैव सर्वकामार्थी निरपेक्षः कथं प्रभुः ॥ *S.S.*, III-7, p.344.

190. अनघगुणौघमेकमवधूतसमाभ्यधिकं स्ववितरणीयसर्वपुरुषार्थमुपास्तिपदम् ।
उपनिषदूषरान्तपरिवर्तनधूसरधीर्न खलु विवेक एष मयि तिष्ठति साधयिता ॥

S.S., III-10, p.346.

191. हृष्यन्ति व्यसनेषु सप्तसु मुधाऽरब्धेषु मत्प्रेरिताः प्रारब्धं न परित्यजन्ति च मुहुः प्रत्यूहवात्याहताः ।

नानादुःखभयानकेऽपि न जहत्यर्थे पुमर्थे रतिं मोहस्याभिनिवेश एकदृगहं कोशाधिकारे स्थितः ॥ *S.S.*, VIII-1, p.664.

192. अवसादप्रसङ्गेषु स्वयमुत्तम्भनोद्यतः ।
अहमार्यस्य लोभस्य भ्राता चरमसंभवः ॥ *S.S.*, VIII-2, p.665.

193. अहो महत्सांपरायिकमुपस्थितमास्माकस्यान्ववायस्य यदिह विवेकेन प्रथममध्यात्म-विद्यामशिक्ष्यत पुरुषः यच्चासौ मतान्तरदौर्बल्यप्रकाशनेन परब्रह्मप्रकाशके शास्त्रे प्रशमितश्रद्धावैकल्यः यदपि च सपरिकरे मोक्षोपाये संसुखीऋतः विमुखीकृताश्च कामक्रोधादयः विमृष्टं च किमपि संयमस्थानम् अवधारितं च धारणायाः शुभमालम्बनं प्रारिप्सितश्च शमदमवैराग्यादिपरिकर्मितः सालम्बनो महायोगः । *S.S.*, VIII, p.666.

194. प्रिये, कामो जुगुप्सया, कोपस्तितिक्षया,
लोभस्तुष्ट्या, अहंकार आत्मविद्यया । एवमन्येऽपि । *S.S.*, VIII, p.669.

195. गृध्रास्तोरणशैल शृङ्गमभितोऽगृह्णन्नभोमण्डलं वात्यामण्डलखण्डितध्वजपटीशून्यानि सैन्यानि नः ।

शूलप्रासकृपाणमुद्गरधनुःक्रूरैर्मुहुः किंकरैर्दृश्यन्ते परिवारिता इव दिशः संवर्तसंवर्तकैः ॥

S.S., VIII-4, p.672.

196. अमुष्मिन्दिवसे श्वो वा नूनं निर्यातिवैभवात् ।
अमोहमविवेकं वा जगदेतद्भविष्यति ॥ *S.S.*, VIII-7, p.674.

197. इदं किल महाराज, चतुर्दशभुवनचक्रचक्रवर्तिनः द्वापरमन्त्रिनिर्धारितनिखिलकार्यस्य दुर्मतिमतप्रतिष्ठितस्य ।
देवस्य महामोहस्य लोभनाम्ना गणकेन लिखित्वा त्वदर्थं प्रेषितमन्तरङ्गेण मया उपहृतमलनीयं शासनम् ॥ *S.S.*, III, p.382.

198. परोपास्तिश्रद्धावधिकमतिवृत्तं यदिह ते ।
तदैश्चर्यप्राप्त्यै भवतु बहु मन्येमहि तदा ॥ *S.S.*, III, p.384.

199. प्रिये, आकर्णितः किलायं भिक्षुपादप्रसरणन्यायः ।
अथवा स्वाभाव्यमेव शवमुष्टिवत् गृहीतग्राहिता महामोहस्य ।
S.S., III, pp.384-85.

200. विश्वाधिको विलयमेष्यति कस्य भूम्ना वीरः प्रसिद्धमहिमा विबुधेषु कामः ।
क्रोधोदितं यदनुभाववशेन शंभोः शृङ्गारशीतलमभून्नयनं तृतीयम् ॥
S.S., III-39, p.386.

201. कामोऽसौ समवर्तताग्र इति हि ब्रूते समीची श्रुतिः कामादेव जगज्जनिस्थितिलयैराद्यः पुमान्क्रीडति ।
निष्कामोऽपि सकाम एव लभते निःश्रेयसं दुर्लभं कामः कस्य वशे क एष भुवने कामस्य न स्याद्वशे ॥ *S.S.*, III-40, pp.386-87.

202. अप्राणितमहामोहमनङ्गीकृतमन्मथम् ।
विधूतप्रतिघं लोको विवेकं बहु मंस्यते ॥ *S.S.*, III-42, p.388.

203. सुप्तप्रबोधनसमुत्सुकया सुमत्या पत्न्या सहाचरितविश्वहितं विवेकम् ।
जेतुं क एव जगति प्रभवेत्तथापि स्वामी नियोजयति मोह इह स्वयं नः ॥
S.S., III-43, p.389.

204. काव्यस्यात्मा स एवार्थस्तथा चादिकवेः पुरा ।
क्रौञ्चद्वन्द्ववियोगोत्थः शोकः श्लोकत्वमागतः ॥ *Dhvanyāloka*, I. 5.

205. नहि रसादृते कश्चिदपि अर्थः प्रवर्तते । *Nāṭyaśāstra* of Bharata, Chowkhambha Sanskrit Samsthan, Varanasi, Samvat 2037, p.71.

206. G.K. Bhatt, *Bharata-Nāṭya-Mañjarī*, Bhandarkar Oriental Research Institute, Poona, 1975, p.83.

207. यथा बीजाद् भवेत् वृक्षो वृक्षात् पुष्पं फलं तथा ।
तथा मूलं रसाः सर्वे तेभ्यो भावा व्यवस्थिताः ॥ *Ibid.*, NMG 38, p.88.

208. शृंगारहास्यकरुणरौद्रवीरभयानकाः ।
बीभत्साद्भुतसंज्ञौ चेत्यष्टौ नाट्ये रसाः स्मृताः ॥
Nāṭyaśāstram, VI-5, p.69.

209. मुनिना भरतेन यः प्रयोगो भवतीष्वष्टसाश्रयो नियुक्तः ।
ललिताभिनयं तैाद्य भर्ता मरुतां द्रष्टुमनाः सलोकपालः ।।
Vikramorvasīyam, II.18.

210. F. Edgerton, *Indirect Suggestion in Poetry*, Proc. of the American Philosophical Society, Vol. 76, 1936, p.704.

211. Vide, V. Rāghavan, *The Number of Rasas*, Adyar Library Adyar, 1940, p.13.

212. रजस्तमो विहीनात्तु सत्त्वावस्थात् सचित्ततः ।
मनागस्पृष्ट बार्ह्यर्थात् सान्तो रस इतीरितः ।।
Bhāvaprakāśa of Śāradātanaya Ed.: K.S. Rāmaswamy, Gaekwad Oriental Series, No. XIV, Baroda, 1930, p.48.

213. शान्तो रसः स्वतन्त्रोऽत्र पृथगेव व्यवस्थितः ।
शान्तस्य तु समुत्पत्तिर्नृप वैराग्यतः स्मृता ।।
स चाभिनेयो भवति लिङ्गग्रहणस्तथा । सर्वभूतदयाध्यानमोक्षमार्गप्रवर्तनैः ।।
Priyabala Shah, *Viṣṇudharmottara Purāṇa*, Vol. I, Oriental Institue, Baroda, 1958, *Kāṇḍa* 3, p.100.

214. वीरो सिंगारो अंबुओ अ रोद्दो अहोइ बोद्धव्वो ।
वेलणओ बीभच्छो हासो कलुणो पसंतो अ ।।
निद्दोसमणसमाहाणसंभवो जो पसंत भावेणं ।
अविकारलक्खणो सो रसो पसंतो त्ति णायव्वो ।।
Aṇuvogaddaram, Shri Mahavīra Jaina Vidyalaya, Bombay, 1968, p.121.

215. तस्मादस्ति शान्तो रसः । तथा च चिरन्तनपुस्तकेषु 'स्थायिभावान् रसत्वमुपनेष्यामः' इत्यनन्तरं शान्तो नाम शमस्थायिभावात्मकः इत्यादि शान्तलक्षणं पठ्यते । तत्र सर्वरसानां शान्तप्राय एवास्वादः, विषयेभ्यो विपरिवृत्त्या । तन्मुख्यतालाभः केवलं वासनान्तरोपहित इति । अत्र सर्वप्रकृतित्वाभिधानाय पूर्वमभिधानम् । लोके च पृथक् पृथक् सामान्यस्य न गणनमिति स्थाय्यस्य पृथङ् नोक्तः । सामान्यमपि तु विवेचकेन पृथगेव गणनीयमिति विवेचकाभिमतसामाजिकास्वादलक्षणप्रतीतिविषयतया स पृथग्भूत एव । इतिहासपुराणाभिधानकाशादौ च नव रसाः श्रूयन्ते, श्रीमत्सिद्धान्तशास्त्रेऽष्वपि । तथा चोक्तम् —

अष्टानामिह देवानां शृङ्गारादीन् प्रदर्शयेत् ।
मध्ये च देवदेवस्य शान्तं रूपं प्रदर्शयेत् ।।

J.L. Masson & M.V. Patwardhan, *Śāntarasa & Abhinavagupta's Philosophy of Aesthetics*, Bhandarkar Oriental Institute, Pune, 1969, p.118.

216. एको रसः करुण एव निमित्तभेदात् । भिन्नः पृथक् पृथगिवाश्रयते विवर्तान् ।।
आवर्तबुद्बुदतरंगमयान् विकारान् । अम्भो यथा सलिलमेव हि तत्समस्तम् ।।
(III. 47)

217. स्वं स्वं निमित्तमादाय शान्तादुत्पद्यते रसः । पुनर्निमित्तापाये तु शान्त एव प्रलीयते।।
इत्यादिना रसान्तरप्रकृतित्वमुपसंहृतम् ।
Śāntarasa & Abhinavagupta's Philosophy of Aesthetics, p.119.

218. शान्तः शमस्थायिभाव उत्तमप्रकृतिर्मतः । कुन्देन्दुसन्दरच्छायः श्रीनारायणदैवतः।।
अनित्यत्वादिनाऽशेषवस्तुनिःसारता तु या । परमात्मस्वरूपं वा तस्यालम्बनमिष्यते ।।
पुण्याश्रमहरिक्षेत्रतीर्थरम्यवनादयः । महापुरुषसङ्गाद्यास्तस्योद्दीपनरूपिणः ।।
रोमाञ्चाद्याश्चानुभावास्तथा स्युर्व्यभिचारिणः । निर्वेदहर्षस्मरणमतिभूतदयादयः।।
Viśvanātha, *Sāhityadarpaṇa*, Krishnadas Academy, Varanasi, 1989, II.245-248, pp.271-72.

219. अत्र विच्छर्दितमिति स्वर्गभोगनिमित्तामृतस्य हेयत्वलक्षणया
शान्तरसो व्यज्यत इति न जुगुप्साश्लीलतादोषः ।। *S.S.*, VII, p.628.

220. एवं शान्तरसविभावा उक्ताः । तदुक्तं संगीतरत्नाकरे —
''संसारभीरुता दोषदर्शनं विषयेषु च ।
योगिसङ्गे मुनीनां च कृपाशमदमक्षमाः ।।
अध्यात्मविषया गोष्ठी तापसास्तापसाश्रयाः ।
भूरिनिर्झरझांकारिवारितीर्थानि तीर्थकाः ।
विष्णुभक्तिप्रदा विद्या विभावा यत्र संगताः।।" *Prabhāvilāsa*, X, p.801.

221. अथ शान्तरसानुभावानाह — तदुक्तं भरतेन मन्दस्पन्दं बहिश्चित्तमानन्दाश्रुल्पुते दृशौ।
रोमाञ्चकञ्चुका मूर्तिर्मोक्ष शास्त्रार्थचिन्तनम् ।।
ब्रह्मविद्योपदेशश्च संगमस्तत्त्वगोचरः ।
नासाग्रमागते नेत्रे ज्ञानमुद्राप्रदर्शनम् ।। *Prabhāvilāsa*, p.817.

222. शृङ्गं हि मन्मथोद्भेदस्तदागमनहेतुकः ।
उत्तम प्रकृतिप्रायो रसः शृङ्गार इष्यते ।।
Viśvanātha, *Sāhitya Darpaṇa,* III-183, p.228.

223. चन्द्रचन्दनरोलम्बरुताद्युद्दीपनमतम् ।
Viśvanātha, *Sāhitya Darpaṇa,* III-185, p.229.

224. दर्शनस्पर्शनादीनि निषेवेते विलासिनौ।
यत्रानुरक्तावान्योन्यं संभोगोऽयमुदाहृतः।।
Viśvanātha, *Sāhitya Darpaṇa,* III-210, p.251.

225. यत्र तु रतिः प्रकृष्टा नाभीष्टमुपैति विप्रलम्भोऽसौ ।
Viśvanātha, *Sāhitya Darpaṇa,* III-187, p.230.

226. विकृताकारवाग्वेपचेष्टादेः कुहकाद्भवेत् ।
हास्यो हासस्थायिभावः श्वेतः प्रथमदैवतः ॥ 214 ॥
विकृताकारवाक्चेष्टं यमालोक्य हसेज्जनः ।
तमत्रालम्बनं प्राहुस्तच्चेष्टोद्दीपनं मतम् ॥ 215 ॥
अनुभावोऽक्षिङ्कोचवदनस्मेरतादयः ।
निद्रालस्यावहित्थाद्या अत्र स्युर्व्यभिचारिणः ॥ 216 ॥
ज्येष्टानां स्मितहसिते, मध्यानां विहसितावहसिते च ।
नीचानामपहसितं तथातिहसितं तदेष षड्भेदः ॥ 217 ॥

Viśvanātha, *Sāhitya Darpaṇa,* III, pp.254-55.

227. इष्टनाशादनिष्टाप्तेः करुणाख्यो रसो भवेत् ।
धीरैः कपोतवर्णोऽयं कथितो यमदैवतः ॥ 222 ॥
शोकोऽत्रस्थायिभावः स्याच्छोच्यमालम्बनं मतम् ।
तस्य दाहादिकावस्था भवेदुद्दीपनं पुनः ॥ 223 ॥
अनुभावा दैवनिन्दाभूपातकन्दितादयः ।
वैवर्ण्योच्छ्वासिनःश्वासस्तम्भप्रलपनानि च ॥ 224 ॥
निर्वेदमोहापस्मारव्याधिग्लानिस्मृतिश्रमाः ।
विषादजडतोन्मादचिन्ताद्या व्यभिचारिणः ॥ 225 ॥

Viśvanātha, *Sāhitya Darpaṇa,* III, pp.258-59.

228. रौद्रः क्रोधस्थायिभावो रक्तो रुद्राधिदैवतः ।
आलम्बनमरिस्तत्र तच्चेष्टोद्दीपनं मतम् ॥ 227 ॥
मुष्टिप्रहारपातन विकृतच्छेदावदारणेश्चैव ।
संग्रामसंभ्रमाद्यैरस्योद्दीप्तिभवेत् । ॥ 228 ॥
प्रौढा भ्रूविभङ्गौष्ठनिर्दश बाहुस्फोटनतर्जनाः ।
आत्मावदानकथनमायुधोत्क्षेपणानि च ॥ 229 ॥
अनुभावास्तथाक्षेपक्रूरसंदर्शनादयः ।
उग्रतावेगरोमाञ्चस्वेदवेपथवो मदः ॥ 230 ॥
मोहमर्षादयस्तत्र भावा स्युव्यभिचारिणः ।

Viśvanātha, *Sāhitya Darpaṇa,* III, pp.260-61.

229. उत्तमप्रकृतिर्वीर उत्साहस्थायिभावकः ।
महेन्द्रदैवतो हेमवर्णोऽयं समुदाहृतः ॥ 232 ॥
आलम्बनविभावास्तु विजेतव्यादयो मताः ।
विजेतव्यादिचेष्टाद्यास्तस्योद्दीपनरूपिणः ।
अनुभावस्तु तत्र स्युः सहायान्वेषणादयः ।
सञ्चारिणस्तु धृतिमतिगर्वस्मृतितर्करोमाञ्चाः ।
स च दानधर्मयुद्धैर्दयया च समन्वितश्चतुर्धास्यात् ॥ 234 ॥

Viśvanātha, *Sāhitya Darpaṇa,* III, p.263.

230. भयानको भयस्थायिभावो कालाऽधिदैवतः ।
स्त्रीनीचप्रकृतिः कृष्णो मतस्तत्त्वविशारदैः ॥ 235 ॥
यस्मादुत्पद्यते भीतिस्तदत्रालम्बनं मतम् ।
चेष्टा धोरतरास्तस्य भवेदुद्दीपनं पुनः ॥ 236 ॥
अनुभावोऽत्र वैवर्ण्यगद्गदस्वरभाषणम् ।
प्रलयस्वेदरोमाञ्चकम्पदिकप्रक्षणादयः ॥ 237 ॥
जुगुप्सावेगसंमोहसंत्रासासग्लानिदीनताः ।
अङ्कापस्मारसम्भ्रान्तिमृत्वाद्या व्यभिचारिणः ॥ 238 ॥
Viśvanātha, *Sāhitya Darpaṇa,* III, pp.266-67.

231. जुगुप्सास्थायिभावस्तु बीभत्सः कथ्यते रसः ।
नीलवर्णो महाकालदैवतोऽयमुदाहृतः ॥ 239 ॥
दुर्गन्धमांसरुधिरमेदांस्यालम्बनं मतम् ।
तत्रैव कृमिपाताद्यमुद्दीपनमुदाहृतम् ॥ 240 ॥
निष्ठीवनास्यवलननेत्रसङ्कोचनादयः ।
अनुभावास्तत्र मतास्तथा स्युर्व्यभिचारिणः ॥ 241 ॥
Viśvanātha, *Sāhitya Darpaṇa,* III, pp.268-69.

232. अद्भुतो विस्मयस्थायिभावो गन्धर्वदैवतः ॥ 242 ॥
पीतवर्णो वस्तु लोकातिगमालम्बनं मतम् ।
गुणानां तस्य महिमा भवेदुद्दीपनं पुनः ॥ 243 ॥
स्तम्भः स्वेदोऽथ रोमाञ्चगद्गदस्वरसंभ्रमाः ।
तथा नेत्रविकासाद्या अनुभावाः प्रकीर्तिताः ॥ 244 ॥
वितर्कवेगसंभ्रान्तिहर्षाद्या व्यभिचारिणः ॥
Viśvanātha, *Sāhitya Darpaṇa,* III, pp.269-70.

233. न कान्तमपि निर्भूषं विभाति वनितामुखम् । *Kāvyālaṅkāra*, 1-13.

234. अलंकारान्तरस्यापि प्रतीतौ यत्र भासते ।
तत्परत्वं न वाच्यस्य नासौ मार्गे ध्वनेर्मतः ॥
Krishnamoorthy, K., *Anadavardhana's Dhvanyāloka*, Karnatak University, Dharwad, 1974, II-27, p.90.

235. काव्यं शोभाकरान् धर्मान् अलंकारान् प्रचक्षते ॥ *Kāvyādarśa*, II-1.

236. काव्यंग्राह्यं अलंकारात्, सौन्दर्यम् अलंकारः ।
Kāvyālaṅkāra sūtra I-12.

237. अनुप्रासः शब्दसाम्यं वैषिम्येपि स्वरसाम्यात् ।
Viśvanātha, *Sāhitya Darpaṇa,* X-3, p.768.

238. च्छेकोव्यञ्जन संघस्य सकृतसाम्यं अनेकधा । *Ibid.,* X-3, p.769.

239. साधर्म्यमुपमा भेदे ।

Mammaṭa, *Kāvyaprakāśa,* ed. A.B. Gajendragadkar, Bombay, 1959, p.34.

240. तद्रूपकम् अभेदो यः उपमानोपमेयोः । *Kāvyaprakāśa,* p.47.

241. श्लेषः स वाक्ये एकस्मिन् यत्रानेकार्थता भवेत् । *Kāvyaprakāśa,* p.55.

242. निगीर्याध्यवसानं तु प्रकृतस्य परेण यत् ।
प्रस्तुतस्य यदन्यत्वं यद्यर्थोक्तौ च कल्पनम् ॥ *Kāvyaprakāśa,* p.63.

243. अभवन् वस्तुसंबन्ध उपमापरिकल्पकः । *Kāvyaprakāśa,* p.56.

244. परोक्तिर्भेदकैः श्लिष्टैः समासोक्तिः । *Kāvyaprakāśa,* p.55.

245. सामान्यं वा विशेषो वा तदन्येन समर्थ्यते ।
यत्र सोऽर्थान्तरन्यासः साधर्म्येणेतरेण वा ॥ *Kāvyaprakāśa,* p.75.

246. विशेषोक्तिः अखण्डेषु कारणेषु फलावचः । *Kāvyaprakāśa,* p.74.

247. अनुमानं तदुक्तं यत् साध्यसाधनयोः वचः । *Kāvyaprakāśa,* p.91.

248. पर्यायोक्तं विना वाच्यवाचकत्वेन यद्वचः । *Kāvyaprakāśa,* p.85.

249. तत् सिद्धिः हेतौ एकैकस्मिन् यत्रान्यत् तत्करं भवेत् समुच्चयोऽसौ ।
Kāvyaprakāśa, p.87.

250. काव्यलिङ्गं हेतोर्वाक्यपदार्थता ॥ *Kāvyaprakāśa,* p.83.

251. विशेषणैः यत् साकूतैः उक्तिः परिकरस्तु सः । *Kāvyaprakāśa,* p.92.

252. क्वचित् यदतिवैधर्म्यान्न श्लेषो घटनामियात् ।
कर्तुः क्रियाफलावाप्तिर्नैवानर्थश्च यद् भवेत् ॥40॥
गुणक्रियाभ्यां कार्यस्य कारणस्य गुणक्रिये ।
क्रमेण च विरुद्धे यत् स एष विषमो मतः ॥41॥ *Kāvyaprakāśa,* p.103.

253. उपमानाद् यदन्यस्य व्यतिरेकः स एव सः । *Kāvyaprakāśa,* p.68.

254. अत्र पूर्वाद्रेः क्षरतीति प्रसिद्धगङ्गाव्यतिरेकात्
व्यतिरेकालंकारो व्यज्यते ॥ *Prabhāvilāsa*, p.420.

255. भ्रान्तिमानन्यसंवित् तत्तुल्यदर्शने ॥ *Kāvyaprakāśa,* p.110.

256. निषेधो वक्तुमिष्टस्य यो विशेषाभिधित्सया ।
वक्ष्यमाणोक्त विषयः स आक्षेपो द्विधा मतः ॥ *Kāvyaprakāśa,* p.72.

257. सूच्यार्थं सूचनं मुद्रा प्रकृतार्थपरैः पदैः ।
Appayya Dīkṣita, *Kuvalayānanda*, Chowkhamba Vidya Bhavana, Varanasi, 1995, p.232.

258. अत्र नृवरेत्यादि पदप्रयोगसंभवेऽपि रक्षणप्रार्थनायां ।
वरदेति पदस्याभिजाततया मुद्रा नामालंकारः ॥ p.597.

259. प्राप्तिः सा समुदायस्य ज्ञानं यच्चैकदेशतः । An example of this *Alaṅkāra* is found in *Prabhavilāsa,* p.254.

260. वचसा कर्मणा प्रीतिर्यस्मिन्ननुनयो हि सः । We have an instance of this *Alaṅkāra* in *Prabhavilāsa,* p.289.

261. उद्दिष्टं स्यात् परोक्षे च प्रत्यक्षे चार्थकीर्तनम् । इत्यमृतानन्द वचनात् ।
This *Alaṅkāra* may be illustrated from *Prabhavilāsa,* p.313.

262. दाक्षिप्यं श्लक्ष्णया वाचा परचित्तानुवर्तनम् ।
A speciman of this *Alaṅkāra* is found in *Prabhavilāsa,* p.326.

263. गर्हणं गुणविच्छेदाद् दोषोद्भेदेन कीर्तनम् ।
Prabhavilāsa, provides the above *Alaṅkāra*, p.354.

264. पश्चात्तापोऽनुतापस्तु कृत्वा कार्यान्तरं यथा ।
Prabhavilāsa, provides this type of *Alaṅkara*, p.377.

265. The definition of this *Alaṅkāra* may be gleaned from *Prabha-vilāsa* as follows.
अथ विषाद प्रमादकर्तव्यामान्तरीं ध्रुवामाह वितमसीति । तदुक्तम्-
"विषादे विस्मृतौ क्रोधे प्रमादे संगमेऽपि च ।
दोषप्रच्छादनादौ च गीयते या तु सान्तरी ॥" (p.441)

266. परिहारस्तु विज्ञेयः कृतानुचितमार्जनम् ।
The above citation of *Alaṅkāra* is drawn from *Prabha-vilāsa*, pp.498-99.

267. न्यायानुवृत्तिरेवात्र नीतिरित्युच्यते यथा ।
This *Alaṅkāra* is taken from *Prabhavilāsa,* p.504.

268. This *Alaṅkāra* is defined as :
"अभासत्त्वे विरोधस्य विरोधाभास इष्यते ।" *Kuvalayānanda,* p.141.
The second line of the love verse illustrates this *Alaṅkāra.*

269. *Prabhāvilāsa*, explains this *Alaṅkāra* which arises when a certain cause is described with reference to the corresponding effect.
"क्रिययाः कारकं हेतुर्मुख्यो गौण इति द्विधा ।
मुख्यहेतुर्द्विधा तत्र कारकज्ञपकक्रमात् ॥" (p.644)
This is here explained thus : अत्राट्टहासाद्नुतानां प्रह्लादहर्षादिहेतुत्वोक्त्या कारकहेतुर्नामालंकारः । (p.644)

270. In his *Kuvalayānanda*, Appayya Dīkṣita has identified *Preyolaṅkāra* with Bhāvālaṅkāra, where he says प्रेयोऽलंकार एव भावालंकार उच्यते। (p.270) Besides *Prabhavilāsa* defines this *Alaṅkāra* as प्रेयः प्रियतराख्यानम् । (p.249), which means narration of a thing causing happiness. In the verse above the protection of *Śruti* is described and this itself is subject of creating joy in the present context.

271. This is defined as below :
परिणामः क्रियार्थश्चेद्विषथी विषयात्मना । प्रसन्नेन दृगब्जेन वीक्षते मदिरेक्षणा ।।
Appayya Dīkṣita, *Kuvalayānanda*, p.22.
In the *Prabhavilāsa* it is illustrated thus : "अत्र रत्नघृणिष्वारोप्यमाणस्यारात्रिकत्वस्य प्रकृतोपयोगात् परिणामालंकारः।" p.307.

272. This is an example of *Vākyovākyālaṅkāra* as it is in the form of a dialogue between two characters, *i.e.* Tumburu and Nārada. The latter clarifies the point put by the former. *Prabhāvilāsa* writes that अस्य श्लोकस्योक्तिः प्रत्युक्तिरूपतया वाक्योवाक्यमलंकारः ।

Chapter V

Philosophical Doctrines Reflected in the Drama

As the *Saṅkalpasūryodaya*, is an Allegorical drama, it variably consists of philosophy of ethics and Vedānta. The philosophical aspect of the drama is however another face of the drama. Perhaps Vedānta Deśika indicates and refutes the views of different philosophical systems including *Advaita Vedānta*. In the second phase the dramatist establishes the supremacy of the *Viśiṣṭādvaita Vedānta*.

As it is stated in the drama itself, Lord Nārāyaṇa is the Supreme Being. Devotion to Him leads to *Mokṣa*. And His auspicious will makes the devotee free from *Saṁsāra*. Thus, he who is imparted with the knowledge of *Aṣṭākṣaramantra* by competent preceptor, he conquers the demon called *Avidyā*.[1] Still a man aspiring for knowledge gets his intellect affected by listening to insignificant and fallacious doctrines of different systems as such the Knot of devotion to Lord becomes loosened. When seeker's advancement of Knowledge and devotion is impeded due to such deluding doctrines, it is the duty of the preceptor to rescue such seeker by avoiding the obstructions.

Of course such systems are rather deluding systems. These systems spread the darkness after the setting of Sun like knowledge. These systems cannot stand the test of *Pramāṇas*, and deceive the folk of demon natured persons. Before the Sun of the knowledge these systems are like darkness bound to disappear.[2]

The disputants following such a systems cause a terrible knowledge but insensible like the sound heard at the time of churning milky ocean. These disputants make vain efforts to silence even Bṛhaspati. As elephants destroy of grooves of plantain trees, these disputants also, with their own fallacious arguments try to root out the faith in the path of righteousness. But these elephants like disputants should be driven away by a lion like scholar endowed with irresistible strength with the help of its five sharp claws of logical reasoning such as *Ātmaśraya, Anyonyāśraya, Cakrāśraya, Anavasthā* and *Aniṣṭaprasaṅga*. And such a lion like a scholar can dispel the darkness with its two well-displayed teeth of *Parapakṣopālambha, i.e.* refutation of false doctrine and *Svapakṣasthāpana, i.e.* the establishment of right doctrine.

For achieving this end, a lion like scholar has to hold a debate of scholars of different systems of Thought. Hence, it is significant on the part of the dramatist that he has entertained the scene wherein *Guru* and *Śiṣya* are engaged in philosophical debate. With a view to showing weak and fallacious views of other systems, the dramatist points to such doctrines and refutes them in a cogent manner.

When a scholar is engaged in such philosophical debate he should avoid *Vitaṇḍavāda*. And he should refute opponents views and through which he has to establish the right theory. This is the ethics of the debate highlighted by Vedānta Deśika. Just as Rāma authorised by Viśvāmitra took the help of *mantras Bala* and *Atibala* to conquer the demons, a debator too is aloud to employ the methods of

Vitaṇḍa and *Jalpa* to defeat foes speaking ill of the *Vedas* and of God.[3]

In this context, the dramatist Vedānta Deśika suggests a rule for disciple to be followed in the discussion, *i.e.* when discussions are held with the persons of our own school of Vedānta one should argue accepting the authority of scriptures held in common by both. Bearing this discipline in the mind, one should argue with the support of *Pramāṇas* in a manner which would appeal to the hearts of the audience.

So far as, generally accepted order of the systems of Indian Philosophy, Cārvāka school comes first. Then other schools like Jaina, Bauddha, Nyāya-Vaiśeṣika, Sāṅkhya, Yoga and Advaita come one after the other. But in this order appears to be dishevelled in the drama. As a matter of fact, Vedānta Deśika's method of following the order of rival schools is not insignificant. He chooses *Sāṅkhya* school first for refutation in the drama. He says, the discourse of *Sāṅkhyas* is taken first because that school is close to the Upaniṣadic Thought; श्रुतिशिरः प्रत्यासन्नतया प्रथमसमुत्थितानां संप्रति स्वमतोऽपन्यासम् ।

1. SĀṄKHYA AND YOGA SCHOOL OF THOUGHT

Sāṅkhya system of thought has been propounded by Sages such as Kapila, Āsuri and Pañcaśikha. They maintain the view that Prakṛti or matter is different from *Puruṣa* or the Individual Self. But they do not accept the existance of the Supreme Being because of their sinful-mindedness.[4] The dramatist refutes suggestively that upholding two *tattvas* *Prakṛti* and *Puruṣa* and rejecting *Paramapuruṣa* is not coherent to the Upaniṣadic Thought. If Sāṅkhyas reject *Paramapuruṣatattva* then they become equal to either *Vaiśeṣika* who accept *Paramāṇus* causality of the world and reject *Prakṛti* or to *Cārvākas* who uphold the view that there is no Individual soul other than the body. In this way, the dramatist wards off the theory of *Prakṛti* and *Puruṣa* as upheld by *Niriśvarasāṅkhyas*.

Even in case of *Śeśvarasāṅkhyas* their views become defective because they accept the existence of Supreme Being, but as possessing glories and powers only within certain limits. Thus *Śeśvarasāṅkhyas* are in close confirmity with Yoga system. However, this veiw of limiting the glories and powers of the Lord is baseless. Yoga system holds the view that the glory of the Lord resembles the nature of the reflection in a mirror.[5] Hence according to them Lord's glory is as true as the reflection. This view goes against the Upaniṣads. Hence, both *Śeśvarasāṅkhyas* and Yoga stand refuted.

2. VAIŚEṢIKA SCHOOL OF KAṆĀDA

Next, *Vaiśeṣika* school of Thought is taken up for exmination. Kaṇāda's *Vaiśeṣika* Thought accepts the creation of a new object which did not exists before as pots from mud the followers of Kaṇāda hold that when mud or potsherds are united to form a pot, the potsherds disappear and a new object, *i.e.* pot is created. Vedāntins say that pot is only a modification of clay or of the pot-sherds. This school applies the casuality to *Paramāṇus* and rejects Brahman's causality which is supported by scriptures. Moreover, Kaṇādas school maintains *Mokṣa* is not resemblance to the Supreme Being which is blissful. But, according to them *Mokṣa* is the attainment of a state similar to that of a stone. Therefore, Kaṇādas view is defective. Therefore, Kaṇāda system survives only in name.[6]

3. BUDDHISTIC SCHOOL OF THOUGHT

Further, the view of Buddhists is refuted. Veṅkaṭanātha calls these Buddhists *Vaināśikas*, because they hold that there is nothing permanent and that everything has a momentary existence and perishes afterwards. Of the Buddhists, *Vaibhāśikas* hold that the Universe has only a momentary existence and *Sautrāntrikas* think that the external world preserves only from inference and not for preception. And the knowledge has different forms. But Yogācāras assert that the external world is illusory, and the *Mādhyamikas* consider that there is nothing real in world at all. Thus these different views of differnt Buddhistic schools contradict one another. When declaring everything is void, *Mādhyamika* is impetuous in his power of arguing that it is possible to determine the truth of falsehood of anything. It is as improper as saying 'मम जननी वन्ध्या.'[7] Therefore, they stand defeated. Therefore, there is no need of pointing out any fallacy in their argument as it is like the trouble taken in beating down with a hammer, a man who is already dead.

4. JAINA SCHOOL OF THOUGHT

Afterwards Jaina school is refuted. Jainas hold the validity of sense perception and inference. They hold the exposition based on *Saptabhaṅgī, i.e.* a thing might be or might not be everything depending on the angle from which it is perceived. The inconṣistency of their own words.[8] Also it is true that these Jains deceive men by imposing their own theories like *Ādityasthambhana, Pāṣāṇasphoṭana, Pratimājalpana* etc. It is said that they have no distinction between what should be eaten and what should not be. They say that Vedic path is defective. Also they ordain plucking out the deep rooted hairs on their heads. This type of religion punishes the followers thereof. Therefore, Vedānta Deśika says that the gods in anger at their vilification of the Vedic way of life have inflicted on them this punishment.[9]

5. ADVAITA SCHOOL OF ŚAṄKARA

Then the dramatist refers to the *Advaita* school of philosophy. As is said Advaitins resemble the Jainas as they hold the views opposed in the Vedas. But appear as observing hard vows and penances; They attempt to destroy the crops growing in the fields of the Vedas; प्रथमगणानुकारिणः केचन दुराचारः। एते च नैगमिकधर्मकमलोपमर्दितः कंडंकरीया इव दूरपरिहरणीयाः।

According to the Advaitins owing to the powerful influence of *Avidyā*, the world appears an illusory imposition on Brahman, which can neither be called the sentient Self, nor the external (non-sentient) thing, like the cloud-city seen in the sky (in maintaining this doctrine) they have to phase contradictions, which, far from being unreal, are stronger than even the Vindhya mountains. They are therefore, to be classed among the heralds who sing the praise of monarchs born of barren women.[10]

But the truth is that all *Pramāṇas* like *Pratyakaṣa* etc. subject the things which possess distinguishing features. Therefore, the application of *Nirviśeṣatva* to Brahman becomes opposed to all *Pramāṇas*. And all the things in the world have one or the other quality by which they can be distinguished from one another. This is the experience of one and all. Hence, there cannot be a thing which is *Nirviśeṣa*. Therefore, Brahman who is full of auspicious qualities and who is free from all blemishes should be accepted as worthy of worship, is accepted at first by these disputants, who (afterwards) deny all attributes and qualities in Brahman. If this is the only course left open to us from the nature of case, the contention, arising from the desire to maintain the theory of a Brahman free from all distinguishing features and qualities which is opposed to all *Pramāṇas* like sense-perception is impossible of being sustained".[11]

Besides, the Advaitins try to create an additional and unique *Mokṣa* to the released Soul who is eternal and is characterised in his essential nature by an absence of distinguishing features. In doing so, he will surely be able to create a new sweetness to the taste of the honery in the flower seen in a dream.[12]

There is a story that, when a man came to house for alms the daughter-in-law told him that he could not be given any. The mother-in-law felt hurt that daughter-in-law should have presumed to do so. So, she called the man back and said, "She has no right to say 'no'. I am saying 'no' as I alone have the right." The Advaitins who are, as it were, the relatives of *Rākṣasas* may be called *Rāhu-mīmāṁsakas* (because they attach importance only to the Upaniṣads which are *Vedaśiras* and not to the *Karmakāṇḍa*) (It is like the head without the trunk). They condemn others for rejecting the Upaniṣads while, like the mother-in-law in the story, they also reject them. They are like the ignorant man, who wanted to say in an assembly (that in him there was no *Sabhākampā* but blurted out, that in him, there was no *bhāsakampa*). We are ashamed even to enter into discussion for refuting them as their speech is ridiculous. The *Śrutis* (themselves) whose (role) object is to protect the three worlds refute them. These *Saṁnyāsins* who are suited to *Kaliyuga* deny the truth concerning the three "Reals", *Cit, Acit* and *Īśvara*. They say that as a preliminary to the study of Vedānta, there should be four qualifications such as: (1) the power to discriminate between what is eternal and what is transcient, (2) the qualities of control of the body and mental serenity, (3) the absence of the desire for the pleasures of this world and *Svarga* and (4) the desire for *Mokṣa*. But, as a matter of fact, good men who have observed their actual conduct ridicule them by saying that their four qualifications are in reality. (1) the Want of discrimination in distingtuishing what is eternal from what is not, (2) love and hatred as efficient means, (3) averseness to the performance of the rites ordained fot the world and for religious welfare and (4) the desire to enjoy (the pleasures of life)."[13]

Thus, these Advaitins explain the existence of world illusion due to *Avidyā* and create much confusion in interpreting the scriptual statements like *Tattvamasi* by denoting opposition in the *Śruti* texts.

6. CĀRVĀKA SCHOOL OF PHILOSOPHY

In the fifth Act, with a view to stultifying the efforts of Viveka, Mahāmoha adhers to Cārvāka philosophy and propogates its teachings. And in this context, the dramatist mentions the teachings of Cārvāka philosophy as below. According to Cārvāka philosophy, there are four 'reals' such as earth, water, fire and air and from their combination with one another consciousness arises. According to them *Śarīra* itself is the soul. Because when the body has disintegrated there cannot be pleasure of any kind. This doctrine is propounded by Bṛhaspati. These doctrines are as per the experience of one and all.[14]

According to this system, only *Pratyakṣa Pramāṇa* is accepted. The Vedas prate of something or other as if it were true. This is just like thousand images of the Sun can never put the Sun to shame. The death of the body is *Mokṣa*. Sexual pleasure itself is the heavenly bliss on the earth and women who are endowed with youth and who give that pleasure are the deities. It is suggested that their teachings of Bṛhaspati impose no strain nor any painful on the society. Therefore, this philosophy appears superior to all schools of philosophy including Vedāntạ. Also it is signified that Cārvāka philosophy is otherwise called

Asuropaniṣat, which was first advised by Brahmā to Virocana.[15]

The refutation of this philosophy is implied through the speech of Mahāmoha himself, *i.e.* Durmati asks that how is it that though Cārvāka philosophy protects the world of *Jīvas* the adherents of rival systems entertain an irrational hostility to that philosophy? In response to this Mahāmoha in a polite manner as it were says न खलु पठच्चराः प्रकृतिं मुञ्चन्ति । न चाप्रमत्तमतयस्तैरुपहन्यन्ते, *i.e.* "Wicked persons cannot change their nature, but careful persons can never be injured by them." This sentence indicates that Cārvākas are really the thieves who so not change their nature and the persons following the path of righteousness, *i.e.* Vedāntins can never be injured by their teachings because they possess the knowledge of discrimination. Further, पठन्तस्त्रय्यन्तान्परिहसनकाकुं विदधतां, *i.e.* "Let the Vedantins mock at us by posing questions". This sentence signifies that Cārvāka philosophy is fit to be rediculed. Then another statement : भजन्तस्ताटस्थ्यं परिभवितुमिच्छन्तु महतः, *i.e.* "Let them pretend to be impartial while wishing to put greatmen to shame." This speech denotes that Vedantins are greatmen and neglect this philosophy of atheism. Another statement उदन्तः शान्तानामयमिति च जल्पन्त्वभिमतं, *i.e.* "Let them prate as they please, saying — this is the considered view of goodmen with a serene outlook. This sentence denotes that Vedāntins are very good at heart with a serene outlook. Therefore, for the good of society, they consider Cārvāka Philosophy as meaningless. The last statement किमन्तर्दुर्दान्तैः कृपणकथ कैरेभिरिह नः । *i.e.* "What have we to do with these wretched disputants and inwardly arrogant ?" This statement suggests that Cārvākas are indeed wretched disputants and inwardly arrogant. So, Vedāntins have nothing to do with them. In essence it means that although the teachings of Cārvāka philosophy are quite attractive to the people of mundane world, they lead the person to the sorrowful condition. Realising this point, Vedāntins redicule this philosophy. Before Vedāntins, the Cārvāka's are butt of redicule. Really this is the considered view of good men with a serene outlook. Thus, Cārvākas are wretched disputants.[16]

7. MĪMĀṀSĀ SCHOOL OF KUMĀRILABHAṬṬA

Mīmāṁsakas' attempt to defend the authority of the (former part of the) Vedas, but have given up the Vedānta (the latter portion of Vedas). The philosophy of Vedānta or the Upaniṣads is the head of the Vedas. Therefore, Mīmāṁsakas should not have neglected the concluding part of the Vedas also. As such, accepting lower part of the body and rejecting upper part of the body, put the Mīmāṁsakas to the condition of headless body. As a matter of fact, the devotees of Lord Viṣṇu should give up all the rituals intended to secure worldly desires and should perform all rituals *Nitya* and *Naimittika*. Therefore, all good men consider that former portion of the Vedas dealing with *Karma Mīmāṁsā* and the latter portion of the Vedas dealing with *Brahmamīmāṁsā* form a single *Śāstra*.

Besides, other schools like Pāśupata Prabhākara, Bhāskara and Yādavaprakāśa have been just named and said that their views are not valid. In this manner, the rival schools of *Sāṅkhya,* Yogas, Vaiśeṣikas, Bauddhas, Janis, Advaitins, Mīmāṁsakas etc. have been referred together with mentioning their important tenets, then those tenets are refuted and showed meaningless.

On the otherhand, Vedānta Deśika has reflected the ideals of Pañcarātra school, one of the branches of Śrīvaiṣṇava religion.

It however appears that Vedānta Deśika has brought in here the philosophy of Pāñcarātra *Āgamas* which are regarded as valid as Vedic texts, to synthesise the teachings of both Teṅgalai and Vaḍagalai sects of Śrīvaiṣṇava religion.

As is found in the literature of Śrīvaiṣṇavism, Vaḍagalai section has all sastric texts including Pāñcarātra *Āgama* as its basis; while Teṅgalai sect has Dravidian *Saṁhitās* written in Tamil as the basis of its religion. Belonging to the Vaḍagalai sect, Vedānta Deśika has made many efforts to unite both the sects showing the integration of the philosophical thoughts and the themes of the rituals. It is for this reason, that Vedānta Deśika has explained the teachings of Pāñcarātra *Āgama* as a separate section though it is part and parcel of Viśiṣṭādvaita Vedānta.[17]

As given in the drama, this Pāñcarātra *Śāstra* is composed by Vyāsa, as being valid as conferring glory, as holy and as being extremely beneficial. This is composed by him for the benefit of the devotees. Therefore, this *Śāstra* is faultless and all authoritative.[18] Thus, there leaves no doubt regarding its validity. This text closely establish the *Siddhānta* view. When there appears due to wrong notion an inconsistancy or contradiction between Veda and Pāñcarātra, the erroneous idea should be dispelled and should show the consistency between both the scriptures.[19]

After setting aside all the views of rival schools of Philosophy, Vedānta Deśika enumerates the sailent features of Viśiṣṭādvaita Vedānta establishes its supremacy over all schools of Philosophy.

8. VIŚIṢṬĀDVAITA SCHOOL OF RĀMĀNUJA

It is universally admitted fact that Rāmānuja is the founder of Viśiṣṭādvaita school of philosophy. He has been regarded as the prime teacher of all Śrīvaiṣṇavites. It is stated that there is no other fate than the preceptor. Lord Hayagrīva shines always on the throne of the tip of the

Ācāryas to tongue. Here *Ācārya* is none other than Rāmānuja himself. Lord Nārāyaṇa himself has incarnated as Rāmānujācārya in order to lift the *jīvas* up from the ocean of *Saṁsāra*.[20]

Lord Nārāyaṇa in the form of Śrīnivāsa dwelling on the heads of Tirumalai has been the *Ārādhya* deity of Rāmānuja. It is considered by wise men on the strength of appropriate proofs that the bell in the temple of Tirupati, which frightens away all enemies of the gods and which was used by four-faced Brahmā in the service of the Lord, is took the incarnation for the betterment of the society. And it is that Vedānta Deśika the author of the *Saṅkalpa-sūryodaya*, great exponent after Rāmānuja to propogate the philosophy of Viśiṣṭādviata Vedānta at large.[21] It is really a note worthy point because this is highlighted by Vedānta Deśika himself.

These preceptors have laid down the tradition on the basis of the scriptural statements. It is that Lord Nārāyaṇa being worshipped by means of *Yāga, Dāna, Homa, Arcanā, Bharasamarpaṇa, Dhyāna* etc. grants to all embodied beings, the fruits of their actions, in accordance with each individuals *Varṇa* and *Āśrama*. This tradition is pointed out in the drama.[22]

This Viśiṣṭādvaita philosophy propounded by Rāmānuja is well in tune with the philosophy of the Upaniṣads. Therefore, it is free from blemishes. Still some perverted persons find faults in his philosophy; but by doing so they themselves become blameworthy. It is just like one who tries to make the sky impure by mire raised by his own hands, that mire ooz down his own limbs but the sky does not get impure.[23] So far as the essence of the Vedānta is concerned, Vedānta Deśika states that by the study of the sculptures, the pure Soul turns away his mind from the pleasures of the world. As such his intellect becomes more matured for the cultivation of meditaion and for the other *Niṣkāma Karmas*. This makes him eligible to gain the grace of the Lord. He cultivates *Bhakti* and steps ahead as *Prapanna*. Thereby, that individual Soul attains salvation.[24]

When *Jīva* adopts the means of realisation, preceptors favour is quite essential to win. Because just as evil spirits bind a child, *Kāma, Krodha, Ahaṅkāra* etc. catch hold of the individual Soul. And as a great magician makes the child free from the grip of evil spirits, the preceptor also destroys *Kāma, Krodha* etc. of a individual soul whom surrenders unto him for protection. And through the grace of the preceptor, his path of realisation becomes unobstructed.

The seeker should always approach such a preceptor who can remove his ingnorance and shower pure knowledge on him. Therefore, individual selves seeking knowledge can learn all the truths from such preceptor with care and attention. Thus, the role of preceptor in the life of a seeker is very important. Such preceptor instructs to his disciple the essence of Upaniṣadic texts as upheld by Rāmānuja.

This secret doctrine taught in the Upaniṣads is highlighted by Vedānta Deśika. The *Bhedi Śruti* texts declare that the three *tattvas Cit, Acit* and *Īśvara* are different from ane another. But the sacred *Śruti* texts declare the unity of all these *tattvas* and declare that these *tattvas* are his body or attributes of the Lord. The Supreme Brahman is the inner ruler and controller of the entire Universe. There is no over lord for him. This is the purport serene of the sacred texts.[25] This dececive knowledge of the three *tattvas* clearly with the help of three *Pramāṇas* accepted by Rāmānuja they are *Pratyakṣa, Anumāna* and *Āgama*.

According to the philosophy of Viśiṣṭādvaita *Jīva*'s are three fold; *i.e. Baddha, Mukta* and *Nitya*. Also there are three kinds of non-sentient things such as *Prakṛti, Kāla* and *Śuddhasattva*. Lord Nārāyaṇa alone can grant all the four objects, *i.e. Dharma, Artha, Kāma* and *Mokṣa*. Just as all rivers meet in the ocean, all beneficient streams of Vedic texts have the eternal and natural substratum, *i.e.* the Supreme Being.

In the philosophy and religion of Viśiṣṭādvaita the place of god Garuḍa, the king of the birds is remarkable for he is ever eager to bring Lord Nārāyaṇa with great speed to the houses of those who have surrendered themselves to Him. Vedānta Deśika makes it clear that Garuḍa who is ever at the sevice of the Lord, is adorned with the serpants as ornaments and enables the seekers who obtain the essence of the truths contained in the ocean of the scriptures.[26] He is endowed with Supreme Power. Therefore in his childhood; Garuḍa made the mountains break to pieces, the four oceans were convulsed and his wings were wet with their water. The stars in the sky were split and scattered and made the interior *Brahmāṇḍa* from the nether world to the top of *Satyaloka* moving round.[27]

Garuḍa dwells in the nest of all the Vedas his shoulders are the seat of the Lord, when he is bent on making his enemies suffer. Further, he is glorified that when Garuḍa's wives Rudra and Sukīrti who are full of joy at his arrival in their homes, embraced him closely pressing their breasts against chest. Thereby the serpants worn as ornaments suffer pain tremble and the rows of the gems on their foots move about in circular forms as if for ritual of *Nīrājana*. Because of this Garuḍa's body becomes more resplendent with the stream of brilliance.[28] This verse is repeated in the *Garuḍa pañcāśata stotra* by the same author.[29]

In order to show the greatness of Garuḍa, it is further explained that when Garuḍa, was snatching away the nectar from the King of Gods, he was hit by Indra's *Vajra*, but the scar left by the edge of Indra's *Vajra*, is borne by him as an ornament. He strikes everyone with astonishment when he rises resembling the tempest at the end of Kalpa. His glory is well understood from his occupying the victorious banner of Lord Viṣṇu. He is the form of Saṅkarṣana and is the deity presiding over and directing the five *Prāṇas* such as *Prāṇa, Apāna, Vyāna, Udāna* and *Samāna*. He assumes five forms such as *Satya, Suparṇa, Vijaya, Tārkṣya* and *Vighneśvara*.

Furthermore, it is glorified that Garuḍa can make accessible to the seeker the spiritual meditaion called *Upāsanās* in the Upaniṣads. Garuḍa's *Pañcākṣaramantra* which has *Praṇava* before the word, *Pakṣi* and *Svāha* at the end make the Puruṣārathas fruitified. He has incarnated to fulfill the vow of *Vālakhilyas* who regard fiercely at the insult of the offered to them by Indra. In the *Pāñcarātra Āgamas*, it is declared that the *Sannāha* or equipment and *Saṅkalpa* or resolve of Lord Hari appear as visible manifestation in the form of Garuḍa and *Sudarśanacakra* respectively.

Garuḍa is regarded as one of the eternal *Jīvas* by the Viśiṣṭādvaits. He is eternal *Jīva* because His consciousness is devoid of contraction, in as much as his activities are never opposed to the will of the Lord. The ancarnations of Garuḍa and other eternal *Jīva*s like Ananta, Viṣvaksena etc. are determined by their own will like the incarnation of the Lord. Moreover, his duties have been fixed from time without beginning by the eternal will of the Lord.[30]

In this manner glory of God Garuḍa has been proclaimed by Vedānta Deśika.

As has been pointed out before, God Garuḍa is identified with Saṅkarṣaṇa form of Supreme Brahman. For favouring the devotees of different religions, Lord Nārāyaṇa dwells in various places of India. As such they are known as holy places. Such places are rather shrines of different forms of the Supreme Brahman. From the long past, these places have been recognized as piligrim centres by the Śrīvaiṣṇavites. The glory of these places is described in such a way that any reader of this portion of the drama would become a devotee of Lord Viṣṇu. The places described in the *Saṅkalpasūryodaya* find their home in the sixth act. Those are : Meru mountain, Kailāsa, Gandhamādana mountain, Himālaya mountain, region of Gaṅges, Vindhya forest, Ayodhyā, Mathurā, Sāligrāma, Vāraṇāsī, Sahyadrī Mountains, Yādavācala, Nārāyaṇagiri, Melukote, Malaya mountain, Pāṇḍya country, Vṛṣācala, Coḷa country, Śrīraṅgam, Tuṇḍīramaṇḍalam, Veṅkaṭācala etc. Obviously, all these regions are not the shrines of Lord Nārāyaṇa. Still as Nārāyaṇa is *Cidacitviśiṣṭa* all the regions either it be a forest or a river or a mountain or a temple all these form the body of the Supreme Nārāyaṇa in essence.

With regard to the concept of Supreme Brahman, Lord Nārāyaṇa is explained by Vedānta Deśika as the Controller of All, the Principle of all the worshipped in every act, the bestower of all fruits, etc. To bring the light, the magnificient power of Lord Viṣṇu, Vedānta Deśika describes different aspects of Brahman one of such aspects is that the dramatists describes Lord Nārāyaṇa's *Vibhava*. It means Lord Nārāyaṇa in different forms similar to that genes. Thus, Lord Nārāyaṇa's *Vibhava* is of ten types. They are those ten particular *Avatāras* such as Matsya, Kūrma, Varāha, Nṛsiṁha, Vāmana, Paraśurāma, Rāma, Balabhadra, Kṛṣṇa and Kalki. All these *Avatāraṣ* are Nārāyaṇa, are well described in the seventh Act of the drama, wherein Puruṣa thinks of proper form of the Supreme Brahman for meditation. "According to *Viśvakṣena Saṁhitā* and *Lakṣmītantra* all the *Avatāras* descend from the fourth *Vyuha*, namely Aniruddha, but *Padmatantra* declares that of the ten *Vibhavas*, *Matsya*, *Kūrma* and *Varāha* descend from Vāsudeva, the *Nṛsiṁha*, *Vāmana*, *Śrī Rāma* and *Paraśurāma* from Saṅkarṣaṇa, Balarāma from Pradyumna, Śrī Kṛṣṇa and Kalki from Aniruddha." [31]

Of these *Avatāras*, Nārāyaṇa assumes *Matsya* form for restoring the Vedas. By supporting the mountain *Mandara* Brahman incarnated as *Kūrma* for generating nectar which was the means for immortality of the Gods. He manifested in *Varāha* form with a view to protecting his own consort Bhūmi and with desire to save humanity sunk in the ocean of phenomenal existence. Lord Viṣṇu appear in the form of *Nṛsiṁha* through the pillar for the destruction of Hiraṇya-kaśipu and to save his devotee Prahlāda. The *Vāmana* incarnation was assumed for the protection of the world, by cleansing its sins with the Ganges arising from his Lotus-feet when he became Trivikrama. Then Lord Nārāyaṇa took the form of *Paraśurāma* for annihilation of the wicked *Kṣatriyas*. Further, he took the incarnation of *Rāma* for the establishment of *Dharma*, *Balabhadra* manifestation of Nārāyaṇa is for the destruction of the demons like Pralambha etc. Lord *Kṛṣṇa* incarnation was taken by Him for pointing out to the humanity, the means for liberation. The last, *i.e. Kalki* incarnation which will take place, is for the establishment of *Dharma* in its entirity by the destruction of unrighteous, and for liberating the world from the clutches of Kali. Thus, all these incarnations taking place as per the will of Lord Nārāyaṇa are for the protection of the good and the destruction of the wicked.[32]

When describing the holy places of Śrī Vaiṣṇavites, the dramatist describes Lord Nārāyaṇa as *Arcāmūrtti*. He dwells in the Nārāyaṇagiri in the *Arcā* form. To quote "Here dwells the Omniscient (as *Arcā*) bearing on His Person, Lakṣmī and the gem Kaustubha, and vouchsafing bliss (to His worshippers) even without speech as he does to the inhabitants of *Śvetadvīpa.* The Lord resides here on the scene of the victory of the prince of *Saṁnyāsins*, where the thousand waves of Vidyās cause as much excitement as in the ocean of milk.[33]

Arcāvatāra means the special form of Nārāyaṇa without remoteness of space and time. In *Avatāra* the Lord assumes the body chosen by the devotees and descends with a non-material body. He becomes dependent on the worshipper for bath, food etc. He bears everything and is replete with Knowledge and with other attributes. He recites in houses, villages, towns, sacred places, hills etc.[34] Thus *Arcā* is a special form of the Lord, who accepts any substance for body.[35] Further, All-Indwellership of the Lord is thus extolled "When Bhagavan is seen in the mirror of the *Vyāpaka mantras* which disclose His All-Pervasiveness, one will see that the Universe (which we perceive with our senses) is absolutely dependent upon Him for its existence, and continuance and, likewise, for its activity and the fruit or result arising from it, since the Universe is supported and controlled by Him and is also solely for the fulfilment of his purpose, one will understand that it is the body of the Primeval Creator. By realizing this relationship of the Universe being the body of the Creator, one is enabled to reach the heart of the *Śrutis,* which were not composed by anyone and which have the deepest significance."[36]

Also the *Bhagvadgītā* statement तेन विना तृणमपि न चलति is illustrated in the following verse :

"When the Lord does not permit, even the great storm of *Pralaya,* cannot move a blade of grass. So also (when He does not permit) the fire at the end of the *Kalpa* cannot consume the blade of grass. The other deitics are all below Him and have their beginning and end and are subject to the pairs of opposites (heat and cold, pleasure and pain etc.), Puruṣa now knows these truths and neither finds pleasure in anything nor falls unto despair at anything."[37] This description signifies the Lord as All-Controller. The Lord controls everything sportively. This idea is brought out as below.

"The existence of all things mentioned below and other similar things, their continuance and their activities are entirely dependent on the Lord's will and it is by the encircling waves of His *Leela* that the wind blows strong, the stars move fast in the sky, the fire burns, the ocean does not cause the earth to shake, and the earth shows herself fit to bear things that move not and beings that move".[38]

In the Viśiṣṭādvaita Philosophy and religion Goddess Lakṣmī is given prime importance next to Lord Nārāyaṇa. Vedānta Deśika enlaces this *tattva* also in the garland of other important tenets. This *tattva* is described as below :

"The Goddess Lakṣmī is the divine wealth of Viṣṇu who is the Celestial Cow that yields whatever is asked for by the world, who is the fullest treasure of all lovely and auspicious things, who is the extreme limit of compassion and who is the eternally fragrant garland on the head of the Vedas (*i.e.*, the Upaniṣads).[39] It is further said that Goddess Lakṣmī, the Consort of Lord Nārāyaṇa assumes different forms appropriate to the forms of the Lord in his manifestaions.[40] This role of Goddess Lakṣmī points to Her *Nityāviyogittva* with the Lord.

So far as the concept of *Jīva* is concerned, Vedānta Deśika refers to another type of the *Jīva, i.e. Baddha* or the bound *Jīva*. The bound *Jīvas* are those who are not freed from the empirical existence. These bound *Jīvas* are again divided into many groups. The Puruṣa or the Individual Soul who is boosted up from all corners in the drama by Viveka comes under the group of *Dharmapara Jīvas* who are devoted to none other than Lord Nārāyaṇa. The Puruṣa spoken of in the drama may be called *Jijñāsu* or the seekers of knowledge. Such a seeker of knowledge is a votary of self realization and of release from *Saṁsāra*. Self-realization arises from pure Knowledge of Brahman. The votaries of *Mokṣa* are the devotees of Lord as well as *Prapannas, i.e.* those who have completely surrendered themselves to God and through the means of *Prapatti* attain *Mokṣa*.

The Viśiṣṭādvaita Vedānta ordains some means to liberation when the *Jīva* is treading the path of *Mokṣa*, he has to offer eight flowers to the Lord, *i.e.* he has to observe *Ahiṁsā, Indriyajaya, Dayā, Kṣamā, Jñāna, Tapas, Dhyāna* and *Satya*. By following all these disciplines strictly, all sins are removed. He should possessed unstinsted devotion to Lord Nārāyaṇa alone. So, that future transgression will not stain him. Then he should undertake the course of deep meditation of no one but the Lord. Then he becomes eligible for the attainment of eternal bliss in *Vaikuṇṭha*. At this stage, will of the Lord arises and the *Jīva* becomes liberated.

When the *Jīva* ascends the steps of meditation, he should win over all the evil effects of the mind, *i.e.* he should win over *Kāma* by *Virakti, Krodha* by *Kṣānti, Lobha* by *Tuṣṭi, Moha, Dambha, Darpa, Asūya, Īrṣā,* etc. by *Viveka*. This discipline is highlighted in the whole of the battle scene in the eighth Act of the drama. And the seeker can enter into a deep meditation if he has cultivated the qualities like *Śama, Dama, Uparati,* etc. and by the blessings of the preceptor. To a person engrossed in meditation, future sins will not cling, and his past sins are destroyed. The meditation in its beginning stage may be obstructed.

"Even though true knowledge (concerning matter, the individual self and the Supreme Self and their relations to one another) has nipped the rise of sins at the bud, even though the mind with proper concentration on itself has clearly withdrawn the activities of all the other senses, even though that of monkey, the mind, has given up its usual fickleness, yet the bad impressions due to past Karma which still continue to remain in a subtle form within the mind like sparks of fire hidden in ashes, kindle into a flame on occasion like being insulted by others, and weaken the meditation or *Samādhi* which is slowly taking shape and rising."[41]

When seekers meditation is impeded, he tries to transgress them with the help of the knowledge of Brahman that he has acquired. At this stage he can be said as extremely fortunate as he shines like the very embodiment of the sentiment of the *Śānta*. When such a seeker completely surrenders to God, the later destroys all sins, so that it may not sprout again.[42]

When such *Jīva* in his life of meditation come its any sin, it will cling to his enemy and the fruits of the meritorious deeds which have been given up by him, will be experienced by his friends.[43] Vedānta Deśika makes it explicit that all sins of the *Jīva* will be destroyed by the will of the Lord. Still *Prārabdha Karma* remains to be experienced. After expe-riencing all *Prārabdha Karmas, Sthūla Śarīra* of *Jīva* will be left away after the fall of the body of the *Jīva.* The *Sūkṣma Śarīra* which he possesses even then, that will be left away after taking bath in the river Virajā.[44] Thus, the *Jīva* comes out of the prison house of the body constituted of water, blood, flesh, fat, bones, marrow and semen and like a prince emerging from within the hut of the hunter and hastening to climb up the palace of his father, the emperor, the *Jīva* ascends to *paramapada* through the path of *Devayāna* accessible to none else. Then he is escorted to the region beyond *Tamas*.[45]

At every step of *Jīva's* path leading to *Paramapada* grace of Lord Nārāyaṇa is essential. This grace is technically called *Icchāśakti* of Nārāyaṇa.[46]

9. CONCEPT OF VIṢṆUBHAKTI AND PRAPATTI

According to Viśiṣṭādvaita Vedānta, *Bhakti* and *Prapatti* are the only means for release. *Bhakti* is continuous stream of rememberance of God, uninterrupted like the flow of oil. It is generated by seven fold disciplines such as *Viveka, Vimoka, Abhaya, Kriyā, Kalyāṇa, Anavasāda* and *Anuddharṣa.* And *Bhakti* denoted by such terms as *Vedana, Dhyāna, Upāsanā,* etc. transforms itself into successive forms of *Parābhakti, Parajñāna* and *Paramabhakti*, it has *Prapatti* as a limb.[47]

This element of *Bhakti* which is very much emphasised by Rāmānuja in his philosophy is described by Vedānta Deśika highlighting its characteristics in this manner. Viṣṇubhakti bestows to a higher spiritual life those who have been reduced, as it were to ashes by the fire of *Saṁsāra*. It is well known to be the origin of all righteous conduct. It is highly extolled by all men of wisdom. It is deep and pure in its course. It is accessible to only the men of wisdom.[48] Further, Viṣṇubhakti is described as like a branch of *Kalpaka* Tree in granting the fulfilment of the life. She is adored by the hosts of *Siddhas* whose minds are pure and who cherish no other interests than the attainment of the Lord.[49]

As described in the drama, *Bhakti* is cherished by those who are endowed with spiritual serinity and the source of the ripe fruit of the creeper of knowledge. It is the perfect development of the *Śrutis* and the abiding place of purity.

She is just like the dawn dispelling the darkness of *Ajñāna* and the fear of *Saṁsāra*.[50]

In fine, Bhakti is the contemplation of the glory of God. Being the next step to *Bhakti*, in Rāmānuja's philosophy, the doctrine of *Prapatti* plays very important role. *Prapatti* is the realisation of Divine Grace. It is the sacrifice of the inner being which is dumb in deep love for the God. It is otherwise called *Nyāsavidyā*.[51]

Accordingly, Vedānta Deśika, states that the path of *Bhakti* and *Prapatti* is essential to give the grace of the Lord. "The Lord is declared in the Upaniṣads to be Himself she means *Upāya* of attaining Him. The ways of *Bhakti* and *Prapatti* are indicated for winning His grace. The adoption of these ways is the result of the great ripening of meritorious deeds (done in the past) and, even for this, the Lord, who has ability to create everything is Himself the cause."[52] The primary element of *Prapatti* is *Śaraṇāgati*. Referring to this Vedānta Deśika says :

"The embodied being is deluded with the dance of *Māyā* or *Prakṛti*; and Supreme Brahman, who is the Lord of everything and whose greatness is unequalled, is besides Himself with Compassion, which is bent on saving him and with the snow of the worship of His feet (*Śaraṇāgati*) quenches the fires of his suffering, and cancels his sins."[53]

The person who has recoursed to the path of *Prapatti*, is protected by the Lord in all respects, from even the servants of Yama. It is so described in the Drama. "The servants of Yama tremble before him and even Time which destroys all (not expecting Indra and Brahmā) is in dread of him. The gods of *Svarga* are afrais that he might displace them from their seats. *Rākṣasas, Anuras, Yakṣas, Guhyakas* and others flee in fear to a great distance. And all this is the result of his having surrendered his self at the two lotus-like feet of the Lord of Lakṣmī.[54]

Prapanna does not beg of the Lord, the pleasure of this world nor of *Svarga* nor *Kaivalya* nor even *Mokṣa*. He praise that he should have the grace of Pure and firm minded *Bhāgavatas*, who are like the chaste wives of the royal harem, because their grace is like the dawn which heralds the day of the splendour of *Mokṣa*.[55]

Though the person, who dreams the path of *Prapatti* in a strict manner, cannot gain realisation due to the *Prārabdha karma* to be worked out.[56]

However, Vedānta Deśika, suggests the emotions in the realisation of the bliss of *Prapatti*. The basic emotion of *Prapatti* consists oin an implicit faith in Divine goodness and Divine mercy. It is called *Mahāviśvāsa*. The dramatist has very effectively put this idea into the poetry as below :

दुरासेधस्थेम्ना दुरितपरिपाकेन भविनः
प्रमाथी संसारः प्रशमरहितोऽयं प्रभवति ।
निरोधे तस्यैका निरुपधिककारुण्यघटित-
स्वतन्त्रेच्छाशक्तिः स्वयमुपधिमाधाय रमते ।।

S.S., I-75, pp.151-52.

This idea of *Mahāviśvāsa* is so sweet that the imagination of Vedānta Deśika comes to relish it.

मिथः कलहकल्पनाविषमवृत्तिलीलादया-
परिग्रहणकौतुकमथितपारवश्यः प्रभुः ।
खलक्षितसमुद्गमे सुकृतलक्षणे कुत्रचित्
घुणक्षतलिपिक्रमादुपनिपातिनः पाति नः ।। *S.S.*, I-67, p.138.

Besides Vedānta Deśika suggests the subsidiary emotions of *Prapatti* equally well. He suggests the divine impulse due to be dutiful to God.

सत्त्वावस्तान्निभृतः प्रसादय सतां वृत्तिं व्यवस्थापय
त्रस्य ब्रह्मविदागमस्तृणमिव त्रैवर्गिकान्भावय ।
नित्ये शेषिणि निक्षिपन्निजभरं सर्वंसहे श्रीसखे
धर्मं धारय चातकस्य कुशलिन् धाराधरैकान्तिनः ।।

S.S., II-38, pp.250-51.

Further stimulus to this emotion is embodied in the resolve to follow the dictates of divine conscious floods. It brings about mental peace tranquility. It brings to fruition the desire to grow into divine consciousness. It is the wisdom of all wisdoms, the purity of all purities, the joy of all joys.

When this sort of feeling gathers force, it leads to another kindered feeling which consists in giving up all that is prejudicial to divine love and divine service. This crisis in divine love with all emphasis is mentioned by the dramatist.

विषमधु बहिष्कुर्वन् धीरो बहिर्विषयात्मकं
परिमितरसस्वात्मप्राप्तिप्रयासपराङ्मुखः ।
निरवधिमहानन्दब्रह्मानुभूतिकुतूहली
जगति भविता दैवात् कश्चिज्जिहासितसंसृतिः ॥

S.S., III-25, p.365.

When this stage of divine love is passed there comes the stage in which one wants to fall prostrate at the feet of the Lord and remain subservient to Him in mind, heart and soul. Service of God and of humanity are not mutually conflicting ideals. This is emphasised when the dramatist says.

किं विज्ञानैः किं तपोदानयज्ञैः किं वाऽन्यैश्चत्वत्परित्यागदीनैः ।
ज्ञातुं द्रष्टुं तत्त्ववश्च प्रवेष्टुं शक्यं ब्रह्मानन्यभाजा त्वयैव ॥

S.S., X-94, p.884.

The last stage in the culture of *Prapatti* is self-abnegation in love of the god.

स्वापोदोधव्यतिकरनिभे भोगमोक्षान्तराले
कालं कञ्चिज्जगति विधिना केनचित्स्थाप्यमानाः ।
तत्त्वोपायप्रभृतिविषये स्वामिदत्तां स्वनिष्ठां
शेषां कृत्वा शिरसि कृतिनः शेषमायुर्नयन्ति ॥ *S.S.*, IX-27, p.768.

In the light of this Supreme realisation, the service of God and the service of humanity become one and the same thing.

10. IMPORTANCE OF DIVINE WILL

As explained in the *Pañcarātra Āgama,* some men of wisdom say that *Saṅkalpa* or Divine Will is *Kriyāśakti* or Power of Action of the Lord. Some others say that *Saṅkalpa* is *Manas-tattva* of the Lord. Others still declare that *Saṅkalpa* is Lord Himself endowed with *Kriyāśakti* etc. But it is an admitted fact that *Saṅkalpa* is ever great and manifested itself as the great destroyer of the ocean of *Saṁsāra.*

क्रियाशक्तिं केचिद्दनुजमथनीं हेतिमपरे
मनस्तत्त्वं चान्ये मधुविजयिनस्त्वामभिदधुः।
तमेवैके तत्तत्पदविषयजुष्टं तदिह नः
सदोत्तुङ्गः प्रादुर्भवसि भवसिन्धुप्रमथनः॥ *S.S.*, X-57, p.846.

Thus, it is evident that unless and until the Sun of Divine will do save the Soul rises, the horizon of a humanity cannot be brightened with the hue of *Bhakti* and *Prapatti.* Therefore, Vedānta Deśika hopes to see the rising of the Sun.

यस्मिन्विस्मयनीयभूमनि मनागुन्मीलिते नैकधा
सिध्यन्त्यस्य सितासितस्य जगतः स्वर्गापवर्गादयः।
ऐशः सोऽहमवासरात्ययभवन्मायामहायामिनी-
सत्ताशेषसुषुप्त बोधनपटुः संकल्पसूर्योदयः॥ *S.S.,* X-20, p.813.

However, the rise of the Sun of Divine will inherits a greater assurance of Universal Truth than the *Prabodha-candrodaya* which Kṛṣṇa Miśra views rising up.

किं वाप्तं किमपोहितं किमुदितं किं वा समुत्सारितं ।
स्यूतं किं नु विलयितं नु किमिदं किञ्चिन्न वा किञ्चन ॥
यस्मिन्नभ्युदिते वितर्कपदवीं नैवं समारोहति ।
त्रैलोक्यं सहजप्रकाशदलितं सोऽहं प्रबोधोदयः॥ *P.C.*, VI-29, p.238.

Devotion to God is ordained as the preparation for the rise of *Saṅkalpasūrya.*

प्रकृतः क्रियया धिया च योगः परमैकान्त्यपरिष्कृतस्य पुंसः ।
निधिदर्शनवन्निरूढहर्षं प्रणिधत्ते विशदं परप्रकाशम् ॥*S.S.,* X-28, p.819.

Such devotion is a greater strength of human heart then the sudden onrush of knowledge which the *Prabodha-Candrodaya* emphasises.

> एषोऽस्मीति विविच्य नेतिपदतश्चित्तेन सार्धं कृते
> तत्त्वानां विलये चिदात्मनि परिज्ञाते त्वमर्थे पुनः ।
> श्रुत्वा तत्त्वमसीति वाधितभवध्वान्तं तदात्मप्रभं
> शान्तं ज्योतिरनन्तमन्तरुदितानन्दः समुद्योतते ।। *P.C.*, VI-27, p.235.

In this manner, for *Prapanna* to attain *Paramapada* Divine will is everything.

> अविरलगुणच्छाया मायाऽऽतपप्रतिरोधिनी
> परिहृतरजः पङ्क तापैरसङ्घटिता त्रिभिः ।
> मधुरिपुदयामूर्तिर्दिव्या निराकृतकण्टका
> वहति निगमादूर्तन्येका पुरीमपराजिताम् ।। *S.S.*, I-83, p.265.

When a *Prapanna* is endowed with all qualities making him eligible for *Mokṣa*, he should remain himself engrossed in *Dhyāna, Stotra, Praṇāma* etc. and should wait for the Grace of the God. At the fulfilment of the *Sādhanas* the seeker is blessed with *Mokṣa* by the Lord. Therein he attains Lord's *Sāmya.*

"In the *Jīvātmā* who like an actor playing for the Lord's amusement, enacts many a part in the drama of *Saṁsāra*, under this authority, and who has succeded in giving him pleasure (at last) by acting the part of a *Prapanna* (who has surrendered everything to Him) — to that *Jīvatmā* the Lord vouchsafer, in *Paramapada*, perfect resemblence to Himself except in regard to those marks and activities of His which are eternally unique to Him."[57]

11. CONCEPT OF MOKṢA

Mokṣa is the ultimate goal of the life. The person who practices *Bhakti* and *Prapatti* does attain *Mokṣa* at the dawn of the Divine will regarding the nature of *Mokṣa* in the

Visiṣṭādvaita Vedānta, *Jīva* attains equal positions to that of the Lord. It is explicated by Vedānta Deśika in the drama. This idea is further emphasizes as below :

"He gets all his doubts cleared; desirous of destroying Moha, he studies Vedānta thoughtfully and reads about those observances or duties which lead to *Mokṣa*. He cultivates virtues like self control and guards his policies from being known to others (Practicing in secret the repetition of *Aṣṭākṣara*) and is always trying to understand *Gīta* undivided devotion."[58]

Thus, in *Paramapada*, *Mokṣa*, *Jīva* experiences the bliss of *Bhagavat-kaiṅkarya*. The glory of the *Paramapada or Vaikuṇṭha* is beatifully described by the dramatist;

"With His left leg stretched downwords and the right leg which removes the sins of his devotees bent a little, with his right hand placed on His knee and the left resting on the body of *Ādiśeṣa* and bearing in his other two arms the Conch and *Cakra* for overthrowing his enemies, the Lord of *Vaikuṇṭha* in the company of His Concerts (Lakṣmī and Nīlā) and adorned with ornaments like the *Kaustubha*, promotes the happiness of all the worlds."[59]

It is also suggested that, as the liberated Soul is always engaged in *Bhagavat-kaiṅkarya* his intellect does never get contaminated by any defects. Thus the qualities Viveka, Sumati, Viṣṇubhakti remain latent for ever, in the heart of the liberatd soul.[60]

In short, all cardinal doctrines of the *Viśiṣṭadvaita Vedānta* propounded by Rāmānuja have been well set in the frame work of different types of plot constructions. A close perusal of the drama makes it evident that the teachings of *Viśiṣṭādvaita Vedānta* have the basis of knowledge of descrimination, which is here personified as Viveka in the drama. That is why Viveka's role in the drama is of primary importance. He is the head of all characters. He is the hero the drama. Thus, one can see in the *Saṅkalpasūryodaya* a culmination of human psycosis and of human realisation. This is the universal Truth of the Philosophy of *Viśiṣṭādvaita Vedānta*.

REFERENCES

1. परः पद्माकान्तः प्रणिपतनमस्मिन् हितमं शुभस्तत्संकल्पश्चुलकयति संसारजलधिम् ।
झटित्येवं प्रज्ञामुपजनयता केनचिदसावविद्यावेतालीमतिपतति मन्त्रेण पुरुषः ॥
S.S., I-93, p.185.

2. असुरादिमोहनविधौ विहिताः प्रमितावतीतसमयाः समयाः ।
तपनापनेयतिमिरक्रमतः प्रचरन्ति हन्त जगदन्तरतः ॥ *S.S.*, II-12, p.217.

3. त्वया मन्निदेशानुवर्तिना कौशिकनियमितेन राघवेणेव
साधिकारेण यथाविधि वीतरागकथानवसरे ।
वेदेश्वरविदूषकाः सर्वे तत्त्वाध्यवसायसंरक्षणार्थमनुज्ञाताभ्यां
बलातिबलाभ्यामिव जल्पवितण्डाभ्यामपि जेतव्याः ॥ *S.S.*, II, p.226.

4. कपिलासुरिपञ्चशिखादिमुनिप्रतिपादित सांख्यमतप्रवणाः ।
प्रकृतिं पुरुषं च विभज्य परं पुरुषं न पठन्त्यघरुद्धधियः ॥ *S.S.*, II-64, p.282.

5. य एते योगाख्ये कतिचिदपतन्त्रे पठितिनः प्रजल्पन्त्यैश्वर्यं प्रतिफलनकल्पं भगवतः ।
स्वतः सिद्धान् बोधप्रशकनबलादीन् गुणगणान् गुणन्तस्त्रय्यन्ताः
प्रतिभणितिरेषामवितथा ॥ *S.S.*, II- 68, p.286.

6. असद्द्रव्यसृष्टिप्रभृत्यर्थक्लृप्त्या श्रुतिप्रक्रियाणामधिक्षेपतश्च ।
उलूकोपदेशापदेशप्रवृत्तः कथाशेषितोऽसौ कणादप्रणादः ॥ *S.S.*, II-70, p.288.

7. परस्परविघट्टनत्रुटिततर्कशस्त्रत्त्छटातिरस्कृतचमत्कृतिः स्वयमखण्डि वैतण्डिकः ।
किमत्र परिशिष्यते किमपि दूषणोद्भावनं स्वतो निहतमुद्गरप्रहरणप्रयासायते ॥
S.S., II-75, pp.294-95.

8. प्रतिक्षिप्तं विदधतां विहितं प्रतिषेधताम् ।
क इवान्यः प्रतिक्षेपः कार्यः स्ववचनादृते ॥ *S.S.*, II-77, p.296.

9. भक्ष्याभक्ष्यस्वपरसमय स्थापनादूषणादिष्वैकान्त्यं ये जहति विहितं कापि नैते विदन्ति ।
दैवैरेषां निगमपदवीदूषणोदीर्णरोषैर्दत्तो नूनं स्थिरशिरसिजोल्लुञ्छनेनैव दण्डः ॥
S.S., II-78, p.297.

10. अविद्यामाहात्म्यादनहमिदमर्थे जगदिदं गृणन्त्येते भातं गगन इव गन्धर्वनगरम् ।
अवन्ध्यैर्व्याघातैरतिपतितविन्ध्यप्रढिमभिर्निबन्ध्यास्ते वन्ध्यासुतनृपतिवैतालिकगणे ॥
S.S., II-90, p.314.

11. निध्यायन्त्वनमूयवः शुभगुणं निर्दोषमाराध्यमित्यध्वा विश्वविशेष शून्यकथकैरप्यादितः स्वीकृतः।
यद्यर्थस्थितिरेतदेकशरणा सप्रत्यवायो भवत्यध्यक्षादिविरुद्धनिर्गुणकथानिर्वाहगर्वाहवः॥
S.S., II-91, pp.315-16.

12. मुक्तस्यनित्यमविशिष्टतनोरपूर्वां मुक्तिं प्रकल्पयितुमात्तविचारयन्तः।
स्वप्नप्रसूनमकरन्दरसस्य मन्ये स्वादुत्वमन्यदुपपादयितुं क्षमेत॥*S.S.*, II-92, p.319.

13. आलक्ष्यतामयं रजनिचरवंशबान्धवानां राहुमीमांसकानां सुभगाभिक्षुकन्यायः, यदेते निगमान्त-परित्यागिन परानधिक्षिपन्ति, प्रतिक्षिपन्ति च स्वयमेव निगमान्तान्। अतः सभाकम्पाभावप्रतिपादकजडपुरुषप्रयुज्यमानभसापङ्काभाववचनवदपहास्यवचसाममीषां प्रतिक्षेपेऽप्य-पत्रपामहे। श्रुतयस्तु त्रिभुवनसंरक्षणे प्रवृत्ताः प्रतिक्षिपन्ति। यदपि चैतेषां चिदचिदीश्वरयाथात्म्यतस्करणामन्तिमयुगमस्करिणां नित्यानित्यवस्तुविवेकादिसाधन-चतुष्टयाभिधानम्, तच्च तत्त्वातत्त्वविवेकाभावः, रागद्वेषादिसाधनसंपत्, लौकिकवैदिक धर्मानुष्ठानवैमुख्यं, बुभुक्षुत्वं चेति यथानुष्ठानं विपरिणामेन परिहसन्ति सन्तः।
S.S., II, pp.320-21.

14. स्वमतविपरीतमन्यैः क्रोशति हृदये विधीयते स्वैरम्।
अमरगुरुशिक्षितार्थैरस्मत्सार्थैर्यथाहृदयम्॥ *S.S.*, V-47, p.503.

15. चिरसेवनतोषितेन धात्रा निपुणस्थानविदा निवेदितार्थः।
असुरोपनिषद्रहस्यमग्र्यं प्रथयामास विरोचनः प्रजानाम्॥*S.S.*, II-58, p.514.

16. पठन्तस्त्रय्यन्तान्परिहसनकाकुं विदधतां भजन्तस्ताटस्थ्यं परिभवितुमिच्छन्तु महतः।
उदन्तः शान्तानामयमिति च जल्पन्त्वभिमतं किमन्तर्दुर्दान्तैः कृपणकथकैरेभिरिह नः॥
S.S., V-60, p.515.

17. For further details see Krishnaiengar D., Śrī Deśika Sambhāvana, Seventh Century Celebrations Committee of Sri Venkatesha Sabha, Mysore, 1968, p.4.

18. स्वतः सर्वावेक्षी श्रुतिशतशिरस्त्राणचरणः स्वभृत्यान्नस्त्रातुं यदिदमनघं तन्त्रमकृत्।
इदं श्रेयः पुण्यं हिततममितीव व्यपदिशन् मुनिः पाराशर्यः प्रकटयति मानं तदखिलम्॥
S.S., II-86, p.308.

19. आरोहन्त्वनवद्यतर्कपदवीसीमादृशां मादृशां पक्षे कार्तयुगे निवेशितपदाः पक्षे पतद्भयः परान्। सर्वानुश्रवसाददर्शिसशिरःकम्पद्विजिह्वाशनक्रीडाकुण्डलमौलिरन्तघृणिभिः सारात्रिकाः सूक्तयः॥ *S.S.*, II-85, p.305.

20. अध्यासीनतुरङ्गवक्त्राविलसज्जिह्वाग्रसिंहासनादाचार्यादिह
देवतां समधिकामन्यां न मन्यामहे।
यस्यासौ भजते कदाचिदजहद्भूमा स्वयं भूमिकां
मग्नानां भविनां भवार्णवसमुत्ताराय नारायणः॥ *S.S.*, II-63, p.281.

21. वित्रासिनी विबुधवैरिवरूथिनीनां पद्मासनेन परिचारविधौ प्रयुक्ता ।
उत्प्रेक्ष्यते बुधजनैरुपपत्तिभूम्ना घण्टा हरेः समजनिष्ट यदात्मनेति ॥
S.S., I-14, p.40.

22. यथाधिकरणं प्रभुर्यजनदानहोमार्चनाभरन्यसनभावनाप्रभृतिभिः समाराधितः ।
फलं दिशति देहिनामिति हि संप्रदायस्थितिः श्रुतिस्मृतिगुरूक्तिभिर्नयवतीभिराभाति नः ॥
S.S., IX-6, p.752.

23. श्रुतिश्रेणीचूडापदबहुमते तावकमते स्वपक्षस्थान्दोषन्वितथमतिरारोपयति यः ।
स्वहस्तेनोत्क्षिप्तैः स खलु निजगात्रेषु बहुलं गलद्भिर्जम्बालैर्गगनतलमालिम्पति जडः ॥
S.S., II-32, p.244.

24. निरपायदेशिकनिदर्शितामिमां कमलासहायकरुणाधिरोहणीम् ।
क्रमशोऽधिरुह्य कृतिनः समिन्धते परिशुद्धसत्त्वपरिकर्मिते पदे ॥
S.S., II-81, p.161.

25. मिथो भेदं तत्त्वेष्वभिलपति भेदश्रुतिरतो विशिष्टैक्यादैक्यश्रुतिरपि च सार्था भगवती।
इमावर्थौ गोप्तुं निखिलजगदन्तर्यमयिता निरीशो लक्ष्मीशः श्रुतिभिरपराभिः प्रणिदधे॥
S.S., II-94, p.324.

26. नमः पन्नगनद्धाय वैकुण्ठवशवर्तिने ।
श्रुतिसिन्धुसुधोत्पादमन्दराय गरुत्मते ॥ *S.S.*, X-17, p.808.

27. क्षुण्णक्षोणीधराणि क्षुभितचतुरकूपारतिम्यद्दरुन्ति त्रुट्यत्तारासराणि स्थपुटितविबुध-स्थानकानि क्षिपेयुः। पातालब्रह्मसौधावधिविहितमुधावर्तनान्यस्मदार्ति ब्रह्माण्डस्यान्तराले बृहति खगपतेरर्भकक्रीडितानि ॥ *S.S.*, IX-18, p.808.

28. गरुडमखिलवेदनीडाधिरूढं द्विषत्पीडनोत्कण्ठिताकुण्ठवैकुण्ठपीठीकृतस्कन्धमीडे स्वनीडा-गतिप्रीतरुद्रासुकीर्तिस्तनाभोगगाढोपगूढस्फुरत्कण्टकव्रतवेधव्यथावेपमानद्विजिह्वाधिपाकल्प-विष्फार्यमाणस्फटावाटिकारत्नरोचिश्छटाराजिनीराजितं कान्तिकल्लोलिनीराजितम्।
S.S., IX, p.809.

29. *Śrī Vedānta Deśika Stotramala*, Sanskrit Sahitya Sadana, Mysore, 1989, Verse No. 11, p.46.

30. नित्या नाम कदाचिदपि भगवदभिमतविरुद्धाचरणाभावेन ज्ञानसङ्कोचप्रसङ्गरहिता अनन्तगरुडविष्वक्सेनादयः ।तेषामधिकारविशेषा ईश्वरस्य नित्येच्छयैव अनादित्वेन व्यवस्थिताः। एतेषामवतारस्तु भगवदवतारवत् स्वेच्छया ।
Yatindramatadīpikā, p.121.

31. Swami Adidevananda, *Yatīndramatadīpikā* of Srinivasadasa, Sri Ramakrishna Math, Madras, 1967, pp.203-204.

32. Cf. *Yatīndramatadīpikā,* pp.137-38.

33. लक्ष्मीकौस्तुभलक्षणेन वपुषा वाचं विनैव स्वयं श्वेतद्वीपनिवासिनामिव दिशन्संतोषमन्तर्मुखम्। विद्यावीचिसहस्रसंभ्रममिलद्दुग्धार्णवाडम्बरे स्थानं संयमिसार्वभौमविजयस्थाने विधत्ते हरिः ।। *S.S.*, VI-50, p.574.

34. अर्चावतारो नाम देशकालविप्रकर्षरहित आश्रिताभिमतद्रव्यादिकं शरीरतया स्वीकृत्य तस्मिन्नप्राकृतशरीर विशिष्टः सन् अर्चकपराधीन स्नानभोजनासनशयनस्थितिः सर्व सहिष्णुः परिपूर्णो गृहग्रामनगरप्रशस्तदेशशैलादिषु वर्तमानो मूर्तिविशेषः ।।
Yatīndramatadīpikā, p.139.

35. This *Arcā* form is fourfold due to the difference as *Svayaṁvyakta* or self manifest, *Daiva* or concecreted by Divine beings, *Siddha* or concecreted by the sages, and *Mānuṣa* or concecreted by human beings.
Yatīndramatadīpikā, p.139.

36. आधेयत्वप्रभृतिनियमैरादिकर्तुः शरीरं सत्तास्थेमप्रयतनफलेष्वेतदायत्तमेतत् ।
विश्वंपश्यन्निति भगवति व्यपकादर्शदृष्टेः गम्भीराणामकृतकगिरां गाहते चित्तवृत्तिम्।।
S.S., IX-32, p.774.

37. तृणक्षोदं क्षेप्तुं प्रलयपवनो न प्रभवति क्षमस्तन्निर्दग्धं यदनभिमतौ कालदहनः ।
तदर्वाचस्सर्वानजहृदवधिदून्दूनियमान् विदन्नासौ तृप्यत्यथ च न विषादे निपतति ।।
S.S., IX-47, p.789.

38. वायुर्दोधूयते यद्यदयमुडुगणो बंभ्रमीति द्रुतं खे तेजो जाज्वल्यते यद्यदपि न जलधिर्माधवीं दोधवीति । भूर्यद्वा बोभवीति स्थिरचरधृतये तच्च तादृक् च सर्वं स्वायत्ताशेषसत्तास्थितियतनपरब्रह्मलीलोर्मिचक्रम् ।। *S.S.*, IX-5, p.751.

39. कल्याणानामविकलनिधिः कापि कारुण्यसीमा नित्यामोदा निगमवचसां मौलिमन्दारमाला।
संपद्दिव्या मधुविजयिनः संनिधत्तां सदा मे सैषा देवी सकलभुवनप्रार्थनाकामधेनुः।।
S.S., VII-24, p.631.

40. यद्भावेषु पृथग्विधेष्वनुगुणान् भावान् स्वयं बिभ्रती।
यद्धर्मैरिह धर्मिणी विहरते नानाकृतिर्नायिका।। *S.S.*, I-6, p.23.

41. तत्त्वज्ञाने विशुद्धे शमयति दुरितारम्भमात्मावधाने व्यक्ताकृष्टेतराक्षे विरमति च मनोवानरे चापलात्स्वात् ।भस्मच्छन्नाग्निकल्पः परपरिभवनाद्यागमे दीप्यमानः श्लक्ष्णः संस्कारसारस्तरलयति शनैरुज्झिहानं समाधिम् ।। *S.S.*, IX-13, p.757.

42. स्वरक्षणभरार्पणक्षणिकसत्रिणः क्षेत्रिणः प्रवर्त्य कृपया स्थितिं प्रभुरभूतपूर्वोदयाम् ।
जगद्विपरिवर्तनप्रथितनित्यशक्तिः स्वयं क्षिपत्यपुनरङ्कुरं दुरितमस्य लक्ष्मीपतिः।।
S.S. I-80, pp.158-59.

43. सुहृदस्तवाददीरन् सुकृतफलं यत्त्वया परित्यक्तम् ।
दुष्कृतफलं द्विषन्तः प्रारब्धान्ते परं पदं विशतः ।।
S.S., X-60, p.849.

44. अद्य हि परसंकल्पकल्पान्तपावकेन प्रारब्धकर्मलेशपरिशेषउपशोषितः पुरुषस्य दुरितार्णवः प्रकृतिरपि निर्मोककल्पाशेषपरिशुद्धस्वभावं पुरुषमायुषः पारे तमसः पारे च निर्मोक्ष्यति ।। *S.S.*, X, p.865.

45. रसरुधिरपिशितमेदःकीकसमज्ञाशुक्लमयकलेबरकारागारा न्निष्क्रान्तः शबरकुटीरकोटरात्सार्वभौमपितृसदनसौधाधिरोहणाय संत्वरमाण इव । राजकुमारस्तत्तद्देशाधिकारिभिरातिवाहिकैरनितरसुलभेन देवयानेन त्रिगुणमरुकान्तारमतिवाहितस्तमःपारभूतं परमपदमधिरोक्ष्यामि ।।
S.S., X, p.874.

46. दुरासेधस्थेम्ना दुरितपरिपाकेन भविनः प्रमाथी संसारः प्रशमरहितोऽयं प्रभवति । निरोधे तस्यैका निरुपाधिककारुण्यघटितस्वतन्त्रेच्छाशक्तिः स्वयमुपधिमाधाय रमते ।।
S.S., I-75, pp.151-52.

47. भक्तियोगो नाम यमनियमासनप्राणायामप्रत्याहारधारणाध्यानसमाधिरूपाष्टाङ्गवाँस्तैल-धारावदविच्छिन्नस्मृतिसन्तानरूपः स च विवेक विमोकाभ्यासक्रियाकल्याणानवसा-दानुद्धर्षरूपःसाधनसप्तकजन्यः।वेदनध्यानोपासनादिशब्दवाच्या भक्तिः परभक्तिपरज्ञान परमभक्तिरूपक्रमवती प्रपत्त्यङ्गिका च।
Yatīndramatadīpikā, 20-21-24, pp. 95-97.

48. संसाराख्यज्वलनभसितीभूतसंजीवनार्हा धर्मोत्पत्तिप्रथितविभवा धार्यमाणा गिरीशैः । गम्भीरत्वादकलुषगतिर्गम्यतीर्थोपपन्ना गङ्गेवान्या पुरुषजलधिं गाहते विष्णुभक्तिः ।।
S.S., IX-22, p.764.

49. इयमखिलपुमर्थप्रार्थनाकल्पवल्ली सितमतिभिरनन्यैः सेविता सिद्धबृन्दैः । द्युतिभिरविरलाभिर्द्योतयन्ती दिगन्तान् विशति सुमतिसौधं विष्णुभक्तिर्विशुद्धम् ।।
S.S., IX-52, p.793.

50. शमधननिधिः संविद्वल्लीसमग्रफलोदयः श्रुतपरिणतिः शुद्धिस्थेमा सुखप्रतिभूरसि। भवभयतमःप्रातःसंध्या परावरदीपिका भगवति हरौ भक्तिर्दिव्या परिष्कृतिरात्मनः ।।
S.S., X-26, p.818.

51. न्यासविद्या प्रपत्तिः। प्रपत्तिर्नामअनुकूल्यस्य सङ्कल्पः प्रातिकूल्यस्य वर्जनम् । रक्षिष्यतीति विश्वासो गोप्तृत्ववरणं तथा ।। *Yatīndramatadīpikā*, 28, p.99.

52. उपायः स्वप्राप्तेरुपनिषदधीतः स भगवान् प्रसत्त्यै तस्योक्ते प्रपदननिदिध्यासनगती। तदारोहः पुंसः सुकृतपरिपाकेन महता निदानं तत्रापि स्वयमखिलनिर्माणनिपुणः ।।
S.S., X-31, p.821.

53. स्वमायाशैलूषीविहरणपरिभ्रान्ततनुभृत्यरित्राणोद्योगप्रवणकरुणावेशविवशः । प्रतिक्षेप्तुं तापान् प्रभुरयमपर्यन्तमहिमा हिमानीमानीय स्वपदनतिमेनः प्रणुदति ।।
S.S., X-30, p.820.

54. कम्पन्ते यमकिंकराः स्वयमसौ कालश्च सर्वं कर्षः शङ्कन्ते किल निर्जरा

निजपदावष्टम्भनं पाक्षिकम्। रक्षोदानवयक्षगुह्यकमुखा धावन्त्यतो दूरतः पद्मावल्लभपादपद्मयुगलप्रत्य-र्पितस्वात्मनः ॥

S.S., X-49, p.837.

55. नाथे नस्तृणमन्यदन्यदपि वा तन्नाभिनालिकिनीनालीकस्पृहणीयसौरभमुचा वाचा न याचामहे।
शुद्धानां तु लभेमहि स्थिरधियां शुद्धान्तसिद्धान्तिनां मुक्तैश्वर्यदिनप्रभातसमयासत्तिं प्रसत्तिं मुहुः ॥ *S.S.*, X-50, p.839.

56. अपि निर्मुक्तजीवानां कामादीनां बलीयसाम् ।
अविद्या कर्मसंज्ञा तु मृतसंजीवनी स्थिता ॥ *S.S.*, IX-17, p.760.

57. स्वाधीनसंसरणनाट्यनिरूढवृत्तेः संतोषितः प्रणतभूमिकयाऽस्य पुंसः ।
स्थाने विधास्यति विभुः स्थिरचिह्नभेदं क्रीडानटः स भगवान्कृपया स्वसाम्यम् ॥

S.S., I-59, p.121.

58. मुकुलयति विवित्सां मोहविध्वंसमिच्छन् विमृशति निगमान्तान् वीक्षते मोक्षधर्मान् ।
निशमयति च गीतां नित्यमेकान्तभक्त्या गुणपरिषदवेक्षी गुप्तमन्त्रो विवेकः ॥

S.S., I-61, p.123.

59. सव्यं पादं प्रसार्य श्रितदुरितहरं दक्षिणं कुञ्चयित्वा जानुन्याधाय सव्येतरभुजमितरं नागभोगे निधाय। पश्चाद्बाहुद्वयेन प्रतिभटशमने धारयन् शचक्रे देवीभूषादिजुष्टो जनयति जगतां शर्म वैकुण्ठनाथः ॥ *S.S.*, X-85, p.875.

60. विवेकोऽयं तत्त्वेष्ववितथविशेषग्रहतनुः भवोदन्वद्दोषप्रतिगमनिकात्मा च सुमतिः ।
परप्रेमाकारा त्वमिति समवेतास्त्रय इमे तमः पारे त्यक्तत्रिगुणमपि च त्यक्ष्यथ न माम्॥

S.S., X-81, p.871.

Chapter VI

An Evaluation

As is evident from the foregoing study of the *Saṅkalpasūryodaya* Vedānta Deśika, popularly known as Vedānta Deśika has not only presented the teachings of Viśiṣṭādvaita Philosophy and Religion in a comprehensive way, but also displayed his skill of being a successfull dramatist. Therefore, Vedānta Deśika is worthy of honour of being called the Poet-Philosopher.

Vedānta Deśika has a special skill of depicting the techniques of the drama in the various scenes with philosophical truths of Viśiṣṭādvaita Vedānta. This has won him admiration by one and all.

Lengthy descriptions like that of dialogue between *Kāma* and *Rati*, conversation between Guru and Śiṣya and of the battle scene etc., show the loftiness of thought that the dramatist possesses. A close perusal of such descriptions within the frame of long compounds makes it may be said that Vedānta Deśika follows Bāṇa or Śubandhu or Daṇḍin in the art of narration. In addition to the narration of different scenes Vedānta Deśika brings in the description of art-pilgrim centres, ten *avatāras* of Supreme God etc., in a grand and charming style. He has given more scope to describe the essentials of Rāmānuja Vedānta than narrating different scenes. Vedānta Deśika's description can be said as perfectly set with original refreshing images of the goals of human life.

The richness of these descriptions are brightened on account of the apt use of figures of speech. Thus, it is crystal clear, that Vedānta Deśika is equally well versed in the science of rhetorics.

In the beginning of the *Saṅkalpasūryodaya*, Veṅkaṭanātha pays homage to the Supreme God in two verses where in the dramatist has conformed to the rules of Sanskrit dramaturgy in revealing the central theme of the play.

The First Chapter deals with the date, life and works of the Vedānta Deśika. He who became very famous after Rāmānuja, by offering multi-dimensional contribution to the world of Viśiṣṭādvaita Vedānta and its literature, has been shown as the author of one hundred and nine works, credited with academic genious (pp.1-30).

The Second Chapter gives the details of (1) meaning of allegory (p.32), (2) origin of allegorical dramas in Vedic literature (pp.33), (3) the place of *Saṅkalpasūryodaya* in Sanskrit literature (p.39-40), (4) the commentaries on the *Saṅkalpasūryodaya* (p.40-41).

It is here shown that the allegorical interpretations in Vedic and Classical literature inspired the later writers, and they began introducing this technique in Sanskrit dramas too. Drama is a direct objective and impersonal representation of life on the stage. And the allegorical dramas convey a veiled moral meaning, in which various qualities and virtues are personified. This surpassing style goes to the credit of Vedānta Deśika.

The Third Chapter describes the significance of the title of the drama. The word *Saṅkalpasūryodaya* means the 'Sunrise of (God's) Resolve (to save man) or Divine Will'.

The dark night of *Saṁsāra* is warded off by the Will of the Lord which is equated with the rise of the Sun, *Sūryodaya* (pp.51-54).

As a part of the same Chapter, then follows a running summary of all the ten Acts of the drama in a lucid language for better understanding of the theme of the drama. The first Act describes a lengthy conversation between *Kāma* and *Rati* regarding the plans of getting victory for their master Mahāmoha (pp.54-61). The second Act presents the conversation between Viveka and Vyavasāya and others in foiling the attempt of Mahāmoha (pp.61-63). In contrast, another conversation between Guru and Śiṣya follows highlighting the refutation of the views of Nyāya, Vaiśeṣika, Sāṅkhya, Jaina, Bauddha etc. thus substantiating the views of the Viśiṣṭādvaita School. Here, Vedānta Deśika has displayed his keen intellect in highlighting the views of different systems of thought like Cārvāka, Bauddha, Jaina, Sāṅkhya etc.

The Third Act highlights the role of evil ministers of King Mahāmoha, *viz.*, Vasanta, Kāma, Rāga and Dveṣa. They appear on the stage and compliment each other on their prowess in gaining a victory for king Mahāmoha (pp.68-70).

A break-up of the military force of Kāma, Krodha and others and their flight, Kāma and Krodha indulging in mutual praise of their strength and their being joined by Lobha and Tṛṣṇā, constitute the subject-matter of the Fourth Act (pp.78-86).

In the Fifth Act, king Mahāmoha is seen on the stage as being engaged in issuing an order to Dambha and Darpa to divert Puruṣa's meditation. This act is full of satire portrayed through Krodha, Dambha, Darpa and Kuhana. (pp. 86-97).

Then, the Sixth Act describes Puruṣa's search for a suitable place of meditation. Puruṣa keeps his other assistants in the background and engages himself in *Bhakti Yoga;* Viveka and Tarka in their search for a suitable place reach Śrīraṅgam and other places. But, finding that there is a still better place, Viveka and Tarka confine themselves to their heart for meditation (pp.97-105).

The Seventh Act is devoted to the determination of a pure form for Puruṣa's meditation. In the *Śuddha-viṣkambhaka,* a new character of *Saṁskāra* enters the stage and describes the painting on the wall of Brahma Vidyā. Viveka as well as Sumati go round the art gallery where the paintings of the ten *avatāras* of God are displayed (pp.105-110).

The Eighth Act is the climax of the play and is the longest of the scenes. King Mahāmoha is seen in all his pomp and pagentry. But ultimately Puruṣa wins a victory and Mahāmoha's assistants are defeated. Nārada and Tumburu congratulate Viveka on his success against Mahāmoha (pp.110-116).

The Nineth Act depicts Puruṣa in a state of *Samādhi,* to whom the role of Viṣṇubhakti lends support (pp.116-123).

The Tenth Act is the climax and culmination of the play. The characters, *viz., Saṅkalpa,* Viṣṇubhakti, Puruṣa and Viveka come on the stage, exchange their views, and come to the conclusion that liberation is possible only by the grace of God through a Guru. Then Viṣṇubhakti and Viveka get the pleasure of witnessing the liberation of *Jīva.* There ends the play *Saṅkalpasūryodaya* with the *Bharatavākya* (pp. 123-137).

The Fourth Chapter of the thesis is divided into *three sections*. Under the *first section* of *characterisation* a critical estimate of the role played by all major and minor characters is developed in such a way that it encompasses all the details scattered in different scenes of the drama. The high order of philosophic honesty and literary earnestness has been brought to light here.

The *second section* deals with the delienation of sentiments. Vedānta Deśika has developed the *Śāntarasa* as the major *rasa*, and subsequently it is here shown how all other *rasas* like *Śṛṅgāra, Vīra,* etc. have been delineated as subordinate ones. Generally all Rasas are known to have been delineated in Sanskrit dramas. But out of nine *Rasas*, Vedānta Deśika adopted *Śāntarasa* in his play. It is true that *Śāntarasa* cannot be conveyed easily to the readers by the author in a play, because it is one's own experience. However, Vedānta Deśika's attempt in portraying *Śāntarasa* to the extent possible goes to his credit and depiction of other sentiments can also be observed here as subordinates. The following verse substantiates this point :

> असभ्यपरिपाटिकामधिकरोति शृङ्गारिता
> परस्परतिरस्कृतिं परिचिनोति वीरायितम् ।
> विरुद्धगतिरद्भुतस्तदलमल्पसारैः परैः
> शमस्तु परिशिष्यते शमितचित्तखेदो रसः ॥ *S.S.*, I-19, p.48.

"Moreover, *Śṛṅgāra* or the sentiment of love can give pleasure only to those who are unfit to be members of a decent assembly; *Vīra* or the sentiment of heroism in war treats of the attempts to disgrace one another; the sentiment of wonder has to deal with incidents and situations that are difficult to imagine as true. Of what use are the other *rasas* which are of little interest ? There is only one *rasa* that remains, and that alone can bring tranquility to the troubled heart. And that *rasa* is *Śāntarasa* itself."

The *third section* describes dramatist's significant use of various *Alaṅkāras* like *Rūpaka*, *Vyatireka,* etc. In toto, the employment of twenty seven *Alaṅkāras* have been described in the thesis. The reflection of all these *Alaṅkāras* has been precisely shown to mark the scholarship of the author. And it is shown how the dramatist has been successful in employing these different *Alaṅkāras* to make the scenes attractive and appealing.

The Fifth Chapter of the book deals with philo-sophical doctrines reflected in the drama. The philosophical tenets, suggested in the drama, have also been brought to light in the thesis. In the play, the author indicates and refutes the views of philosophical systems namely, Nyāya, Sāṅkhya, Vaiśeṣika, Bauddha, Mīmāṁsā and Advaita Vedānta in the Second Act (pp.317-325). At the end, Vedānta Deśika establishes the superiority of tenets of the Viśiṣṭādvaita school (pp.325-336).

The author, proclaims the significance and utility of Śrīvaiṣṇavism throughout the play. Since the system is also known as qualified monism propounded by Rāmānuja, it provides a form to Brahman and mentions His attributes, Spouse, vehicles and weapons. Evidently Lord Nārāyaṇa is the Supreme Brahman according to Viśiṣṭādvaita school. In this play, Vedānta Deśika brings in a character namely Guru, who is none other than Rāmānuja himself. As an ardent follower of Rāmānuja, Vedānta Deśika lays much stress on Viṣṇubhakti and Prapatti which are the fundamentals of Viśiṣṭādvaita Vedānta.

Now, I would like to offer my findings as below :

It is a hear-say of the tradition that the *Saṅkalpa-sūryodaya* of Vedānta Deśika (1268 to 1369 A.D.) was written within a night on a personal challenge to Kṛṣṇa Miśra (1092 A.D.) of *Prabodhacandrodaya*. But, due to the long gap of time between Kṛṣṇa Miśra and Vedānta Deśika, the point of personal challenge between them is open to absurdity. Rather, it may be conceived that Vedānta Deśika's composition, *Saṅkalpasūryodaya* is a philosophical response to Kṛṣṇa Miśra's *Prabodhacandrodaya*. In both the plays however one does find more similarities like names of the characters, plot-construction, delineation of *Śāntarasa* as principal *Rasa* etc. But, it does not mean that Vedānta Deśika has least originality. As a matter of fact Vedānta Deśika follows the same path, but shows the goal of different nature. This is the originality of Vedānta Deśika.

The *Saṅkalpasūryodaya* adheres to the rules of dramaturgy in Sanskrit. The drama begins with entrance of *Sūtradhāra* after the utterance of the Nāndi verses. (Viśvanātha, *Sāhitya Darpaṇa*, VI-395).

At proper places the dramatist brings in various *Sandhis* which have been described by the author of *Sāhitya Darpaṇa*. They are–

Text	*Page*	*Sandhi*	*Sāhitya Darpaṇa*	*Page*
S.S.	45	आमुख	VI Adh.	402
"	139	परिकर	VI "	435
"	141	परिन्यास	VI "	"
"	162	प्राप्ति	VI "	434
"	207	प्रतिमुख	VI "	420
"	240	विमानं	VI "	429-30
"	350	गर्भ	VI "	431 etc.

Besides he has made use of other techniques too–

Text	*Page*	*Name*	*Sāhitya Darpaṇa*	*Page*
S.S.	1	नांदि	VI Adh.	395
"	18	भारतीवृत्ति	VI "	401
"	70-71	विष्कम्भकः	VI "	417
"	126	मिश्र विष्कम्भकः	VI "	417
"	66	कथोद्घातः	VI "	404
"	196	प्रवेशकः	VI "	419
"	125	बीजम्	VI "	424
"	84	नायक विशेषः	III "	114

Almost *Vaidarbhī* and *Gauḍī* style have been employed by Vedānta Deśika which he indicates in the following verse :

> गौडवैदर्भपाञ्चालमालाकारां सरस्वतीं ।
> यस्य नित्यं प्रशंसन्ति सन्तः सौरभवेदिनः ।। *S.S.*, I-12, p.39.

"His eloquent compositions displaying the beauties of the *Gauḍa*, *Vaidarbha* and *Pañcāla* styles are always spoken of with high praise by good men who can appreciate literary fragrance."

The hero of the *Saṅkalpasūryodaya* Viveka is characterised as *Dhīrodātta* type of the hero. He is shown to be possessing all the qualities mentioned in the books of dramaturgy (pp.162-168). Similarly, *Nāyikā* or heroine that is Sumati is portrayed as a true wife of Viveka (pp.168-172). In a similar manner on the counter part, Mahāmoha is pictured as a *Pratināyaka* in a right manner. Thus, one can say that Vedānta Deśika has followed closely the foot steps of the authors on dramaturgy.

Vedānta Deśika describes the combat scene between two forces but through conversation between Naraḍa and

Tumburu. Yet the picturousque description of which remains before the eyes of audience lively. This is how he follows the rules of dramaturgy faithfully, by not bringing such scenes on the stage directly, and appeals to *Sahṛdayas*.

Indeed the dramatist has kindly stated[1] that the play caters for the mental and spiritual palate of those who have grown into Divine consciousness of self surrendered and selfless love as well as service to Supreme God. Therefore, there is no scope at all to misunderstand that *Saṅkalpasūryodaya* lacks dramatic force. Of course Vedānta Deśika does not wish to claim any dramatic force. Nevertheless he has brought in essential techniques of the drama. He has written this philosophical and devotional work applying to it the technique of the playwrite.

Superseding all the above, the learned dramatist has rightly stated his view of composing the play in the following verse :

> अङ्गीकुर्वन्त्वकलुषधियो नित्यमध्यात्मविद्या-
> माद्यो धर्मः स्पृशतु वसुधामाशिषः पारवर्ती ।
> देवः श्रीमान्निरवधिदयासिन्धुरस्मिन्प्रबन्धे
> वक्ता श्रोता वचनविषयः प्रियतां वासुदेवः ॥ *S.S.*, X-97, p.888.

"Let men of unclouded intelligence ever persue the study of Vedānta. Let the *Dharma* of renunciation characteristic of the first *Yuga,* which is beyond all other blessings, pervail on earth. May Vāsudeva, the lord of Śrī, the boundless ocean of compassion, who is the author, the audience and the subject of this composition be gracious (to all)."

A close observation of all these points emphasise Vedānta Deśika's proficiency in different branches of learning like *Nāṭyaśāstra, Yuddhaśāstra, Alaṅkāraśāstra, Chandaśāstra, Vedāntaśāstra,* etc. This is implied in the following verse :

न तच्छास्त्रं न सा विद्या न तच्छिल्पं न ताः कलाः।
नासौ योगो न तज्ज्ञानं नाटके यन्न दृश्यते॥ *S.S.*, I-20, p.51.

"There is no Scripture, no Subject of Learning, no Art, no Craft, no Yoga or Jñāna that cannot be represented in a dramatic performance."

Vedānta Deśika's flow of thought is dignified and profound. His words and ideas are apt and significant. The soft and melodious sound of *Anuprāsas* find place in his comprehensive style to keep step with the richness of sense.

Vedānta Deśika's attempt to reform society of his days by portraying human emotions and interplay through the several characters in the drama is laudable. The appropriate use of satire in this regard is worthy of appraisal. This is true because the function of literature is not only to delight but instruct.

It is apt and significant to obsreve here that the scholar Veṅkaṭanātha is well-known by the suffix 'Deśika', besides other ones. Out of the latter, it is generally believed that the title '*Vedāntācārya*' was bestowed on Vedānta Deśika by Lord Śrī Raṅganātha Himself.

Another point worhty of note is that his role in the history of Śrī Vaiṣṇavism, particularly is that of a unifying force trying for a useful settlement of conflict between Conservatism and Progressivism, between Veda and Prabandham, between Dharma and Brahman, between *Jñāna* and *Bhakti* and above all between Teṅgalaism and Vaḍagalaism.

Inspite of all these merits one may find a few shortcomings of *Saṅkalpasūryodaya* as a drama, because the play is more poetic than dramatic. It has lengthy speeches in ten acts though the *Śāntarasa* is considered as the principal rasa of *Saṅkalpasūryodaya*, yet its depiction is made through implication. Nevertheless the multitude merits of the *Saṅkalpasūryodaya* over-weigh its short-comings. Thus, the *Saṅkalpasūryodaya* stands the test of all times and climes.

REFERENCE

1. स्तोतुं निंदितुमस्मदुक्तमथवा सोढुं समूढं जगत् किं नश्छिन्नमनन्तचिन्तनरसे सुस्थे सुखं तस्थुषाम् । शिष्याः शिक्षितबुद्धयः श्रुतिपथे येषां वयं ये च न स्तत्संतोष-समर्पणक्षममिदं साडम्बरैः किं परैः ॥ *S.S.*, X, p.889.

   श्रुतिकिरीटविहारजुषा धिया सुरभितामिह नाटकपद्धतिम् ।
   मुहुरवेक्ष्य विवेकमुपघ्नयन् मतमपश्चिमयामि विपश्चिताम् ॥ *S.S.*, I-7, p.26.

Bibliography

ORIGINAL WORKS IN SANSKRIT

Ahobala, *Prabhāvilāsa*, Adyar Library, Madras, 1948.

Ānandaraya Makhin, *Vidyā - Pariṇaya*, Nirṇaya Sagar Press, Kolaphatlane, Bombay, 1930.

Ānandaraya Makhin, *Jivānandam*, Ed. Duraiswami, Aiyangar, Adyar, Library Series, 59, Adyar, 1947.

—— *Aṇuvogaddaram*, Shri Mahāvīrā Jaina Vidyālaya, Bombay, 1968.

Appayya Dīkṣita, *Kuvalayānanda*, Chowkhamba Vidyā Bhavana, Vāraṇāsī, 1995.

Bharata, *Nāṭyaśāstra*, Chowkhamba Sanskrit Samsthana, Vāraṇāsī, Saṁvat 2037.

—— *Nāṭyaśāstra*, Volume 1, 111-112, Oriental Institute, Baroda, 1934.

—— *Bhāgavatapurāṇa*, Skandha IV, Adhyāyas 25-29, Gita Press, Gorakhpur, Vikrama Śaka 2020.

Bhatt, G.K., *Bharata-nāṭya-mañjarī*, Bhandarkar Oriental Reserch Institute, Poona, 1975.

Bharat Pisharoti, E.P., *Ekabhāratam*, Kamadhenu Publication, P.O. Eranallur, Trichur.

Bhūdeva Śukla, *Dharma-vijaya*, Vidyā-vilāsa Press, Gopalamandir lane, Varanasi, 1930.

Dhanañjaya, *Daśarūpakam*, Motilal Banarasidass, Delhi, 1979.

Gaṇapati, S.V., *Sāmaveda*, Āgneyakāṇḍa, IV, 10, Motilal Banarasidass, New Delhi, 1982.

Gaṅgā Prasād Upādhyaya, *Śatapatha Brāhmaṇa*, Volume I, 1-45 , 8-10. The Research Institute of Ancient Scientific Studies, New Delhi, 1962.

Gokulanātha, *Amṛtodayam*, Chowkhamba Sanskrit Series, Com. by Ācarya Ramacandra Miśra, Vāraṇāsi, 1965.

Hari Nārāyaṇa Apte, *Aitareya Brāmhmaṇa*, Ed. 3-12.5. Ānandāśrama, Poona, 1869.

Ilathur Ramaswamy Śāstrī, *Kaivalyavalliparinayam*, Ullur S. Parameswara Iyyar, Vijñānadeepikā, Volume III, Publication, R.T. Pillai and Sons, Chalai, Trivendrum, No. 1122.

Jayantabhaṭṭa, *Āagamāḍambara*, Ed. Raghavan, Mithila, Institute Series, Darbhanga, 1964.

Jīvanyāyatīrtha Bhaṭṭācārya, *Caṇḍatāṇḍava*, Ācārya Panchanama Smṛtigranthalaya, No. 4.

Kavikarṇapura, *Caitanaya - Candrodaya*, Nirṇaya Sagar Press, 23, Kolaphat lane, Bombay, 1917.

Kannampuzha, *Mahābhārata Ādiparva*, (Malayalam com.) 6613-14, S. Krishna Warrior, Śrīmahābhārata Publishing House, Abbanabde, Trichur, 1951.

Kavi Śankarlal Singh, *Dhruvābhyudaya*, Ed. Limbadipura, First Ed., Samvat, 1968.

Kṛṣṇa Miśra, *Prabodhacandrodaya*, Chowkamba Sanskrit Series, Vāraṇāsī, 1968.

Kṛṣṇamācārya, V., *Saṅkalpasūryodaya* of Vedānta Deśika Adyar Library, Madras, 1948.

Mammaṭa, *Kāvyaprakāśa*, Ed. A.B. Gajendragadkar, Bombay, 1959.

—— *Muṇḍakopaniṣat* : III-1.

Menon, M.S., *Pūrṇapuruṣārthacandrodaya*, Subhadrāharaṇa, Brahmadatta Nārāyaṇa, Department of Sanskrit, University of Calicit, 1983.

Max Muller, *Ṛgveda Saṁhitā*, Volume I, The Hon'ble the East India Company, London, 1849.

—— *Municaturvijayam*, Gaekvad Oriental Series, Baroda, 1918.

Nalla Dīkṣita, *Jivanmukti Kalyāṇa*, Śrī Śaṅkara Gurukula Series, No. 10, Sri Vanivilasam Press, Śrīraṅgam, 1944.

—— *Cittavṛtti - Kalyāṇa*, Ed. Municaturvijaya, Central Library, Baroda, 1935,

Omkāranātha, *Śodhaprabandha*, Sanskrit Vibhag, Prayag Visvavidyalaya, Prayag (unpublished), 1967.

Paṇḍit Śrīpāda Damodara Satavalekar, *Atharvaveda Saṁhitā,* VII-43 Swadhayayamandal Paradi city, Gujarat, (Noyan).

Priyabala Shah, *Viṣṇudharmaottara Purāṇa*, Vol. I, Kāṇḍa - 3, Oriental Institute, Baroda, 1958.

Pūrṇasaraswati, *Kamalinīrajahaṁsa*, Kinjunni Raja, The Contribution of Kerala to Sanskrit Literature, University of Madras, 1980.

Ramaswamy, K.S., *Bhāvaprakāśa of Śāradātanaya*, Ed. Gaekwad Oriental Series, No. XIV, Baroda.

Rajarajavarma, *Gīrvāṇavijaya*, Rajarajavara (Vadakkmkur).

—— *Kerala Sanskrit Caritam*, Vol. VI, National Book Stall, Kattayam, 1965.

Radhakrishnan, S., *Chāndogya Upaniṣad*, Vol. I, 6-8, Ten Principal Upaniṣads with Śaṅkara Bhāṣya, Motilal Banarasidass, Delhi, 1964.

Ravidāsa, *Mithyājñānaviḍambanam*, Harischandra Kaviratnadwara, Vidyaratna, Calcutta, 1894.

Raghavan, V., *Vimukti*, Ed. in Sanskrit Pratibha Sahitya Academy, Publication, New Delhi, 1961.

—— *Śukla - Yajurveda*, with Sanātana Bhāṣya Sadguru Gangeshwara International Veda Mission, Bombay, XXXIV, 6.

Sarup, L., *The Nighaṇṭu and Nirukta*, II-4, Motilal Banarasidass, Delhi, 1967.

Śrīrāma, *Subalavajratuṇḍa*, Ullur S. Parameswara Iyyer, Kerala Sahitya caritam, Volume III, University of Kerala, 1963.

Sri Krishna Datta, *Purañjana-caritam*, Vidarbha Saṁśodhana Mandala Granthamala, No. 16, Nagpur, 1961.

Sri Venkitaramanacarya, *Jīvasaṁjīvani-nāṭaka*, V.V. Subbayya and Sons, Publishing House, Bangalore, 1945.

—— *Vikramorvaśīyam*

Sri Vātsya Varadācārya, *Yatirājavijaya-nāṭaka*, Tirupati Devastanam, Tirupati, 1956.

Swami Ādidevānanda, *Yatīndramatadīpikā*, Eng. Srinivasadasa, Sri Ramakrishnamath, Madras, 1967.

Vāmana, *Kāvyālaṅkāra Sūtra*, Chowkhamba Sanskrti Samsthan, Vāraṇāsī, 1976.

Veera Raghavacharya, *Saṅkalpasūryodaya*, Sri Rama Press, Bangalore, 1975.

—— *Yādavābhyudaya*, Ed., Ubhya Vedanta Granthamala, Madras, 1969.

—— *Yogavasiṣṭham*, Volume I, Chenkottukonam, Tiruvanantapuruam, 1985.

Vādicandra Suri, *Jñānasūryodayam*, Government Press, Nagpur, 1926.

Vāsudevashasri Abhyankar, *Sarvadarśana Saṅgraha*, Bhandarkar Oriental Research Institute, Poona, 1978.

Viśvanātha, *Sāhityadarpaṇa*, Chowkhamba Sanskrit Series, Vāraṇāsi, 1989.

Vidyānātha, *Pratāparudrīya*, The Sanskrti Education Society, Madras.

Yaśahpala, *Mohaparājaya*, Municaturvijaya Central Library, Baroda, 1918.

WORKS IN ENGLISH

Bennet, William Rose, *The Readers Encyclopedia*, Thomas, Y. Growell Company New York, 1951.

Edgerton, F., *Indirect Suggestion in Poetry*, Proc. of the American Philosophical Society, Volume 76, 1936.

Epigraphica Indica, Vol. XIII.

Epigraphica Indica, Vol. VI.

Gajendragadkar, A.B., *Abhijñāna Śākuntala of Kālidāsa*, Bombay, 1934.

Janaki, S.S., *Svaranamukta - Saṁvāda* or *Vivāda*, Prof. Kuppuswami Birth Centenary Volume.

Krishna moorthy, K., *Ānandavardhana's Dhvanyāloka*, Karnataka University, Dharwad, 1974.

Krishamacariar, M., *History of Classical Sanskrti Literature*, Motilal Banarasidass, Delhi, 1974.

Massob, J.L. & Patawardhan, M.V., *Śāntarasa and Abhinava-gupta's Philosophy of Aesthetics*, Bhandarkar Oriental Institute, Pune, 1969.

—— *Oxford Advanced Learners Dictionary of Current English*, Oxford University Press, New Delhi, 1982.

Surendranath Dasgupta, *A History of Indian Philosophy*, Vol. III, Motilal Banarasidas, Delhi, 1975.

Satyavrata Singh, *Vedānta Deśika — His Life, Works and Philosophy - A Study*, Chowkhamba Sanskrti Series Office, Varanasi, 1958.

Satnam Talwar, *A study of Allegorical Sanskrit Dramas*, (unpublished thesis), University of Delhi, 1967.

Srinivasachari, S.M., *Advaita and Viśiṣṭādvaita*, Asia Publishing House, Adyar, Madras - 20.

Raja Gopala Iyengar, M.R., *Saṅkalpasūryodaya*, Vedānta Deśika Research Soceity, Madras, 1977.

Raghavan, V., *The Number of Rasas*, Adyar Library, Adyar, 1940.

WORKS IN KANNADA

Bhayankaram Annan, *Saptatriratnamālika*, D. Krishnayyangar, *Śrī Vedānta Deśikaru,* Bangalore, 1964.

Krishnayyangar, D., *Sri Vedānta Deśikaru*, Bangalore, 1964.

Rangachar, S., *Śrī Vedānta Deśika Stotramālā* - Part III, Sanskrit Sahitya Sadana, Mysore, 1989.

JOURNALS AND PERIODICALS

Aśvaghoṣa, *Śariputra Prakaraṇa*, An incomplete manuscript discovered by Lueders from Central Asia, Chinese Literature, Part III, 1956.

Ānandadeva, *Kṛṣṇa-bhakti-candrikā*, Descriptive catalogue of the Government collections of manuscripts, deposited in the Bhandarkar Oriental Research Institute, Poona, 4, Volume XIV, 1937.

Ananta Paṇḍita, *Svānubhuti*, Report of Manuscripts in Rajasthan and Centre India, No. 1904-6.

Dharmadeva, *Dharmodaya*, Gosvami Journal of the Assam Research Society, Volume III-4.

Durgeśvara, *Dharmoddharaṇa*, Karnatak University, Journal, Humanitieis, 1957.

Dāmodarāśrama, *Pāṣaṇḍadharma — Khaṇḍana*, Catalogue of Sanskrti, Pali and Prakrti Books in the British Musueum, Col. No. 316, London, 1906-29.

Ghanaśyāma, *Navagraha-carita*, Gopal S. Journal of the Tanjore Saraswati Mandir Library, Tanjore, No. 3. (Volume - XV).

Kṛṣṇa Baladeva Varman, *Bhartṛharirājyatyāga*, Private Manuscripts, Lucknow, 1806.

Krishnayyangar, D., *Śrī Deśika Sambhāvana*, Seventh Centenary Celebrations Committee, Sri Venkatesa Sabha, Mysore, 1968.

Jayanta Bhaṭṭa, *Sanmata-nāṭaka*, Report of Opertation in Search of Sanskrti Manuscripts in the Bombay circle, by Peterson, Bombay, Vol. V, No. 407.

Jātavedas, *Pūrṇapuruṣārtha-Candrodaya*, Description catalogue of the Sanskrit Manuscripts in the Govertnment Oriental Manu-scripts Library, Madras, No. 125 40-41.

Jivadeva, *Bhaktivaibhava*, Triennial Catalogue Manuscripts collected from the Government Oriental Manuscripts Library, Madras No. 3752; Descriptive Catalogue of Sanskrit Manuscripts in the Adyar Library, Adyar No. 1478.

Narasiṁha, *Śrīnivāsaratha-vijaya-nāṭaka*, A Catalogue of the Sanskrit Manuscripts, British Museum, Cecil Bendak, London, 1902.

Narasiṁhamiśra, *Śivanārāyaṇabhañja-mahodaya Nāṭika*, The Asiatic Society Bengal, 1901, and M.H.

Hariprasad Sastry, Report on search for Sanskrit Manuscripts, 1805-1900.

Nṛsiṁhakavi, *Anumiti-Pariṇaya*, Descriptive Catalogue of the Madras, Govt Oriental Manuscripts Library, No. D. 12463.

Nṛsiṁhadaivajña, *Citsūryaloka*, List of Sanskrit Manuscripts in Private Libraries of Southern India by Bustave oppest. Volume I, Madras, 1906-28.

Rāmānuja Kavi, *Viveka-Vijaya*, Government orient Sanskrit Manuscripts Library, Madras, No. D. 12683.

Ratnakheṭa Śrīnivāsadīkṣita, *Bhāvanapuruṣothama,* Saraswati Mahal Library, Tanjore, No. 4427 / 979.

Ravidāsa, *Mithyājñāna-Khaṇḍana*, (Bombay Branch, R.A.S. 1289-90, No. 10, 4200), 1951.

Sundaradeva, *Muktipariṇaya*, Tanjore New Catalogue, No. 4460, NW Province Catalogue Pt. VII.

Sudarśanācārya, *Siddhāntābherināṭaka*, Catalogue of Sanskrit Manuscripts in Mysore and Coorg.

Śukleśvaranatha, *Prabodhodayam*, Hariprasada Sastri, M. Notices, 11 series, Volume - III, No. 190, p.12224.

Sundarashastri, *Svātma-Prakāśana*, Private Manuscripts, No. 037-38, Chidambaram.

Thedor Aufrecht, *Catalogus Catalogorum*, Part I, Franz Steiner, Veriag GMBH, Wiesbaden, 1962.

Triveni, *Tattvamudrābhadrodaya*, Dr. Krishnamacarya, M. Sanskrit Poetesses, Souvenir of Silver Jubilee of the Trivendrum Sanskrit Series.

Vaijanatha, *Satsaṅga-Vijaya*, Catalogue of Sanskrit Manuscripts in Private Library, Gujarat, No. 64.

Vijayīndratīrtha, *Ubhayagrāsa - rāhūdaya*, A List of Sanskrit Manuscritps in Private Libraries of South India by Gustav, Madras, No. 2504.

Index